Dedicated to

Late Balaram Nag
My father, who had built the foundations of my life.

About the Author

Avishek has a Master's degree in Data Analytics & Machine Learning from BITS (Pilani) and a Bachelor's degree in Computer Science from West Bengal University of Technology (WBUT). He has more than 14 years of experience in different renowned companies like VMware, Cognizant, Cisco, Mobile Iron, etc. He started his career as a Java developer and later moved to the core area of Machine Learning around five years back. He has practical experience in the design & development of Machine Learning systems, starting from inception to production in multiple organizations. Strong foundations in Mathematics/Statistics and substantial experience in product development had helped him to excel quickly in the world of ML & Data Science. He has shared his knowledge & experience through this book, which will help any Software Engineer to kick start in this area. He also writes blogs, and the same can be found at https://medium.com/@avisheknag17

Outside work, he loves spending time in reading books. He also has a fascination for art & sketch work.

Pragmatic Machine Learning with Python

Learn How to Deploy Machine Learning Models in Production

by

Avishek Nag

FIRST EDITION 2020

Copyright © BPB Publications, India

ISBN: 978-93-89845-365

Distributors:

BPB PUBLICATIONS
20, Ansari Road, Darya Ganj
New Delhi-110002
Ph: 23254990 / 23254991

DECCAN AGENCIES
4-3-329, Bank Street,
Hyderabad-500195
Ph: 24756967 / 24756400

MICRO MEDIA
Shop No. 5, Mahendra Chambers,
150 DN Rd. Next to Capital Cinema,
V.T. (C.S.T.) Station, MUMBAI-400 001
Ph: 22078296 / 22078297

BPB BOOK CENTRE
376 Old Lajpat Rai Market,
Delhi-110006
Ph: 23861747

Published by Manish Jain for BPB Publications, 20 Ansari Road, Darya Ganj, New Delhi-110002 and Printed by him at Repro India Ltd, Mumbai

Acknowledgement

I would like to thank team at BPB Publications for giving me this opportunity to write my first book for them.

Preface

Being in the industry for around 14 years, I have seen that there is always a massive gap between what we study& what we implement in practical scenarios. Especially for subjects like Machine Learning, which needs a strong theoretical background in Mathematics, this gap will be more. The biggest challenge here is how to take an abstract mathematical theory of a model to the production environment. I have read many Machine Learning books by famous authors and felt that each one is unique in some sense. I thought, if I could contribute from my experience of Industry & Academics here, then I could build a bridge between the theory & practice. This contribution may help a lot of working professionals. That's the inspiration for writing this book. It is divided into nine chapters. Details of each are given below:

Chapter 1 Introduces the concept of Machine Learning (ML) to the reader at a high level. It explains what do we understand by a Model, life cycle of ML projects. It gives a little & high-level understanding of different ML techniques, which are explained in subsequent chapters in detail. This chapter also gives an overview of different mathematical concepts essential to understanding ML models.

Chapter 2 discusses the classification techniques. It explains the concept of ML pipeline and gives a short introduction to the scikit-learn library of Python as it would be the default choice of implementation of different ML models. This chapter covers Naïve Bayes, Logistic Regression, Decision Tree, and Ensemble model like Random Forest.

Chapter 3 is all about regression techniques. It gives a formal algebraic definition of a regression problem and explains two primary methods of solution: OLS & Gradient Descent. It covers topics like feature selection (Forward & Backward), Polynomial form of regression, regularization (Lasso & Ridge), fact explanation from parametric linear model, etc.

Chapter 4 covers one unsupervised learning technique: Clustering. It gives formal definition object groups and distances and relates these to clusters. Two main approaches of clustering are discussed here: Centroid-based like KMeans and Density-based like DBSCAN. Apart from usual techniques, Hierarchical clustering like the Agglomerative approach is also discussed. In the end, one unique alternative technique of classification using clustering is covered.

Chapter 5 is all about Deep Learning. It starts with the concept of perceptron and defines its components. Then details of Neural networks, its varieties like CNN, Auto encoders are covered. Standard classification & regression using neural network is also discussed.

Chapter 6 covers another two unsupervised learning techniques like Dimensionality Reduction with Principal Components and outlier detection techniques. Clustering, Auto-Encoder & an Isolation tree-based approach are discussed under outlier detection.

Chapter 7 describes how to process text data and how it is different from other data types. It explains several vector space models like TF-IDF, Doc2Vec, Word2Vec, and how to use these in standard text classification & clustering problems. It also covers text visualization techniques using the standard histogram and Word cloud plot.

Chapter 8 describes the techniques of putting ML models into the production environment. It describes probable challenges to do that and possible solutions. Standard specifications like PMML for exporting an ML model in a platform-independent way are described with examples. The architectural technique of scaling up ML models using Big data is also explained.

Chapter 9 contains case studies and techniques of writing data science-based stories. Three models with different datasets are prepared & described as stories with the explanation of facts.

Readers are requested to install **Python 3** and **Jupyter Notebook** while reading this book.

Downloading the code bundle and coloured images:

Please follow the link to download the
Code Bundle and the *Coloured Images* of the book:

https://rebrand.ly/fk35z3l

Errata

We take immense pride in our work at BPB Publications and follow best practices to ensure the accuracy of our content to provide with an indulging reading experience to our subscribers. Our readers are our mirrors, and we use their inputs to reflect and improve upon human errors if any, occurred during the publishing processes involved. To let us maintain the quality and help us reach out to any readers who might be having difficulties due to any unforeseen errors, please write to us at :

errata@bpbonline.com

Your support, suggestions and feedbacks are highly appreciated by the BPB Publications' Family.

Table of Contents

CHAPTER 1
Introduction to Machine Learning and Mathematical Preliminaries

Over the recent years, **machine learning (ML)** is the most discussed topic in computational/software industry. People andcompanies are running behind it. Just by reading the term *machine learning,* the first question comes in our mind, that: *Can a brainless machine learn?* Moreover, who will give the knowledge for learning? Learning itself is an exciting and complex action. When a teacher teaches a group of kids in school about how to identify an animal's picture by showing them many samples, it becomes a typical learning process. Kids learn the animal's name and their corresponding pictures.

In the same way, *Can a machine or a computer learn to do the same task?* Yes, it can. The subject where these techniques of learning are discussed is known as **machine learning.** Humans have a brain, so they learn by intuition without explicitly thinking about the computational or mathematical background behind a learning process. But, in the case of a computer/machine/software program, there is no explicit existence of the brain, so there has to be an explicit existence of the mathematical learning process to compensate this as computers only understands numbers.

Structure

In this chapter, we will discuss

- Objectives of machine learning
- Lifecycle of machine learning as software projects

- Formal definitions of different machine learning techniques
- Mathematical preliminaries required to understand machine learning in-depth

Objective

After reading this chapter, we should be able to:

- Understand machine learning at a high level from a mathematical perspective.
- Understand practical execution cycles of machine learning projects at a high level.
- Understand what do we mean by a machine learning model.
- Differentiate between different techniques of machine learning and types of problems.
- Some mathematical theories in the light of machine learning.

Purpose of machine learning

We understood from the previous section that learning is possible by a machine. But what is the need for it? What benefit can we get by making a machine learn? The benefit is nothing but the automation of human performed tasks or repetitive tasks. For example, a computer can read and understand somebody's facial gestures and use it as a key to open a door for him/her. So, manual innervation is reduced over here.

Similarly, an ecommerce portal can learn a buyer's purchasing pattern and generate recommended items for him/her to purchase. With ML, all of these are possible. Another example could be the validation of a loan borrower from a commercial bank. With ML, it can be checked whether the customer who is borrowing the loan would be a potential defaulter (not able to repay the loan) or not. In general, with ML, a variety of works is possible to do, starting from identification of a picture to recommendation of items and many more things.

What is a machine learning model?

A machine learning model is a mathematical expression/equation or a complex data structure from the theory of computer science or a combination of both. It is an intersection between statistics, core computer science, and software engineering. A model can learn from the actions of humans or nature and can simulate future behavior for some unknown situation. In simple terms, a model can predict future things that can happen. We will be using the term model and machine learning model interchangeably throughout our discussion.

Models can learn from the history of actions, as said above. These actions are stored as records in the database. So, having a dataset is essential for building a model and using it.

What is a dataset?

From the concept of **DBMS (Database Management Systems)**, we can say that a dataset is a collection of records. Each dataset consists of several rows and columns. Each column represents several different aspects of a dataset as defined in DBMS. A simple dataset is precisely like a table in relational DBMS. But, sometimes, the dataset can be complicated, that is, hierarchical or can contain other datasets within it. This situation is precisely like NoSQL DB. A straightforward dataset of an employee is shown below:

	branch	department	designation	id	name	salary	type
0	LA	Accounts	Manager	1	John	20000	permanent
1	New York	Accounts	CA	2	David	15500	contract
2	New York	Marketing	Manager	3	Samantha	18000	permanent
3	LA	Design	Director	4	Jacob	30000	permanent

Figure 1.1: Sample employee dataset

There are five columns (branch, department, designation, id, name, type) and four rows in the dataset (There can be more rows in the dataset. We are just considering four rows for our discussion purpose). An ML model can learn from this dataset and later can give predictions. Having a dataset is evident for a model to be ready and work successfully.

What are the variables and features?

We will be using terms variables and features many times throughout our discussion. In the above dataset, each column itself is a variable. From a database perspective, a column can have multiple values to variable.

Predictor and target variables

For example, if we have to build a machine learning model that can predict the salary of an employee, then salary becomes the target variable, and all other becomes the predictor variable. A machine learning model analyzes predictor variable values and tries to construct a mathematical form/data structure that can predict the values of the target variable.

Predictor variables are often called features. It is not evident that from a dataset, we will take all the features for building a model. There are techniques to choose the appropriate features that we will discuss later.

Types of variables: Continuous and categorical

Majorly, there are two types of variables: continuous andcategorical.

- **Continuous:** Continuous variables can have any values within a specific range or without a range. For example, any real number with decimal places or integer values. In the above dataset, `salary` is a continuous variable.

- **Categorical:** Categorical variables are generally of the string data type. But these can have only a fixed number of different values. For example, the department in the above dataset. It can have values: `Accounts, Marketing,` and `Design` only. These values are real strings. Though string can have characters inside it, we don't consider individual characters as separate values for a specific data type. Instead we consider the entire string as a whole. The number of distinct values for a categorical variable is called the **cardinality** of that. The cardinality of the `department` is 3 in the above dataset.

Apart from these two, there is another type of variable like `Binary, Date,` and more. `Binary` variables are a special type of categorical variable having cardinality 2 (True and False or else 0 and 1 as combinations). The `date` type variable can be decomposed into categorical and continuous variables.

Categorical variables don't need to always be of string type. Numbers can also be treated as categorical ones. There is a special logic of determining which variable is categorical and which one is continuous. We need to measure a ratio as given below:

$$\text{Variable Test Ratio} = \frac{\text{No of distinct values in the dataset for a variable } X}{\text{Total no of records in a dataset}}$$

We can set a threshold for this ratio to decide on considering a variable as continuous or categorical. A higher value of this ratio indicates the possibility of a variable to be considered continuous; otherwise, it should be categorical.

Lifecycle of a machine learning model

Like any software development project, ML model development projects also have a typical lifecycle. But in some areas, it differs a lot with traditional application/ product development. The main reason is the research-oriented nature of work. A typical model goes through several iterations before putting it in a production environment. Generally, ML comes under a broader practice of subject called *data science.* Other than ML, data science involves data discovery, exploration, and normal descriptive analytics. All model development-related research activities come under data science and anything else which helps in rolling out the model to production, scaling, and more, come under *data engineering* activities.

There are four major stages in a typical ML model development, as shown in the below cyclic diagram:

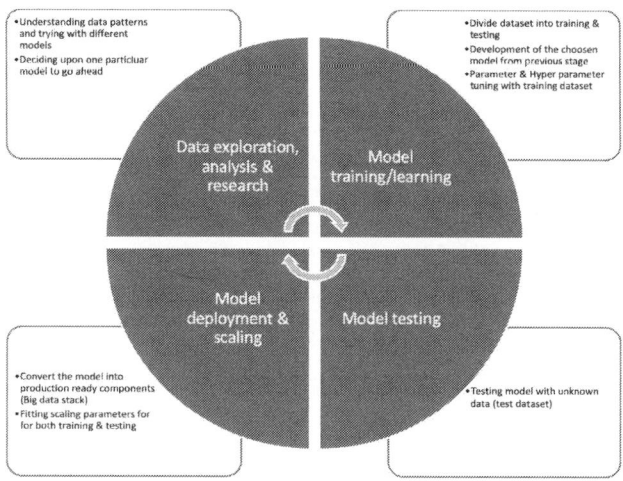

Figure 1.2: *Life Cycle of Machine Learning Project*

- **Data exploration, analysis, and research:** In this stage, ML experts/data scientists get a first taste of the data. Various kinds of slicing, dicing, and visualization are done at this stage by using a proper sample of the total dataset. Trial and error with several models also are done here. In the end, one particular model is chosen to proceed.

- **Model training/learning:** This stage involves tuning parameters and hyper-parameters of the chosen model and makes it repeatedly learn from the provided dataset. Parameters are model required information, and hyper-parameters are for fine-tuning (we will discuss these two in later sections).

- **Model testing:** This stage, as stated above, deals with testing the developed model with an unknown dataset.

- **Model deployment and scaling:** This stage involves converting the model into Big Data technology stack compliant components (like Spark, Hadoop, and more.). The development of proper data engineering platform/framework and finding out optimal scaling parameters and infrastructure are also done in this stage. Scaling is required for handling huge volumes of data. It is never possible without proper hardware and infrastructure support. Model training and testing for production /UAT/staging environments are also done over here.

These four stages are repeated circularly (as shown above) after getting the customer/ stake holder's feedback about the deployed model. The first three stages come under typical data science-related activities, and the last stage comes under data engineering activity.

Pre-conditions of a successful ML project

Machine learning projects are quite different. As it involves a lot of research-related activities, a team of people with the right skill sets is required at first. These projects go through several iterations, and it may happen that after a lot of research and spending a lot of time, no output comes at the end. So, a flexible and open mindset in the project management team is also one of the pre-conditions here. The output or performance of a machine learning project should never be compared with other regular track projects; otherwise, it will create a wrong perception and expectation.

It has been observed many times in the software industry that despite having a good, skillful team, ML projects have failed simply due to the wrong mindset, vision, and expectation of the higher management. As data science/machine learning is a very niche area, lack of knowledge and awareness in the higher management is also a primary reason for these type failures.

Different types of the learning process

There are different types of learning techniques to train a model. Depending on the problem type, these learning techniques are chosen accordingly.

Supervised learning

We already discussed the target variable and the predictor variable in earlier sections. In supervised learning, a dataset containing proper definitions of target and predictor variables are always given. This learning process tries to find out relationships between these two variables. There is a clear-cut segregation between the training and testing stage in this learning technique. Algorithms learn in the training stage and validate themselves in the testing stage. Examples of supervised learning would be classification and regression techniques. We will discuss these in later sections.

Unsupervised learning

In unsupervised learning, algorithms learn by themselves without any external supervision or clear segregation of predictor and target variables. By going through the learning process, algorithms find out hidden relationships between the features (without the existence of any clear definition of predictor or target, all variables is treated as *features* here). Target variables are often defined on the fly or as an output of the algorithm. Unlike a supervised approach, this technique does not very clearly segregate training and testing. Validation also happens while building the model. Examples will be clustering, dimensionality reduction, and more.

A model can take anyone or both of these learning processes to give predictions or finding out hidden patterns from the data.

Parameter and hyperparameter

It is easily understood from our discussion so far that each model is backed up by an algorithm (be it supervised or unsupervised learning). From the concept of computer science and Mathematics, we can say that an algorithm may need some information supplied externally to proceed. These are called **parameters**. For example, let's consider a straightforward algebraic equation like below:

$$y = mx + c$$

Here, m and c are parameters of the equation. An algorithm can be developed to find out optimal values for m and c. Parameters are always required for a model. We can say a model is defined by its statement and parameters. Like in the above example, the equation is defined by the statement and parameters m and c.

Hyperparameters are optional for a model. In the model definition, there is no existence of hyperparameters. But these are required to tune it and make it strong enough to give the optimal result. For example, to solve the above-mentioned simple equation numerically, we may have to run an iterative algorithm, and the number of iterations can be controlled. It may affect the final result. The number of iterations is a hyperparameter over here. But this is never defined or mentioned in above-mentioned algebraic equation itself. The number of iterations can be set from outside while solving the problem.

We will see more detailed examples of parameters and hyperparameters in the respective chapters of different machine learning techniques.

Machine learning models by objective

Machine learning practice can be divided into two types depending on the objective. We will discuss it one by one. By objective, we mean the high-level goal of the problem.

Predictive machine learning

From the name itself, it is clear that this type of machine learning practice is always used for giving any kind of predictions. It can give predictions for the unknown/ unseen data.

Descriptive machine learning

ML models are not only used for predictions, but these can be built to explain some kind of hidden behavior or pattern of the data also. Practicing or building this type of model is known as **descriptive ML**. It can describe a story by analyzing a dataset or multiple datasets. It can discover some hidden patterns which will give a lot of insights to the stakeholders of the model. The same model can be used for both predictive and descriptive purposes. In general, unsupervised learning-based models are good candidates for descriptive ML.

Machine learning models by problem type

Before designing any model, first, we have to make sure what type of problems we are trying to solve. A detailed analysis of the datasets is required for this. At a very high level, we can say, nature of the target variable often decides the problem type. Problem type based on different models is discussed next.

Classification model

When we try to assign a label to a data instance, we call it as classification or tagging. Classification is mostly supervised learning in nature; that is, it will already have a historical dataset with tagged labels. Our model will learn from there, and for any incoming and unknown data instance, it can infer a label for it. It is a typical prediction problem and comes under predictive ML, as discussed earlier. For example, let's consider the `employee` dataset discussed earlier. If we set our target variable as a designation, then it becomes a classification problem. We have to predict an employee's designation by his/her other given information. In mathematical terms, it can be said at high-level that, when a target variable is categorical, then the prediction problem is a classification problem. There are various techniques of classification models like Decision Tree, Logistic Regression, Naïve Bayes, and more. We will discuss it in more detail in *Chapter 2: Classification*.

Regression model

If the target variable is a continuous one, then it becomes aregression model. It also comes under the predictive ML andsupervised learning category. Considering the same `employee` dataset, if weset `salary` as our target variable, then predicting salary from other features becomes a regression problem. Various regression techniques are *linear regression, polynomial regression, decision tree regression*, and more. We will discuss it in more detail in *Chapter 3*: Regression.

Clustering model

Without knowing any target variable, if we have to find out groups or chunks inside the dataset, it becomes a clustering problem. It comes under unsupervised learning and can be of both predictive and descriptive ML types. In a typical clustering model, tightly related data instances are grouped by analyzing its features. These groups are called **clusters**. We will discuss it in more detail in *Chapter 4: Clustering*.

Dimensionality reduction model

We saw a limited number of features in the `employee` dataset. But what if we have a lot of predictor variables that may be in thousands or more than that. Taking all these features into computation simply disturbs the model creation and its perfectness. It may happen that not all features were deciding the target variable value or the model objective (Note: features are also known as dimensions). There are standard techniques to choose only important features or reduce the dimension or map those in separate dimensions. These are known as **dimensionality reduction models**. For example, Principal Component Analysis (PCA), Auto encoder-based reduction, and more. We will discuss it in more detail in *Chapter 6: Miscellaneous Unsupervised Learning*.

Machine learning models by assumptions

Having a set of assumptions is one of the vital important aspects of model development. Some model starts with a strong assumption, and some do not.

Parametric model

Parametric models assume a particular pre-existing statistical/mathematical form of the model and try to find out optimal values of the parameters defined by the model. Parametric model development is often called as **statistical ML** or rather better to say simple statistical techniques. These models, as said above, are solidly backed by a statistical or mathematical formulation. Most of the time, parametric models assume certain statistical distributions about the nature of the data. By these assumptions, it tries to force-fit the model into the data. It works well if the data distribution assumptions or the model form assumptions are correct, but fail drastically for wrong assumptions. Parametric models are better designed by experienced statisticians with good amount domain knowledge about the data rather than machine learning experts in some areas. Examples of parametric models would be linear and polynomial regression, logistic regression, Gaussian mixture models of clustering, and more.

Parametric models are easy to understand and tune. It consumes less memory and processing time and works well with fewer data. These have limitations in understanding non-very well-known data or data from some unknown domain. Results from these come at two extreme ends, either it would be too good or too bad. That's why we have to be very sure before applying this technique.

Non-parametric model

Unlike parametric models, non-parametric models do not assume (or assume very few) any statistical/mathematical form and distributions of the data. It works well for those cases where data distributions are unknown. An example would be *Decision Trees, Regression Trees, K nearest neighbors*, and more.

Non-parametric models work well with much unknown dataset from unknown domains. These have better flexibility as compared to parametric ones. But, running time and resource (memory and CPU) usage are quite high for these models as there are more parameters to train. Also, these models are more complex and difficult to tune.

From the name parametric andnon-parametric, it may seem like one with parameters, and the other one is without parameters. But this is not the case at all. The definition of a parameter is entirely different, and both techniques of model development may or may not have parameters. So, confusion in the names should be avoided.

Accuracy of the ML model

After designing the model, measuring its perfectness is essential to get good results. It is known as **accuracy** in general terms. There are various metrics to compute accuracy and those differences across problem types. Accuracy is measured for training as well as testing dataset. We will just discuss different accuracy metrics for different problem types at a very high-level. Model or problem-specific detailed discussions of accuracy metrics will be done in respective chapters.

Training and testing dataset

For training/building the model and measuring accuracy input dataset is split into two parts: training and testing. The model is trained and built on the training dataset, and the testing dataset is kept as hidden or unknown to the model. Once built, accuracy is generally tested on the testing dataset, that is, on the unknown data. Though measuring accuracy on the training data may be necessary sometimes for an in-depth analysis of the model. We will be doing this train-test splitting in each of the respective chapters for measuring accuracy.

Accuracy for classification

Accuracy for classification is measured by the ratio (no of data instances correctly classified/total no of records). A larger value (maximum can be 1) of this ratio indicates a better classifier. This metric can be used for any kind of classification problems. Other detailed metrics will be discussed in detail in *Chapter 2: Classification*.

Accuracy for regression

As regression deals with predictions of continuous variables, simple ratio/count-based methods of accuracy won't work here, unlike classification. For regression, accuracy should be given in the form of errors. Error term looks like below:

$$error = y - \hat{y}$$

Where y = original value of target variable and $\hat{y}$ = predicted value of target variable.

At a very high-level, by measuring this value, we can get the accuracy of a regression problem. A lesser value of the error indicates a better regression model. More details about other metrics will be discussed in *Chapter 3: Regression*.

Accuracy for clustering

Cluster accuracy is inclined towards relative measures of distances between data points. We see there, how closely data points are scattered, and measure intra-cluster vs. inter-cluster distances. We will see it in more detail in *Chapter 4: Clustering*.

Bias-Variance decomposition

Bias means how much a model is skewed towards a few data instances. In a classification problem, it may happen that a model is classifying a set of data instances as always, some particular labels. For example, in our `employee` dataset, if a classification model (for predicting `designation`) is developed and it always predicts designation of an employee as CA in 90% cases, then depending on the class label distribution, it can be said that the model is biased towards class label CA. Sometimes the presence of highly regular classes creates biases in the model. We generally say that the class distribution is not symmetric in those cases.

In regression also, the same biases can be there for a combination of features, which causes the target variable to have a fixed range of values always. Thus, Bias always creates problems in designing a perfect model. We can also say that an underprepared or less complicated model will have a high bias.

Variance is the exact opposite situation. When a model tries to be too smart and starts giving predictions too accurately for a training dataset, it adjusts itself too much and tunes its parameters alot. Effect of this would be a very complex model which may have less accuracy in testing or unknown dataset. High variance is also a barrier in designing a perfect model. A very highly complex model will have high variance and low bias.

The overall error in a model is composed of both bias and variance. A mathematical expression would be like below:

$$Error = Bias + Variance$$

If we plot Model Complexity vs. *Error*, then it looks like below:

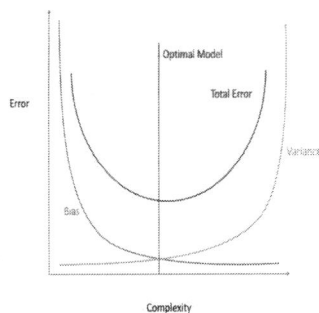

Figure 1.3: Bias vs. Variance plot

From the above plot, we can say that decreasing bias will increase variance, and decreasing variance will increase bias. An optimal model will always be in between with a moderate bias and variance combination.

Underfitting andoverfitting

As an effect of bias and variance, two problems occur in any ML model development. These are known as underfitting andoverfitting.

- **Underfitting:** It occurs due to a shortage of training data, an immature model causing high bias and low variance. An underfitted model fails to predict or work accurately in all situations. Sometimes, even though we have sufficient training data, the number of iterations done for the training is low, which is again causing high bias.

- **Overfitting:** It is the exact opposite situation. Here we have high variance and low bias. Overfitted models are too involved. In the process of making a model too perfect, sometimes over-tuning of parameters or too much iteration on the training data causes this problem. Here, the accuracy obtained with training data may be useful, but the moment a model is tested with unknown/testing data, it starts failing to perform well.

Each ML techniques (classification, regression, and clustering) have their way of handling bias and variance. We will discuss these in the respective chapters.

Mathematical concepts in machine learning

As discussed in earlier sections, ML is a mixture of mathematics-statistics, computer science theory, and software engineering practices. The mathematical-statistical analysis is a key part of the entire story. It is a building block of any model.

Each model needs a proper and definitive structure of data. Once this information is available, it starts processing and gives the data a proper shape before doing the actual work. These steps are known as **pre-processing**. In this next, we will find out an appropriate definition of data, discuss pre-processing steps, and short mathematical tools/metrics which are shared across the models.

Definition of data point

A data point is a record of the dataset. For example, in the `employee` dataset, record no 1 is a data point. Each data point has a set of feature value and can be expressed as a mathematical expression of tuple or vector-like below:

$$x = (x_1, x_2, x_3, ..., x_n)$$

Each data point is an n-dimensional vector over here. The x is a data point consisting of n feature values x_1 to x_n. For the `employee` dataset, there are four features and hence $n = 4$ (without considering `id` and `name`. These are not generally considered as features) if we consider salary as our target variable. So, record no 1 of `employee` dataset can be written as a vector x = ('New York', 'Accounts', 'CA', 'contract'). Similarly, if we consider `designation` as our target variable then we can write record no 1 as vector x = ('NewYork', 'Accounts', 15500, 'contract'). Target variables also can be written as single feature vector like y = (15000) or y = ('CA').

Dataset as a vector space

As we denote each data point as a vector, so the entire dataset constitutes a collection of vectors, a.k.a. **Vector Space**. The number of features decides the dimension of the vector space over here. In ML modeling, everything has to be represented as a vector in a vector space. Be it continuous, categorical, text data, image data, or whatever. And in most of the cases, vectors have to be compared with each other. This comparison metric can be expressed as similarity or distance.

For the convenience of computation and ease of solving problems, feature vectors are imagined as Euclidian Vectors constituting a Euclidean Vector Space. It is a special type of inner product space where the inner product is the dot product of two vectors. Euclidean vectors can have both magnitude and direction. Magnitude anddirection of the sample vector are shown below for a 2-dimensional vector space:

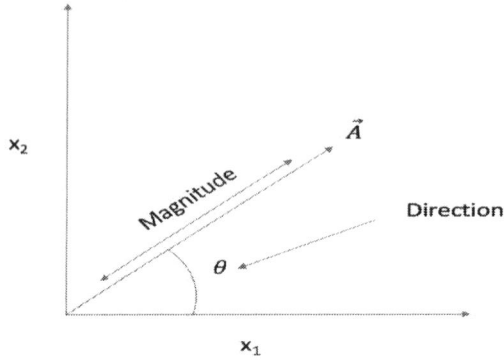

Figure 1.4: *Sample Vector*

The direction is always measured with respect to the origin (0, 0,0), and it is expressed as an angle. Magnitude is the distance between the origin and the end of the vector. There are few metrics to compute the magnitude, direction, and the scalar representative value of Euclidean Vectors.

Norm of a Vector

Norm is a function that gives a strictly positive value of a vector in a vector space. The *p*-norm of a vector is given by the mathematical expression:

$$L_p = \left(\sum_{i=1}^{n} |x_i|^p \right)^{1/p}$$

Where *p* = degree of the norm and *n* = number of dimensions.

Norm is often considered as the magnitude of a vector. Euclidean vectors always have L2 norm, and simple expression is $\sqrt{\sqrt{|x|.|x|}}$. That isthe square root of the dot product with itself.

Euclidean distance

Euclidean distance between two vectors x_i and x_j is the square-root of the sum of the squared differences for all the features. The mathematical expression is given by:

$$Euclide\ an\ Distance\ (x_i, x_j) = \sqrt{\sum_{k=1}^{n}(x_{ik} - x_{jk})^2}$$

Where n is the total number of features.

Euclide an distance works well in measuring the difference in terms of raw magnitude. It is always better to bring down all variables on the same scale before Euclide an computing distance.

Similarity of vectors

Similarity can be expressed by taking the geometric cosine of the angle between vectors. Mathematically cosine similarity expression between two vectors $\vec{A}$ and $\vec{B}$ is given by:

$$cosine\_similarity\ (\vec{A}, \vec{B}) = \frac{\vec{A}.\vec{B}}{\|\vec{A}\|\ \|\vec{B}\|}$$

Where $\vec{A}.\vec{B}$ = dot product of two vectors A & B and $\|\vec{A}\|$ = L2 norm or Euclidean Norm of vector $\vec{A}$, cosine similarity values range from – 1 to 1 (same as the range of cos θ). The cosine similarity does not consider the magnitude of vectors that much. It considers direction or angle between vectors more.

Below diagram is a pictorial representation of cosine similarity and Euclidean distance:

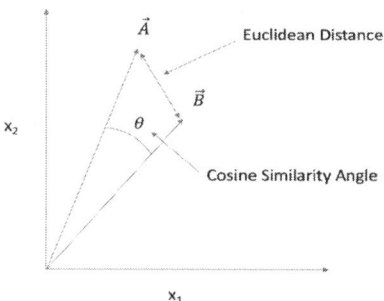

Figure 1.5: *Cosine Similarity & Euclidean Distance*

Both cosine similarity and Euclidean distance can be used as distance metrics. It depends on the use case, which one to prefer over another. If we are more concerned about the raw difference between data point values, then Euclidean distance is a default choice, but if the orientation is a matter of interest, then cosine similarity makes more sense. Euclidean distance can be used in most of the cases, but a few specific subjects like text mining needs cosine similarity to be considered as a metric.

There is a small difference between the interpretation of two metrics. Euclidean distance is a distance metric, whereas cosine similarity is similarity metrics. If we use (1-cosine similarity), then it also becomes a distance metric.

We will now compute the cosine similarity of two 3-dimenstional sample vectors and see an interesting property of it:

1. $V_1 = (-3, 4, 2)$ and $V_2 = (5, -4, -2)$

2. Now, $V_1 \cdot V_2 = [(-3) \cdot 5 + 4 \cdot (-4) + 2 \cdot (-2)] = [(-15) + (-16) + (-4)] = -35$

3. $\quad || V_1 || = \sqrt{\sqrt{(-3)^2 + (4)^2 + (2)^2}} = 5.38$

    and $\quad || V_2 || = \sqrt{\sqrt{(5)^2 + (-4)^2 + (-2)^2}} = 6.7$

4. So, cosine_similarity $(V_1, V_2) = (-35) / (5.38 * 6.7) = -0.97$

5. Now, if V_1 gets multiplied by a scaler factor 2 then $V_1 = (-6, 8, 4)$

6. $V_1 \cdot V_2 = [(-6) \cdot 5 + 8 \cdot (-4) + 4 \cdot (-2)] = [(-30) + (-32) + (-8)] = -70$

7. Then, $|| V_1 || = \sqrt{\sqrt{(-6)^2 + (8)^2 + (4)^2}} = 10.77$

    So, cosine_similarity $(V_1, V_2) = (-70) / (10.77 * 6.7) = -0.97$

So, it is a proof that cosine similarity measure is unaffected by vector magnitude.

Eigenvalues and Eigenvectors

Eigenvalues and Eigenvectors are always computed against a square matrix. A square matrix is analogous to a 2-dimensional vector. Multiplication of Eigenvector with the square matrix has the same result as the multiplication of Eigenvector with a scalar quantity.

To explain it mathematically, if A is a linear transformation, that is, the square matrix, V is a vector, and λ is a scalar quantity, and if the relationship $AV = \lambda V$ holds, then V is called **Eigenvector** and λ is called **Eigenvalue** of A.

Eigenvectors have usage mainly in variable transformations. We will see its usage in *Chapter 6*: Miscellaneous Unsupervised Learning.

Variable transformation andimputation

We already discussed continuous and categorical variables in previous sections. In most of the ML algorithms, a fair amount of pre-processing is. One of the pre-processing is variable transformations. There are various types of transformations available. Each one has its purpose.

Scaling and normalization

Different continuous variables may have a different range of values. Accuracy is profoundly affected by this phenomenon. For example, let's consider there is a two-feature dataset having continuous variables X_1 and X_2. X_1 values range from 1000 to 10000, whereas X_2 values range from 1 to 10.

Distance for two data point $p_1 = (1200, 3)$ and $p_2 = (2000, 7)$ is computed as

Euclidean distance $(p_1, p_2) = \sqrt{\sqrt{(1200 - 2000)^2 + (3 - 7)^2}} \cong 800$

In the same way for another pair of points $p_3 = (1200, 3)$ and $p_4 = (1250, 7)$

Euclidean distance $(p_3, p_4) = \sqrt{\sqrt{(1200 - 1250)^2 + (3 - 7)^2}} \cong 50.15$

Distances are heavily influenced by the X_1 variable because of its higher range. Computation is ignoring the effect of variable X_2. The solution to this problem is variable scaling. We need to bring down all variables to the same scale.

Min-max scaling

The mathematical expression of Min-Max scaling is given by:

$$Z = \frac{X - X_{min}}{X_{max} - X_{min}}$$

Where *Xmin* = Minimum value of X in the dataset, Xmax = Maximum value of X in the dataset. By default, transformed variable values of Min-Max scaling range from 0 to 1. So, no matter whatever be the actual range of any variables, it will always be trimmed down between 0 and 1. We can apply the same for our sample data point p_1 and p_2:

$$Z_1 = \left(\frac{1200 - 1000}{10000 - 1000}, \frac{3 - 1}{10 - 1} \right) = (0.022, 0.22)$$

$$Z_2 = \left(\frac{2000 - 1000}{10000 - 1000}, \frac{7 - 1}{10 - 1} \right) = (0.11, 0.66)$$

Now, the distance between Z_1 and Z_2 can be computed as:

Euclidean Distance (Z1, Z2) $= \sqrt{\sqrt{(0.022 - 0.11)^2 + (0.22 - 0.66)^2}} = 0.619$

Distance values won't be affected by scale factors.

Standard scaling

The mathematical expression of standard scaling is given by:

$$Z = \frac{X - \mu}{\sigma}$$

Where, μ = Mean of X in the dataset and σ = Standard deviation of X in the dataset.

Standard Scaler brings down all features to zero mean and unit variance. It helps many ML algorithms to do proper optimization and give better accuracy. It is an optional pre-requisite of many models.

Categorical to continuous variable transformation

Categorical variables cannot be used directly in some ML models like linear/polynomial regression, or clustering. It has to be converted to a continuous variable. Python libraries like `scikit-learn` cannotunderstand categorical data at all. So, there also this conversion is a pre-requisite.

One-hot encoding

One-hot-encoding is a mechanism where one categorical variable is decomposed into a set of continuous variables.

For example, if a categorical variable X with cardinality 3 has three distinct values A, B, C and we have three data points $P1 = ('A')$, $P2 = ('B')$, $P3 = ('C')$ then X can be decomposed into 3 variables X_A, X_B, and X_C respectively (we can use any name instead of X_A, X_B, X_C). X_A denotes whether a data point p has value 'A' or not, and it can be 0 or 1. Values can be similarly set for X_B and X_C.

So, the transformed dataset will look like:

Datapoint	X_A	X_B	X_C
P1	1	0	0
P2	0	1	0
P3	0	0	1

Table 1.1: Sample one-hot encoded variable

In general, a categorical variable with cardinality n will be decomposed into n continuous/boolean variables, and value for each one will be 0 or 1 depending on the presence of a category.

The result of this transformation definitely will increase dimensionality or number of features of the dataset, but it can be handled with dimensionality reduction techniques.

Continuous to categorical variable transformation

This type of transformation is not so common, unlike one-hot-encoding, but still sometimes has to be done for special cases. A very common technique of doing this is by clustering. Clustering divides the data into different groups. Each group can be stated as a string indicator, and if a data point p has value X_1 for variable X and X_1 belongs to clustered group C, and we can create a new variable and set the value as string C instead of X_1. Details of clustering techniques can be found it *Chapter 4: Clustering*.

Imputation

Imputation is the technique for filling missing values in a dataset. Missing values creates problem while doing any kind of numerical computation like mean, square, and more. For example, if our `employee` dataset has some values of feature `salary` are missing for some rows, then it may create problem while building the regression model. There are different imputation strategies to fill the missing feature values. Most of them are central tendency based. Like filling the missing ones with the mean, median, or mode of other values for that feature. Mean andmedian are used for continuous features, whereas mode is for categorical ones. Missing values in a dataset should be checked before building the actual model, and an appropriate imputation strategy should be applied.

Measures of variance

Variance is a statistical measure of dispersion between data points in a dataset. It helps a lot in the identification of unique data points. Most of the predictive ML models try to uphold the variance present in the data. It is given by the average sum of squares of deviations from the mean, and the expression looks like:

$$Var(x) = \frac{1}{n}\sum_{i=1}^{n}(x_i - \mu)^2$$

And the standard deviation (σ) is the square root of variance:

$$SD(x) = \sqrt{Var(x)}$$

Standard deviation andvariance are used interchangeably in ML-based analysis.

Coefficient of variance (CV)

It is the ratio between the standard deviation and means. It is given by the expression:

$$CV(x) = \frac{\sigma}{\mu}$$

A high value of CV indicates more variability in the data with respect to mean. This metric is used in some models as stopping criteria of the algorithm; that is, the algorithm would try to maintain a certain variability to boost prediction accuracy. This certain value can be externally seeded as a threshold.

Conclusion

In this chapter, we discussed the formal definition and concept of ML, the building blocks of it, the lifecycle of a machine learning project. We also discussed various categories of machine learning techniques and accuracy measures at a high-level.

We learned at a very high level about various ML techniques like classification, regression, clustering, and more. We understood the definition of data and how do we represent it using Vector Space. Our learning curve also touched upon different vector space operations like addition, scaling, measuring distance, and more. We also learned about various preprocessing and variable transformation techniques. These transformations are more or less required in every kind of ML algorithm.

In the next chapter, we will start our detailed discussion with the first ML technique: classification. It is a typical data labeling technique where the target variable is categorical, and our discussion will show how we can give a mathematical shape to it and solve the problem.

CHAPTER 2
Classification

The previous chapter was about the fundamentals of **machine learning(ML)** and its different approaches at a very high level. In this chapter, we will discuss the first ML technique among those: classification. What do we mean by classification? It is a technique of assigning data instances to one or more categories. Here the target variable is of categorical type. Each data instance can be denoted by *atuple* (x, y) where x is a vector of features, and y is the special attribute or target attribute. The goal of the classification algorithms is to learn this tuple relation for each data instance, and when any unlabeled instance comes, it should be able to put it into a relation. Practical examples of classification would be identifying a mail as spam or non-spam, predicting genres from movie plot, identifying whether a loan-borrower would be defaulter or not, and many more. In this chapter, we will discuss the various techniques to solve the classification problem and the corresponding mathematical foundations.

Structure

In this chapter, we will discuss:

- Problem definition and graphical interpretation of classification
- Introduction to `scikit-learn` as a Python library to use for present and all subsequent chapters

- Different parametric and non-parametric classifiers like Decision Tree, Naïve Bayes, Logistic Regression, and more.
- Ensemble models
- Class imbalance problem
- Multi-label classification techniques

Objective

After finishing this chapter, we will be able to:

- Analyze dataset and choose appropriate classification model to solve the problem
- Mitigate class imbalance problem
- Build ensemble models of different classifiers
- Get a practical idea of how to use `scikit-learn` to build pipelines for models

Problem formulation

To formulate the classification problem and understand it from a practical perspective, we will take an example of `employee` dataset from the previous chapter:

	branch	department	designation	id	name	salary	type
0	LA	Accounts	Manager	1	John	20000	permanent
1	New York	Accounts	CA	2	David	15500	contract
2	New York	Marketing	Manager	3	Samantha	18000	permanent
3	LA	Design	Director	4	Jacob	30000	permanent

Figure 2.1: Sample employee dataset

If we want to know the `type` of a new employee from the other features, then `type` becomes the *target* variable, and a classification algorithm will predict either `permanent` or `contract` as value. Each of these values becomes a *Class Label* or simply class.

Binary and multi-class

If the number of total distinct class labels is at max two, then it is a *Binary Classification* problem. As per this, the previous example is suitable for binary classification.

If the number of total distinct class labels is more than two, then it is a *multi-class* classification problem.

Class boundary

Now, the question comes, how we can distinguish theoretically between different data instances with class label tagging. We will try to understand by a graphical plot of any sample dataset.

Let's consider we have a 2-class (*Class A* and *Class B*) or binary classification problem with the dataset having only two features (x_1 and x_2). A sample dataset plot will look like:

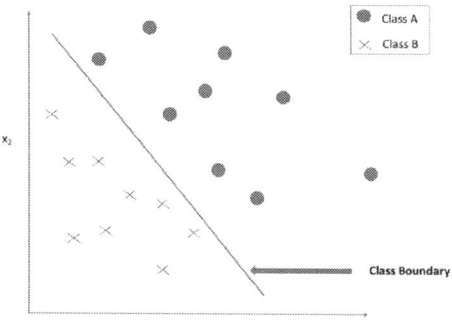

Figure 2.2: Standard class boundary

We can see from the above plot, that we can draw a straight line as a separator between two different sets of points representing each class. This separator is known as *class boundary*. It works as a borderline. As it is a 2-D plot, a separator is a line, but it would be a plane for a 3-D plot and hyperplane for an n-D plot. So, more number of features causes more complex separator.

Linear and non-linear class boundary

When the class boundary is a straight line (2-D case) or hyperplane (n-D case), then it is a *linear class boundary*, as shown in the above example. But, not all the cases are pretty straight-forward and simple like above. Data points belonging to different class labels may not always be separable by a straight line or hyperplane. Below plot explains it:

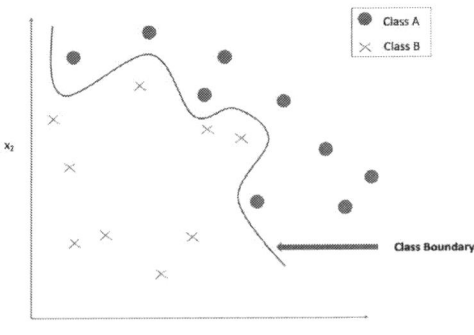

Figure 2.3: *Non-Linear Class Boundary*

It is never possible to draw a straight line, which can separate two classes in the above case. That's why the *class boundary* is a curve and non-linear (For understanding linear and non-linear relationships, please refer to *Chapter 3: Regression*).

The general approach for solving classification

Classification models try to build a relationship between the features set and the target variable from the input dataset. The process of building the relationship is known as a typical *learning process* of the classification problem. The output of this process could result in a mathematical relationship between variables or a data structure that can tell the class labels for an unknown input data. As explained in *Chapter 1: Introduction to Machine Learning and Mathematical Preliminaries*, this process starts with at first dividing the entire dataset into *training and testing*. Learning happens on the training dataset, and the testing dataset is kept unknown to the algorithm. Learning can happen through several iterations, or it can calculate some probabilities (we will see later in detail) required for the model to be built. Once the model building is finished, it's accuracy is tested with a testing dataset. This entire process of training and testing combination is known as an **epoch**. For better accuracy, several epochs can be performed, and then the final model can be released. Though this methodology can vary, more or less, it is followed across different types of *classification* models.

A brief introduction to scikit-learn

Before going through different classification models and their implementation details, we will discuss very briefly about Python's `scikit-learn` package. We will be using it for solving practical ML problems for classification and also for most of the other techniques to be discussed in subsequent chapters. It depends on other Python libraries like `numpy`, `pandas`, `scipy`, and more. The `scikit-learn` provides implementations of some common algorithms for classification, regression, clustering, dimensionality reduction, and deep learning.

This library follows a typical design pattern for both unsupervised and supervised algorithms. The beauty is that it maintains the same programming style for both types of algorithms. Thus, integrations become very easy. We will see a very simple example of DecisionTree classification using `scikit-learn`:

```
from sklearn.datasets import load_iris
from sklearn.tree import DecisionTreeClassifier

iris = load_iris()
clf = DecisionTreeClassifier()
clf = clf.fit(iris.data, iris.target)
predictions = clf.predict(iris.data)
```

Figure 2.4: Code snippet for Sample Decision Tree Classifier using Iris data

Details of the DecisionTree will be explained later in this chapter. For the time being, let's assume that it is a classification algorithm. We will only discuss the programming style of the library by leaving aside all internal mathematical details of the algorithm here.

Training process – fit function

In the above example, we are loading a sample dataset named `iris` available inside the `scikit-learn` package. Then we are creating an instance of `DecisonTreeClassifier` and calling a fit function on the instance with features and target labels as defined in the iris dataset as parameters. The fit function trains the model with the data available. This training process includes finding out optimal parameters that define the model through several iterations. It holds for any kind of ML model under the `scikit-learn` library.

Each of the *classification* algorithm implementations has been done by creating a class by extending `BaseEstimator`and `ClassifierMixin` classes in `scikit-learn`. For example, `DecisionTreeClassifier` also extends from these two classes. `BaseEstimator` provides some basic functions of parameter processing, and `ClassifierMixin` provides a `score` function for calculating the average accuracy of the current classifier. If we want to create our custom classification algorithm, then also we have created a class by extending `BaseEstimator`and `ClassifierMixin`.

Testing/validation process – predict function

Once the model is trained, it is ready for actual execution. And this is done by calling `predict` function. It applies the trained model on the unseen input data to find out class labels and returns the results as an array or `pandas` data frame. Each classification algorithm under `scikit-learn` has to implement this `predict` function and so as `DecisonTreeClassifier`.

Concept of pipeline

Creating and leveraging `pipelines` for supporting large scale integration and reusability is an essential part of ML practice. A `pipeline` is a collection of different reusable components that can be stacked together in the proper sequence to create a composite but single computing unit while implementing an ML algorithm. These reusable components are called *stages* of the pipeline. A stage can be a data transformation operation, scaling operation, or any kind of data pre-processing operation or the actual ML algorithm itself. We already saw several data transformation and scaling options in *Chapter 1: Introduction to Machine Learning and Mathematical Preliminaries*. Those can be used as pipeline stages on a requirement basis. The primary usage of pipeline stages is for data pre-processing. A sample pipeline will look like below:

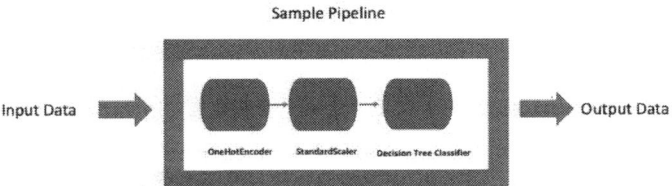

Figure 2.5: Sample ML pipeline

Each of these `One Hot Encoder, Standard Scaler, and Decision Tree Classifier` are pipeline stages. The bounding box in the above diagram becomes a composite component but can work as a single computing unit that can be invoked in a single shot instead of maintaining the lifecycles of each stage separately. All pipeline stages follow a standard common interface. Each ready-made stage component under `scikit-learn` extends from the same `BaseEstimator`, as mentioned earlier. Even if we want to make our custom stage, we have to create a class by extending `BaseEstimator`.

The `scikit-learn` has a class named `Pipeline`, which should be constructed with all stages as arguments to create a real pipeline. This one also extends from `BaseEstimator` and have `fit, predict, and transform` as major functions. The `transform` function does the actual transformation for any data pre or post-processing work. We will see all these through an example. Again, for the time being, we will ignore internal algorithmic details of the components and study only the programming style. Later, detail discussions will come one-by-one.

Without pipeline

If pre-processing is needed, then each stage has to be created and invoked separately. Result of one stage also has to be passed to the next stage:

```
from sklearn.linear_model import LogisticRegression
from sklearn.preprocessing import StandardScaler

logit_clf = LogisticRegression()
sc = StandardScaler()

sc.fit(iris.data)
iris_transformed = sc.transform(iris.data)

logit_clf.fit(iris_transformed, iris.target)
logit_predictions = logit_clf.predict(iris_transformed)
```

Figure 2.6: Sample Logistic Regression without pipeline

In the above example, fit and `transform` of the `StandardScaler` stage are called, and the result is passed to the `LogisticRegression` stage. More stages definitely will create a longer and repetitive code sequence, which could also be error-prone.

With Pipeline

`Pipeline` class in the `scikit-learn` library works as a holder for all stages, and it is itself an estimator which extends from `BaseEstimator` like others. One sample pipeline construction is shown below:

```
from sklearn.pipeline import Pipeline

pl = Pipeline(steps = [('standard_scaler',StandardScaler()),
                       ('logit', LogisticRegression())]
             )
pl.fit(iris.data, iris.target)
pipeline_predictions = pl.predict(iris.data)
```

Figure 2.7: Sample Logistic Regression with pipeline

We created a pipeline instance and set the stages as an array of Python tuples. Each tuple contains a name for the stage and an instance of `BaseEstimator`. Just a single call of fit function trains the entire model with pre-processed data. Calling a fit function on a pipeline instance makes repetitive internal calls of fit for all stages sequentially. Order of calls will be the same as the order of stages as those are created inside array while constructing the pipeline instance. A similar effect will be on calling the `transform` function. Calling `predict` on the pipeline instance makes the call of `predict` of the last stage. Thus number of calls gets reduced to a single call.

The Bayesian approach of classification

This technique is all about analyzing the probabilistic relationships between features and target class labels. And it is primarily based on the statistical theory of *Bayes Theorem*. Let's first have a small introduction of Bayes theorem before applying it in solving the real problem.

If X and Y are two random and dependent variables, the probability of X taking a value x_1 and Y taking a value y_1 is given by the joint probability (or the intersection):

$$P(X = x_1, Y = y_1) = P(X = x_1) = P(Y = y_1 \mid X = x_1)$$

Or,

$$P(X = x_1, Y = y_1) = P(Y = y_1) = P(X = x_1 \mid Y = y_1)$$

In the first case, Y is dependent on X, and in the second case, X is dependent on Y. $P(Y = y_1 \mid X = x_1)$ or $P(X = x_1 \mid Y = y_1)$ is known as conditional probability. Now from the above two expressions, we can write:

$$P(X = x_1) \times P(Y = y_1 \mid X = x_1) = P(Y = y_1) \times P(X = x_1 \mid Y = y_1)$$

So,

$$P(Y = y_1 \mid X = x_1) = \frac{P(Y = y_1) \times P(X = x_1 \mid Y = y_1)}{P(X = x_1)}$$

Or,

$$P(X = x_1 \mid Y = y_1) = \frac{P(X = x_1) \times P(Y = y_1 \mid X = x_1)}{P(Y = y_1)}$$

Thus, we can compute conditional probability given that we know the values of the left-hand side for both of the cases.

Applying Bayes theorem in classification

The above-formulated theorem can be applied to determine the class labels of a data instance. We can formalize the classification problem in terms of Bayes Theorem. Let X denote the feature set, and Y denotes the class label set or the target variable. We can compute the relationship between features and target variable using $P(Y \mid X)$ like above.

Prior and posterior probability

In Bayes Theorem, we saw the right-hand side expression is known to us, that is,

$P(X = x_1)$, $P(Y = y_1)$, $P(X = x_1 \mid Y = y_1)$ are pre-computed and known to us. These probabilities are known as **prior probabilities**.

And the conditional probabilities that need to be computed to derive a decision are known as **posterior probability**. $P(Y = y_1 \mid X = x_1)$ is an example of this.

Formulation

Conditional probability $P(Y \mid X)$ gives us the chances that a data instance having features X will have class label Y. There will be a number of $P(Y \mid X)$ for all possible class labels. In general, the predicted class label of a data instance is that one for which the conditional probability $P(Y \mid X)$ is maximum.

Mathematically:

$$P(Y = y_C) = \max \{P(Y = y_i \mid X = x_j)\}$$

Where C = predicted class label. The training process of the Bayesian approach involves prior computing probabilities from the dataset. Prior probabilities and the Bayes Theorem formulae work as a model over here. This model spits out the output as posterior probabilities, which determine the class labels.

Naïve Bayes classifier

In practice, variable X in the Bayes Theorem formulae will be composed of different sub-variables, that is, as X is the feature set, it is made of a vector of features and can be written as $X = \{X_1, X_2, ..., X_n\}$ where n is the total number of features in the dataset. Computing $P(X)$ and $P(X \mid Y)$ as prior probabilities are done with a naïve assumption that all features are conditionally independent of each other. By the law of probability:

$$P(X) = \prod_{i=1}^{n} P(X_i)$$

$$= P(X_1) \times P(X_2) \times ... \times \times P(X_n) \times$$

And,

$$P(X \mid Y) = \prod_{i=1}^{n} P(X_i \mid Y)$$

$$= P(X_1 \mid Y) \times P(X_2 \mid Y) \times ... P(X_n \mid Y)$$

So, the probability of a data instance having a set of feature values is the product of all individual probabilities of each feature value. The same rule is applicable for computing conditional probability $P(X \mid Y)$.

Conditional independence

As per conventional probability theory, two events X and Y are said to be conditionally independent with respect to third event Z if and only if below condition is satisfied:

$$P(X,Y \mid Z) = P(X,Z) \times P(Y,Z)$$

In Naïve Bayes classifier also, as said earlier, all features are conditionally independent with respect to target variable Y. That means if we set the target variable Y at a fixed value, any two features X_1 and X_2 do not get influenced by each other's value.

Conditional independence is a strong assumption for Naïve Bayes Classifier. If this criterion is not satisfied, probability computations will go wrong, and so as predicted class labels.

Accuracy

As discussed in *Chapter 1: Introduction to Machine Learning and Mathematical Preliminaries*, computation of accuracy for classification problems is straightforward and simple. It is defined by the ratio:

$$\text{Accuracy} = \frac{\text{Number of records predicted correctly}}{\text{Total number of records}}$$

It is a probability metric, and value ranges from 0 to 1. A higher value infers a better accuracy and classification model. It also can be expressed in terms of percentages like probability.

We will be using this metric throughout our discussion for all classification models.

Example using an abstract dataset

Let us consider a fictional dataset representing weather conditions for playing `golf`.

Outlook	Humidity	Temperature	Windy	Play Golf
Rainy	High	Cold	Yes	Yes
Rainy	High	Hot	Yes	No
Overcast	High	Hot	No	Yes
Sunny	High	Mild	No	Yes
Sunny	Normal	Cold	No	Yes
Sunny	Normal	Cold	Yes	No
Rainy	High	Mild	No	No
Rainy	Normal	Cold	No	Yes

Sunny	Normal	Mild	No	Yes
Overcast	Normal	Hot	No	Yes

Table 2.1: Sample dataset for Golf Playing conditions

Here features are *Outlook, Humidity, Temperature, Windy*, and target variable is *Play Golf*. Our objective is to predict *Play Golf* value from other features. As it is a classification problem, so *Play Golf* is, as usual, a categorical variable, and it has two class labels: *Yes* and *No*. But in this case, all other features are also categorical. We chose this type of dataset for our convenience and to understand Naïve Bayes Classifier easily.

We need to compute two posterior probabilities for deciding the class label. These are P(*Play Golf* = *Yes* | X) and P(*Play Golf* = *No* | X). Now, X = {*Outlook, Humidity, Temperature, Windy*} and from the theory of Naïve Bayes Classifier:

$$P(X) = P(\text{Outlook}) \times P(\text{Humidity}) \times P(\text{Temperature}) \times P(\text{Windy})$$

Training process

Prior probabilities for each feature & target variable values need to be computed now. One of those is P(*Outlook* = 'Rainy'). We can see there isa total of 10 records in the dataset, and 5 of them having '*Rainy*' as the value of *Outlook* attribute.

So,   *P(Outlook = 'Rainy') = 5/10 = 0.5.*

In similar fashion,

> *P(Outlook = 'Sunny') = 4/10 = 0.4*

> *P(Outlook = 'Overcast') = 2/10 = 0.2*

> *P(Humidity = 'High') = 5/10 = 0.5*

> *P(Humidity = 'Normal') = 6/10 = 0.6*

> *P(Temperature = 'Cold') = 4/10 = 0.4*

> *P(Temperature = 'Hot) = 3/10 = 0.3*

> *P(Temperature = 'Mild') = 4/10 = 0.4*

> *P(Windy = 'Yes') = 4/10 = 0.4*

> *P(Windy = 'No') = 6/10 = 0.6*

And, for target variable Play Golf,

$$P(Play \ Golf = 'Yes') = 7/10 = 0.7$$

$$P(Play \ Golf = 'No') = 3/10 = 0.3$$

Training is complete now with the computed prior probabilities as model.

Validation with a data instance

Let's say, a data instance X comes with features values *Outlook = 'Sunny', Humidity = 'Normal', Temperature = 'Mild', Windy = 'No'*.

Now, conditional probabilities need to be computed:

$$P(X \mid PlayGolf = 'Yes') = P(Outlook = 'Sunny' \mid PlayGolf = 'Yes')$$
$$\times P(Humidity = 'Normal' \mid PlayGolf = 'Yes')$$
$$\times P(Temperature = 'Mild' \mid PlayGolf = 'Yes')$$
$$\times P(Windy = 'No' \mid PlayGolf = 'Yes')$$

There are three records where Outlook is Sunny given the condition that Play Golf is Yes.

So,

$$P(Outlook = 'Sunny' \mid Play \ Golf = 'Yes') = 3/10 = 0.3$$

Similarly,

$$P(Humidity = 'Normal' \mid Play \ Golf = 'Yes') = 5/10 = 0.5$$
$$P(Temperature = 'Mild' \mid Play \ Golf = 'Yes') = 4/10 = 0.4$$
$$P(Windy = 'No' \mid Play \ Golf = 'Yes') = 6/10 = 0.6$$

So,

$$P(X \mid PlayGolf = 'Yes') = 0.3 \times 0.5 \times 0.3 \times 0.4 \times 0.6 = 0.0108$$

Again,

$$P(X) = P(Outlook = 'Sunny') \times P(Humidity = 'Normal')$$
$$\times P(Temperature = 'Mild') \times P(Windy = 'No')$$
$$= 0.4 \times 0.6 \times 0.4 \times 0.6 = 0.0576$$

Now, we can compute the posterior probability to get the predicted label:

$$P(PlayGolf = 'Yes' \mid X) = \frac{P(PlayGolf = 'Yes') \times P(X \mid PlayGolf = 'Yes')}{P(X)}$$

$$= \frac{0.7 \times 0.0108}{0.0576} = 0.13$$

As the sum of total probability, space is one, and this is a two-class problem, so we don't have to compute *P* separately *(Play Golf = 'No' | X)*. We can get it easily

$$P(PlayGolf = 'No' \mid X) = 1 - P(PlayGolf = 'Yes' \mid X) = 1 - 0.13 \cong 0.87$$

Predicted class label for *Play Golf* is *No* as *P(Play Golf = 'No' | X) > P(Play Golf = 'Yes' | X)*.

For multi-class problems, we still would have to compute all possible posterior probabilities and then compare the values.

Laplace estimation

If, by any chance, while posterior computing probabilities, any of the conditional probabilities come out as zero, then the entire posterior probability becomes zero. In the previous example, if *P(X | Play Golf = 'Yes')* comes out as zero, then posterior probability *P(Play Golf = 'Yes' | X)* becomes zero due to multiplication effect. This problem simply wipes out all information coming from other prior probabilities and gives us a wrong estimate. That's why conditional probabilities should be regularized by adding 1 to the feature count (in the denominator) and adding k to the total number of records (*k* is the number of features or attributes).

$$Estimated\ Condtional\ Probablity = \frac{count + 1}{n + |features|}$$

This is known as **Laplace estimation**, and thus zero probability is always avoided. It is always better to do Laplace estimation as a pre-processing step while using Naïve Bayes Classifier.

Handling continuous attributes

So far, our discussion has always rotated around categorical variables as features. But how to use Naïve Bayes for continuous variables as features. Simple count based probability estimates won't work because continuous variables can take an infinite number of possible values, especially for real number based features. Counting for all combinations is simply impossible and incorrect. There are two ways to handle this situation:

1. We can assume a continuous probability distribution for that variable and estimate the parameters from the training data. A Gaussian distribution is the usual choice for estimating probability. The mean of the Gaussian distribution is estimated by the computing sample mean of the feature variable and so as the variance or standard deviation. Formulae for Gaussian

distribution is given by:

$$f(X) = \frac{1}{\sigma\sqrt{2\pi}} \exp\left(-\frac{(X-\mu)^2}{2\sigma^2}\right)$$

Where μ is computed mean, and σ is the computed standard deviation from the training data. For example, if a continuous variable X_1 takes a value 45.78, then conditional probability and prior probability can be computed as:

$$P(X_1 = 45.78) = f(X = 45.78) = \frac{1}{\sigma\sqrt{2\pi}} \exp\left(-\frac{(45.78-\mu)^2}{2\sigma^2}\right)$$

Gaussian is a very generic distribution, so if we specifically know the particular probability distribution for that continuous variable, then it is always better to use that one instead of Gaussian. For scientific research or financial data, knowing the exact probability distribution for any continuous variable may be possible, but in most cases, it may not be, and hence Gaussian estimate is the default choice. But doing so definitely will hamper the result to some extent.

2. We can convert the continuous variable to a categorical one and apply conventional Naïve Bayes on that. The clustering technique (refer *Chapter 6: Miscellaneous Unsupervised Learning*) can be used for this. Cluster number can be used as a category, and normal count based probability estimates can be easily done on that.

If the implementation library only supports continuous variables, then having a Gaussian estimate, that is, approach 1 is the only generic option.

Naïve Bayes Classifier using Python

We will use scikit-learn's built-in libraries for applying Naïve Bayes Classifier for prediction from a real dataset. For this example, we will use *Online Shoppers Intentions Dataset* from Kaggle (https://www.kaggle.com/roshansharma/online-shoppers-intention). At first, let's try to explore the dataset, see its contents, and formulate the problem statement.

The dataset is available as a `csv` file and below Python code can read the contents:

```python
import pandas as pd

page_visits_df = pd.read_csv('./data/online_shoppers_intention.csv')
page_visits_df.head()
```

	Administrative	Administrative_Duration	Informational	Informational_Duration	ProductRelated	ProductRelated_Duration	BounceRates	ExitRates	PageValues
0	0.0	0.0	0.0	0.0	1.0	0.000000	0.20	0.20	0.0
1	0.0	0.0	0.0	0.0	2.0	64.000000	0.00	0.10	0.0
2	0.0	-1.0	0.0	-1.0	1.0	-1.000000	0.20	0.20	0.0
3	0.0	0.0	0.0	0.0	2.0	2.666667	0.05	0.14	0.0
4	0.0	0.0	0.0	0.0	10.0	627.500000	0.02	0.05	0.0

Figure 2.8: Online Shoppers Intentions Dataset for Classification

From the description available at Kaggle and content shown above, we can understand that this dataset represents a different type of page visit counts and actual revenue generated indicator from an ecommerce portal. The objective is to understand whether visiting a page in the portal results in a purchase from there by a user or not. There is an attribute named `Revenue` of Boolean type indicates whether revenue is generated or not from the page visits. We have to build a classifier that can predict the value of `Revenue` from other attributes or features.

We can first separate features and target variable:

```
page_visits_x = page_visits_df[page_visits_df.columns[0:17]]
page_visits_y = page_visits_df[['Revenue']]
```

Figure 2.9: Feature and target variable split

Once we have raw features ready, we have to jump into the pre-processing part, as discussed next.

Pre-processing

There are three categorical variables: Month, `Visitor Type` and `Weekend` respectively, in the dataset. The `scikit-learn` cannot understand categorical data, so these have to be converted to numerical features. From the knowledge of *Chapter 1: Introduction to Machine Learning and Mathematical Preliminaries*, we can say that `OneHotEncoder` can be used over here for this purpose. The `pandas` library also provides a function `get_dummies` for this type of conversion. First, we will use it to see the effect:

```
pd.get_dummies(page_visits_x, columns=['Month','VisitorType','Weekend']).head()
```

th_Mar	Month_May	Month_Nov	Month_Oct	Month_Sep	VisitorType_New_Visitor	VisitorType_Other	VisitorType_Returning_Visitor	Weekend_False	Weekend_True
0	0	0	0	0	0	0	1	1	0
0	0	0	0	0	0	0	1	1	0
0	0	0	0	0	0	0	1	1	0
0	0	0	0	0	0	0	1	1	0
0	0	0	0	0	0	0	1	0	1

Figure 2.10: One Hot Encoded decomposition of categorical variables

The `get_dummies` takes the data frame and the categorical feature names as input and returns the converted dataset. It leaves numerical features as it is but converts the categorical ones. We can see that the `VistiorType` feature has been decomposed into three numerical features: `VisitorType_New_Vistor`, `VisitorType_Other`, `VisitorType_Returning_Vistor`, and each one have value `1` or `0`. Similar conversions are there for Month and Weekend also. But we will not use pandas utility for this. Instead, I will stick to `scikit-learn's OneHotEncoder` class.

Training and testing set

We will then divide the data into training and testing. The model will be built and trained on the training dataset, and testing dataset will help us to compute the accuracy:

```
from sklearn.model_selection import train_test_split

train_x, test_x, train_y, test_y = train_test_split(page_visits_x, page_visits_y, test_size=0.2)
```

Figure 2.11: Code snippet for train-test split

For subsequent examples in other chapters also, we will use this `train_test_split` function. It accepts the `test_size` ratio. We kept it `0.2` here; that is, 20% data of the entire dataset will be used for testing only and not for training.

Building the pipeline

As discussed earlier, a pipeline consists of pre-processing, post-processing, and ML algorithms as stages. For the current use case, stages would be `OneHotEncoder` and the Naïve Bayes Classifier itself. One problem with `scikit-learn's` one hot encoder is that it cannot work by itself without the help of `LabelEncoder`, which assigns unique integers in place of category strings. We can wrap everything inside a `ColumnTransformer`, which is the recommended approach as per the latest `scikit-learn` specification. Also, we need to convert the transformed 2D array into a dense matrix rather than sparse. So, we will create a custom stage by extending `BaseEstimator`. We need to override the `fit` and `transform` method accordingly:

```
from sklearn.preprocessing import OneHotEncoder
from scipy.sparse import csr_matrix
from sklearn.compose import make_column_transformer
from sklearn.base import BaseEstimator

class CategoricalVariableEncoder(BaseEstimator):

    def __init__(self, categorical_features):
        self.preprocessing_transformer = make_column_transformer((OneHotEncoder(handle_unknown="ignore"),
                                                                  categorical_features))

    def fit(self, X, y=None):
        self.preprocessing_transformer.fit(X)
        return self

    def transform(self, X):
        preprocessed_x = self.preprocessing_transformer.transform(X)
        return csr_matrix(preprocessed_x).todense()
```

Figure 2.12: Code snippet of Custom transformer for One-Hot-Encoder

Now, we can use an instance of `CategoricalVariableEncoder` as a stage in a pipeline. To create an instance, we just need to pass the list of categorical feature names.

There are two flavors of Naïve Bayes supported by `scikit-learn`: Gaussian and Multinomial.

Gaussian Naïve Bayes

Gaussian Naïve Bayes computes prior and posterior probabilities by Gaussian Distribution approximation. It works well when all or most of the features are continuous. We already discussed the techniques of approximation in the previous section:

```
from sklearn.pipeline import Pipeline
from sklearn.naive_bayes import GaussianNB

gnb_clf_pl = Pipeline(steps = [
                      ('cat_var_encoder',
                       CategoricalVariableEncoder(categorical_features=['Month','VisitorType','Weekend'])),
                      ('nb_clf', GaussianNB())
                      ]
            )
gnb_clf_pl.fit(train_x, train_y)

/Users/avnag/Library/Python/3.6/lib/python/site-packages/sklearn/utils/validation.py:724: DataConversionWarning: A co
lumn-vector y was passed when a 1d array was expected. Please change the shape of y to (n_samples, ), for example usi
ng ravel().
  y = column_or_1d(y, warn=True)

Pipeline(memory=None,
         steps=[('cat_var_encoder',
                 CategoricalVariableEncoder(categorical_features=None)),
                ('nb_clf', GaussianNB(priors=None, var_smoothing=1e-09))],
         verbose=False)
```

Figure 2.13: Code snippet of the pipeline for Gaussian Naïve Bayes

We can ignore the warning.

Now, we can use this model on the test data to compute the accuracy. `Pipeline` class has a `score` function that computes `accuracy` from the last stage configured. In our case, it will be the classifier accuracy metric, as discussed earlier:

```
gnb_clf_pl.score(test_x, test_y)
```

```
0.6261151662611517
```

Figure 2.14: Code snippet of Accuracy of Gaussian Naïve Bayes

Gaussian Naïve Bayes is giving 62.6% accuracy of the data. The reason for a little bit of low accuracy is the presence of decomposed categorical features. Gaussian approximation of probabilities is not a very good fit for categorical features. It should be used for the use cases where the majority of the features are continuous. Sometimes, even though there are only one or very few numbers of categorical features as compared to continuous, but if the cardinality of categorical features is too large, then after decomposition, too many continuous features are created, which may distort the model building. All these factors have to be considered before deciding on using *Gaussian Naïve Bayes*.

Multinomial Naïve Bayes

It assumes the probability distribution of features as Multinomial. It works well when most of the features are categorical. Multinomial distribution computes probability by counting feature values; that is, it is a type of discrete probability distribution and has a **PMF (Probability Mass Function)** instead of **PDF (Probability Density Function)**, unlike Gaussian distribution. PMF of Multinomial Distribution is given by the following expression:

$$f(X) = \frac{\left(\sum x_i\right)!}{\prod x_i!} \prod p_i^{x_i}$$

Where, $X = (x_1, x_2, ..., x_n)$ is a feature vector, p_i = probability of event i.

Now, the question may come what event is and what is the relationship of feature vector with it. If we think in terms of categorical data, an event i is the value of a categorical variable, and pi is the probability of occurrence of that value in the entire dataset. Feature vector X is the count of each categorical value for a feature.

In the first example of Naïve Bayes, we used a fictional dataset named *weather conditions for Golf*. There we always computed the probability of a categorical feature by counting records having a particular value. For theoretical understanding, that works well. But in a practical scenario, each categorical variable will be transformed by *One-Hot-Encoding*, and then *Multinomial Naïve Bayes* can be applied on top of that. Ultimately, both two approaches will produce the same result.

This can be explained by an example. We computed posterior probability *P(Outlook = 'Sunny' | Play Golf = 'Yes')* as *0.3* for data instance *I* = { *Outlook* = 'Sunny', *Humidity* = 'Normal', *Temperature* = 'Mild', *Windy* = 'No'}. We will see how same value can be computed by multinomial distribution. By *One-Hot-Encoding, Outlook* can be decomposed into 3 features: (*Outlook_Sunny, Outlook_Overcast, Outlook_Rainy*). For data instance *I*, this decomposed feature vector X can be written as $X = \{1, 0, 0\}$ where $x_1 = 1$, $x_2 = 0$, $x_3 = 0$. As 'Sunny' occurs only once in *I*, that's why its count is 1. Now, probability $p_1 = 3/10 = 0.3$, $p_2 = 2/10 = 0.2$, $p_3 = 2/10 = 0.2$. Now, we can write

$$\left(\sum x_i\right)! = (1 + 0 + 0)! = 1! = 1$$

$$\prod x_i! = (1 \times 0 \times 0)! = 0! = 1$$

$$\prod p_i^{x_i} = (0.3)^1 \times (0.2)^0 \times (0.2)^0 = 0.3$$

So, by the PMF of Multinomial Distribution:

$$f(X) = 0.3$$

That proves correctness of Multinomial Distribution based computation.

The `scikit-learn` provides API similar for Multinomial Naïve Bayes as similar to Gaussian one. We have to do a similar kind of pre-processing using `CategoricalVariableEncoder` and build the pipeline with the same dataset as below:

```
from sklearn.naive_bayes import MultinomialNB

mnnb_clf_pl = Pipeline(steps = [
                        ('cat_var_encoder',
                         CategoricalVariableEncoder(categorical_features=['Month','VisitorType','Weekend'])),
                        ('nb_clf', MultinomialNB())
                      ]
                    )
mnnb_clf_pl.fit(train_x, train_y)
/Users/avnag/Library/Python/3.6/lib/python/site-packages/sklearn/utils/validation.py:724: DataConversionWarning: A co
lumn-vector y was passed when a 1d array was expected. Please change the shape of y to (n_samples, ), for example usi
ng ravel().
  y = column_or_1d(y, warn=True)

Pipeline(memory=None,
         steps=[('cat_var_encoder',
                 CategoricalVariableEncoder(categorical_features=None)),
                ('nb_clf',
                 MultinomialNB(alpha=1.0, class_prior=None, fit_prior=True))],
         verbose=False)
```

Figure 2.15: Code snippet of the pipeline for Multinomial Naïve Bayes

And accuracy can be computed similarly:

```
mnnb_clf_pl.score(test_x, test_y)
```

0.8394160583941606

Figure 2.16: Code snippet of Accuracy of Multinomial Naïve Bayes

It gives far better accuracy (83.9%) than Gaussian one. So, the theory is proved once again; the presence of a large number of decomposed categorical features is a good reason for using the *Multinomial Naïve Bayes Classifier*.

Advantage of Naïve Bayes Classifier

- Easy to implement, and it is based on a simple probabilistic model and theoretically supports both linear and non-linear class boundary problems.
- Works well even there is less training data. It is better to use Naïve Bayes techniques rather than others where we don't have sufficient training data.
- It converges quickly rather than other models. The training process is so simple that it does not need rigorous parameter tuning and lots of iteration, unlike other parametric models.
- Highly scalable as the training process is very simple.

The disadvantage of Naïve Bayes Classifier

- Heavily dependent on the conditional independence criteria of the features. If conditional independence is broken, it starts giving higher probability estimates.
- As it is a very simple model, it fails to capture complex relationships between features and many times suffers from low accuracy for very large dimensional datasets.

Naïve Bayes is a very simple classifier. Due to its simplicity and assumption oriented nature, it mostly comes under parametric models. It works well for text classification problems (refer to *Chapter 7: Text Mining*).

Logistic Regression Classifier

We discussed Naïve Bayes in the previous section. Let's consider; there is a scenario that our classification problem is two-class or binary, and we have many continuous features. Estimating probability directly with Gaussian approximation for that many variables definitely would not give a good prediction. We may have to re-shape the traditional two-class Naïve Bayes differently.

Let's say, we have two classes C_1 and C_2 and feature set X, the posterior probability $P(C_1 \mid X)$ can be written from Bayes theorem:

$$P(C_1 \mid X) = \frac{P(X \mid C_1)P(C_1)}{P(X)}$$

As we only two classes, $P(C_1) + P(C_2) = 1$ (sum of probability space is always 1).

That's why; $P(X)$ is the summation of conditional probabilities of class C_1 and C_2:

$$P(X) = P(X \mid C_1) P(C_1) + P(X \mid C_2) P(C_2)$$

So,

$$P(C_1 \mid X) = \frac{P(X \mid C_1)P(C_1)}{P(X \mid C_1) P(C_1) + P(X \mid C_2)P(C_2)}$$

$$= \frac{1}{1 + \dfrac{P(X \mid C_2) P(C_2)}{P(X \mid C_1) P(C_1)}} \qquad \text{(Dividing both sides by P(X | C1) P(C1))}$$

If we define $Z = \log_e \dfrac{P(X \mid C_1) P(C_1)}{P(X \mid C_2) P(C_2)}$, then $\dfrac{P(X \mid C_2) P(C_2)}{P(X \mid C_1) P(C_1)} = \exp(-Z)$

We can re-write the posterior probability expressed as a function of Z, that is, σ(Z):

$$P(C_1 \mid X) = (Z) = \frac{1}{1 + \exp(-Z)}$$

If we plot Z vs σ(Z), it looks like an S-shaped curve like below:

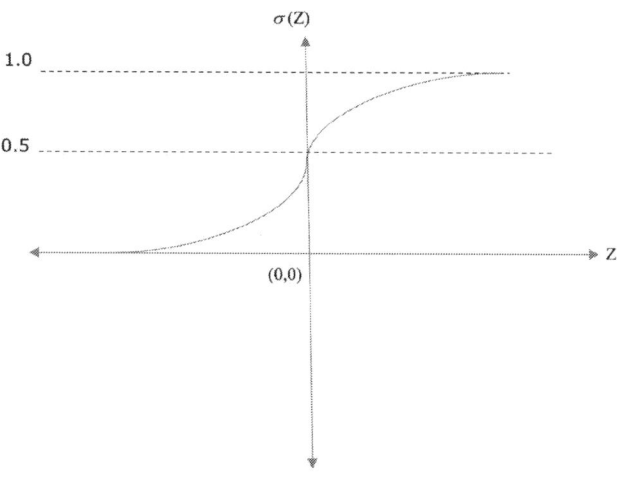

Figure 2.17: Logistic Sigmoid function

It is known as **logistic sigmoid** function. As, this is a binary classification problem:

$$P(C_2 \mid X) = 1 - P(C_1 \mid X)$$

From the expression of *P(C1 | X)*, we can see that if we can estimate Z, then we can have the value of σ(Z), that is, *P(C1 | X)*. As Z is a continuous variable in nature this would be a regression problem (details given in *Chapter 3: Regression*). That's why, even being classification in nature, we call it *logistic regression*, that is, regression to estimate probabilities for classification using a *logistic sigmoid* function.

This Z can be estimated by a generalized additive linear combination of features X $(x_1, x_2, \ldots, x_k)$ and the expression can be written as a linear regression model:

$$Z = b_0 + \sum_{i=1}^{k} b_i x_i$$

$$= b_0 + b_1 x_1 + b_2 x_2 + \sigma + b_k x_k$$

Where b_i is the regression coefficient corresponding to each feature x_i, the b_0 is known as *bias* term.

All the details of how to solve these types of regression problems are explained in *Chapter 3: Regression*. For the time being, let us assume that it is solvable. As we are assuming a statistical form of the model and trying to fit features into it, that's why logistic regression comes is considered a highly parametric type and supervised model.

Now, the question can come, why are we estimating Z that involves a logarithm? Instead, we could have estimated the probability ratio $P(X | C_1) P(C_1) / P(X | C_2) P(C_2)$ directly via regression technique. This probability ratio has a value range 0 to 1, whereas the logarithm has ranged from $-\infty$ to $+\infty$. So, taking a logarithm gives us higher upper and lower bounds of the target variable, and it helps to achieve better accuracy and avoid early convergence.

Training process

Training for Logistic Regression is the same as the normal Linear Regression problem. We will see that in detail in *Chapter 3: Regression*. Training is an iterative process which will adjust regression coefficients accordingly to reach the desired target variable value (which in this case is the pre-computed logarithmic ratio of posterior probabilities). There are different techniques for this type of training, for example, Newton-Raphson, Limited Memory, Large Linear Classification, Saga and more. Discussing each of those is out of scope here. The output of the training process is the model, which contains the regression equation in terms of the set of coefficients.

This model is used to predict the Z value of an unknown data instance and using that we get $\sigma(Z)$, which is the posterior probability of a class label.

Logistic Regression Classifier using Python

We will use scikit-learn's built-in Logistic Regression API to build a pipeline similar to previous Naïve Bayes example. Splitting into training and testing sets is required as it is.

Pre-processing and building the pipeline

Like the previous example, one hot encoding transformation for converting categorical to numerical features is required over here. Additionally, as a recommended pre-processing of any kind of regression problem, `StandardScaler` for scaling down all features to the same level (refer *Chapter 3: Regression* for regression techniques) should be added. It ensures better accuracy. So, the pipeline and the model can be built like below:

```
from sklearn.pipeline import Pipeline
from sklearn.linear_model import LogisticRegression
from sklearn.preprocessing import StandardScaler

logit_clf_pl = Pipeline(steps = [
                        ('cat_var_encoder',
                         CategoricalVariableEncoder(categorical_features=['Month','VisitorType','Weekend'])),
                        ('standard_scaler', StandardScaler()),
                        ('logit_clf', LogisticRegression())
                        ]
                )
logit_clf_pl.fit(train_x, train_y)
```

```
/Users/avnag/Library/Python/3.6/lib/python/site-packages/sklearn/linear_model/logistic.py:432: FutureWarning: Default
solver will be changed to 'lbfgs' in 0.22. Specify a solver to silence this warning.
  FutureWarning)
/Users/avnag/Library/Python/3.6/lib/python/site-packages/sklearn/utils/validation.py:724: DataConversionWarning: A co
lumn-vector y was passed when a 1d array was expected. Please change the shape of y to (n_samples, ), for example usi
ng ravel().
  y = column_or_1d(y, warn=True)
```

```
Pipeline(memory=None,
         steps=[('cat_var_encoder',
                 CategoricalVariableEncoder(categorical_features=None)),
                ('standard_scaler',
                 StandardScaler(copy=True, with_mean=True, with_std=True)),
                ('logit_clf',
                 LogisticRegression(C=1.0, class_weight=None, dual=False,
                                    fit_intercept=True, intercept_scaling=1,
                                    l1_ratio=None, max_iter=100,
                                    multi_class='warn', n_jobs=None,
                                    penalty='l2', random_state=None,
                                    solver='warn', tol=0.0001, verbose=0,
                                    warm_start=False))],
         verbose=False)
```

Figure 2.18: *Pipeline for Logistic Regression classifier*

Jupyter console prints out the classifier model details with all parameters. We can see one interesting parameter **penalty** with **l2** added. We will discuss it later.

We can now use this model to validate both training and testing datasets. With testing dataset:

```
logit_clf_pl.score(test_x, test_y)
```

```
0.8600973236009732
```

Figure 2.19: *Logistic Regression Accuracy with test*

With training dataset:

```
logit_clf_pl.score(train_x, train_y)
```

```
0.8415450121654501
```

Figure 2.20: *Logistic Regression Accuracy with train dataset*

So, testing accuracy is 84.99%, and training accuracy is 84.40%, which is quite close to each other.

Overfitting and regularization

From the discussion of *Chapter 1: Introduction to Machine Learning and Mathematical Preliminaries*, we can say that overfitting happens when training accuracy is very high as compared to testing. An overfitted model is complex in and with a little bit different dataset, it starts performing poorly. We will try to understand the overfitting concept with respect to class boundaries.

Below two diagrams are showing class boundaries for appropriate and overfitted solution respectively:

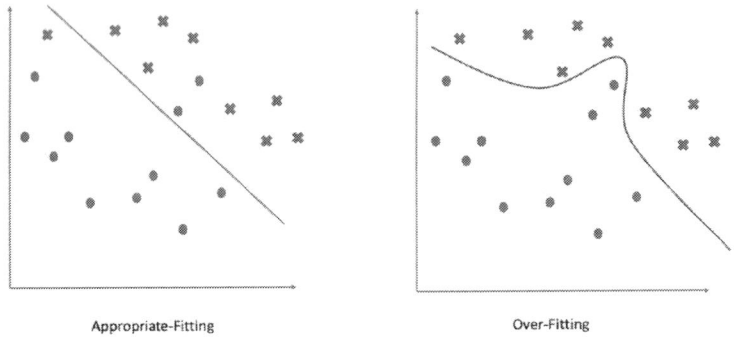

Figure 2.21: Appropriate-fitting andoverfitting in 2-D feature space

The above one is a two-class problem. For our understanding, let us consider cross sign denotes class 1 and circle denotes class 0 in the above diagrams. In the first diagram, the class boundary is linear, and it separates most of the data points, leaving a few. The class boundary in the second diagram may look a perfect one, which successfully separates all data points.

Now, if three unknown test data points of class 1 are added, then let's see how both of the solutions treat those (Unknown test data points are shown in red).

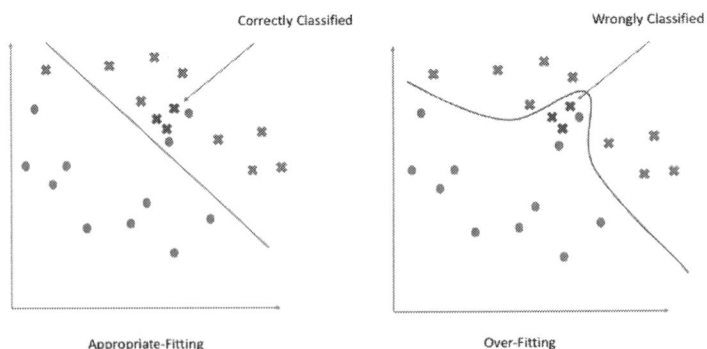

Figure 2.22: Classification of unknown data point for overfitted and appropriate-fitted models

We can see, the first solution rightfully predicts all of three as class 1 and puts those in the region of class 1 only. But, the second solution could not predict correctly and puts those in the region of class 0. That's the problem of overfitted solutions. If any data point comes, which is(are) a little bit different from the training dataset data points, there is no guarantee that the solution will work perfectly. An overfitted model tries to minimize errors while training, which spoils the solution. It gives better accuracy for the training dataset, but for testing or validation datasets, it performs poorly, which is not desirable. Whereas an appropriate-fitted solution leaves a fair amount of training error as it is without trying to reduce it and does not make the models overly complex. It gives good results with testing/validation datasets.

Regularization

Regularization is a technique that makes sure that models don't overfit. It may sound a little crazy, but, indeed, a little amount of error is forcefully introduced at training time so that the direction of parameter tuning remains correct. And this trick works well.

As currently discussed Logistic Regression model actually uses regression techniques internally, and model function is also of a regression model, so *L1* and *L2* regularization techniques are applicable here. Mathematical details of these two will be discussed in *Chapter 2: Regression*. These do nothing but add a penalty term to the objective or error function of a regression model, and the entire expression is used for training. And the result is the mitigation of the overfitting effect.

`LogisticRegression` class of `scikit-learn` takes one parameter named as `penalty` for the same. Its value can be either `l1` or `l2`. By default, the instance of the `LogisticRegression` is created with an *L2* penalty. The *L1* penalty is good for models with too many features. It helps to reduce unnecessary features by zeroing out the coefficients. We will see the details of this again in *Chapter 2: Regression*.

Multi-Class Logistic Regression

From the mathematical model, it is clear that by default, Logistic Regression is designed to handle binary classification problems. However, it can handle multi-class problems as well with some enhanced approaches. There are two ways to do it as discussed below:

1. **One vs. Rest approach**

    If there are *K* number of classes in the dataset, then *K* Logistic Regression classifier models can be built separately to handle the problem. The model building is done with a *one vs.* rest approach and can be explained with an example.

Suppose we are dealing with a dataset having fourclasses: C_1, C_2, C_3, and C_4 We have to decompose the main problem into four binary Logistic Regression subproblems so that separate models can be designed for each. Decomposition is done with the help of 3 binary questions as given below

a. Is the data instance a C1 or not?

b. Is the data instance a C2 or not?

c. Is the data instance a C3 or not?

d. Is the data instance a C4 or not?

Here, four separate target variables can be created, which can have value 0 or 1 as the answer to the above questions. For example, one target variable Y_1 can be there, which will have one if any data instance belongs to class C_1 or else 0 if it belongs to others (C2, C3, C4) as an answer to the first question. Similarly, there can be Y2, Y3 & Y4 for the other two questions. Once this new variable creation and dataset transformation are done, four binary logistic regression models can be trained with target variables Y1, Y2, Y3, and Y4, respectively. Each target variable will have only two transformed class labels: 0 and 1.

One test data instance is fed through each of the binary Logistic Regression models and we keep track of the posterior probabilities of transformed class label 1 for each. The predicted class label will be the one that gives the maximum probability. This maximum probability approach, similar to the posterior probability estimation approach of the Naïve Bayes Classifier.

Python implementation

The scikit-learn's `LogisticRegression` class has one parameter multi-class. In the previous sample code, it was set with the value to `warn` as the problem was binary. But for real multi-class problems which have to be solved with the currently discussed *one-vs-rest* approach, value ovr has to be set. `LogisticRegression` API internally will handle the decomposition part.

2. **SoftMax Activation approach**

We saw the expression of posterior probability for a two-class case:

$$P(C_1 \mid X) = \frac{P(X \mid C_1) P(C_1)}{P(X \mid C_1) P(C_1) + P(X \mid C_2) P(C_2)}$$

Now, we can re-write the generalized form of the above for a multi-class scenario, that is, expression of the posterior probability of class C_k:

$$P(C_k \mid X) = \frac{P(X \mid C_k) P(C_k)}{\sum_j P(X \mid C_j) P(C_j)}$$

Where,

$$Z_k = \log_e \left(P(X \mid C_k) \, P(C_k) \right)$$

This expression of $P(C_k \mid X)$ is known as Normalized Exponential and can be regarded as a multi-class version of Logistic Sigmoid function. Normalized Exponential is also known as SoftMax Activation Function. So, by this, we can get posterior probabilities for each class, and the predicted class label will be that one which has a maximum probability. It is quite analogous to the multi-class Naïve Bayes classifier.

The training process of SoftMax can be done via a network, as shown below:

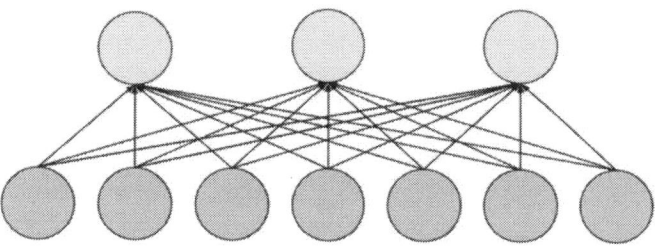

Figure 2.23: Network structure of SoftMax function

Output and input nodes are shown as cyan and saffron-colored, respectively. The number of output nodes is equal to the number of classes present in the dataset, and each output node contains the value of Zk corresponding to a class k. We have to estimate the values for each output node. So, it is a multi-output regression problem where multiple coefficients have to be optimized accordingly for multiple target variables. Standard Stochastic Gradient Descent or normal Gradient Descent algorithm can be used to solve this, and Z is regressed against the set of features X of the dataset.

Python implementation

Similar tothe one-vs-rest approach, the SoftMax approach can be chosen by setting `multinomial` as value for the multi-class parameter of `LogisticRegression` API.

Advantage of Logistic Regression Classifier

- Easy to implement, and it is based on a simple probabilistic model and theoretically supports both linear and non-linear class boundary problems (Provided non-linear features are taken as a linear combination. For more details, see, Polynomial Regression section of *Chapter 3: Regression*).
- The ideal choice for binary classification for most of the problems as the default base model is binary in nature.
- Works well when most of the features are continuous.

The disadvantage of Logistic Regression Classifier

- It requires more time to train due to its iterative nature.

- It does not work well for very non-linear class boundaries, which are not even possible to handle with polynomial features.

- It does not work well when features don't follow a normal distribution, as it is a basic assumption of the linear regression model.

Data scientists and ML experts prefer this logistic regression alongside with Naïve Bayes to build a first-hand model of the dataset. As logistic regression is an actual regression inside, it is easy to apply all linear regression related fine-tuning on top of it. It is also possible to know the importance of each feature and the impact it on the class probabilities. This technique will be discussed in *Chapter 3: Regression*.

Decision Tree Classifier

More or less, we all are familiar with algorithmic flowchart. At each stage, it asks questions and depending on *yes, no,* or other answers, some other stage or process is executed. The entire flowchart looks like a tree. Its *yes* or *no* based decision paths are branches, and processing instructions are nodes. In the end, there is a terminating node where the flowchart ends. There may be more than one terminating nodes. If we use these types of trees for solving classification problems, then the model is known as the **Decision Tree Classifier**.

Decision Tree is built by a series of carefully drafted questions about the features of a data instance. Each time a question is asked, an answer is received, a follow-up question is again asked until we receive the class label of the data instance. Now the big question is, what is the question to be asked? These questions are nothing but about getting the value of an attribute or feature of the dataset. Depending on the value, the next question will be asked about another attribute. These questions are stacked together hierarchically in the form of a tree structure consisting of nodes and edges.

Anatomy of a Decision Tree

Like any general tree data structure, the Decision Tree has nodes and edges as usual. But the interpretation of these is very specific to the classification problem. There are three types of nodes in a Decision Tree as given below:

- **Root node:** The starting point of the algorithm. It contains the first attribute or feature from the dataset to be checked. It can have two or more number of outgoing edges and zero incoming edges.

- **Intermediate node:** All nodes coming in between the root node and the last level are Intermediate nodes. These contain the attributes or features to checked consecutively after the root node attribute. These nodes have exactly one incoming edge and two or more outgoing edges.

- **Leaf node:** It is the actual decision-making node. Each leaf node refers to a particular class label. These nodes have two or more incoming and zero outgoing edges.

Let us consider a practical example to understand this more clearly. A Bank or any financial institution verifies customers' credibility before sanctioning a loan amount to them. The bank checks whether a particular customer would be a potential defaulter or not. It is a typical classification problem. Practically, there are many factors (or features in better terms) that influence the decision of the bank or determining whether the customer would be a defaulter or not. But to simplify the problem statement and our understanding, we will consider only three features of the customer: income range, family size, and city where income range and city are categorical, and family size is real numbered feature.

Let's consider different values for income range are *>=5000, <5000*, and for the city, these are *A, B,* and *C*. Our target variable is *loan sanctioned*, and it can have class labels as yes or no. So, leaf nodes should have yes or no values.

Theoretically, more than one decision tree can be built from the information provided above. But, for our convenience, let us consider the below one:

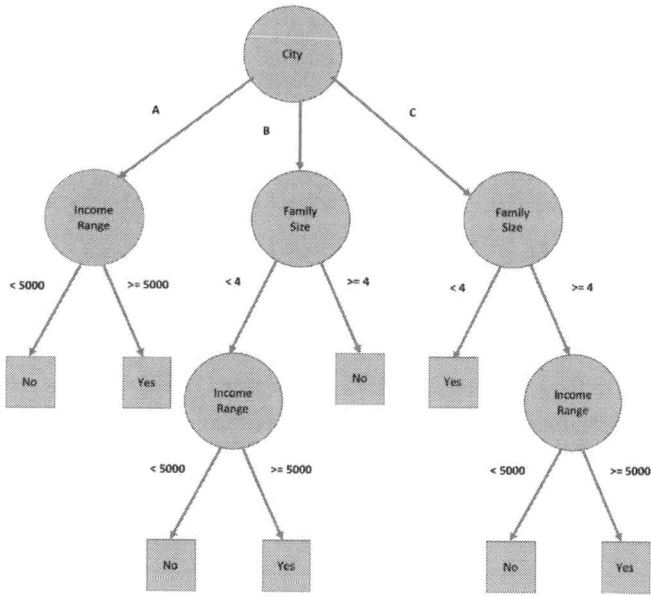

Figure 2.24: Sample Decision Tree Model

From the decision tree, we can observe that not all attributes are checked all the time. It depends on the value of an attribute to decide on a path.

Classifying a test data instance is straightforward once the tree is built. We have to apply the test condition (that is, attribute values) from the root node and follow the path until any of the leaf nodes are reached. Leaf node obviously will give us the predicted class label. We may not have to check all the attributes every time. For example, a test data instance coming with *City* as *A* and *Income Range* as *>=5000* can be directly predicted yes as the value of loan sanctioned. In this case, checking *Family Size* was not required. We will take another example and try to trace the path of prediction with a test data instance having *City = 'B,' Family Size < 4, Income Range >=5000*. The traced path will look like below (dashed arrow line in red):

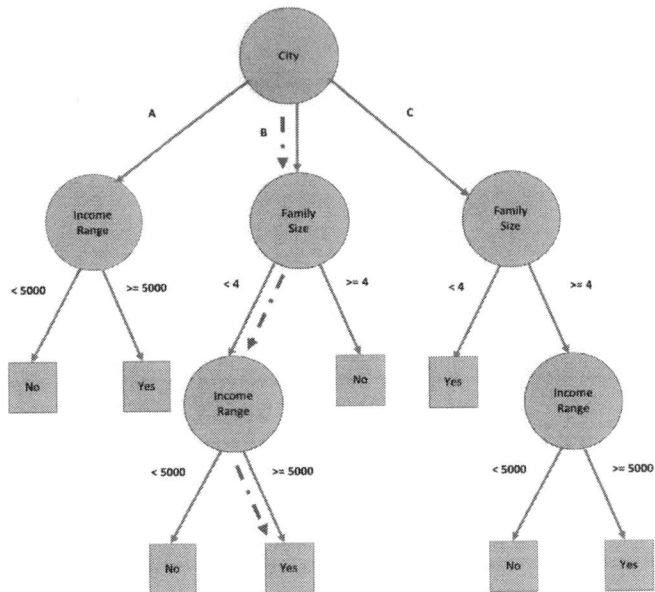

Figure 2.25: One decision path of the sample Decision Tree Model

So, the predicted label is *yes*. In this case, all three attributes are needed to make a decision.

Handling continuous and categorical attributes

Each node of the decision tree must provide a technique to split an attribute into different parts so that it can be represented by a set of branches. Each branch will carry a value of the attribute. Decision Tree is by default designed for handling categorical attributes, but with the transformation, it can also handle continuous ones as described in the next section.

Categorical attribute

Categorical attributes can be easily split into different values. The number of branches coming out from a categorical attribute node is equal to the cardinality of that. In the previous example, variable *City* has cardinality three and can have values: *A*, *B* and *C*. So, there will be three branches coming out from node *City*, as shown below:

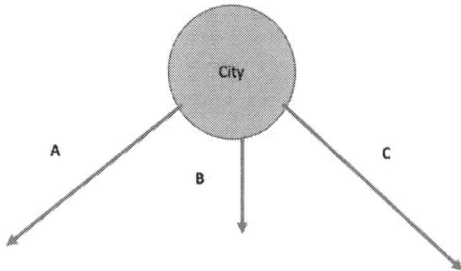

Figure 2.26: One sample node and its branches of the Decision Tree

Continuous attribute

Continuous attributes cannot be directly split into different branches. First, conversion to categorical from continuous has to be done for each of those. This type of variable transformation was already discussed in *Chapter 1: Introduction to Machine Learning and Mathematical Preliminaries*. Once the transformation is applied, we get categorical variables as value ranges; for example, Annual Income is {6000,7000}, that is, it is between 6000 and 7000. We consider each range as a single value of the attribute. In this case {6000, 7000} is considered a value. Similarly Annual Income can have values as {10000, 20000}, {25000-40000}, {70000, 100000}, and more. So, it will be split into branches like below:

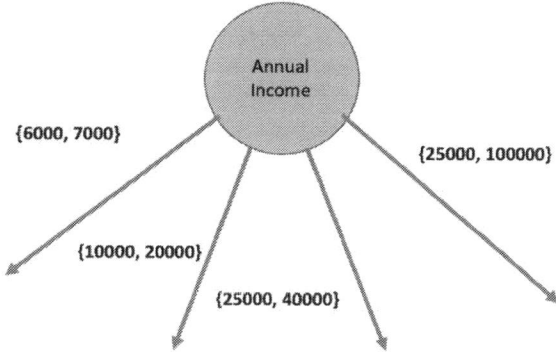

Figure 2.27: One node with continuous feature and its branches of a decision tree

In our previous example, dataset Income Range variable had only two values: *<5000* and *>=5000*, and hence it had two branches.

In both of the categorical and continuous variables, we saw that variables are always getting split into *K* number of branches where *K* is the cardinality. But, it may not be the case always. Some special decision tree algorithm like CART always creates a binary split, that is, two branches by considering $2K - 1 - 1$ way of binary splits of K attributes values.

Measure and technique of splitting a node

Technically what do we understand by splitting a node? Splitting is a filtering operation on the dataset by a condition. It is analogous to running a SQL query like this: `SELECT * FROM TABLE T1 WHERE T1.ATTRIBUTE1 = VAL1`. It divides the dataset into multiple partitions to make our computation easier. In our customer loan sanctioning problem, we have chosen *City* as the first attribute to check and split. But on what basis? We could have chosen *Annual Income* or *Family Size*. But we did not do that. There is a proper mathematical procedure to decide which attribute to be chosen at what level. Depending on that *City* was chosen at level 1, *Family Size*, and *Income Range* at level 2 and only *Family Size* at level 3. But, no attribute should be repeated in a single path of the tree.

The decision to choose a node for splitting is driven by the class distribution of the data. In a typical two-class (binary) problem, if p is the probability of class 1, then $1 - p$ would be the probability of class 2. In this case, class distribution or class ratio is $p : 1 - p$, or it can be written as a tuple $(p, 1 - p)$. Similarly, for a multi-class problem, the class distribution would be $(p1, p2,..., pk)$. For a given filtered dataset at any node of the decision tree, class distribution can be computed by counting the number of data instances corresponding to each class.

Impurity and mathematical measures

We always try to create a node where class distribution would be heavily skewed;that is, there should be a higher number of data instances for a particular class rather than others. Skewed class distribution helps us to identify the class of an unknown data instance while using the decision tree model. This process continued for all nodes of the tree, and ultimately at the end, leaf nodes are created, each of which contains data instances for a particular type of class only. The phenomenon of mixing of different types of classes at each intermediate node is known as **Impurity**. The more skewed class ratio or distribution indicates less impurity. For example, a class ratio (0, 1) for a node says there is no impurity. Our objective is to reduce impurity as much as possible.

If *pi* is the probability of class *i* for a given node *t* then three types of impurity measures for that node *t* can be computed as given below (*k* is class cardinality):

$$Entropy\ (t) = -\sum_{i=1}^{k} p_i \log_2 \log_2 p_i$$

$$Gini(t) = 1 - \sum_{i=1}^{k} [p_i]^2$$

$$Classification\ Error(t) = 1 - \max_{k} \max_{k} \{p_i\}$$

For our discussion, we will only consider Entropy as our measure of impurity.

The decision of choosing the right attribute for splitting a node depends on the amount of impurity reduction between before and after the split. This reduction can be measured as the difference of impurity between the parent node and weighted average impurity of the probable child nodes after splitting. It is known as *Information Gain* (δ) and mathematically can be written as:

$$\delta = I(t_p) - \sum_{t \in T} p(t)\, I(t)$$

Where, t_p = parent node,

t = current child node

T = total number of possible splits under parent node (basically, the cardinality of the parent node attribute)

$I(t)$ = Impurity measure of node t

$p(t)$ = probability of the number of records with node t

Decision tree building algorithms try to maximize δ. Conceptually, maximization of Information Gain makes sure that a single node contains records of a single class, which ultimately helps to reach leaf nodes which are responsible for prediction.

ID3 algorithm of building Decision Tree

ID3 is an iterative algorithm for building a decision tree. It starts with the complete dataset and computes Information Gain (δ) for each unused attribute. Then it selects the one with maximum δ and again repeats the same process until it creates a node with $\delta = 0$ or δ = some predefined threshold value or if there are no more attributes to check.

Step by step, it can be stated as follows. Let S is the set of all unused attributes:

1. Compute entropy of the current node t as $I(t)$.

2. Iterate through S and for each attribute compute δ

3. Pick the attribute which gives maximum δ and remove it from *S*.

4. Check if *S* is empty or not otherwise check if δ = 0 or δ = *predefinedthreshold*.

5. If anyone of the condition in Step 4 is true and repeat Step 1 otherwise end.

We will illustrate the algorithm by computing all the steps manually with the Weather condition dataset for Golf as discussed for Naïve Bayes Classifier. We will go via step-by-step.

1. We will start with the root node and compute the overall entropy of the system. There are two class labels Yes and No for target variable Play Golf.

   So, *P*(Play Golf = Yes) = 7/10 = 0.7 (7 records are there where Play Golf = Yes)

   P(Play Golf = No) = 3/10 = 0.3

   Hence, Entropy(troot) = $-\sum p \log (p)$ = $-$ [(0.7 × log 0.7) + (0.3 × log 0.3)] = $-$ 0.61

2. If we select Outlook as first attribute to check then we can have three branches: Rainy, Overcast and Sunny. For each of these we have to compute entropy from the split and then overall gain.

   If we filter entire dataset with Outlook = Rainy, then

   P(Play Golf = Yes) = 2/4 = 0.5

   P(Play Golf = No) = 2/4 = 0.5

   Entropy(*t* Outlook = Rainy) = $-$ [(0.5 × log 0.5) + (0.5 × log 0.5)] = $-$ 0.69

   Probability of number of records with *t*Outlook = Rainy = 4/10 = 0.4

   Similarly,

   Entropy(*t*Outlook = Overcast) = $-$ [(1 × log 1) + (0 × log 0)] = 0

   Probability of number of records with tOutlook = Overcast = 2/10 = 0.2

   Entropy(*t*Outlook = Sunny) = $-$ [(0.75 × log 0.75) + (0.25 × log 0.25)] = $-$ 0.56

   Probability of number of records with tOutlook = Sunny = 4/10 = 0.4

   Now, information gain for attribute Outlook

   δOutlook = Entropy(troot) $-$ [0.4 × ($-$ 0.69) + 0.2 × 0 + 0.4 × ($-$ 0.56)] = $-$ 0.11

   Similarly we can get

   δHumidity = $-$ 0.03

   δTemperature = $-$ 0.01

   δWindy = $-$ 0.12

   So, at first level, maximum δ is given by attribute Temperature and the partial tree will look like:

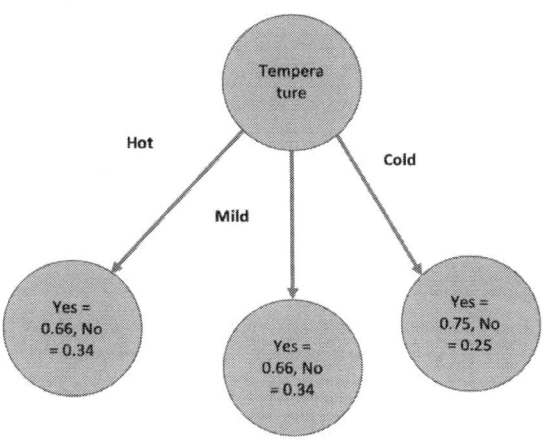

Figure 2.28: Partial formation of decision tree

Each child node contains probabilities of Yes and No for that branch.

3. At the second level, lets first consider the node corresponding to branch Cold. We have to apply the same procedure as Step 2.

Here, Entropy(tTemperature = Cold) = $-$ [0.75 × log 0.75 + 0.25 × log 0.25] = $-$ 0.562

We can now start applying filters and compute entropy for all other attributes except Temperature as it is already applied and first level of the tree in that path.

Let' start again with attribute Outlook. Our first test composite filter will be Temperature = Cold & Outlook = Rainy.

Here, P(Play Golf = Yes) = 2/2 = 1

P(Play Golf = No) = 0/2 = 0

Entropy(tTemperature = Cold, Outlook = Rainy)

$$= - [(1 \times \log 1) + (0 \times \log 0)] = 0$$

Probability of number of records with tTemperature

$$= \text{Cold, Outlook} = \text{Rainy} = 2/4 = 0.5$$

Similarly,

Entropy(*t*Temperature = Cold, Outlook = Overcast) = 0

Probability of number of records with *t*Temperature

$$= \text{Cold, Outlook} = \text{Overcast} = 0/4 = 0$$

Entropy(*t*Temperature = Cold, Outlook = Sunny)

$$= - [(0.5 \times \log 0.5) + (0.5 \times \log 0.5)] = - 0.69$$

Probability of number of records with tTemperature

$$= \text{Cold, Outlook} = \text{Sunny} = 2/4 = 0.5$$

Now, information gain for the path Temperature – > Outlook

δTeperature, Outlook = Entropy(tTemperature)

$$- [0.5 \times 0 + 0 \times 0 + 0.5 \times (-0.69)] = -0.217$$

Similarly,

δTeperature, Humidity = – 0.082

δTeperature, Windy = – 0.082

So, we can choose any one between Humidity and Windy as both of these are giving maximum information gain and our partial tree at next level will look like below (if we choose Humidity):

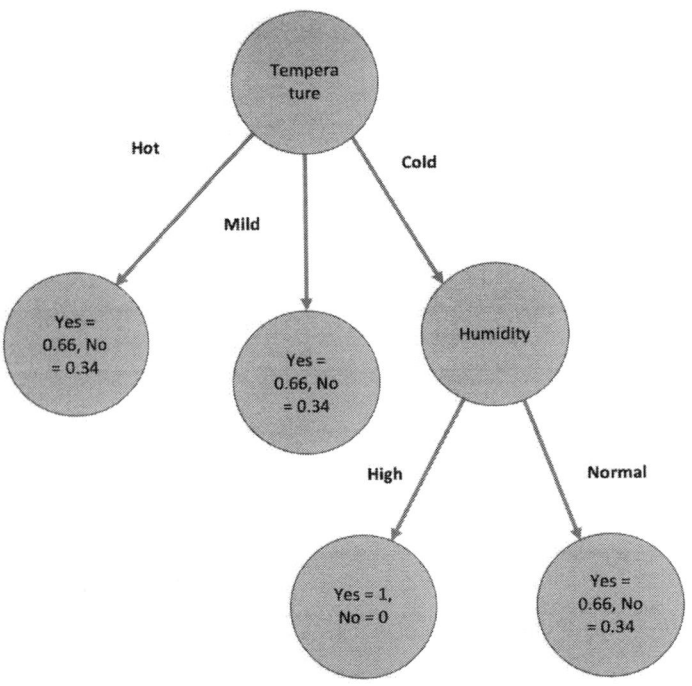

Figure 2.29: Partial formation of decision tree

As the path Temperature (Cold) – > Humidity(High) is producing a node with impurity 0, we can stop further exploring any other attribute for that path and declare that node a leaf node which is giving class label Yes.

We can repeat the same steps and further expand the tree as much as required. Readers can try it on their own.

CART is another model for representing decision trees. It always splits a node into two branches, each of which represents a binary question on an attribute. Most of the time, each intermediate node checks a value, whether it is greater than a threshold or not. It should return an answer in terms of yes or no. In that sense, CART is much simpler than ID3. Here the objective is to find out that threshold for each node.

Python implementation of the Decision Tree

We will use scikit-learn's built-in Decision Tree Classifier API to build a pipeline similar to previous Naïve Bayes and Logistic Regression example with the same Online Shoppers Intentions Dataset. Splitting into training and testing sets is required as it is.

Pre-processing and building the pipeline

Like the previous example, one hot encoding transformation for converting categorical to numerical features is required over here. Unlike logistic regression, `StandardScaler` is not required as it is probability-based. So, the pipeline and the model can be built like below:

```
from sklearn.pipeline import Pipeline
from sklearn.tree import DecisionTreeClassifier
from sklearn.preprocessing import StandardScaler

decision_tree_model = DecisionTreeClassifier(criterion='entropy')
dt_clf_pl = Pipeline(steps = [
                        ('cat_var_encoder',
                        CategoricalVariableEncoder(categorical_features=['Month','VisitorType','Weekend'])),
                        ('decision_tree_clf', decision_tree_model)
                        ]
                    )
dt_clf_pl.fit(train_x, train_y)

Pipeline(memory=None,
        steps=[('cat_var_encoder',
                CategoricalVariableEncoder(categorical_features=None)),
                ('decision_tree_clf',
                DecisionTreeClassifier(class_weight=None, criterion='entropy',
                            max_depth=None, max_features=None,
                            max_leaf_nodes=None,
                            min_impurity_decrease=0.0,
                            min_impurity_split=None,
                            min_samples_leaf=1, min_samples_split=2,
                            min_weight_fraction_leaf=0.0,
                            presort=False, random_state=None,
                            splitter='best'))],
        verbose=False)
```

Figure 2.30: Code snippet for the pipeline with Decision Tree classifier

We have used `entropy` as an impurity measure. Apart from this, we may also set `gini` over here. There are few hyperparameters like `max_depth`, `min_impurity_split` is important over here. The `max_depth` says what would be the depth of the decision tree. That may sound a little peculiar, right? Because we saw a decision tree grows until we reach a zero impurity node. But the built model may be complex, and the tree can grow really big. To restrict this, we can set a certain height, which will allow the tree to grow till that level.

Let's see how accurate the above model is:

```
dt_clf_pl.score(test_x, test_y)
```

0.8422546634225466

```
dt_clf_pl.score(train_x, train_y)
```

0.8460056772100568

Figure 2.31: Code snippet for accuracy of train & test dataset for a Decision Tree model

It gives 84% accuracy with the test dataset and almost the same with the training dataset. With hyperparameter tuning and we can always improve the accuracy.

Visualization of the Decision Tree using Python

We can plot the tree using the `export_graphviz` function of `scikit-learn`. It takes the `decision_tree_model` created above and exports it as a dot file like below:

```
from sklearn.tree import export_graphviz
from pydotplus import graph_from_dot_data
from IPython.display import Image

dot_file = export_graphviz(decision_tree_model, out_file=None,
                filled=True, rounded=True,
                special_characters=True)
graph = graph_from_dot_data(dot_file)
Image(graph.create_png())
```

Figure 2.32: Code snippet for visualizing Decision Tree model

And the above (*Figure 2.32*) produces the following image:

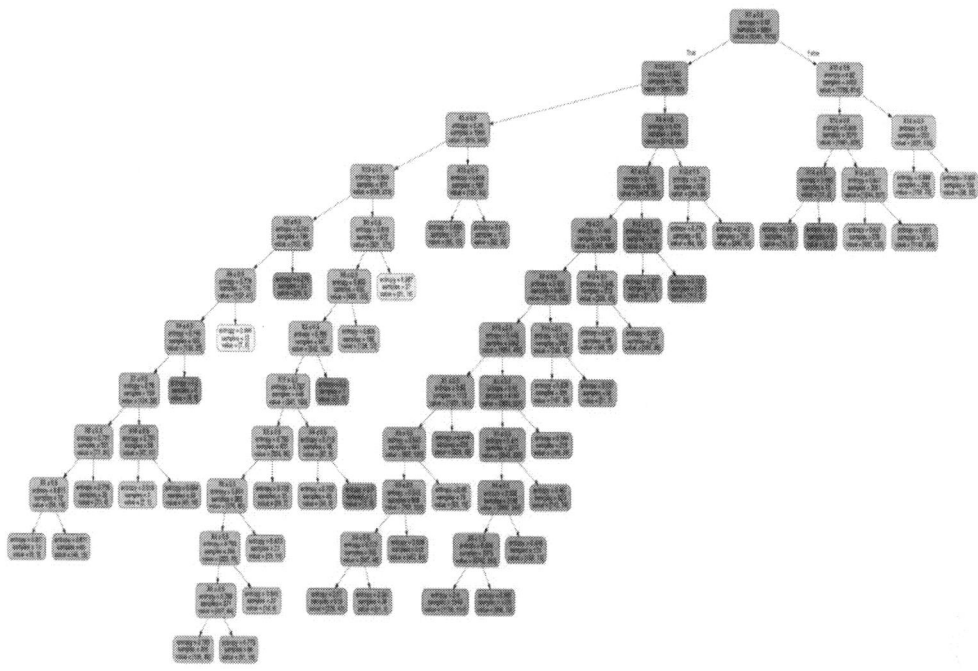

Figure 2.33: *Decision Tree model in the tree structure*

It may be difficult to see the content as the tree is too big. So, let's maximize the image and see one part of the tree (a few nodes) more closely:

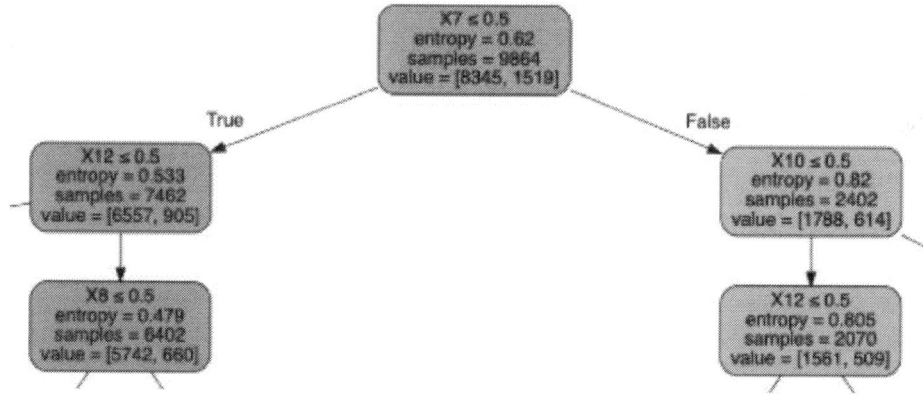

Figure 2.34: *Partial view of the Decision Tree model in the tree structure*

The `scikit-learn` uses CART as a tree building algorithm. We can see from the tree structure (*Figure 2.32*) that each transformed attribute X* is split into two branches. The left branch denotes True, and the right one is for `False`. The threshold is chosen as 0.5 for each node.

Advantage of Decision Tree Classifier

- It is a simple model, and visualization is very easy to understand. Its non-mathematical approach of visualization is quite self-explanatory to a person without an ML background.

- It is a non-parametric model and does not assume any statistical distribution of the data. Decision Tree works well with very non-linear problems.

- Variable scaling is not needed for Decision Tree as it is probability-based.

- It can automatically choose which features are important and which are not. At the end of the algorithm, it can be observed that some features are not at all used as nodes. It is the beauty of impurity computation that can cancel out not so important features.

The disadvantage of Decision Tree Classifier

- Very sensitive to data. A little variation on the dataset may produce a completely different tree.

- It may not work well with too many continuous variables as the default model is explained for categorical variables.

- Decision Tree sometimes becomes too complex and cannot give good predictions. Complex tresshave to be handled by cutting the trees short by hypermeter tuning or using multiple trees at a time in an ensemble.

Decision Tree is well suited for problems related to an unknown domain where data distributions or pattern is not that much well-known beforehand. It is also used in very real-time scenarios in production environments where fast response is needed or better to say a tight SLA is there.

Class imbalance problem

The frequency distribution of class labels in a dataset may not be evenly balanced or symmetric in nature. For example, a credit card fraud detection system may have very few fraudulent transactions, whereas the number of valid transactional records will be very high. Hence, it is a typical binary classification problem, and there are two class labels: fraud or non-fraud. If we take the ratio fraud vs. non-fraud, that would be heavily skewed with a value close to almost zero. This phenomenon often misleads us to get a perfect classifier. The objective of credit card fraud detection is to identify fraud transactions perfectly. A standard classifier with a good accuracy definitely will be able to classify non-fraud transactions in most of the cases as it is the frequent class, but it may fail to identify fraud records which belong to the infrequent class. So, for example, with 95% accuracy also, a classifier may not be able to predict rare classes and thus creates the *class imbalance problem*.

Conventional accuracy metrics like the ratio of correctly classified vs. the total number of records may not be well suited for imbalanced class datasets, as explained above. For example, with a dataset where only 1% credit card transactions are fraudulent, then it is quite obvious that a very good classifier that predicts all non-fraudulent transactions with 99% accuracy may fail to identify fraudulent ones. So, the result is higher accuracy, but still, fraudulent transactions remain unidentified, and the objective is not satisfied. We will discuss next how to use alternative metrics to test and techniques to build a classifier suitable for imbalanced datasets.

Alternative metrics

Traditional simple right vs. total ratio based accuracy measures treat every class as equally important. But in some cases, one or more class labels in entire class distribution might have more importance than other ones. For example, Fraud class label in credit card fraud detection problem has more importance than Non-fraud as the system is only interested in detecting frauds. A different nomenclature is used for important and not important classes in imbalanced class distribution. These are known as positive and negative classes, respectively.

Confusion Matrix

To understand the performance & behavior of a general classifier with the imbalanced class dataset, a confusion matrix can be constructed. It is a comparative analysis of Actual Class vs. Predicted Class given in the form of a matrix. For example, if there are two classes in our dataset P(Positive) and N(Negative), then a sample confusion matrix may look like below:

	Predicted P(Positive)	**Predicted N(Negative)**
Actual P(Positive)	TP	FN
Actual N(Negative)	FP	TN

Table 2.2: Confusion Matrix Structure

Following terminology is used (also shown above) in Confusion Matrix:

- **True Positive (TP):** Number of records whose actual class and predicted class is positive.
- **False Negative (FN):** Number of records whose actual class is positive and predicted class is negative.
- **False Positive (FP):** Number of records whose actual class is negative and predicted class is positive.
- **True Negative (TN):** Number of records whose actual class and predicted class is negative.

Ratio based metrics

From the above definitions, we can say that only TP and TN records are correctly predicted. All these four numbers are nothing but counts. We know that accuracy is expressed in terms of ratio for normal cases. Similarly, there are few ratio-based metrics which can judge the correctness of a classifier for imbalanced classes as given below:

- **True Positive Rate (TPR):** It is the ratio of correctly predicted positive records vs. the total number of positive records and is given by:

$$TPR = \frac{TP}{TP + FN}$$

  TPR is also known as Recall (r).

- **False Positive Rate (FPR):** It is the ratio of incorrectly predicted negative records vs. the total number of negative records and is given by:

$$FPR = \frac{FP}{FP + TN}$$

- **True Negative Rate (TNR):** It is the ratio of correctly predicted negative records vs. the total number of negative records and is given by:

$$TNR = \frac{TN}{TN + FP}$$

- **False Negative Rate (FNR):** It is the ratio of incorrectly predicted positive records vs. the total number of positive records and is given by:

$$FNR = \frac{FN}{FN + TP}$$

- **Precision (p):** It is the ratio of actual correctly predicted positive records vs. the total number of predicted positive records and is given by:

$$Precision(p) = \frac{TP}{TP + FP}$$

From all the ratios, we can say that a low FPR is always desirable, and that defines the goodness of a classifier. For example, in the case of credit card fraud detection, a good classifier should never predict a fraudulent transaction as a valid one, which can affect the business. Similarly, a high Recall or TPR is also expected from a good classifier.

As a practice, we always mix precision (p) and recall (r) in a single metric and expressed it as the harmonic mean of both. It is known as the F1 score, and the expression is given by:

$$F_1 = \frac{2}{\dfrac{1}{r} + \dfrac{1}{p}} = \frac{2rp}{r + p}$$

A good classifier will always give a high F_1 score, and its value ranges between 0 and 1. We will consider the F_1 score as a standard metric to overcome the class imbalance problem.

The scikit-learn's metrics module provides a function `f1_score` to compute the same. It takes actual and predicted target variable values as parameters:

```
from sklearn.metrics import f1_score

predicted_y = logit_clf_pl.predict(test_x)
f1_score(test_y, predicted_y, average='micro')
```

0.8600973236009732

Figure 2.35: Code snippet for F1 score computation

Accuracy metric for multi-class and imbalanced dataset

F_1 score can be used for multi-class use cases also. If one or more classes are rare in the multi-class dataset, then two different strategies can be taken to compute the F_1 score: Macro and Micro. The theoretical basis is the same for both one, that is, compute basic TPR, FPR or F_1 with a one-vs-rest approach (similar to multi-class Logistic Regression):

- **Macro average:** Average precision and recall is computed from the set of precision and recalls for each class label (considering that label is positive class and the rest of all as negative), and then F_1 is computed using the conventional formulae:

$$\text{Average Precision } \bar{p} = \frac{1}{K} \sum p_i$$

$$\text{Average Recall } \bar{r} = \frac{1}{K} \sum r_i$$

$$F_1 \text{ Macro} = \frac{2\,\bar{r}\bar{p}}{\bar{r} + \bar{p}}$$

Where K = the total number of class labels.

- **Micro average:** Individual true positive, false negative, and false positives are counted for each class label and all summed up together to compute overall precision and recall. Then final *F1* is computed using the conventional formulae:

$$Precision\ Micro\ p_{\mu} = \frac{\sum TP}{\sum TP + \sum FP}$$

$$Recall\ Micro\ r_{\mu} = \frac{\sum TP}{\sum TP + \sum FN}$$

$$F_1\ Micro = \frac{2r_{\mu}\ p_{\mu}}{r_{\mu} + p_{\mu}}$$

Python function `f1_score` takes a parameter average whose value can be set as macro or micro.

Receiver Operating Characteristic Curve (ROC)

ROC is a graphical plot of TPR vs. FPR for a model across the dataset. TPR and FPR are plotted across the *Y* and *X*-axis, respectively. For a model, there should be only one TPR and FPR. Then, how can we get a series of TPR, FPR values for a model in both axes? To understand this, let us see two sample ROCs for comparing two models, as shown below:

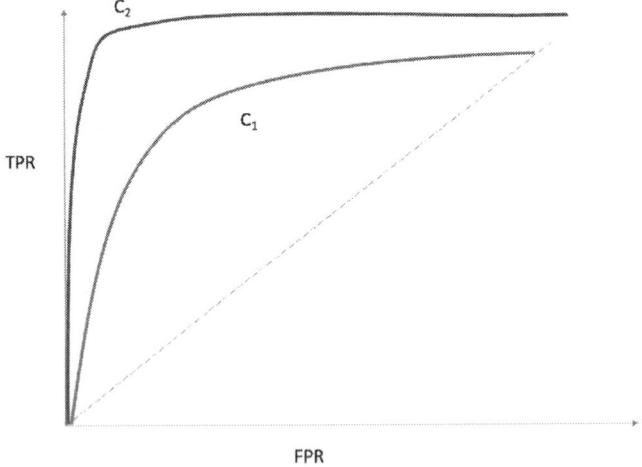

Figure 2.36: *ROC Structure*

Generally, ROCs are reversing elbow-shaped. In the above diagram, we can see there are two curves for two different hypothetical classifiers C1 and C2.

Every classifier can give scores either as probability or some distance metric like Euclidean distance. These scores are easily obtained by running a trained classifier on a dataset for prediction. If T is the threshold score (probability or distance) for being a positive or negative record, then we can have a series of TPR and FPR values for a set of varying T. As the T is changing, the definition of positive and negative will also change, and it will produce different values of TPR and FPR. It shows how the classifier is getting affected by T or how well it is solving the class imbalance problem. We can judge the goodness of the classifier by looking at the ROC. The classifier, which covers more **Area Under Curve (AUC)**, is considered better. It is quite justified and can be explained. We know from the definition of TPR & FPR that a good classifier will tend to have high TPR and low FPR. From the ROC, we can see that more inclination towards the top-left corner of the co-ordinate space indicates a high TPR and low FPR value, and also it covers more area (AUC). So, a classifier that covers more area (AUC), that is, has a high AUC value is always better.

Python implementation of ROC generation

We will now see a utility function which can generate ROC from sample data:

```python
import matplotlib.pyplot as plt
from sklearn.metrics import roc_curve, auc

def plot_roc(model, x, y, title):
    plt.figure(figsize=(12,6))
    probs = model.predict_proba(x)[:,1]
    model_fpr, model_tpr, thresholds = roc_curve(y, probs)
    roc_auc = auc(model_fpr, model_tpr)

    plt.plot(model_fpr, model_tpr,lw=2, label='AUC = %0.2f' % roc_auc)

    plt.plot([0, 1], [0, 1], color='navy', lw=2, linestyle='--')
    plt.xlim([0.0, 1.0])
    plt.ylim([0.0, 1.05])
    plt.xlabel('False Positive Rate')
    plt.ylabel('True Positive Rate')
    plt.title(title)
    plt.legend(loc="lower right")
    plt.show()
```

Figure 2.37: Code snippet of plot_roc function

Above function uses several Python library functions as explained below:

1. `predict_proba` function of the model returns the desired probability score required to generate ROC.

2. `roc_curve` function computes FPR, TPR from the probability scores with varying thresholds, and returns everything as three elements tuple.

3. auc function computes the area under the curve (AUC) from model TPR and FPR values. It is expressed as a percentage of the total area of the coordinate space (which equals 1).

4. At last, FPR and TPR values are plotted in the graph.

Function plot_roc can be called by passing the logistic regression model that we built in the earlier section like below:

```
plot_roc(logit_clf_pl, test_x, test_y, 'ROC for test data')
```

Figure 2.38: Code snippet for generating ROC using plot_roc function

And it will produce the following graph:

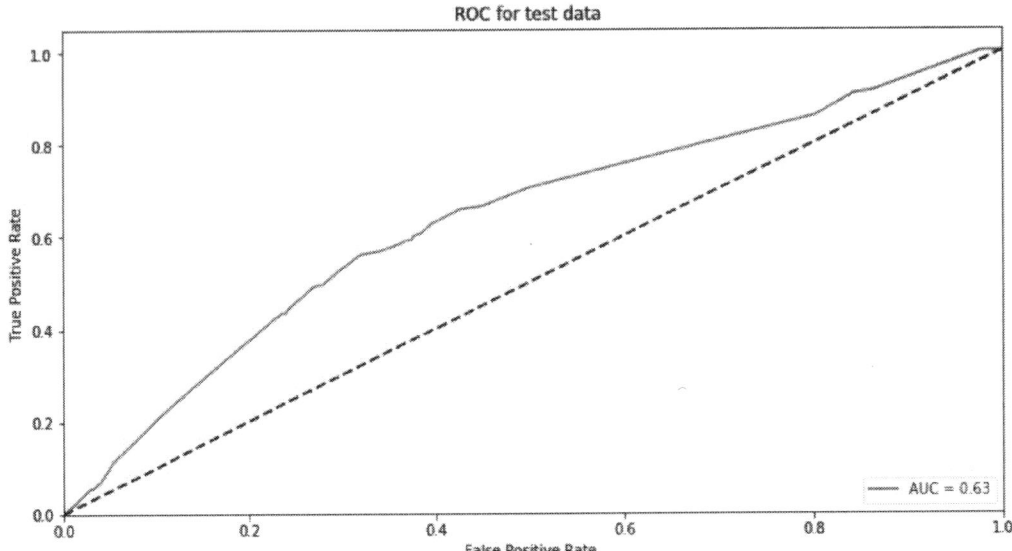

Figure 2.39: ROC generated from plot_roc function

So, AUC is 0.63 or 63%.

Mitigating class imbalance problem

We saw how to evaluate a classifier having a class imbalance problem. But how will we reduce this problem? Evaluation does not solve the problem yet, and it just gives an indication that the model is not perfect, and some action needs to be taken. We will discuss two major techniques of class imbalance mitigation.

Class weight adjustment approach

Class weights are externally supplied arguments that can influence the optimization direction of the objective function of the classifier. These weights are generally kept proportional to the importance of the class label. One of the very common approaches is using balanced weights. This approach uses reciprocal of class frequency as weight; that is, if fK is the frequency of class K, then the corresponding weight would be $1/fK$. This one ensures that more dominant or frequent classes get fewer weights, and rare classes get more weight. It helps in solving problems where finding rare class events are the ultimate objective. The previously discussed credit card fraud detection problems would be an example.

The usage of class weights varies from model to model. In a linear model like Logistic Regression, class weights can be multiplied with the error function. As an effect, if there is an error in identifying a rare class in training time, this multiplication will enhance it and guide the optimization process of the classifier accordingly. In the case of a Decision Tree, class weights can be multiplied with impurity computation function, and it will have an effect of enhanced or reduced impurity accordingly.

The scikit-learn's classifiers argue `class_weight` in the constructor. It takes a value as a string literal *balanced* or a Python dictionary like `{0:2, 1:4}`. Here 0 and 1 are class labels, and 2 and 4 are weights. By default, it does not take any value and is kept as None.

Sampling-based approach

The purpose of sampling is to modify the skewness in the class distribution to that the rare class events are well represented in the dataset. Two of the very common sampling techniques are undersampling and oversampling.

The undersampling technique removes records of majority class and fixes the skewness in class ratio. It can be a good choice when we have a lot of training data, and the reduction of some of that does not hamper the overall solution.

The scikit-learn's utils module has a function named as resample, which can do the undersampling. But, before that, we need to know the class frequency ratio. We will use the same Online Shoppers Intentions Dataset:

```
page_visits_df_true = page_visits_df[page_visits_df.Revenue == True]
page_visits_df_false = page_visits_df[page_visits_df.Revenue == False]
page_visits_df.Revenue.value_counts()
```

```
False    10422
True      1908
Name: Revenue, dtype: int64
```

Figure 2.40: Code snippet for finding class counts of Online Shoppers Intentions Dataset

We divided the dataset depending on the target variable value, True or False. And it shows quite a bit of skewness. Now, with resample, we can set the sample size equals to true data size and filter it accordingly:

```
from sklearn.utils import resample

false_upsampled = resample(page_visits_df_false,replace=True,
                           n_samples=len(page_visits_df_true))
upsampled = pd.concat([page_visits_df_true, false_upsampled])
upsampled.Revenue.value_counts()
```

```
True     1908
False    1908
Name: Revenue, dtype: int64
```

Figure 2.41: Code snippet for the under-sampling approach of class imbalance mitigation

We can see that the true and false ratio is now 1:1. Now we can use the unsampled dataset for training. The Oversampling technique adds more records of the minority class. It is a good choice when there is a shortage of data, and we cannot afford the removal of it.

Oversampling can be done similarly:

```
true_oversampled = resample(page_visits_df_true,replace=True,
                            n_samples=len(page_visits_df_false))
oversampled = pd.concat([page_visits_df_false, true_oversampled])
oversampled.Revenue.value_counts()
```

```
True     10422
False    10422
Name: Revenue, dtype: int64
```

Figure 2.42: Code snippet for oversampling approach of class imbalance mitigation

It is sometimes preferable to combine both under-sampling and oversampling in a single strategy. Generally, the under-sampling stage follows oversampling to build the proper balanced dataset.

Ensemble classification models

All the classification techniques we discussed so far use a single algorithm to predict class labels of an unknown record. We can achieve better classification accuracy by using a set of classifiers instead of a single one. This technique is known as ensemble classification techniques or ensemble classification models. An ensemble model is made of a set of base classifiers, each of which is built individually from the training data. The overall prediction process is performed by taking a vote on the predictions done by base classifiers.

Mathematically, for example, if *CE* is the ensemble model *Ci* is the individual base classifier then for a record *X* output *CE(X)* is given by

$$C_E(X) = MajorityVote\{C_1(X), C_2(X), ..., C_K(X)\}$$

The Majority vote is obtained by counting the number of times each class label is predicted in the whole set. The class label whose count or vote is maximum is returned as the final predicted result.

There are various techniques to construct an ensemble of classifiers. We will discuss one of them in short.

Bagging

Bagging a.k.a Bootstrap Aggregating is an ensemble technique that repeatedly samples the data from the whole training dataset and builds several classifiers on each of the sample sets. Data sampling is performed according to a uniform probability distribution. For example, if we are given a dataset of 1000 records, then a general workflow of bagging works like below fashion:

1. Create ten random sub-samples of 100 records each from the dataset.
2. Train and build ten different base classifiers for each of the datasets.
3. Given a new record, predict the class label by taking a majority vote among ten predictions from 10 base classifiers.

Bagging reduces the overfitting problem by cutting down the variance present in the models. The performance of bagging depends on the stability of the base classifiers. The sub-sampling procedure helps to reduce the instability present in the base classifiers.

RandomForest model

It is a bagging based ensemble model made of several decision tresses as base classifiers. The normal bagging based tree model has a problem of ending up creating an array of decision trees which are co-related. It considers all features of the dataset into consideration while building the trees. RandomForest based approach instead takes special steps to make the base classifiers less co-related. It does so by choosing only a subset of features from the dataset for each base model. A typical pictorial view of the workflow of RandomForest is like below:

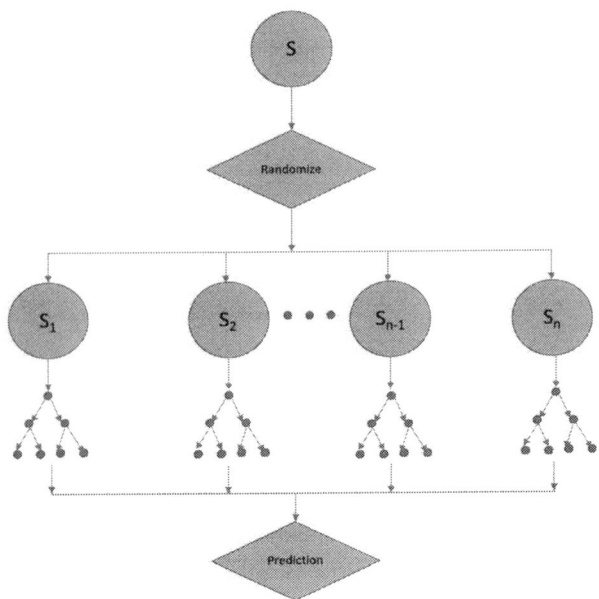

Figure 2.43: Sample workflow of a typical Random Forest model

From *Figure 2.43*, we can see that RandomForest is a fork-join based technique. Forking happens while building the model with separate training datasets and joining is nothing but the prediction process which combines all outputs.

Python implementation of RandomForest

The `scikit-learn` has a built-in RandomForest model that can be used in an exactly similar way to other discussed models. Like the decision tree, RandomForest also does not need any kind of variable scaling. Only one-hot-encoding transformation is sufficient as the pre-processing stage. We will keep using the same dataset, and `CategoricalVariableEncoder` class created earlier for one-hot-encoding.

The pipeline can be created and trained as below:

```python
from sklearn.pipeline import Pipeline
from sklearn.ensemble import RandomForestClassifier
from sklearn.preprocessing import StandardScaler

rf_clf_pl = Pipeline(steps = [
                        ('cat_var_encoder',
                         CategoricalVariableEncoder(categorical_features=['Month',
                                                                          'VisitorType',
                                                                          'Weekend'])),
                        ('rf', RandomForestClassifier())
                        ]
            )
rf_clf_pl.fit(train_x, train_y)
```

Figure 2.44: Code snippet of the pipeline with Random Forest

And the accuracy can be computed:

```
rf_clf_pl.score(test_x, test_y)
```

```
0.8341443633414436
```

Figure 2.45: Code snippet of accuracy computation

Decision Tree and RandomForest have similar kinds of hyper-parameters as conceptually; both are the same. But especially for RandomForest, there is a hyper-parameter n_estimator (see above code), which decides the number of base classifier trees in the forest, that is, the over model. By default, its value is kept as ten by scikit-learn (version 0.21.3).

Multi-label classification models

So far, we have seen class labels are mutually exclusive. Mathematically, A target variable Y can take anyone, and maximum one class label from the set {C1, C2, ..., CK} of size K. It is known as single-label classification and already discussed in previous sections in detail. But, what if Y takes more than one class label from the defined set? Mathematically, it is possible. But, practically, is it meaningful? Of course, it is. Let's think about the problem of movie genre prediction. A movie can have multiple (one or more) genres attached to it. For example, one movie can have action, comedy, and romance together as genres. It is a classification problem with multiple labels and hence is known as **multi-label classification**.

Problem formulation

One-Hot encoding transforms a categorical variable into several single continuous ones, and it produces a binary string representation like 010..0. Only one bit should be set as one here, and others would be zero. The target variable of single-label classification can be transformed like this. But, for multi-label multiple bits should be set to 1, and one such example could be 0100110..0. There can be N number of 1s in a multi-label target variable where $1 <= N <= K$ and K is the total number of classes. The length of the binary string also would be K. One single-label classifier can predict only one 0 or 1. A conventional single-label classifier alone cannot predict N number of 1s in a multi-label problem.

Problem decomposition and Umbrella classification scheme approach

In multi-label classification, we can think of each bit of the target variable binary string as a result of different problems. Hence the main problem can be decomposed into a set of sub-classification problems, each of which individually is a binary classifier. Let us elaborate this with the context of the movie genres prediction problem. If there are K different types of genres available then the target variable will be a binary string of length K. If different genres are for example action, comedy, horror, science-fiction, romance, and more, then K number of individual binary subproblems will look like following:

- 1) Is the movie of type action? 0 or 1
- 2) Is the movie a type ofcomedy? 0 or 1
- K) Is the movie of type romance? 0 or 1

(For all cases, 0 indicates No and 1 indicates Yes)

These K number of binary classifiers can be designed using any standard classification model like discussed earlier like Decision Tree, Logistic Regression, Naïve Bayes, and more or else any ensemble model. In general, one particular model is chosen and built for several subproblems. For our example, if we choose Logistic Regression as our model, then the total K number of Logistic Regression models should be designed.

There are two types of schemes which should be applied on top of these base classification models. These can be called as **Umbrella classification schemes**.

Binary relevance scheme

Binary relevance is a simple scheme where each model is trained on a particular class label, ignoring others. It is similar to the one-vs-rest approach of multiclass logistic regression, as discussed earlier. Each model will produce 0 or 1 as predicted output, where one means the class label is present in the data instance, and 0 means it is not present. In the end, only 1s from all classifiers and corresponding class labels are returned as total predicted output. In our example, if the predicted genres for a movie are 11000...0, then we will say that the movie is of type action and comedy.

Classifier chain scheme

This scheme uses the output of previous classifiers as extra features in the next classifier. These features keep getting added, and the last classifier will have *K-1* extra features in addition to the normal features it has. By this, as a general statement we can say that classifier, *i* will have *i*-1 extra feature where *1 <= i <= K*. The solution can be shown by the below diagram:

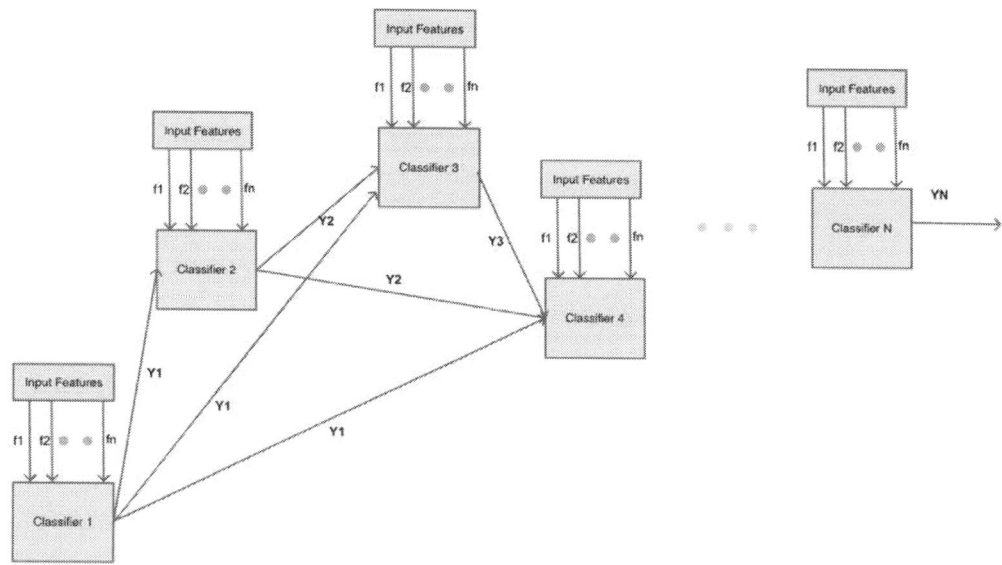

Figure 2.46: *Architecture of Classifier Chain Scheme*

The above diagram almost resembles the LinkedList data structure. Y_1, Y_2, ..Y_N are the response variables of each classifier. Response from all previous classifiers is seeded into the next classifier and become extra feature along with original input features $(f_1, f_2, ...f_n)$. In general, at any stage classifier, *i* will be built on complete feature set $f_1, f_2, ...f_n, Y_1, Y_2, ..Y_{i-1}$.

Now, the question may come regarding the order of the classifier chain. Which classifier will be chosen as 1st, 2nd, 3rd, and so on? There are different statistical techniques for doing that as given below:

- **The ensemble of Classifier Chains:** It is an ensemble of classifier chains based on random sampling. Randomly selected different chains are used, and in the end, a majority voting scheme is applied to get the prediction like the RandomForest model.
- **Monte-Carlo Classifier Chains:** It applied Monte-Carlo simulation for optimal classifier sequence generation.

Detailed discussion for both of the methods is out-of-scope.

Label powerset scheme

The fundamental concept of *Binary Relevance* and *Classifier Chain* is the same, that is, based on the output of a sequence of sub classifiers. But label powerset does not decompose the problem into subproblems. It considers each unique combination of target variable value present in the dataset as a separate single class label and builds a single classifier on top of it. For example, (1100…0), (010…0), (00…110) are considered as separate class labels as a whole. In the context of movie genre prediction example, we can say that Label Powerset considers combinations like (action, comedy), (comedy, romance) and (science-fiction) as a separate class label if these are present in the dataset. This technique does not consider any random combination as a class label if that one is not present in the dataset. That's why the predicted class label of an unknown data instance will always be a combination that is already there in the training dataset.

Comparison of each scheme

- **Binary Relevance** is a very simple approach and applicable for all cases where class labels are independent of each other; that is, the occurrence of one class label does not influence the occurrence of another. It does not consider label inter-dependency and often fails to identify hidden relationships.

- **Classifier Chaincan** handle class label interdependencies. As it takes the output of previous classifies as an input feature, it takes the relationship information along with. It is a good choice for use cases where there exist some kind of parent-child relationships between class labels; that is, child labels can only occur if and only if parent label is there. But this scheme is quite complex as the number of features will be proportional to the class space. Especially is class space is large, and then complexity increases a lot.

- **Label Powerset** works well for cases where numbers of unique combinations of class labels present in the dataset are quite less as compared to the number of classes. Unlike the previous two schemes, detailed, and decomposed analysis is overkill and not required here.

Accuracy metrics

There are different metrics to judge the performance of the multi-label classifier. The standard way of measuring the right prediction vs.the total number of records ratio gives a high-level estimate of the multi-label classifier and the ratio is known as **subset accuracy** in a multi-label case. But it is fully reliable. For example, if a movie has genres science-fiction, action, adventure, and the predicted genres are action, adventure, romance, then can we say the prediction is completely right or wrong? It is neither. So, we have to measure in a different way to capture the partial correctness.

Hamming loss metric

Hamming *loss* can measure the partial correctness of the multi-label classifier's prediction. It computes the average loss generated in the binary bit string of class labels during prediction. It does so by performing XOR operation between the original binary string of class labels and predicted class labels for each data instance and computes the average across the dataset. Its expression is given by:

$$Hamming\ Loss = \frac{1}{|N| \cdot |L|} \sum_{i=1}^{|N|} \sum_{j=1}^{|L|} XOR\left(y_{i,j}, \widehat{y_{i,j}}\right)$$

Where,

|N| = number of data instances, |L| = number of unique class labels,

$y_{i,j}$ = actual bit of class label j in data instance i

$\widehat{y_{i,j}}$ = predicted a bit of class label j in data instance i

The Hamming loss value ranges from 0 to 1. As it is a loss metric, a lower value indicates a better score.

We can also measure accuracy using the F1 score, as discussed in earlier sections like multi-class scenario. We should use either a macro or micro strategy based F1 score. Scores should be computed for each separate class labels, and then a macro or micro strategy should be applied to get a concrete score. It is always a better metric to use if there is a class imbalance in a multi-label case.

Python implementation of multi-label classifier

There is a separate library named scikit-multilearn which has modules and functions for multi-label classifier schemes. A complete use case is given in *Chapter 9: Case Studies and Storytelling* for predicting the movie genres. Readers can refer there for full implementation.

Conclusion

In this chapter, we discussed what a classification problem, its mathematical interpretation, different classifiers and their theoretical foundation, as well as Python implementation using open-source datasets, is.

We learned about class imbalance problems, alternative metrics to measure it, and its resolution mechanisms. We also saw how to build a pipeline using Python `scikit-learn` library. This knowledge will be beneficial for us while discussing subsequent chapters.

In the next chapter, we will see how to build an ML model when the target is a continuous variable.

CHAPTER 3
Regression

We discussed about how to predict a categorical target variable from a set of features, that is, a typical classification problem in this chapter. Now, if we have to do the same thing for numerical / continuous target variables, then how will weproceed? First of all, this is known as a *Regression problem*. Let's take a simple example from our software industry itself. The problem statement is: Can we predict a software engineer's salary from his/her years of experience, technologies he/she has worked, no of companies he/she has changed, and more. Here, salary is a continuous variable having real/positive numbers. So, we have to estimate salary in with the help of other features of the dataset. This is a typical regression problem. In this chapter, we will discuss it in detail.

Structure

In this chapter, we will discuss:

- Mathematical form of regression: linear vs. non-linear relations
- Solution of linear regression using OLS and Gradient Descent approach
- Technique for feature selection: forward and backward
- Regularization techniques: Lasso and Ridge
- Regression tree-based approach

Objective

After finishing this chapter, we will be able to:

- Build linear and polynomial regression models with a proper feature selection technique.
- Decide which regression model is appropriate for different use cases.
- Explain the importance and impact of the change of each feature on the target variable.

Mathematical problem definition of Regression

Inthe introduction, we discussed the problem of estimating the salary of a software engineer. Now, let's try to write an algebraic equation for this problem:

*salary = 1.5 * years of exp + 1.7 * technology stack + 2 * no of companies + 0.4 * city*

From our perception of ML so far, we can understand that years of Exp, technology stack, and more, are nothing but independent variables, and salary is the dependent variable. But what are these real numbers: 1.5, 1.7, 2, and more? These are coefficients or weights. How to get these weights we will discuss in subsequent sections. From the above equation, we can easily get an estimate of the salary of a software engineer if the values of independent variables are provided.

We can write the above equation in a much more generic format like below:

$$y = b_0 + \sum_{i=1}^{n} b_i x_i$$

This is the equation of a typical linear regression. The b_0 is known as **intercept** and b_1, b_2 and more, are known as coefficients of independent variables x_1, x_2...x_n.

Linear vs.non-linear relationships

The previously discussed equation is of a linear relationship. Why isit called linear? Let's simplify the problem and take only one dependent variable x and re-write the equation with $b_0 = 3$ and $b_1 = 10$

$$y = 3 + 10x$$

We can plot the relationship between Y and X by randomly generating some values for X and computing corresponding Y values. Below, Python code snippet can help us in doing that.

```
from numpy.random import randint
import matplotlib.pyplot as plt

X = randint(low=10, high=650, size=(50, 1))
Y = 3 + 10 * X
plt.scatter(X, Y)
plt.xlabel('X')
plt.ylabel('Y')
plt.show()
```

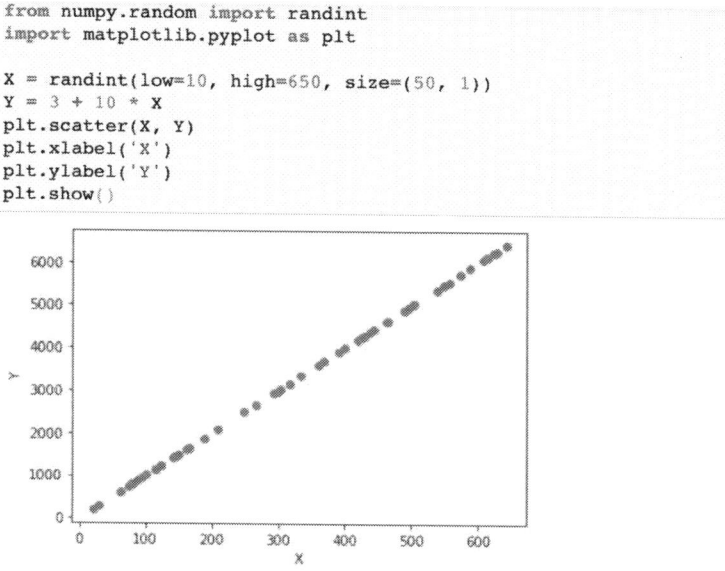

Figure 3.1: *Plot of a sample linear relationship*

Though we did a scatter plot, but it clearly shows the shape of a straight line. Gradient or Slop of this type of linear relationship is constant. This is for just two variables. But if we consider *n* number of feature variables like *X*, then what will happen? Then this straight line will become a hyperplane in n-dimension.

Now, let's change the equation and consider the following:

$$y = 3 + 10x^2$$

And the plot will look like a curve below:

```
Z = 3 + 10 * X * X
plt.scatter(X, Z)
plt.xlabel('X')
plt.ylabel('Y')
plt.show()
```

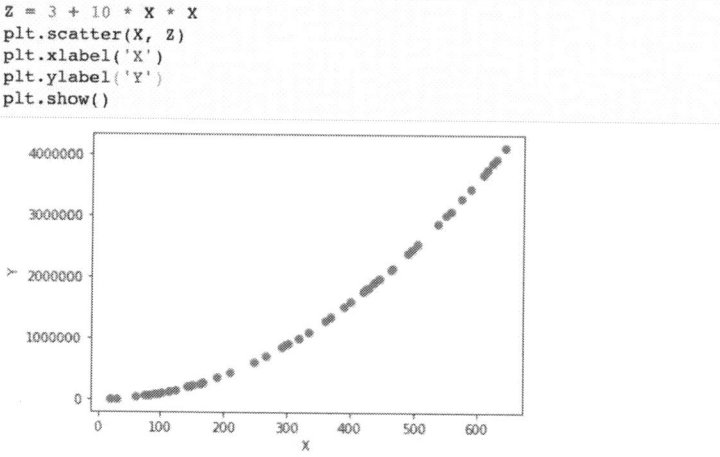

Figure 3.2: *Plot of a non-linear sample relationship*

This curve will become a Sphere and hypersphere for 3-*D* and *n-D* case, respectively. Here gradient is $10x$, which is a variable itself. So, we can say that the above equation is for a non-linear relationship between Y and X.

The main difference between linear and non-linear relationship is the gradient (constant vs. variable). And we can say that these relationships are always with respect to other variables and of very relative nature.

Conversion between linear and non-linear relationships

If we change/transform one variable, then the relationship changes drastically. A nonlinear one becomes linear and vice-versa.

For the previous equation, if we consider w as x_2 and the equation becomes:

$$y = 3 + 10w$$

Plotting above equation will produce below a line like below:

```
W = X * X
Z1 = 3 + 10 * W
plt.scatter(W, Z1)
plt.xlabel('W')
plt.ylabel('Y')
plt.show()
```

Figure 3.3: Plot of a sample transformed non-linear relationship

So, transforming one variable to others can change the nature of the relationships. A non-linear can become linear and vice versa.

Building a linear regression model

We saw the formal algebraic form of Linear Regression, which is an equation. Now, the question is, how can we build the model and find optimal values of coefficients

b_0, b_1, b_2, ..., b_n. There are different techniques fordoing it. We will discuss one of them in the next section.

General approach tosolving linear regression

We can think of linear regression as an optimization problem. Our objective is to minimize the errors generated in the prediction. If $\widehat{y}_i$ are the predicted value, and y_i is the actual value of the target variable, then objective function, a.k.a. the cost function can be written as:

$$E = \frac{1}{N} \sum_{i=1}^{N} (\widehat{y}_i - y_i)^2$$

Error is nothing but is an average of the square of differences between predicted and actual values of continuous variable y. We can visualize the concept of this error from the estimated regression line and scatter plot for one feature variable and one target variable case. The plot is shown below:

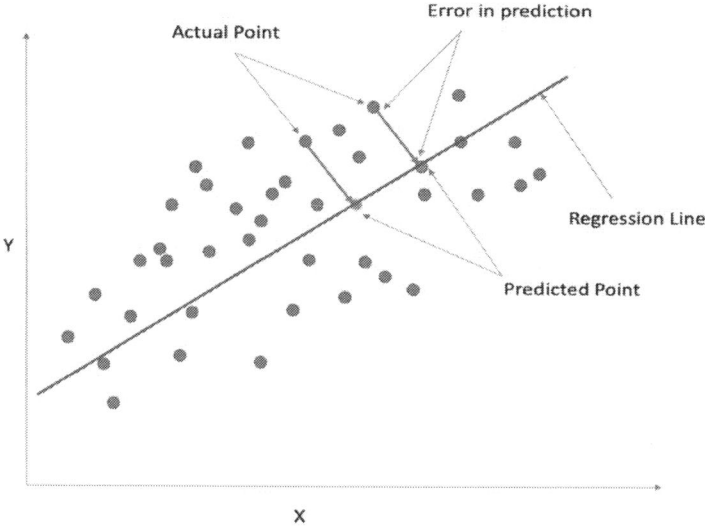

Figure 3.4: Scatter plot of sample dataset and the estimated regression line

If we have to find the equation for the regression (be it a line or hyperplane), then error E has to be minimized, and optimal values of b_0 to b_n have to be determined. From calculus and abstract mathematical point of view, this problem can be solved in numerous ways. We will discuss two of the techniques next.

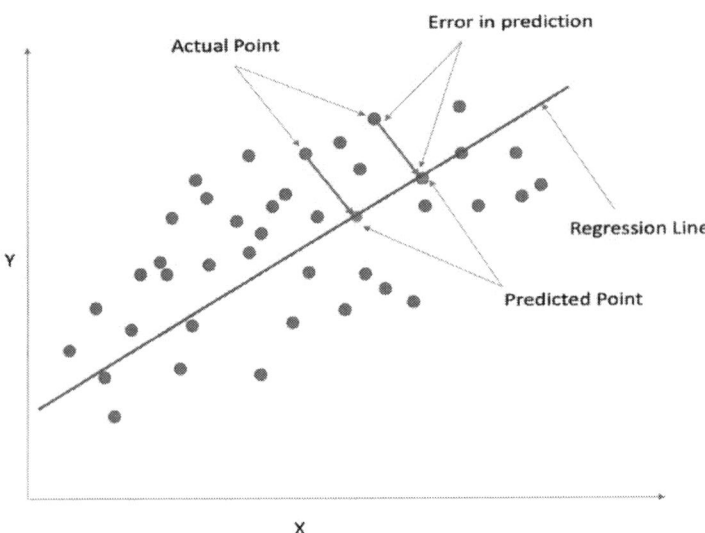

Ordinary Least Squares (OLS)

For a one feature variable (x) andone target variable (y) case, a good estimate of b in OLS approach is given by:

$$\hat{b} = \frac{Cov(x, y)}{\sigma_x^2}$$

For a general *n*-features case, this estimate comes from matrix algebra:

$$\hat{b} = (x^T x)^{-1} x^T \ y$$

Where, x^T = transpose of feature matrix, x^{-1} = inverse of matrix x.

This estimate minimizes the cost function E.

OLS approach is easy to compute and works well for large datasets. It is strongly parametric assumes that errors are fully uncorrelated to features. But this strong assumption does not hold good in many use cases, and that's the weak point of this approach.

The `scikit-learn` provides a class named `LinearRegression` for building the model using the OLS approach.

We will take a sample dataset and build a model. We will be using the Combined Cycle Power Plant Data Set from the UCI Machine Learning repository (https://archive.ics.uci.edu/ml/datasets/Combined%2BCycle%2BPower%2BPlant). Let's first read the data and see how it looks like:

```
import pandas as pd

cpp_df = pd.read_csv('../data/Folds5x2_pp.csv')
cpp_df.head()
```

	AT	V	AP	RH	PE
0	14.96	41.76	1024.07	73.17	463.26
1	25.18	62.96	1020.04	59.08	444.37
2	5.11	39.40	1012.16	92.14	488.56
3	20.86	57.32	1010.24	76.64	446.48
4	10.82	37.50	1009.23	96.62	473.90

Figure 3.5: *Code snippet to read Power Plat Data and the result*

Here the problem is to predict **net hourly electrical energy output (PE)** from other attributes. PE is a continuous attribute, so, it is a regression problem.

It is better to scaled-down all features using a `StandardScaler` to give them unit variance and create the pipeline after that. A typical training process is finding out the optimal b values using OLS. Calling a fit function on the training data does that (splitting data into train and test set is essential before that).

```
from sklearn.model_selection import train_test_split

target_y = cpp_df['PE']
features_x = cpp_df.drop('PE', axis = 1, inplace=False)

train_x, test_x, train_y, test_y = train_test_split(features_x, target_y, test_size=0.2)
```

Figure 3.6: *Code snippet to separate feature and target and splitting of train and test data*

Now, we can build the pipeline like below:

```
from sklearn.linear_model import LinearRegression
from sklearn.preprocessing import StandardScaler
from sklearn.pipeline import Pipeline

lr_model = LinearRegression()
lr_pl = Pipeline(steps=[('scaler', StandardScaler()),('lr',lr_model)])
lr_pl.fit(train_x, train_y)
print('Co-eficients: ',lr_model.coef_)
print('Intercept: ',lr_model.intercept_)

Co-eficients:  [-14.70451068  -3.01753432   0.38345152  -2.33328595]
Intercept:  454.36970474498327
```

Figure 3.7: *Code snippet to build the pipeline of the linear regression and the model coefficients as output*

We got the value of intercept b_0 and other b_i values as an array. Finally, the derived regression equation of the model will look like below:

$$y = 454.36 - 14.7x - 3.01x_2 + 0.38x_3 - 2.33x_4$$

Her x_1, x_2, x_3 and x_4 are transformed (Standard Scaled) AT, V, AP, and RH, respectively.

Gradient Descent

Mathematically, this can be done by taking partial derivatives with respect to each coefficient bi and equating the derivative to zero to solve for bi. Series of these derivative equations can be written as:

$$\frac{\partial E}{\partial b_0} = 0, \frac{\partial E}{\partial b_1} = 0, \ldots, \frac{\partial E}{\partial b_n} = 0$$

These derivatives are nothing but Gradientsof E.

If we replace E with actual expression, then the gradients for b_0 and b_1 would look like below:

$$\frac{\partial E}{\partial b_0} = -\frac{2}{N} \sum_{i=1}^{N} \left(\widehat{y}_i - \left(b_0 + \sum_{j=1}^{n} b_j x_j \right) \right)$$

$$\frac{\partial E}{\partial b_1} = -\frac{2}{N} \sum_{i=10}^{N} x_1 \left(\widehat{y}_i - \left(b_0 + \sum_{j=1}^{n} b_j x_j \right) \right)$$

Where N = total number of data points, n = number of feature variables.

We can have similar expressions for other coefficients b_2 to b_n. But, numerical and iterative methods are required to implement it practically.

There is a standard algorithm for Gradient Descent for its numerical execution. Steps are given below:

1. Get the algebraic expression of the partial derivative of the coefficient.
2. Set some initial value for the coefficient.
3. Repeat steps 4 to 6 for a number of predefined iterations.
4. Repeat steps 5 to 6 for each training data instance.
5. Evaluate the rate of change the coefficient (a.k.a Gradient) by substituting y and x attributevalues coming from training data.
6. Update coefficient value with a learning rate adjustment.
7. Repeat from Step 1 to 6 for other coefficients.

Through the above process, Gradient Descent tries to minimize the objective function E. It reaches an optimal point where the gradient is zero, and error E is minimum. In the process, it keeps on updating coefficient b. If we plot E vs. b, it looks like an inverted parabola like below:

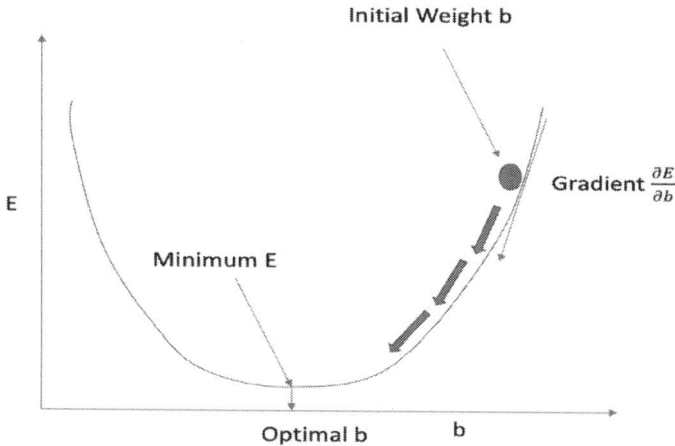

Figure 3.8: *Plot of Error vs. Coefficient of the Linear Regression*

Accuracy wise Gradient Descent technique works pretty well and is better than OLS. But, it has a performance problem with large datasets. Its complexity is O(mn), where m is the number of iterations, and n is dataset size just for one coefficient. Each time it iterates over the entire dataset to reach a locally optimal point (for computation of error E), and at last, it spits out the global optimal point.

Probably for this weakness, it is not very preferable to use in the practical use case. The `scikit-learn` also does not provide any implementation for it. But, we will write a class for it for our understanding:

```
from sklearn.base import BaseEstimator
import numpy as np

class GradientDescentLinearRegression(BaseEstimator):

    def __init__(self, learning_rate=0.1, n_iterations=100):
        self.learning_rate = learning_rate
        self.n_iterations = n_iterations
        self.errors_ = []
        self.coef_ = None
        self.intercept_ = None

    def _compute_gradients_(self, X, error, n, n_features):
        coeff_gradient = np.zeros(n_features)
        intercept_gradient = -(2/n) * np.sum(error)
        for coeff_index in range(n_features):
            coeff_gradient[coeff_index] = -(2/n) * np.dot(X[:,coeff_index], error)

        return intercept_gradient, coeff_gradient

    def fit(self, X, y):
        n = len(y)
        n_features = len(X[0])
        self.intercept_ = 0.0
        self.coef_ = np.zeros(n_features)
        for iteration in range(self.n_iterations):
            predicted_y = np.add(self.intercept_, np.dot(X, self.coef_))
            error = np.subtract(predicted_y, y)
            self.errors_.append(np.dot(error, error) / n)
            intercept_gradient, coeff_gradient = self._compute_gradients_(X, error, n, n_features)
            self.intercept_ = self.intercept_ + (self.learning_rate * intercept_gradient)
            self.coef_ = np.add(self.coef_, np.multiply(self.learning_rate, coeff_gradient))

        return self

    def predict(self, X):
        return np.add(self.intercept_, np.dot(X, self.coef_))
```

Figure 3.9: *Code snippet of GradientDescentLinearRegression class as Estimator*

We can see that inside `_compute_gradients_` function, and gradients are being computed for both intercept and coefficients as per the expressions of derivatives we discussed earlier. Each iteration updates the coefficients and intercepts with these computed gradient multiplied by a learning rate. There are no fixed stopping criteria for this algorithm. It depends on how do we want to control it. The defined `GradientDescentLinearRegression` class does it by limiting the number of iterations. We can also do it by setting a threshold on the errors computed by the objective function.

We can add `GradientDescentLinearRegression` inside a pipeline along with a `StandardScaler` and train the model:

```
from sklearn.preprocessing import StandardScaler
from sklearn.pipeline import Pipeline

gd_lr = GradientDescentLinearRegression()
gd_pl = Pipeline(steps=[('scaler', StandardScaler()),('gd_lr', gd_lr)])
gd_pl.fit(train_x, train_y)

Pipeline(memory=None,
         steps=[('scaler',
                 StandardScaler(copy=True, with_mean=True, with_std=True)),
                ('gd_lr',
                 GradientDescentLinearRegression(learning_rate=0.1,
                                                 n_iterations=100))],
         verbose=False)
```

Figure 3.10: *Code snippet of the pipeline using GradientDescentLinearRegression*

We used a 0.1 as a default `learning_rate` and 100 as `n_iterations`. These two can be taken as Hyperparameters and with different combinations; different models can be built to pick the best one.

We can get the intercept and coefficients values:

```
print('Intercept: ', gd_lr.intercept_)
print('Coefficients: ', gd_lr.coef_)
```

```
Intercept:  454.30816410059964
Coefficients:  [-13.73252155  -3.68987019   0.56570365  -1.99717584]
```

Figure 3.11: Coefficients of the trained model using GradientDescentLinearRegression

So, the regression equation will look like below:

$$y = 454.3 - 13.73x_1 - 3.68x_2 + 0.56x_3 - 1.99x_4$$

The equation almost looks similar to the one generated by the OLS approach. We can also plot the squared errors generated at each iteration.

```
%matplotlib inline

import matplotlib.pyplot as plt

pd.DataFrame(gd_lr.errors_).plot()
plt.xlabel('Iteration')
plt.ylabel('Error')
plt.show()
```

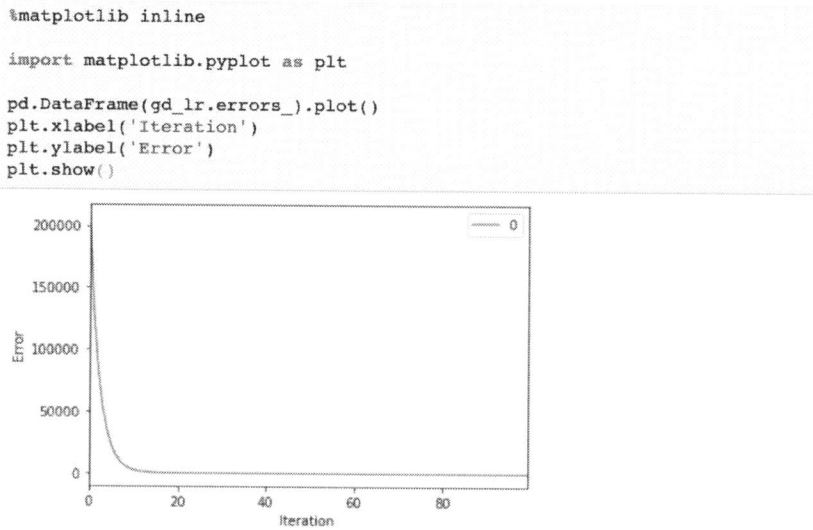

Figure 3.12: Plot of Error vs. Iteration of the trained model

Squared error is decreasing exponentially and gets stabilized at later iterations.

Accuracy of linear regression (R2 measure)

We saw the objective function of a linear regression that captures errors in prediction. To compute accuracy, we consider a more simplified version of the error. It is known as residual, and the expression is given by:

$$e = \widehat{y_i} - y_i$$

Where, $\widehat{y_i}$ = predicted value of data instance *i*. We need to capture some statistical metrics to derive a final accuracy metric as given below:

$$Total\ Sum\ of\ Squares\left(SS_{Tot}\right) = \sum(y_i - \overline{y})^2$$

Where, $\overline{y}$ = mean of the observed *y*:

$$Explained\ Sum\ of\ Squares(SS_{Reg}) = \sum(\widehat{y_i} - \overline{y})^2$$

$$Residual\ Sum\ of\ Squares(SS_{Res}) = \sum e^2$$

R^2 metric is given by the expression:

$$R^2 = 1 - \frac{SS_{Res}}{SS_{Tot}} = \frac{SS_{Reg}}{SS_{Tot}}$$

R^2 Value ranges between 0 to 1, and higher value indicates a better model. It can also be expressed as a percentage, and it says that how much percentage of variance in the data is explained by the model.

From, R^2 expression, we can also see that:

$$SS_{Tot} = SS_{Reg} + SS_{Res}$$

SS_{Reg} is the normal variance present in the data.

We can compute the accuracy of the designed model in the previous section. The `scikit-learn` provides a function named `r2_score` to get the R2 metric value from the actual & predicted data. Before that, we have to get the predicted y values from the test dataset. We have already overridden the predict function of the pipeline. We can use that to get the predicted y values.

```
from sklearn.metrics import r2_score

predicted_y = gd_pl.predict(test_x)
r2_score(test_y, predicted_y)
```

0.9301405683939182

Figure 3.13: Code snippet to get the accuracy of the trained model

So, almost 93% of the variance is explained by the model.

Selection of features in linear regression

So far, we have considered all feature variables for building the model. But, this is not the right approach to doing it. It may affect the accuracy of the model and increase the complexity unnecessarily. Datasets with a large number of features have to be properly analyzed before building the final model. We will discuss a technique of selecting the right number of features from which is the correct predictors of the model. Before that, we will know a metric which can guide us here.

Adjusted R2

It gives a filtered version of the R^2 metric by considering the number of feature variables used in the model. It may happen that even we include more features, but the model R^2 does not improve that much. It indicates the fact that some features may be irrelevant and are not influencing the determination of target variable value. Those can be excluded while building the final model. Adjusted R^2 metric is given by the following expression:

$$R^2_{Adjusted} = 1 - \frac{(1-R^2)(n-1)}{n-k-1}$$

Where n = number of records or dataset size, k = number of feature variables.

A higher value of $R^2_{Adjusted}$ indicates a better model. $R^2_{Adjusted}$ will decrease if k is increased, but there is not that much significant increment in normal R^2. So, it takes care of the model complexity. We can avoid an overly complex model that does not give very good R^2 value.

Let's take an example. For a dataset of size 1000, R^2 is 90% with five feature variables and 90.25% with 40 feature variables, respectively. We will compute Adjusted R^2 values now.

Adjusted R^2 with five feature variables = $1 - \dfrac{(1-0.90)(1000-1)}{1000-5-1} = 0.899$

Adjusted R^2 with 40 feature variables = $1 - \dfrac{(1-0.9025)(1000-1)}{1000-40-1} = 0.898$

Though there is a big change in feature variables (5 vs. 40, the change might have occurred due to inclusion of a categorical variable with cardinality 35, and it is transformed into 35 extra continuous variables by one-hot-encoding), there is not that much significant change in R^2 (0.25%), and that's why Adjusted R^2 decreased. So, the model is five feature variables that are more optimal and less complex.

We will now discuss a few techniques for selecting feature variables next.

Forward selection

This technique starts by building a collection of k models with each single feature variable where k is the total number of features. As a next step, it chooses the best scoring one with the selected feature variable, adds another variable from remaining, and the process continues until no improvement on the scoring is visible. As a scoring metric, *Adjusted R^2* is used instead of normal R^2. The entire algorithm can be stated step by step, as given below:

1. Initialize `selected_set` with empty, `remaining_set` with all independent variables (x_1 to x_n), `adjusted_r2_diff=1` and `last_adjusted_r2 = 0`.

2. Take one variable randomly from `remaining_set`, remove it from `remaining_set`, add it to `selected_set` and build a linear regression model and compute `current_adjusted_r2`, and remove the current variable from `selected_set`.

3. Set `adjusted_r2_diff = current_adjusted_r2 - last_adjusted_r2`.

4. Repeat from Step 2 and until all variables of `remaining_set` are tested and keep the combination of variables in `selected_set`, which is giving maximum `adjusted_r2_diff`.

5. Reset `last_adjusted_r2 = current_adjusted_r2` and add back all variables to `remaining_set` that are not there in `selected_set`.

6. Repeat from Step 2 until `adjusted_r2_diff < 0` or `remaining_set` is empty.

The `scikit-learn` does not provide any support for variable selection using a forward selection approach. We will write a custom class for that.

```
from sklearn.base import BaseEstimator
from sklearn.linear_model import LinearRegression
from sklearn.metrics import r2_score

class ForwardSelectionLinearRegression(BaseEstimator):

    def __init__(self):
        self.optimal_predictors_ = None
        self.optimal_model_ = None

    def fit(self, X, y=None):
        current_predictors = []
        if not isinstance(X, pd.DataFrame):
            X = pd.DataFrame(X)
        remaining_predictors = list(X)
        adjusted_r2_diff = 1
        last_adjusted_r2 = 0

        while True:
            best_predictor, adjusted_r2, r2 = self._get_next_best_predictor_(X=X,Y=y,
                                                current_predictors=current_predictors,
                                                remaining_predictors=remaining_predictors)
            adjusted_r2_diff = round(adjusted_r2 - last_adjusted_r2, 2)

            if adjusted_r2_diff <= 0.00 or len(remaining_predictors) <= 0:
                break

            current_predictors.append(best_predictor)
            remaining_predictors.remove(best_predictor)
            last_adjusted_r2 = adjusted_r2

        self.optimal_predictors_ = current_predictors
        self.optimal_model_ = LinearRegression().fit(X[self.optimal_predictors_], y)


    def _adjusted_r2_score_(self, r2_val, n, k):
        return (1 - (((1 - r2_val) * (n - 1)) / (n - k - 1)))
```

Figure 3.14: Partial code snippet of ForwardSelectionLinearRegression class as Estimator

The _get_next_best_predictor_ function does the combination checking of variables and picks up the best one. Its content is given below (it is also declared in class ForwardSelectionLinearRegression):

```
def _get_next_best_predictor_(self, X, Y, current_predictors=None, remaining_predictors=None):
    max_adjusted_r2_val = 0
    adjusted_r2_val = 0
    best_r2_val = 0
    r2Val = 0
    best_predictor = None
    n = len(X)

    for predictor in remaining_predictors:
        lr = LinearRegression()

        predictors = []
        predictors.extend(current_predictors)
        predictors.append(predictor)

        lr.fit(X[predictors], Y)
        predY = lr.predict(X[predictors])
        r2Val = r2_score(Y, predY)
        adjusted_r2_val = self._adjusted_r2_score_(r2Val,n,len(predictors))
        if max_adjusted_r2_val < adjusted_r2_val:
            best_predictor = predictor
            max_adjusted_r2_val = adjusted_r2_val
            best_r2_val = r2Val

    return best_predictor, max_adjusted_r2_val, best_r2_val

def predict(self,X):
    if not isinstance(X, pd.DataFrame):
        X = pd.DataFrame(X)
    X = X[self.optimal_predictors_]
    return self.optimal_model_.predict(X)
```

Figure 3.15: Partial code snippet of ForwardSelectionLinearRegression class as Estimator

The `predict` function of the custom estimator only chooses the selected optimal features from the data frame and delegates the call to actual the `predict` function of the optimal model. Variable `optimal_predictors` gives us the names of the feature variable to be used finally in model building.

We can test the above component with a fresh dataset. This time, we will use Predicting Comprehensive Strength of Concrete dataset from Kaggle (https://www. kaggle.com/pavanraj159/concrete-compressive-strength-data-set). It describes the number of ingredients used in the production of concrete and concrete strength. The objective is to predict concrete strength from the ingredients used there. Dataset looks like below:

```
import pandas as pd

csr_df = pd.read_csv("../data/Concrete_Data_Yeh.csv", header=0)
csr_df.head()
```

	cement	slag	flyash	water	superplasticizer	coarseaggregate	fineaggregate	age	csMPa
0	540.0	0.0	0.0	162.0	2.5	1040.0	676.0	28	79.99
1	540.0	0.0	0.0	162.0	2.5	1055.0	676.0	28	61.89
2	332.5	142.5	0.0	228.0	0.0	932.0	594.0	270	40.27
3	332.5	142.5	0.0	228.0	0.0	932.0	594.0	365	41.05
4	198.6	132.4	0.0	192.0	0.0	978.4	825.5	360	44.30

Figure 3.16: Code snippet to read Concrete Data Strength and the result

The `csMpacolumn` is our target variable, which is continuous.

We can do the splitting of feature and target variable, train, and test dataset generation in a similar fashion as earlier. We will now directly jump into the building pipeline of the model using `ForwardSelectionRegression`:

```
from sklearn.preprocessing import StandardScaler
from sklearn.pipeline import Pipeline

fs_lr = ForwardSelectionLinearRegression()
fs_lr_pl = Pipeline(steps = [('scaler', StandardScaler()),
                             ('forward_selection_model', fs_lr)])
fs_lr_pl.fit(train_x, train_y)

Pipeline(memory=None,
         steps=[('scaler',
                 StandardScaler(copy=True, with_mean=True, with_std=True)),
                ('forward_selection_model',
                 ForwardSelectionLinearRegression())],
         verbose=False)
```

Figure 3.17: Code snippet of the pipeline using ForwardSelectionLinearRegression

We can get the list of optimal predictors:

```
list(csr_df.iloc[:,fs_lr.optimal_predictors_])

['cement', 'superplasticizer', 'age', 'slag', 'water', 'flyash']
```

Figure 3.18: Code snippet to print a list of optimal predictors

The `coar seaggregate` and fine `aggregate` were not selected as predictors, as these are insignificant.

Backward selection

It works on similar principles, but it works in the opposite direction. It starts with all or a probable set of predefined important variables instead of a single one, unlike *forwarding selection* and removes one by one by checking the changes in adjusted $R2$ values. Stopping criteria is the same as the *forward selection*.

Forward or backward: When to use what

Forward selection works better when we don't have any domain knowledge about the data, that is, the importance of variables from the domain perspective. But if no variables are too many, then it becomes a quite time-consuming process. Whereas backward selection is good when we have sufficient knowledge about the domain, and we can start with a good set of important variables. On average most of the time, it is less time-consuming than forwarding Selection when no of the variables is large.

Though both forward and backward selection gives accurate results, due to its high time complexity, these are not preferable techniques with practical high-volume datasets. Theoretically, these are very much correct, but in practice, standard regularized techniques are mostly used for variable selection (will be discussed in later sections).

Key points to remember in linear regression

Before deciding to use linear regression, we have to remember a few things which will help us to build a proper model. These are discussed below:

1. Residuals or errors should not have any pattern. If we observe some patterns there, then the model is unable to explain the significant variance and not optimal.

   Let's a scatter plot of the residuals from the Gradient Descent Model we designed:

```
import seaborn as sns

residuals = predicted_y - test_y
sns.scatterplot(data=residuals)
plt.xlabel('Data Instance')
plt.ylabel('Residual')
plt.show()
```

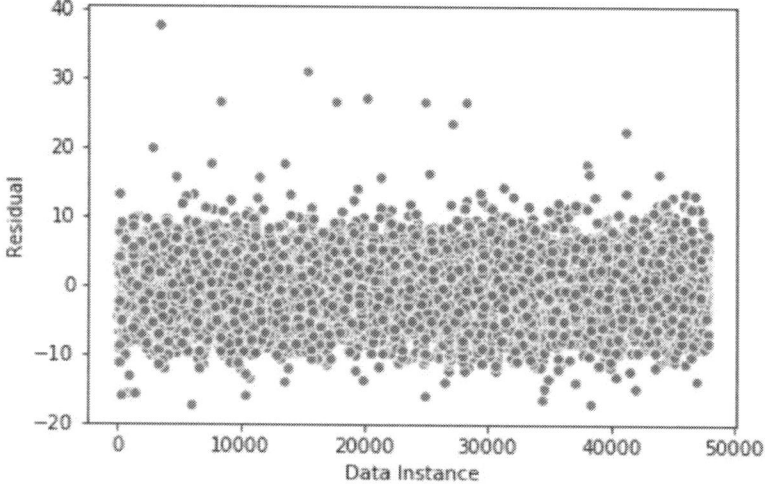

Figure 3.19: Code snippet to plot residuals of the model

2. All feature variables should follow a normal distribution and should be transformed to the same scale.

   It is always better to apply a transformation (refer *Chapter 1: Introduction to Machine Learning*) to the independent variables before modeling. Transformation should be StandardScaler; that is, after applying it; the independent variable should be a Normal distribution with zero mean and unit variance. If some or all of the independent variables don't follow Normal distribution, then this transformation also may not have any effect on the model, and it will still be wrong.

   Building a linear regression model forcefully with features not following normal distribution may result in poor accuracy.

3. Linear Regression model is defined for continuous variables, so categorical ones should be transformed into continuous using a one-hot-encoding scheme. Though this process may increase model building time, without this is a pre-requisite.

4. There should be minimum or no multi co-linearity between feature variables.

   Multi co-linearity means to what extent any variable is related to other ones.

The presence of it affects the accuracy of the model. It should be calculated for each feature variable. Practically it is measured by building a series of test linear regression models between feature variables without considering the actual target variable. For each model, one feature is made as a target, and others are made as features. Here the objective is to discard the feature, which can be determined by other features. There is a formal mathematical metric to measure factor of determination of a feature as given below:

$$Variance\ Inflation\ Factor\ (VIF) = \frac{1}{1 - R^2}$$

This R^2 comes from a linear regression model built by considering that feature as a target. So, if there are k features, then k number of these types of models can be built, and *VIF* can be computed. For example, if there are four features x_1, x_2, x_3, x_4, then the first model should be built considering x_1 as target and x_2, x_3, x_4 as features, the second model should have x_2 as target and x_1, x_3, x_4 as features and so on. At the end of the process, few features will be discarded. The decision to discard a feature depends on the *VIF* value. A very general convention is there for that.

A VIF > 10 denotes high multi-collinearity. So, the feature should be discarded at any cost. A VIF <=5 is considered good, and we can keep an independent variable in our set for that case. For any other values, domain knowledge helps to make the decision. From the VIF expression, it is clear that a high R^2 in between features produces a high VIF.

In a practical scenario with a very large dataset, this process of building test models and VIF analysis may take a very long time to come to a conclusion and build the final model. So for that, instead of doing *VIF* analysis, *Principal Components* (see *Chapter 6: Miscellaneous Unsupervised Learning*) are extracted and used as features. PCs bind all co-linear features in a single feature that can be used directly. So, co-linearity is absorbed there.

Linear regression is simple to understand and tune. Data scientists and ML experts often prefer it as a first-cut model. But as discussed above, due to its statistical assumption, it may not work well in most of the cases. A more specialized approach, like polynomial regression, may be applied, which is discussed next.

Polynomial regression

We have seen how to build a regression with a linear equation. Nonlinear equations have already been discussed in previous sections, and we have seen how to convert from nonlinear to linear. Now, we will discuss how we can use this nonlinearity in regression models. Let's take an example linear regression model of two independent variables x_1 and x_2. What if we write the equation of a newly proposed model like this:

$$y = b_0 + b_1 x_1 + b_2 x_2 + b_3 x_1^2 + b_4 x_2^2$$

Definitely, with respect to x_1 and x_2, this regression model is non-linear, and it will form a hypersphere in three-dimensional space (y, x_1, x_2). We could have added any extra terms containing x_1 and x_2. There can be infinite no of nonlinear forms, and it is very difficult to decide which one to choose for modeling.

Generally, for convenience, only n^{th} degree polynomials are chosen for nonlinear parametric regression modeling. The general form of nth degree polynomial with x_1 and x_2 is given below:

$$y = b_0 + b_1 x_1 + b_2 x_2 + b_3 x_1^2 + b_4 x_2^2 + .. + b_{2n-1} x_1^n + b_{2n} x_2^n$$

So, a 3-degree polynomial with x_1 and x_2 will look like

$$y = b_0 + b_1 x_1 + b_2 x_2 + b_3 x_1^2 + b_4 x_2^2 + b_5 x_1^3 + b_6 x_2^3$$

Normal linear regression techniques, like Gradient Descent, cannot be directly applied here. We need to do variable transformations before that. We can do the following replacements and rewrite the 3-degree polynomial equation like this:

$$w_1 = x_1^2, \; w_2 = x_2^2, \; w_3 = x_1^3, \; w_4 = x_2^3$$

$$y = b_0 + b_1 x_1 + b_2 x_2 + b_3 w_1 + b_4 w_2 + b_5 w_3 + b_6 w_4$$

Now, it is a linear regression problem with six independent variables (x_1, x_2, w_1, w_2, w_3, w_4). w_1, w_2, w_3, and w_4 are known as virtual dummy variables. We can introduce as many dummy variables as per the degree of the polynomial.

As a general rule, $k(n - 1)$ number of extra dummy variables is required to generate an nth degree polynomial with k original feature variables. After the variable generation, normal Gradient Descent or any other linear techniques can be applied to train the model. Gradients of the new variables would be computed like $\partial \dfrac{\partial E}{\partial w_1}$, $\partial \dfrac{\partial E}{\partial w_2}$, And so on.

We can simply use the existing linear regression API to build these types of models. We can write a custom estimator which generates these dummy features and build the model using normal linear regression API.

```
class PolynomialRegression(BaseEstimator):

    def __init__(self, degree=2):
        self.degree = degree
        self.poly_reg_model = LinearRegression()

    def _generate_polynomial_features_(self, X):
        new_columns = []
        columns = list(X)
        for c in columns:
            for d in range(2, (self.degree+1)):
                new_c = str(c) + '^' + str(d)
                X[new_c] = pow(X[c], d)
        return X

    def fit(self, X, y=None):
        if not isinstance(X, pd.DataFrame):
            X = pd.DataFrame(X)
        X = self._generate_polynomial_features_(X)
        self.poly_reg_model.fit(X, y)

    def predict(self,X):
        if not isinstance(X, pd.DataFrame):
            X = pd.DataFrame(X)
        X = self._generate_polynomial_features_(X)
        return self.poly_reg_model.predict(X)
```

Figure 3.20: Code snippet of PolynomialRegression as Estimator

We will use the same Predicting Comprehensive Strength of Concrete dataset from Kaggle to build and test this model. We can write a pipeline similarly:

```
poly_reg = PolynomialRegression(degree=3)
poly_lr_pl = Pipeline(steps = [('scaler', StandardScaler()),
                               ('poly_reg', poly_reg)])
poly_lr_pl.fit(train_x, train_y)

Pipeline(memory=None,
         steps=[('scaler',
                 StandardScaler(copy=True, with_mean=True, with_std=True)),
                ('poly_reg', PolynomialRegression(degree=3))],
         verbose=False)
```

Figure 3.21: Code snippet of the pipeline using PolynomialRegression

We have used a 3-degree polynomial. We can get the total number of features used from the length of the coefficient array:

```
len(poly_reg.poly_reg_model.coef_)
```

24

Figure 3.22: Code snippet to print coefficients of the trained polynomial model

The number of higher degree features generated is 16 as the number of original features was 8 (24 – 8 = 16). It validates the expression $k(n-1)$ ($k = 8$, $n = 3$).

Now, we can test this with a test data set:

```
predicted__poly_y = poly_lr_pl.predict(test_x)
r2_score(test_y, predicted__poly_y)

0.8123267652415588
```

Figure 3.23: Code snippet to test the accuracy of the polynomial model

Polynomial models are known to give known results in some very typical non-linear use cases. But knowing the appropriate degree of the model to be built is very difficult. The trial and error process can help over here.

Regularization

Before going into the details of *regularization*, we will discuss the Auto MPG Prediction dataset available from UCI (https://archive.ics.uci.edu/ml/datasets/Auto+MPG). It is a regression problem of predicting target variable **mpg** for fuel consumption. Dataset is not given here in a proper CSV format; rather, it is space-separated. It also has many missing values. So, we will write a small pre-processing function that can parse the file and prepare a semi-preprocessed dataset for us.

```python
import pandas as pd
import re
import numpy as np

def prepare_auto_mpg_dataset(file_name):
    mpg_records = []
    file = open(file_name, 'r')
    lines = file.readlines()
    for index, line in enumerate(lines):
        mpg_record = {}
        tab_parts = re.split('\t',line)
        feature_parts = re.split('\\s+', tab_parts[0])
        mpg_record['mpg'] = feature_parts[0]
        mpg_record['cylinders'] = feature_parts[1]
        mpg_record['displacement'] = feature_parts[2]
        if (feature_parts[3] == '?'):
            mpg_record['horsepower'] = np.nan
        else:
            mpg_record['horsepower'] = feature_parts[3]
        mpg_record['weight'] = feature_parts[4]
        mpg_record['acceleration'] = feature_parts[5]
        mpg_record['model year'] = feature_parts[6]
        mpg_record['origin'] = feature_parts[7]

        mpg_records.append(mpg_record)
    file.close()
    return pd.DataFrame(mpg_records)
```

Figure 3.24: Code snippet to prepare & format Auto-MPG dataset

We can now see the content as a data frame:

```
mpg_df = prepare_auto_mpg_dataset('../data/auto-mpg.data')
mpg_df.head()
```

	acceleration	cylinders	displacement	horsepower	model year	mpg	origin	weight
0	12.0	8	307.0	130.0	70	18.0	1	3504.
1	11.5	8	350.0	165.0	70	15.0	1	3693.
2	11.0	8	318.0	150.0	70	18.0	1	3436.
3	12.0	8	304.0	150.0	70	16.0	1	3433.
4	10.5	8	302.0	140.0	70	17.0	1	3449.

Figure 3.25: Code snippet to view Auto-MPG dataset

The `cylinders, model year,` and `origin` are categorical variables, and rest is continuous (as per UCI dataset specification). We can use the same `CategoricalVariableEncoder` class as a pipeline stage (as defined in *Chapter 2: Classification*) for converting those to continuous ones. Some values for horsepower features are missing. We have marked those missing values as `NaN` inside `prepare_auto_mpg_dataset` function. But it will create problem while doing any sort of computation. For that, we have to use a mean-based imputation mechanism (refer to *Chapter 1: Introduction to Machine Learning*) to fill these missing values. We can use the `SimpleImputer` class from `scikit-learn` and add it as a step in the pipeline.

Before doing anything, we need to separate features and `target` variable and prepare the dataset for training and testing like below:

```
from sklearn.model_selection import train_test_split

mpg_df_x = mpg_df[['acceleration','cylinders','displacement','horsepower','model year','origin','weight']]
mpg_df_y = mpg_df['mpg']
train_mpg_df_x, test_mpg_df_x, train_mpg_df_y, test_mpg_df_y = train_test_split(mpg_df_x, mpg_df_y)
```

Figure 3.26: Code snippet to separate feature and target variable and split the dataset into train and test

Now, the entire pipeline and training process would look like below:

```
from sklearn.impute import SimpleImputer

auto_mpg_pl = Pipeline(steps=
                    [('one_hot_encoder', CategoricalVariableEncoder(categorical_features=
                                                        ['cylinders','model year','origin'])),
                     ('imputer',SimpleImputer(missing_values=np.nan, strategy='mean')),
                     ('scaler', StandardScaler()),
                     ('lr', LinearRegression())])

auto_mpg_pl.fit(train_mpg_df_x, train_mpg_df_y)
```
```
Pipeline(memory=None,
        steps=[('one_hot_encoder',
                CategoricalVariableEncoder(categorical_features=None)),
               ('imputer',
                SimpleImputer(add_indicator=False, copy=True, fill_value=None,
                              missing_values=nan, strategy='mean',
                              verbose=0)),
               ('scaler',
                StandardScaler(copy=True, with_mean=True, with_std=True)),
               ('lr',
                LinearRegression(copy_X=True, fit_intercept=True, n_jobs=None,
                                 normalize=False))],
        verbose=False)
```

Figure 3.27: Code snippet to build the pipeline of Linear Regression using SimpleImputer and others

We can test the model with the testing dataset:

```
test_mpg_df_predicted_y = auto_mpg_pl.predict(test_mpg_df_x)
r2_score(test_mpg_df_y, test_mpg_df_predicted_y)
```

```
0.7892633164421352
```

Figure 3.28: Code snippet to measure the accuracy of the model on the test dataset

Now, the same accuracy test with the training dataset itself.

```
train_mpg_df_predicted_y = auto_mpg_pl.predict(train_mpg_df_x)
r2_score(train_mpg_df_y, train_mpg_df_predicted_y)
```

```
0.7974154888423302
```

Figure 3.29: Code snippet to measure the accuracy of the model on train dataset

Training accuracy is a little bit higher than testing accuracy. Though, in our case, the accuracy is differing by 0.01 or 1%, but in some cases, it may differ by 30-40%, which is quite a significant difference. This difference will result in poor accuracy for unknown data, and the overall solution will be less stable. As discussed in *Chapter 1: Introduction to Machine Learning*, it is the case of low bias and high variance problem. So, now the question is: how do we overcome this?

As the bias is low, can we introduce a forceful bias from outside, increase it a bit, and fix the issue? Yes, we can. There is a mathematical model for that. Before discussing that, let's see first how does overfitting induce additional complexity in a model.

For our convenience, we will see it with a simple 1-feature *n*-degree polynomial like below:

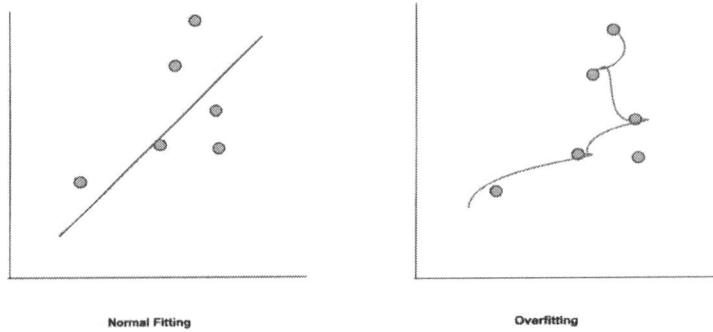

Figure 3.30: Visual interpretation of Normal vs. Overfitted model

An overfitted solution is trying to cover all data points as much as possible. Now if a new unknown data point comes and we have to predict its `target` variable value, the situation could be like below:

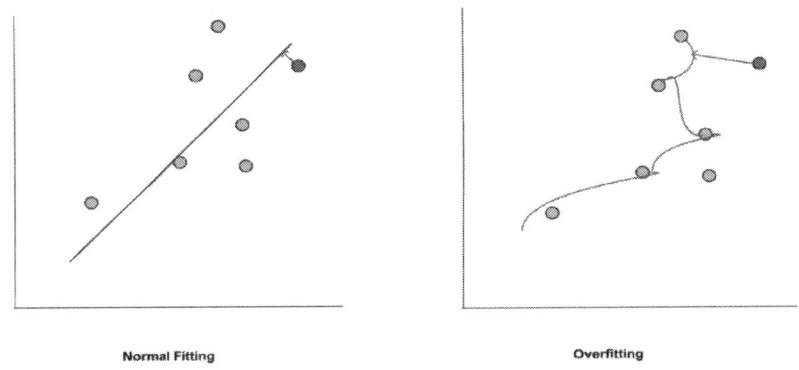

Figure 3.31: Prediction of an unknown data point in both Normal & Overfitted model

We can see, for the unknown blue point, the prediction error is much more in the overfitted solution (the amount of error is indicated by the distance covered by arrow). It resembles the situation in the previous example: testing accuracy is 1% is less than the training accuracy.

We can reduce overfitting by introducing an extra error or bias term in the overall objective/error function of the model. This bias term will be the norm (refer *Chapter 1: Introduction to Machine Learning*) of the coefficient vector of the regression model. Mathematically the entire objective function can be written as:

$$E = \sum_{i=1}^{N}(\widehat{y_i} - y_i)^2 + \left(\sum \left|b_j\right|^p\right)^{\frac{1}{p}}$$

As b_j is the coefficient of the regression expression, the second term of the above equation is known as a *regularization term*. By default, Gradient Descent may start its process with this modified error term. As we are adding extra error in overall error, it will mitigate the effect of finding a quick and local solution to the overall problem. This is, in general, known as *Lp regularization*. There are different types of it. We will discuss it next.

L1 regularization or Lasso

If we set $p = 1$, then it becomes L_1 *regularization or Lasso regression*. Error becomes

$$E = \sum_{i=1}^{N}(\widehat{y_i} - y_i)^2 + \sum \left|b_j\right|$$

Here λ is the additional hyperparameter to control the regularization term. When we $\lambda = 0$, then the effect is zero, and it becomes a normal linear/polynomial model. Lasso tends zeroing out coefficients of less important predictors. Less important predictors get vanished automatically by this process.

So, it can be used as a more effective and alternative variable selection technique rather than time-consuming *forward* or *backward* selection. We will build a Lasso based pipeline model on the same Auto MPG Prediction dataset. Other steps of the pipeline should remain the same asthe previous one. The `scikit-learn` provides a class named `Lasso` for the same.

```
from sklearn.linear_model import Lasso

lasso_model = Lasso()
lasso_auto_mpg_pl = Pipeline(steps=
                [('one_hot_encoder', CategoricalVariableEncoder(categorical_features=
                                                ['cylinders','model year','origin'])),
                ('imputer',SimpleImputer(missing_values=np.nan, strategy='mean')),
                ('scaler', StandardScaler()),
                ('lr', lasso_model)])

lasso_auto_mpg_pl.fit(train_mpg_df_x, train_mpg_df_y)

Pipeline(memory=None,
        steps=[('one_hot_encoder',
                CategoricalVariableEncoder(categorical_features=None)),
               ('imputer',
                SimpleImputer(add_indicator=False, copy=True, fill_value=None,
                              missing_values=nan, strategy='mean',
                              verbose=0)),
               ('scaler',
                StandardScaler(copy=True, with_mean=True, with_std=True)),
               ('lr',
                Lasso(alpha=1.0, copy_X=True, fit_intercept=True,
                      max_iter=1000, normalize=False, positive=False,
                      precompute=False, random_state=None, selection='cyclic',
                      tol=0.0001, warm_start=False))],
        verbose=False)
```

Figure 3.32: *Code snippet to build the pipeline of Lasso Regression using SimpleImputer and others*

We will now test the model for both testing and training dataset:

```
test_mpg_df_predicted_y_lasso = lasso_auto_mpg_pl.predict(test_mpg_df_x)
r2_score(test_mpg_df_y, test_mpg_df_predicted_y_lasso)
```

```
0.6715265490064688
```

```
train_mpg_df_predicted_y_lasso = lasso_auto_mpg_pl.predict(train_mpg_df_x)
r2_score(train_mpg_df_y, train_mpg_df_predicted_y_lasso)
```

```
0.6750000493825794
```

Figure 3.33: Code snippet to measure the accuracy of the model on the train and test dataset

Though the accuracy decreased, the difference between training and testing accuracy reduced a lot, and both are almost the same. It reduces bias ness in the model. For a huge amount of unknown data, its accuracy at least will not change drastically.

Now, let's see how many feature variables are there in the model. We can get it from the length of the coefficient array:

```
len(lasso_model.coef_)
```

```
21
```

Figure 3.34: Code snippet to get the number of coefficients of the Lass model

These 21 features include one-hot-encoded transformed categorical variables. We can get also get the number of features having non-zero coefficients:

```
len(lasso_model.coef_[lasso_model.coef_ != 0.00])
```

```
9
```

Figure 3.35: Code snippet to get the number of non-zero coefficients of the Lass model

So, only nine features are important. Though the model contains the other 12 features, its value will be nullified after multiplication by zero coefficients.

L2 regularization or Ridge

If we set $p = 2$, then it becomes L_2 *regularization or Ridge regression*. Error becomes:

$$E = \sum_{i=1}^{N}(\widehat{y_i} - y_i)^2 + \sum b_j^2$$

Ridge helps heavily in improving the overall accuracy of the solution. It prevents coefficients from rising too high values. But it cannot zero out irrelevant features like Lasso. The `scikit-learn` provides a class named Ridge for doing Ridge regression.

The rest of the implementation can be done exactly in a similar fashion, like Lasso. Readers can try it on their own.

Parametric regression models to explain facts

Parametric models (like linear/polynomial regression) are great at explaining facts. Without even using the model for prediction, it is possible to tell the change in target variables just by looking at the model. Let's analyze the mathematical expression of linear regression:

$$y = b_0 + b_1 x_1 + b_2 x_2 + \ldots + b_n x_n$$

Let's say, we change the value of x_1 from δ_1 to δ_2 keeping all other variable values same, then corresponding y values would be:

$$y_1 = b_0 + b_1 \delta_1 + b_2 x_2 + \ldots + b_n x_n$$

$$y_2 = b_0 + b_1 \delta_2 + b_2 x_2 + \ldots + b_n x_n$$

Subtracting y_1 from y_2 would produce:

$$y_2 - y_1 = b_1 (\delta_1 - \delta_2)$$

It can be simplified and generalized for variable xi more like this:

$$\Delta y = b_i \Delta x_i$$

So, the change in y can be estimated from only a change in one feature x1 without even knowing the other feature values.

It also depends on the sign of the coefficient bi that on which direction the change will happen. If coefficient b_i is positive, then a change in x_i would result in an increment of $\Delta b_i x_i$ in target variable y; otherwise, a decrement of $b_i \Delta x_i$ would happen. These facts are very useful in some use cases handling sales or profit/loss dataset. Analysts can easily estimate a positive or negative change in sales due to a change in any of the features (or dimensions in business terms) just by looking at the model. We will discuss one of these types of use cases in *Chapter 9: Data Science Storytellingchapter*.

Changes are also affected by scaling. Most of the time, we transform the features using *StandardScaler* to give those a unit variance and zero mean. If μ_1 and σ_1 are the mean and variance of the original variable $\widehat{x_1}$ then we know that:

$$x_1 = \frac{\widehat{x_1} - \mu_1}{\sigma_1}$$

So, in general,

$$\Delta x_i = \frac{\widehat{\Delta x_i}}{\sigma_i}$$

And the change in y can be captured with respect to the original variable $\widehat{x_i}$

$$\Delta y = \frac{b_i \widehat{\Delta x_i}}{\sigma_i}$$

The above formulae can be used whenever `StandardScaler` is applied before building the model.

In short, it can be said that after building the model, these change characteristics can be captured just by analyzing the coefficients. We don't have to execute the model through the entire real dataset and waste a lot of time there. These facts of changes can be shared as stories that may help analysts to make a lot of business decisions.

Tree-based regression

In *Chapter 2: Classification* chapter, we have seen how Decision Tree and Random Forest are used for predicting class labels. For the regression problem also, this tree-based approach can be used for model building. Unlike Linear equation-based regression, we don't assume any statistical nature or formulae and try to fit the data into the model. The tree-based approach is non-parametric and fact-based. Facts could be the information present in the data in terms of probability or any other metrics.

In a classification problem, we have seen the Entropy and Gini index have been used as impurity measure. Both of these are probability-based, and it calculates mixtures of different class labels in a dataset. But in regression, the problem is little different, and probability has less importance there as we deal with actual value prediction instead of class label.

So, is there any alternative metric by which we can measure the impurity of continuous values? Of course, yes. From the statistical concept, we can say, an impurity for a continuous array of values is the amount by which those differ from mean of the values, that is, variance. We can use variance or **MSE (Mean Squared Error)** as an *impurity measure* for deciding on splitting a node of the tree. The mathematical expression is given by:

$$MSE\left(Mean\ Squared\ Error\right) = \frac{1}{N}\sum_{i=1}^{N}(y_i - \widehat{y_i})^2$$

Where yi = actual value of the target variable, $\hat{y}$ = predicted value of target variable (sample mean)

A higher value of MSE or variance indicates more impurity in the data. Its minimum possible value is zero, which means all values are the same, and there is no impurity.

Like Decision Tree Classifier, we will check for all features at each stage and will choose the one which is causing the highest variance reduction, that is, the least impurity. In a classification problem, the predicted class label is obtained from the leaf node having no impurity or a threshold impurity value. But, in regression, reaching zero impurity level is almost least probable. Hence maintaining a threshold is essential over here.

The entire training process is known as the same ID3 algorithm as Classification.

Stopping criteria of the node splitting in ID3 algorithm:
1. No more attributes are pending for node splitting.
2. A threshold percentage of the 'statistical coefficient of variation' is reached.
3. Only one data sample is pending in the node.

At last, the average value of all data points of the leaf node becomes the predicted/regressed value of the regression problem.

We will see this procedure through an example of a dataset having categorical data as feature variables.

For our convenience, let's create a random dataset of 10 records containing five categorical feature variables (f1, f2, f3, f4, and f5) and one target continuous variable (y). This dataset looks like below:

```
reg_tree_df = pd.read_csv("../data/decision_tree_regressor_sample_data.csv", header=0)
reg_tree_df
```

	f1	f2	f3	f4	f5	y
0	A1	B2	C6	D1	E4	200
1	A2	B4	C2	D2	E1	300
2	A1	B2	C6	D1	E4	134
3	A4	B1	C5	D1	E3	500
4	A1	B3	C1	D2	E4	222
5	A3	B1	C4	D1	E1	125
6	A1	B2	C3	D1	E2	211
7	A2	B1	C1	D1	E3	121
8	A1	B3	C2	D2	E4	115
9	A2	B2	C6	D1	E1	332

Figure 3.36: Code snippet to read sample dataset for decision tree regressor

We need to predict y from feature variables.

We will use the following notations of a few necessary statistical measures for our convenience:

Mean(Y) = Mean of target variable Y at any node of the tree

Var(Y) = Variance of target variable Y at any node of the tree

SD(Y) = Standard Deviation of target variable Y at any node of the tree

CV(Y) = Coefficient of variance of target variable Y at any node of the tree = SD(Y) * 100 /Mean(Y)

$Var(Y, X) = \sum_{c \in X} P(c) Var(c)$ = Variance with respect to variable X. Here, $P(c)$ denotes the probability of attribute value c in the dataset and $Var(c)$ denotes variance of Y having $X = c$

$VarReduction(Y, X) = Var(Y) - Var(Y, X)$

Instead of simple Variance, we will use the *Coefficient of Variance (CV)* as an impurity measure, which is more appropriate.

The same mechanism as Decision Tree classifier is applicable here also at a high level. We will choose one feature at a time and check the value of *VarReduction(Y, X)*. The feature responsible for maximum reduction in variance is chosen as the splitting attribute. If at any node certain threshold *CV* is reached or there is no more pending attribute to check, then the process stops there. Let's see this in a step-by-step way with our current dataset.

1. Mean(Y) = 226

    Var(Y) = 13471.6

2. Testing with attribute $f1$:

    Var $(Y, X(f1 = A1))$ = P $(f1 = A1)$ Var($X(f1 = A1)$)

    $\qquad\qquad\qquad\qquad$ = (5/10) * (1888.24)

    $\qquad\qquad\qquad\qquad$ = 944.12

    Var $(Y, X(f1 = A2))$ = P $(f1 = A2)$ Var($X(f1 = A2)$)

    $\qquad\qquad\qquad\qquad$ = (3/10) * (8620.66)

    $\qquad\qquad\qquad\qquad$ = 258.62

    Var $(Y, X(f1 = A3))$ = P $(f1 = A3)$ Var($X(f1=A3)$)

    $\qquad\qquad\qquad\qquad$ = (1/10) * (0)

    $\qquad\qquad\qquad\qquad$ = 0

    Var $(Y, X(f1=A4))$ = P $(f1 = A4)$ Var($X(f1=A4)$)

    $\qquad\qquad\qquad\qquad$ = (1/10) * (0)

    $\qquad\qquad\qquad\qquad$ = 0

So,   Var (Y, X) = 944.12 + 258.62 = 1202.74

VarReduction (Y, X) = 1371.6 – 1202.74 = 168.86

Similarly, for attribute *f2*, VarReduction (Y, X) = – 2802; attribute *f3*, VarReduction (Y, X) = – 6214; attribute *f4*, VarReduction (Y, X) = – 4703; and attribute *f5*, VarReduction (Y, X) = – 7365

Attribute *f1* is giving us the highest variance reduction. Hence the root node split will be based on *f1*. We can see graphically:

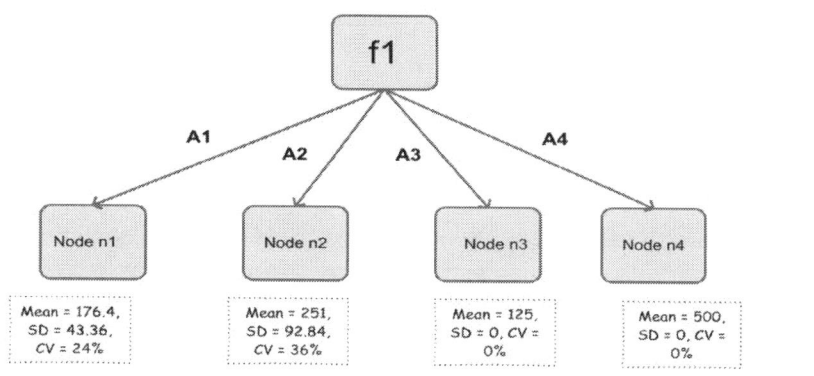

Figure 3.37: Partial Regression Tree built from the dataset

There are four branches from the root node carrying values of attribute *f1*. As CV and SD of the 3rd and 4th branch are zero, the process stops there, and Node *n3* and *n4* become leaf node. But for the 1st and 2nd branches, further splitting is required, and the same process will continue recursively by checking other attributes apart from *f1*. It will stop if some threshold value of CV (let's say 10% which can be set as hyper-parameter) is reached for any node or all attributes are tested in that branch. Reaching 0% CV like Node *n3* or *n4* is less likely to happen. That's why it is always preferable to set a certain threshold for CV as termination criteria. All nodes will be the leaf node at the last level of the tree. Now for example, if a data point comes with a value A3 for attribute *f1*, directly we can go to Node 3, and as it is a leaf node, no more exploration is possible, we can say that the predicted value for *Y* would be 125 (125 is the mean value of the leaf node).

The `scikit-learn` provides a `DecisionTreeRegressor` class as like `DecisionTreeClassifier`. It internally uses the same CART algorithm (discussed in *Chapter 2: Classification* chapter). All categorical features have to be converted into continuous ones to be processed by `scikit-learn`. The pipeline should consist of two steps, one hot encoding and the `DecisionTreeRegressor` itself:

```
from sklearn.tree import DecisionTreeRegressor

X_dt_reg = reg_tree_df[['f1','f2','f3','f4','f5']]
Y_dt_reg = reg_tree_df[['y']]
dt_reg_model = DecisionTreeRegressor()
sample_dt_reg_pl = Pipeline(steps=
                    [('one_hot_encoder', CategoricalVariableEncoder(categorical_features=
                                                        ['f1','f2','f3','f4','f5'])),
                     ('dt_reg',dt_reg_model),
                     ])

sample_dt_reg_pl.fit(X_dt_reg, Y_dt_reg)

Pipeline(memory=None,
        steps=[('one_hot_encoder',
                CategoricalVariableEncoder(categorical_features=None)),
               ('dt_reg',
                DecisionTreeRegressor(criterion='mse', max_depth=None,
                                    max_features=None, max_leaf_nodes=None,
                                    min_impurity_decrease=0.0,
                                    min_impurity_split=None,
                                    min_samples_leaf=1, min_samples_split=2,
                                    min_weight_fraction_leaf=0.0,
                                    presort=False, random_state=None,
                                    splitter='best'))],
        verbose=False)
```

Figure 3.38: Code snippet of the pipeline of the regression tree model

We can visualize the entire tree using `graphviz` API:

```
from sklearn.tree import export_graphviz
import pydotplus
from IPython.display import Image

dot_file = export_graphviz(dt_reg_model, out_file=None,
                filled=True, rounded=True,
                special_characters=True)
graph = pydotplus.graph_from_dot_data(dot_file)
Image(graph.create_png())
```

Figure 3.39: Code snippet to view a regression tree model

The plotted tree would like below:

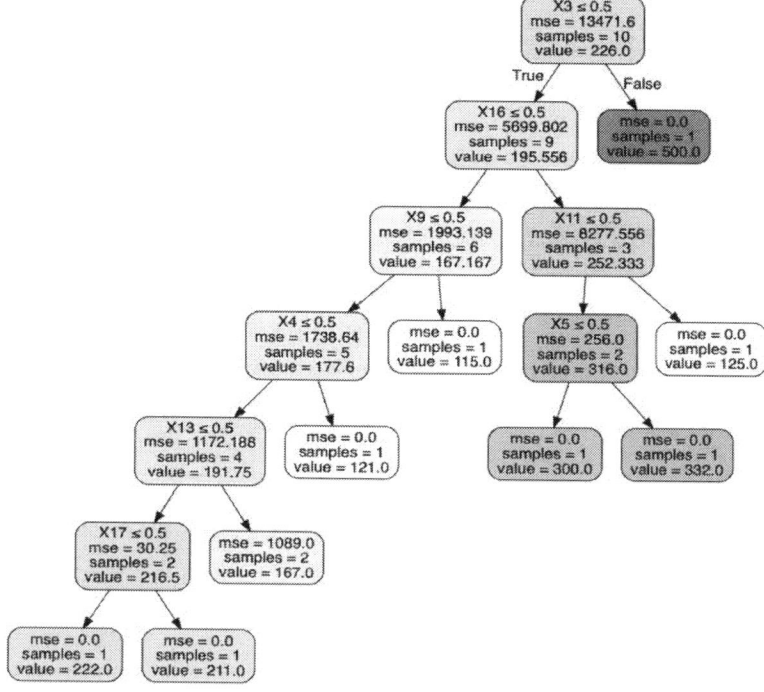

Figure 3.40: *Plot of the trained regression tree model*

All leaf nodes have `mse` as 0.0, that is, with zero impurity.

We will now create a sample data instance and get the predicted y value from the model:

```
test_x_1 = pd.DataFrame([{'f1':'A1','f2':'B2','f3':'C3','f4':'D2','f5':'E1'}])
sample_dt_reg_pl.predict(test_x_1)
```

```
array([300.])
```

Figure 3.41: *Code snippet to test model with an unknown data instance*

We can design a similar pipeline to build the model for Auto MPG Prediction dataset:

```
dt_reg_auto_mpg_model = DecisionTreeRegressor()
auto_mpg_dt_reg_pl = Pipeline(steps=
                    [('one_hot_encoder', CategoricalVariableEncoder(categorical_features=
                                                        ['cylinders','model year','origin'])),
                    ('imputer',SimpleImputer(missing_values=np.nan, strategy='mean')),
                    ('dt_reg_model', dt_reg_auto_mpg_model)])

auto_mpg_dt_reg_pl.fit(train_mpg_df_x, train_mpg_df_y)

Pipeline(memory=None,
        steps=[('one_hot_encoder',
                CategoricalVariableEncoder(categorical_features=None)),
                ('imputer',
                SimpleImputer(add_indicator=False, copy=True, fill_value=None,
                              missing_values=nan, strategy='mean',
                              verbose=0)),
                ('dt_reg_model',
                DecisionTreeRegressor(criterion='mse', max_depth=None,
                                      max_features=None, max_leaf_nodes=None,
                                      min_impurity_decrease=0.0,
                                      min_impurity_split=None,
                                      min_samples_leaf=1, min_samples_split=2,
                                      min_weight_fraction_leaf=0.0,
                                      presort=False, random_state=None,
                                      splitter='best'))],
        verbose=False)
```

Figure 3.42: *Code snippet of the pipeline of the regression tree model using Auto MPG dataset*

We can similarly generate the plotted tree, and it will look like below:

Figure 3.43: *Plot of the trained regression tree model of Auto MPG dataset*

The tree looks quite big due to its number of features. We can get the accuracy by using the model on test data:

```
predicted_mpg_dt_reg_y = auto_mpg_dt_reg_pl.predict(test_mpg_df_x)
r2_score(test_mpg_df_y, predicted_mpg_dt_reg_y)
```

```
0.7147510044465863
```

Figure 3.44: Code snippet to test the accuracy of the model on the test data

For the tree-based model, the traditional $R2$ metric may not be that much relevant as tree models are non-parametric. We can also use standard MSE as accuracy in place of $R2$.

Comparison of different regression techniques

Linear/non-linear parametric (refer *Chapter 1: Introduction to Machine Learning*) models are straight forward to implement and tune. But here, we have to know the pattern, data distribution, and relationships beforehand so that one mathematical/ statistical expression can be formed. Like in the case of linear/polynomial regression, we assume a formal algebraic equation-based relation between variables, and then by standard techniques available, we find out its parameters. This gives very good results if, in the true sense, variables have that kind of relationship.

In some cases, we know the data distributions of variables beforehand. One example could be data from the banking/financial industry. Most of the cases, banking/ financial data follows standard statistical distributions, and we can assume several parametric models (both linear/non-linear), and it gives very good results there. Parametric techniques of regression are heavily affected by high/low values. We always have to do proper scaling/noise removal of all variables before building the model.

Non-parametric and non-linear models like the regression tree do not assume any formal distribution of the data. It does not try to fit the data into any predefined algebraic form. Rather, it builds the model by an intuitive analysis of the data with the help of some mathematical metrics like probability, variance, or mean. So, it is always better to apply these techniques where data distribution is unknown to us. Most of the cases, these are preferable over parametric/equation-based techniques where the domain is unknown to us.

Conclusion

In this chapter, we discussed how we could predict a continuous or numerical target variable using regression techniques. We saw a wide variety of regression techniques starting from a parametric linear model to non-parametric techniques like a decision tree. We discussed the regularization technique like Lasso and Ridge to prevent overfitting. A detailed analysis of the accuracy metric is also covered.

We learned the formal algebraic definition of linear and polynomial regression. We implemented several custom classes for these, which can work as Estimators in pipelines. Variable selection and important factor analysis are very important in descriptive machine learning practice. We learned techniques of doing these using forward, backward selection, and Lasso. In the end, the regression tree gives us an idea of how to build a non-parametric regression model. We also learned a nice visualization technique of regression using the standard Python library.

In the next chapter, we will learn about an unsupervised technique named clustering, where labels like classification problem or numerical values like regression problem won't be provided beforehand. Discovery of patterns there have to do without any prior knowledge.

CHAPTER 4
Clustering

Previous chapters helped us in learning mostly supervised **machine learning(ML)** techniques. In this chapter, we will discuss an unsupervised approach to extracting meaningful information from the data. We already saw a very brief definition of clustering in *Chapter 1: Introduction to Machine Learning*. It is a technique of finding groups in the data without any information about the hidden pattern. The objective of clustering is to find patterns and groups. That's why it is completely unsupervised. Unlike classification or regression, there is no tagged information about any target variable.

Structure

In this chapter, we will discuss:

- Formal definition of clustering
- Different types of clustering techniques like centroid-based (*K* Means), density-based (DBSCAN)
- Details of *X* Means clustering
- Hierarchical clustering
- Clustering as a classification technique

Objective

After finishing this chapter, we will be able to

- Apply specific clustering techniquesbased on use case and do appropriate visualization of clusters.
- Use clustering as an alternative classification technique.

Formal definition of clustering

Clustering is a process of creating meaningful groups of records or objects having common characteristics. These common or similar characteristics can be found out by visual observation or by some mathematical formulation. Any visual observation of the data to form clusters can be explained by an underlying mathematical or statistical theory. We can manually find out groups present in the data from a scatter diagram. We try to match objects based on the information found there. Through ML, this manual process can be automated by the cluster analysis technique.

Concept of cluster

A cluster can be thought of as a labeled group or class and quite analogous to a classified object in classification but an unsupervised manner. And the process of making clusters is known as **clustering**. Classification models are built from the dataset already tagged with class labels. Dataset for clustering does not come with tagged class labels. A clustering algorithm can find those hidden class labels and treat those as separate clusters. Objects or records are assigned to those clusters depending on similarity or match score with each of the clusters. We can see three different clusters shown in the two-dimensional scatter diagram below:

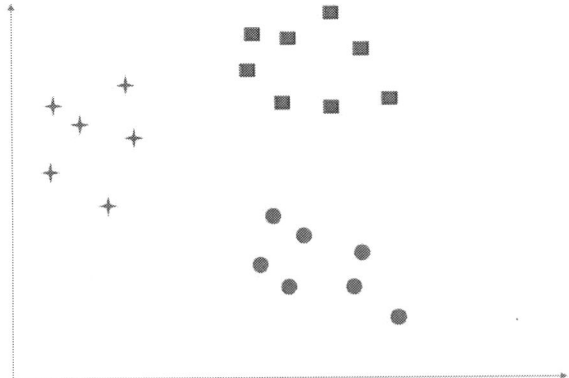

Figure 4.1: Sample Clusters

- **Well-separated cluster:** In this type of cluster setup, data points of each group are quite far from the other group. A thresholding mechanism can be used to specify the closeness of the data points, and that will determine the boundary lines. Below plot is an example of a well-separated cluster in 2D space:

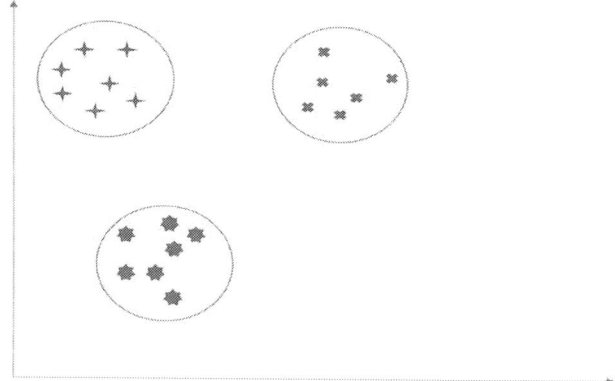

Figure 4.2: Sample well-separate cluster

- **Overlapped cluster:** This setup contains which may have common data points across different clusters. Theoretically, a data point can belong to more than one cluster in this type of clustering technique. Below plot is an example of it:

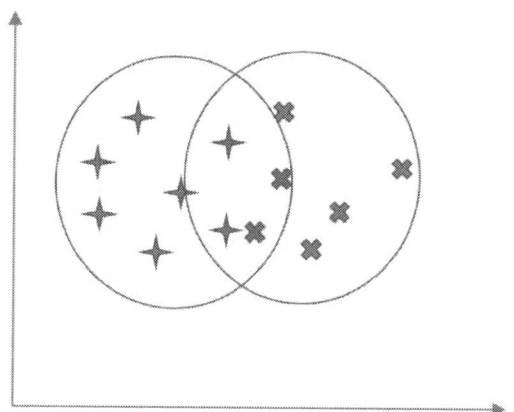

Figure 4.3: Sample well-separate cluster

Red data points in the scatter plot belong to both of the clusters.

Similarity metrics

One very important part of most of the clustering algorithm is the computation of distance or similarity between the data points. Either one of distance or similarity can be taken as a measure. Conceptually these two are opposite or reciprocal to each other. It is the similarity/distance measure that determines the membership of a data point to a cluster. Most of the algorithms compute distance by Euclidean Distance or similarity by Cosine Similarity (refer *Chapter 1:Introduction to Machine Learning*). The metric (1-Cosine Similarity) or (1/ Cosine Similarity) can also be taken as a **distance metric**.

Center-based clustering

It is a type of clustering approach where one representative data point is chosen for each cluster. All other data points evolve around these sets of representative data points. Practically, for the dataset with mostly continuous attributes, the representative is nothing but the mathematical centroid. From the concept of Physics, we know that centroid is the center point of mass where the object can be perfectly balanced. And geometrically, it is the arithmetic mean of all points of a geometric figure or object. In most cases, centroids don't have a physical existence;that is, it may not be an existing data point among the entire dataset. It may be conceptual. For a multi-dimensional figure, centroid should be computed for each dimension. On a similar note, the composite centroid of a set of multi-dimensional data points in a Euclidean Space can be computed by:

$$Centroid_{ki} = \frac{1}{n_k} \sum_{j=1}^{n_k} x_{kij}$$

$$Centroid_k = (Centroid_{k1}, Centroid_{k2}, ..., Centroid_{kd})$$

Where d = number of dimensions

$Centroid_{ki}$ = Centroid of the ith dimension of kth cluster

$Centroid_k$ = Composite centroid of all dimensions of kth cluster

n_k = number of data points in the kth cluster

x_{kij} = i^{th} dimension of jthdata point of the kth cluster in Euclidean Space

Center-based clusters tend to be spherical. Some examples of the centroid are shown in below cluster plot (centroids are shown in red):

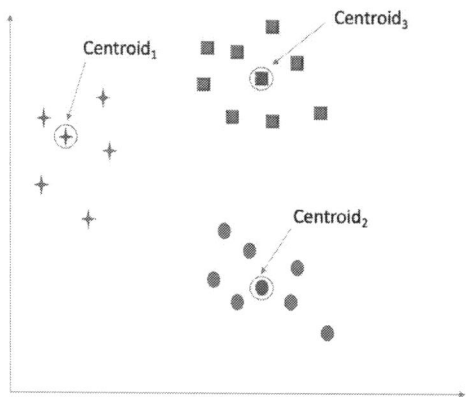

Figure 4.4: *Sample Centroid based clusters*

We can observe that Centroid3 is not a real data point; rather, it is conceptual.

K-means clustering

K-means is the most popular center-based clustering algorithm. It completely works on the concept of the centroid, as explained in the previous section. Its working principle starts with an assumption/initialization of *K* center points or centroids from the dataset. Here *K* is the user-supplied parameter. Other data points then start getting assigned to the closet centroid. The collection of points assigned to a centroid form a cluster. Centroids are re-computed after this and are matched with the previously assigned values. If re-computed centroids are close enough or the same, then the process stops; otherwise, it continues. There are some hyper-parameters to control the number of times it should loop through or the threshold to determine centroid's closeness.

Basic K-means algorithm

1. Select *K* data points from the dataset as initial cluster centroids.
2. Compute distances from centroids for each other data points.
3. Assign a data point to the cluster having minimum distance.
4. Re-compute the centroids for all *K* clusters.
5. Re-compute *K* centroids and compare them with previous values.
6. Repeat from Step 2 if centroids change otherwise end.

Hyper-parameters

There can two high-level hyper-parameters to control the algorithm. Practically, it is very difficult to check if previous and current centroids values are the same or not because of floating-point arithmetic. That's why one *threshold* is kept as hyper-parameter to set the minimum difference in centroid values. If the absolute difference in current and previously computed centroids is greater than this threshold, then only the algorithm will continue; otherwise, it will stop. Centroids computed in the last iteration will be final cluster centers.

The number of iterations can also be set as hyper-parameter to control the looping. In this case, the threshold may be overlooked or vice versa.

Python implementation of K-means clustering

The `scikit-learn` has a library for KMeans clustering. As per the `scikit-learn` standard, it follows the same `fit`, `predicts`, and `transform` function signatures, and the KMeans itself works as `Estimator` and `Transformer`, which can be added as a step in a pipeline.

We will use Wholesale Customer's dataset from the UCI Machine Learning Repository (https://archive.ics.uci.edu/ml/datasets/Wholesale+customers) for applying the KMeans clustering algorithm. Let's explore the dataset first:

```python
import pandas as pd

df = pd.read_csv('../data/Wholesale customers data.csv')
df.head()
```

	Channel	Region	Fresh	Milk	Grocery	Frozen	Detergents_Paper	Delicassen
0	2	3	12669	9656	7561	214	2674	1338
1	2	3	7057	9810	9568	1762	3293	1776
2	2	3	6353	8808	7684	2405	3516	7844
3	1	3	13265	1196	4221	6404	507	1788
4	2	3	22615	5410	7198	3915	1777	5185

Figure 4.5: Code snippet to display Wholesale Customer's dataset

This dataset holds information about product wise sales across different channels and regions. From the description available in the UCI portal, we can observe that `ChannelandRegion` are categorical variables, and rest are all continuous. Our objective is to study and visualize the clusters of sales data inclusive of all features:

Pre-processing

We have to convert the categorical variables to continuous using `OneHotEncoder` and apply `StandardScaler` to available continuous variables only. We will use the same `ColumnTransformer`as earlier use cases:

```
from sklearn.compose import ColumnTransformer
from sklearn.preprocessing import StandardScaler

preprocessor = ColumnTransformer(
    transformers=[
        ('numerical', StandardScaler(), ['Fresh','Milk','Grocery','Frozen','Detergents_Paper','Delicassen']),
        ('categorical', OneHotEncoder(handle_unknown='ignore'), ['Channel','Region'])])
```

Figure 4.6: *Code snippet to convert categorical feature to continuous*

Pipeline creation

We will use the preprocessor instance and the `KMeans` itself as pipeline stages. For our understanding, we can set cluster size as 5 (by `n_clusters` parameter):

```
from sklearn.pipeline import Pipeline
from sklearn.cluster import KMeans

kmeans_pl = Pipeline(steps = [
                        ('col_preprocessor', preprocessor),
                        ('kmeans', KMeans(n_clusters=5))
                    ]
                )
kmeans_pl.fit(df)

Pipeline(memory=None,
        steps=[('col_preprocessor',
                ColumnTransformer(n_jobs=None, remainder='drop',
                                  sparse_threshold=0.3,
                                  transformer_weights=None,
                                  transformers=[('numerical',
                                                 StandardScaler(copy=True,
                                                                with_mean=True,
                                                                with_std=True),
                                                 ['Fresh', 'Milk', 'Grocery',
                                                  'Frozen', 'Detergents_Paper',
                                                  'Delicassen']),
                                                ('categorical',
                                                 OneHotEncoder(categorical_features=None,
                                                               categories=None,
                                                               drop=None,
                                                               dtype=<class 'numpy.float64'>,
                                                               handle_unknown='ignore',
                                                               n_values=None,
                                                               sparse=True),
                                                 ['Channel', 'Region'])],
                                  verbose=False)),
               ('kmeans',
                KMeans(algorithm='auto', copy_x=True, init='k-means++',
                       max_iter=300, n_clusters=5, n_init=10, n_jobs=None,
                       precompute_distances='auto', random_state=None,
                       tol=0.0001, verbose=0))],
        verbose=False)
```

Figure 4.7: *Code snippet to build pipeline for KMeans cluster*

The fit function computes centroid distances and does the actual learning part of the algorithm:

As discussed, the KMeans algorithm assigns one cluster membership for each data record. The `predict` function will give us those details as cluster indices (0 to 4):

```
kmeans_pl.predict(df)

array([0, 0, 0, 2, 1, 0, 0, 0, 2, 0, 0, 2, 0, 0, 0, 2, 0, 2, 0, 2, 2, 2,
       1, 0, 0, 0, 2, 2, 0, 1, 2, 2, 2, 1, 2, 0, 1, 0, 0, 1, 1, 2, 0, 0,
       0, 0, 0, 4, 0, 0, 2, 2, 1, 0, 2, 2, 4, 0, 2, 2, 0, 4, 0, 0, 2, 4,
       2, 0, 2, 2, 1, 1, 2, 1, 0, 2, 2, 0, 2, 2, 2, 0, 0, 2, 0, 4, 4, 1,
       2, 1, 2, 2, 4, 1, 0, 2, 0, 2, 2, 2, 0, 0, 0, 1, 2, 2, 0, 0, 0, 0,
       2, 0, 1, 2, 2, 2, 2, 2, 2, 2, 2, 2, 0, 1, 1, 1, 0, 2, 1, 2, 2, 2,
       2, 2, 2, 2, 2, 2, 2, 2, 2, 1, 1, 2, 2, 0, 2, 2, 2, 1, 2, 2, 2, 2,
       2, 0, 0, 2, 0, 0, 0, 2, 2, 0, 0, 0, 0, 2, 2, 2, 0, 0, 2, 0, 2, 0,
       1, 2, 2, 2, 2, 1, 0, 3, 2, 2, 2, 2, 0, 0, 2, 2, 2, 0, 2, 1, 1, 0,
       2, 2, 0, 0, 1, 2, 2, 0, 2, 0, 2, 0, 2, 4, 2, 0, 0, 0, 2, 0, 2, 2,
       2, 2, 2, 2, 2, 2, 0, 2, 2, 2, 2, 2, 2, 2, 2, 2, 2, 2, 2, 2, 1, 1, 2,
       2, 2, 2, 0, 2, 2, 2, 2, 2, 4, 2, 1, 2, 1, 2, 2, 1, 1, 2, 2, 2, 2,
       0, 0, 0, 2, 0, 2, 2, 2, 2, 1, 2, 2, 1, 1, 2, 0, 2, 0, 1, 1, 1, 1,
       2, 2, 2, 1, 2, 2, 2, 0, 2, 2, 2, 0, 0, 2, 0, 0, 0, 0, 0, 0, 0, 2,
       2, 0, 2, 1, 0, 2, 2, 0, 2, 2, 2, 0, 2, 2, 2, 2, 1, 2, 2, 2, 2, 2,
       2, 0, 2, 4, 1, 0, 2, 2, 2, 2, 0, 0, 2, 0, 2, 2, 0, 0, 2, 0, 2, 0,
       2, 0, 2, 2, 2, 0, 2, 2, 2, 2, 2, 2, 2, 0, 2, 2, 2, 2, 1, 1, 2, 0,
       2, 2, 0, 1, 2, 0, 1, 1, 1, 2, 0, 2, 2, 2, 2, 2, 2, 2, 2, 1, 2, 2,
       0, 2, 2, 2, 2, 1, 2, 2, 2, 2, 1, 0, 0, 2, 2, 2, 2, 1, 2, 0, 0, 2,
       0, 2, 0, 0, 2, 2, 0, 1, 0, 1, 2, 2, 2, 1, 2, 2, 2, 1, 1, 0, 2, 2],
      dtype=int32)
```

Figure 4.8: Code snippet to predict cluster indices of the dataset

The predict function can be used for any unknown/new data instance to determine its cluster membership. Once a new data point is given, it computes Euclidean distances from all centroids of the cluster setup and assigns the data point to the cluster whose centroid is closest.

Clustering as new feature space

A center-based clustering algorithm like KMeans, can be used to generate a new feature space for the dataset. Any dataset can be transformed into a K-dimensional feature space by applying the KMeans algorithm. Each transformed feature for a data point is obtained by computing its distance from each of K cluster centroids.

The transform function of KMeans can do it:

```
kmeans_pl.transform(df)

array([[ 1.21324982,  2.8771171 ,  1.90411194, 18.95148826,  7.2656983 ],
       [ 0.88171365,  3.01158625,  1.95925167, 18.72683871,  7.04820962],
       [ 2.40821901,  3.50040771,  3.05451543, 16.87984844,  7.39898674],
       ...,
       [ 2.65953653,  4.94505617,  4.72870864, 18.80205956,  3.94223618],
       [ 2.5277389 ,  2.48926033,  0.67959373, 18.935351  ,  8.54508298],
       [ 2.58704184,  3.17934941,  0.87138495, 19.72784094,  8.62955702]])
```

Figure 4.9: Code snippet to use KMeans as new feature space

As we had set n_clusters as 5, transformed feature space will be 5-dimensional. It can be used as a high-level dimensionality reduction technique.

The sensitivity of KMeans with centroid initialization

KMeans is highly sensitive tothe initial allocation of cluster centroids. It greatly influences cluster formation. With a random initialization strategy, different runs of KMeans may produce different cluster setup with varying accuracy. So, it is preferable to keep initial centroid allocation fixed and seeded externally instead of random allocation. It will help to generate consistent clusters in scenarios where multiple runs of the algorithm with an increasing dataset are needed.

As an alternative, KMeans++ strategy can be used. It works as follows:

1. Select one single centroid C randomly from the dataset.
2. Compute the distance $DC(x)$ from each other point x to the closest centroid C.
3. Select the next centroid with a weighted probability directly proportional to $[DC(x)]^2$
4. Go to Step 2 if the number of selected centroids is less than K otherwise end.

KMeans++ tries to select widespread centroids as much possible. It ensures to capture greater variability of the data. The sciki-learn's KMeans class, by default, initializes centroids with KMeans++ approach.

Visualization of clusters

As we have a total of 11-dimensions (including transformed categorical variables), it is not possible to visualize clusters with all of those together easily. There are two approaches to view clusters in a 2D scatter diagram, as discussed next.

- **Using any two variables and cluster indices**

  We can plot the clusters against any two desired variables from the dataset. Though the while doing cluster computation, we considered all variables, but here we will try to visualize those cluster patterns with respect to any two variables and the same computed cluster indices. For our use case, we will choose `Milk` and `Grocery` as variables and view the cluster.

  The `seaborn` library has a function `scatterplot`, which takes X and Y variable names, original data frame as the source, color codes as hue parameter to draw scatter diagrams. We can mention `cluster_labels` itself variable as hue as we need different colors for five different clusters:

```
import matplotlib.pyplot as plt
import seaborn as sns

plt.figure(figsize=(25,15))
sns.scatterplot(x="Milk", y="Grocery", data=df, hue=cluster_labels, size=cluster_labels, sizes=(20, 300))
plt.title('Cluster Visualization with Milk & Grocery', fontsize=16)
plt.ylabel('Grocery', fontsize=16)
plt.xlabel('Milk', fontsize=16)
plt.xticks(rotation='vertical');
```

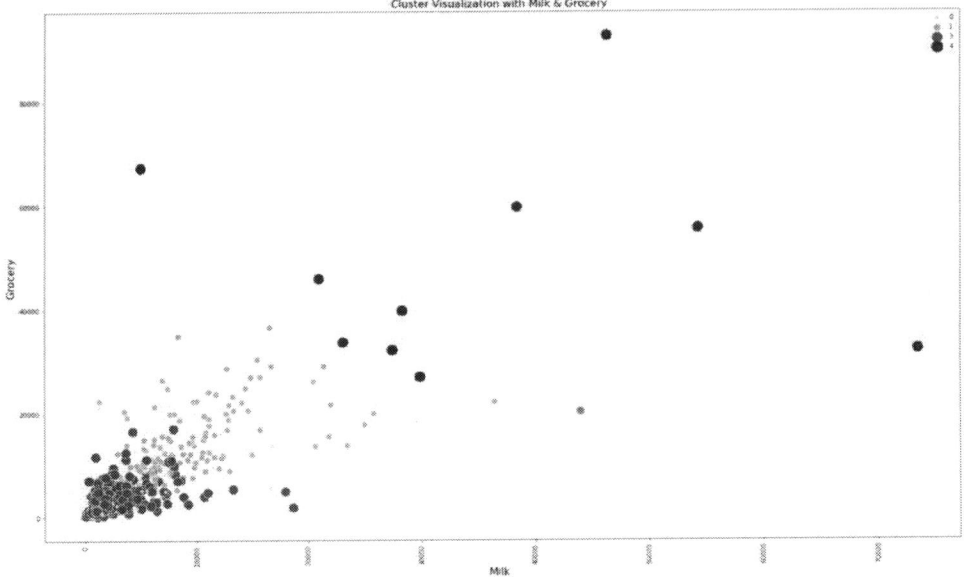

Figure 4.10: Code snippet to plot KMeans cluster

We can see that there a concentration of clusters (especially cluster index 3) in the range 0-20000 for `Grocery` and 0-10000 for `Milk`. So, `Milk` and `Grocery` were sold more within these ranges. We can also get cluster patterns with respect to other remaining variable pairs in a similar fashion.

- **Using the first two principal components and cluster indices**

  We can use PCs to generate the two most important virtual dimensions and use these to re-run the KMeans algorithm. These 2 PCs can be plotted in a scatter diagram along with newly generated cluster indices to view formed clusters.

  We can use a pipeline with the same preprocessor defined earlier and PCA as another step:

```
from sklearn.decomposition import PCA

pca_pl = Pipeline(steps = [    ('col_preprocessor', preprocessor),
                               ('pca', PCA(n_components=2))
                          ]
                 )
pca_vectors = pca_pl.fit_transform(df)
pca_vectors
```

```
array([[ 4.56510987e-01, -4.15233235e-01],
       [ 6.90371107e-01, -4.13859584e-01],
       [ 9.86235647e-01,  7.46248727e-01],
       [-9.07106282e-01,  6.34782984e-01],
       [ 3.35755338e-01,  1.13006219e+00],
       [ 1.19396372e-01, -4.41716878e-01],
       [-3.80732985e-02, -6.87171852e-01],
       [ 4.02827403e-01, -3.49837686e-01],
       [-5.74674443e-01, -6.28149912e-01],
       [ 1.83178373e+00, -7.01265659e-01],
       [ 8.92241713e-01, -4.66822617e-01],
       [-6.27745123e-01, -4.47404670e-01],
       [ 1.16474959e+00,  6.41779558e-01],
       [ 1.07665725e+00, -1.32861412e-01],
       [ 1.05696458e+00,  1.03528532e-01],
       [-1.00284796e+00, -5.12217369e-01],
       [ 8.52259604e-01, -1.08773107e+00],
       [-4.68200766e-01,  2.39988299e-01],
       [ 5.30761279e-01,  3.30717861e-01],
```

Figure 4.11: Code snippet to compute first 2 Principal Components of the dataset

We will apply KMeans on top of these `pca_vectors` to generate clusters:

```
cluster_labels = KMeans(n_clusters=5).fit_predict(pca_vectors)
cluster_labels
```

```
array([0, 0, 0, 2, 1, 2, 2, 0, 2, 0, 0, 2, 0, 0, 0, 2, 0, 2, 0, 2, 2, 2,
       1, 3, 0, 2, 2, 2, 0, 1, 2, 2, 2, 1, 2, 0, 1, 0, 0, 1, 1, 2, 0, 0,
       0, 0, 0, 3, 0, 0, 2, 2, 1, 0, 2, 2, 3, 0, 2, 2, 2, 3, 2, 0, 2, 3,
       2, 0, 2, 2, 1, 1, 2, 1, 2, 2, 2, 0, 2, 2, 2, 0, 0, 2, 2, 3, 3, 1,
       2, 1, 2, 1, 3, 1, 0, 2, 2, 2, 2, 2, 0, 0, 0, 1, 2, 2, 0, 0, 0, 0,
       2, 0, 1, 2, 2, 2, 2, 2, 2, 2, 2, 2, 0, 1, 1, 1, 0, 2, 1, 2, 2,
       2, 2, 2, 2, 2, 2, 2, 2, 1, 1, 2, 2, 0, 2, 2, 2, 2, 2, 2, 2, 2,
       2, 0, 0, 2, 0, 0, 2, 2, 0, 0, 0, 0, 2, 2, 2, 0, 2, 0, 2, 0, 0,
       1, 2, 2, 2, 2, 4, 0, 4, 2, 2, 2, 2, 0, 0, 2, 2, 2, 0, 2, 1, 1, 0,
       2, 2, 0, 0, 1, 2, 2, 0, 2, 0, 2, 0, 2, 3, 2, 2, 0, 0, 0, 2, 0, 2,
       2, 2, 2, 2, 2, 2, 2, 2, 2, 2, 1, 2, 2, 2, 2, 2, 2, 2, 2, 1, 1, 2,
       2, 2, 2, 0, 2, 2, 2, 2, 2, 3, 2, 2, 1, 2, 2, 2, 1, 1, 2, 2, 2, 2,
       0, 1, 0, 1, 0, 2, 2, 2, 2, 1, 2, 2, 1, 1, 2, 0, 2, 2, 1, 1, 1, 2,
       2, 1, 2, 1, 2, 2, 2, 0, 2, 2, 2, 2, 0, 2, 2, 0, 0, 0, 0, 0, 0, 2,
       2, 0, 1, 2, 0, 2, 2, 0, 2, 2, 2, 0, 2, 2, 2, 2, 2, 4, 2, 2, 1, 2,
       2, 0, 2, 3, 1, 0, 2, 2, 1, 2, 0, 0, 2, 0, 2, 2, 0, 0, 2, 0, 2, 0,
       2, 0, 1, 2, 2, 0, 1, 2, 2, 2, 2, 2, 0, 2, 2, 2, 2, 2, 1, 1, 2, 2,
       2, 2, 0, 1, 2, 2, 2, 1, 1, 2, 0, 2, 2, 2, 2, 2, 2, 2, 1, 2, 2,
       0, 2, 2, 2, 2, 1, 2, 2, 2, 2, 1, 0, 2, 2, 2, 2, 1, 2, 0, 0, 2,
       0, 2, 0, 2, 2, 2, 2, 1, 0, 1, 2, 2, 2, 1, 2, 2, 2, 1, 1, 0, 2, 2],
      dtype=int32)
```

Figure 4.12: Code snippet to apply KMeans on PCA features

We can plot `pca_vectors` against the cluster indices like below:

```
import matplotlib.pyplot as plt
import seaborn as sns
plt.figure(figsize=(25,15))
sns.scatterplot(x=pca_vectors[:, 0], y=pca_vectors[:, 1], hue=cluster_labels_pca, size=cluster_labels_pca,
                sizes=(20, 300))
plt.title('Cluster setup with first 2 PC', fontsize=16)
plt.ylabel('Principal Component 2', fontsize=16)
plt.xlabel('Principal Component 1', fontsize=16)
plt.xticks(rotation='vertical');
```

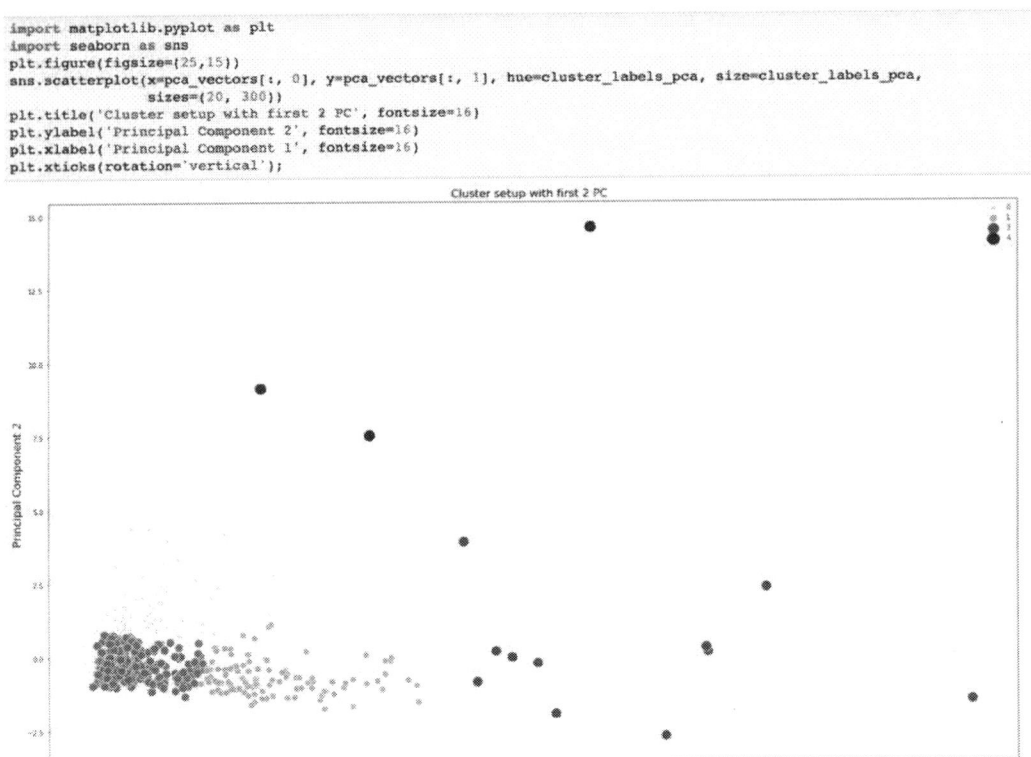

Figure 4.13: Code snippet to plot PCA features with clusters

As we know, principal components do not specify the underlying physical attributes, and it may not be possible to infer which attribute is contributing significantly to it. From the cluster plot, we can see there is a high concentration of data points in value range around (– 1.25) – (+ 1.25) for PC 2 and (– 2) – 0 for PC 1. Mostly within these ranges, data points fall under cluster index 1.

From the visualization, it is clear that clustering can reveal a lot of hidden information which are not available at first hand. This information can be used to study data and seeded into other systems or models. That's the sole objective of clustering.

Accuracy metrics

Like other ML models, clustering models also have metrics to judge accuracy. As mostly clustering algorithms deal with distance, so total error generated in distance computation could be a metrics to judge the quality of clustering. This is known as **SSE (Sum of Squared Errors)** of a cluster. SSE is given by computing error for each data point, that is, its Euclidean distance from the centroid of its cluster and summing up altogether. Its expression is given by:

$$SSE = \sum_{i=1}^{k} \sum_{x \in C_i} (x - \mu_i)^2$$

Where k = number of clusters

C_i = set of data points in a cluster i

μ_i = centroid of cluster i

SSE is quite an absolute measure and gives a very high-level estimate of cluster quality. But, it ignores two very important quality aspect of center-based clustering as discussed next.

Cohesion andseparation of clusters

Cohesion is a cluster quality measure that defines how much compact each cluster is. It can be obtained by computing the sum of all pairwise distances of data points within a cluster. Pictorially, a cluster's cohesion can be shown as:

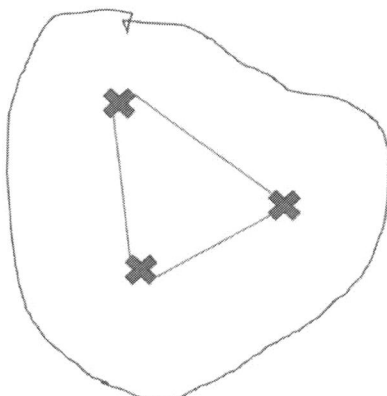

Figure 4.14: Cohesion of clusters

A lower cohesion indicates cluster is more compact, and there is less error present in each cluster.

Separation defines how many wells separated clusters are from each other. It can be obtained by the sum of distances between each data point pair of clusters. It can be shown as below:

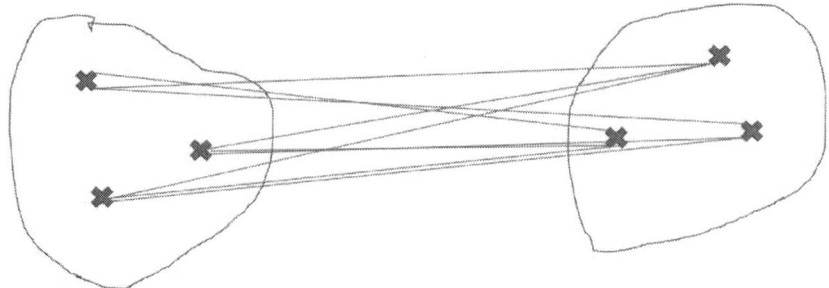

Figure 4.15: Separation of clusters

A higher separation indicates a better cluster setup.

Silhouette coefficient

It combines concepts of both *Cohesion* and *Separation* in a single measure and can work as a uniform and unit independent metric of cluster quality. *Silhouette Coefficientis* considered as a standard metric for center-based clusters and is independent of the distance unit. Silhouette Coefficient for the ith data point is given by the expression:

$$Silhouette\ Coefficient_i = \frac{b_i - a_i}{\max(b_i, a_i)}$$

Where,

a_i = average distance between the ith data point and all other data points within the same cluster that data point i belongs to.

b_i = minimum of the all average distances between the ith data point and all other data points of all other clusters that i do not belong to.

In short, we can say that a_i is the intra-cluster distance and b_i is the inter-cluster distance of data point i.

Silhouette Coefficient of the entire cluster setup is the average of coefficients of all data points and is given by:

$$Silhouette\ Coefficient_{All} = \frac{1}{N} \sum_{i=1}^{N} Silhouette\ Coefficient_i$$

Where N = the size of the total data set.

Value for any Silhouette Coefficient ranges between – 1 to +1. A bigger value indicates bigger inter-cluster distance and lesser inner-cluster error and thus a better overall cluster setup. A negative Silhouette Coefficient for a data point indicates that it has been assigned to a wrong cluster, and overall negative measure says most of the data points are wrongly assigned.

Python implementation of cluster metric

The `scikit-learn` provides two functions for computing the overall Silhouette Coefficient of the complete cluster setup as well as individual Silhouette Coefficient for each data point. It takes features and predicted cluster labels as input. We will use computed `pca_vectors` in the previous section as features:

```
from sklearn.metrics import silhouette_samples, silhouette_score

silh_mean_score = silhouette_score(pca_vectors, cluster_labels)
silh_mean_score
```

```
0.4929231633101926
```

Figure 4.16: Code snippet to computer Silhouette Coefficient of the entire cluster setup

So, the overall score is 0.49, which is moderate. Now, we can get scores for all data points as an array:

```
silh_scores = silhouette_samples(pca_vectors, cluster_labels)
silh_scores
```

```
array([ 0.12114483,  0.32282963,  0.0896917 ,  0.2198748 ,  0.29826668,
        0.24764841,  0.33781969,  0.04230122,  0.65149252,  0.62299237,
        0.44680142,  0.70090393,  0.22295241,  0.44455907,  0.37530081,
        0.7369608 ,  0.46670279,  0.46691479,  0.000742  ,  0.56856192,
        0.44428521,  0.71680607,  0.54625455,  0.00154322,  0.09070631,
        0.17943594,  0.68834058,  0.72103452,  0.49531715,  0.25246894,
        0.27109578,  0.72869032,  0.686882  ,  0.40875966,  0.6921836 ,
        0.24363898,  0.4478888 ,  0.53704238,  0.6199559 ,  0.4490586 ,
        0.53846898,  0.27156344,  0.56301178,  0.57651782,  0.30894592,
```

Figure 4.17: Code snippet to computer Silhouette Coefficient for each data point

(Array was shown partially)

Advantages of KMeans

- It is quite simple to use and can be applied to a wide range of data without having sufficient domain knowledge about the data source.
- It does get affected that much with the high-dimensional dataset, that is, can work efficiently even though the number of features is quite high.
- It can detect clusters well if these are globular or spherical.

KMeans can be used as a general-purpose clustering algorithm at first hand. Data scientists and machine learning experts often use it to get an initial view of the patterns.

Disadvantages of KMeans

- It is highly dependent on cluster initialization in the first step. If initialized cluster centroids are wrongly chosen, then it can end up generating a poor cluster setup.

- KMeans is heavily affected by noise/outliers in the data. Statistical measure Mean is greatly influenced by extreme (very high or low) values present in data and so as centroids computed in KMeans (as centroid is multi-dimensional mean). One example of these extreme values and how does it affect centroid is shown below:

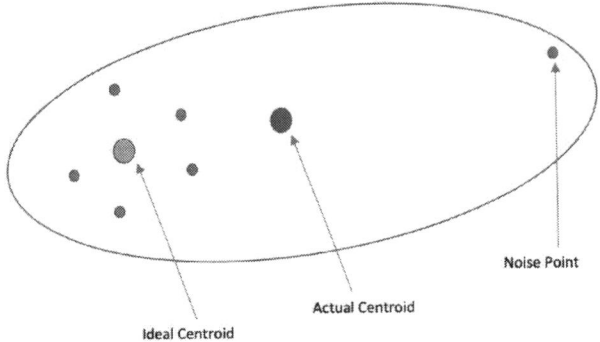

Figure 4.18: Effect of an outlier on KMeans

Due to the presence of a single noise point, computed centroid falls far away from most of the data points in the cluster. As centroid is democratic and it is a representative of the majority, it should have been close to most of the points, and its ideal location is shown in the above cluster plot (as green data point). Wrongly computed centroids due to the presence of noise point increase cluster SSE because ofthe poor cluster setup.

- KMeans cannot produce good clusters if the inherent shapes present in the data are not spherical. It will try to give spherical shape forcefully, which can spoil the setup.

- It also fails to handle clusters that have varying densities.

If there is sufficient domain knowledge, then it is better to use other very specific clustering algorithms rather than KMeans.

Determining optimal K in KMeans

In KMeans, the value of K is seeded from outside. But, how to know the best guess for K? KMeans algorithm does not provide any mechanism to get optimal K by itself. If we choose K too low, cluster SSE will be too high, and it is considered underfitted, whereas a very high K would produce many miniature clusters, which causes overfitting. So, we need an optimal K.

Elbow method

There is a technique to find out optimal K from a predefined range of values. For each K, different cluster setups are generated by running KMeans repeatedly, and cluster SSEs are computed. A minimum value of K will give maximum cluster SSE whereas a maximum K causes minimum cluster SSE. So, there will be changes in SSE for a changing K. Optimal K will be that one for which there will maximum change in SSE. If we plot SSE vs. K, it will look like an elbow-shaped curve, and the elbow point will hold optimal K. Graph looks like below:

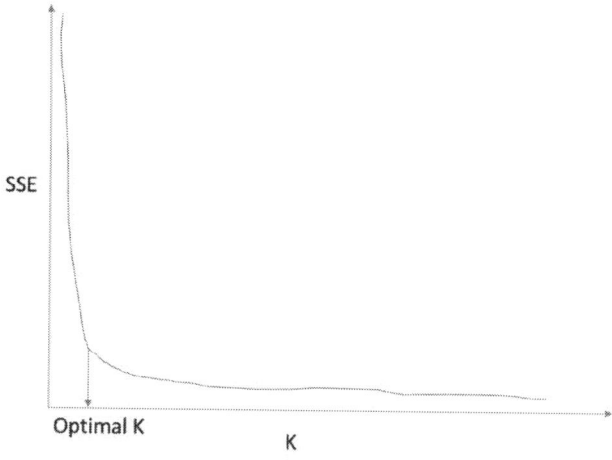

Figure 4.19: *SSE vs. K plot for KMeans and Elbow point*

Visual confirmation of elbow point may look fine for a small dataset, but to automate the entire process at production-grade systems, we need an iterative algorithm to find the elbow point. One very general approach would be to try out a range of K and keep computing the change in SSE for a pair of consecutive K values. Optimal K will be the one for which change in SSE is maximum. This approach looks very simple but has a time and resource complexity and hence not very popular.

XMeans clustering

As SSE is not considered a very good metric for judging cluster quality, applying the elbow method directly may not give us the right optimal K. We have to consider other statistical measures to reach the optimal point.

Bayesian Information Criterion (BIC) can find the optimal model that gives a minimum score. XMeans clustering algorithm loops through the given range of values for K and returns the optimal K by computing the BIC score.

The idea of XMeans is originally published in a paper (https://www.cs.cmu.edu/~dpelleg/download/xmeans.pdf) by *Dan Pelleg* and *Andrew Moore*. BIC is computed by the expression as given below:

$$BIC = L - \frac{p}{2} \log \log R$$

WhereL is the log-likelihood of the model, p is the number of parameters, and R is the total number of data points being considered.

Computation of Log-likelihood

Rather than using any cluster accuracy metric, *XMeans* tries to optimize cluster foundation using statistical measures. Its objective is to maximize posterior probability $P(Mj \mid D)$ where Mj is the current model, and D is the set of all data points. It also assumes that data points follow Gaussian distribution and as per the paper the **maximum likelihood estimate (MLE)** of the data variance for K^{th} cluster given by:

$$\hat{\sigma}^2 = \frac{1}{R-K} \sum (x_i - \mu)^2$$

Probability of a data point assigned to a cluster i is a joint event of choosing the cluster and Gaussian probability estimate of the data point. The expression of this joint probability for a data point xi is given by:

$$\hat{P}(x_i) = \frac{R_i}{R} \frac{1}{\hat{\sigma}^M \sqrt{2\pi}} \exp\left(-\frac{1}{2\hat{\sigma}^2} \|x_i - \mu\|^2 \right)$$

Where R_i is the number of data points under the cluster, i belongs to.

$P(x_i)$ should be maximized for all data points. Joint probabilities for all data points is the multiplication of all individual probabilities, that is, $\prod P(x_i)$. Maximizing this is equivalent to maximizing the $(\log \prod P(x_i))$, and it is known as the log-likelihood estimate L (as given in BIC expression).

After mathematical computation, maximized estimate $\hat{L}$ is given by:

$$\hat{L} = Max\_Estimate\left(\log \log \left(\prod P(x_i) \right) \right)$$

$$= -\frac{R_n}{2} \log \log (2\pi) - \frac{R_n \cdot M}{2} \log \log \hat{\sigma}^2 - \frac{R_n - K}{2}$$

$$= +R_n \log \log(R_n) + R_n \log \log R$$

Where R_n is the number of data points assigned to cluster n, R is the total number of data points, K is the total number of clusters, M is the number of the parameters for the cluster n. Above estimate $\hat{L}$ is computed for each cluster in the entire setup.

The total number of parameters p in BIC expression can be roughly estimated by (M * K). The BIC score of each cluster is computed, and the overall score of the entire cluster setup is obtained by summing up all scores. We will use this overcall score as a metric to judge the cluster setup and pick the K, which gives maximum value.

There are two techniques of BIC computation for a varying K. First approach is the simpler one and starts from 2 to maximum possible clusters we want. This number of maximum possible cluster (max K) has to be supplied externally. It is an iterative process and may work slowly for a large amount of data. The second approach follows divide and conquer. It starts with randomly selecting n clusters and then runs local K-means on each of the child clusters. Each time, cluster setup with & without the child is tested against BIC score, and a better setup is chosen. This process is complex to implement, but overall runtime complexity is less than the first approach. For our convenience, we will only implement the first approach in Python.

Python implementation of XMeans

The `scikit-learn` does not have library support for XMeans. So, we can write a custom estimator by extending `BaseEstimator` of `scikit-learn`:

```python
from sklearn.base import BaseEstimator
from math import log, pi
from sys import maxsize
from sklearn.metrics.pairwise import euclidean_distances

class XMeans(BaseEstimator):

    def __init__(self, max_k):
        self.optimal_clusterer = None
        self.max_k = max_k
        self.optimal_k = None

    def fit(self, X, y=None):
        n = len(X)
        max_bic_score = -maxsize
        M = len(X[0])
        for k in range(2,(self.max_k + 1)):
            current_clusterer = KMeans(n_clusters = k)
            current_clusterer.fit(X)
            cluster_centers = current_clusterer.cluster_centers_
            cluster_labels = current_clusterer.predict(X)
            bic_score_k = self._compute_bic_score_(X, n, k, M, cluster_centers, cluster_labels)

            if bic_score_k > max_bic_score:
                max_bic_score = bic_score_k
                self.optimal_k = k
                self.optimal_clusterer = current_clusterer

        return self

    def predict(self, X):
        return self.optimal_clusterer.predict(X)
```

Figure 4.20: Partial code snippet of XMeans class as Estimator

Overridden fit function of **XMeans** class tries out different **KMeans** with a varying K between 2 to **max_k**. BIC score is computed for each KMeans model, and the one that gives minimum score is chosen as final and **optimal** K. We can get this value from the `optimal_k` variable of **XMeans** class. We have also defined two private functions `_compute_bic_score_` and `_compute_log_likelihood_` inside the class **XMeans**. These are used within the fit function:

```
def _compute_log_likelihood_(self, r, rn, sigma2_mle, M, k):
    L1 = -(rn * 0.5 * log(2.0 * pi))
    L2 = -((rn * M) * 0.5 * log(sigma2_mle + 1))
    L3 = -((rn - k) * 0.5)
    L4 = rn * log(rn + 1)
    L5 = -rn * log(r)
    return (L1 + L2 + L3 + L4 + L5)


def _compute_bic_score_(self, X, n, k, M, cluster_centers, cluster_labels):
    all_bic_scores = []
    for cluster_index in range(k):
        current_cluster_center = cluster_centers[cluster_index]
        cluster_k_X = X[cluster_labels == cluster_index]
        rn = len(cluster_k_X)
        total_squared_distance = euclidean_distances(cluster_k_X,
                                   current_cluster_center.reshape(1, -1), squared=True)

        sigma2_mle = sum(total_squared_distance) / (n - k)
        L = self._compute_log_likelihood_(n, rn, sigma2_mle, M, k)

        p = M * k
        bic_score = L - (p * 0.5 * log(n))
        all_bic_scores.append(bic_score)

    return sum(all_bic_scores)
```

Figure 4.21: Partial code snippet of XMeans class as Estimator

μ in the expression of MLE $\hat{\sigma}^2$ is nothing but the individual cluster centres. The expression $\sum (x_i - \mu)_2$ can be computed by summing up squared Euclidean distances of all data points from their cluster centres.

We will use this XMeans as a pipeline stage and test the `predict` function with the same Wholesale Customer's dataset.

```
from sklearn.pipeline import Pipeline

xm = XMeans(max_k = 15)
xm_pl = Pipeline(steps = [
                    ('col_preprocessor', preprocessor),
                    ('xmeans', xm)
                    ]
            )
xm_pl.fit(df)

Pipeline(memory=None,
        steps=[('col_preprocessor',
                ColumnTransformer(n_jobs=None, remainder='drop',
                                 sparse_threshold=0.3,
                                 transformer_weights=None,
                                 transformers=[('numerical',
                                              StandardScaler(copy=True,
                                                            with_mean=True,
                                                            with_std=True),
                                              ['Fresh', 'Milk', 'Grocery',
                                               'Frozen', 'Detergents_Paper',
                                               'Delicassen']),
                                             ('categorical',
                                              OneHotEncoder(categorical_features=None,
                                                           categories=None,
                                                           drop=None,
                                                           dtype=<class 'numpy.float64'>,
                                                           handle_unknown='ignore',
                                                           n_values=None,
                                                           sparse=True),
                                              ['Channel', 'Region'])],
                                 verbose=False)),
               ('xmeans', XMeans(max_k=15))],
        verbose=False)
```

Figure 4.22: Code snippet of the pipeline for XMeans cluster

And we can get the optimal K from **XMeans** instance:

```
xm.optimal_k
```

```
5
```

Figure 4.23: *Code snippet to get optimal K of XMeans*

So, the optimal number of clusters, in this case, is 5. We can now get the predicted cluster indices:

```
xm_p1.predict(df)
```

```
array([1, 1, 1, 4, 0, 1, 1, 4, 1, 1, 4, 1, 1, 1, 4, 1, 4, 1, 4, 4, 4,
       0, 1, 1, 1, 4, 4, 1, 0, 4, 4, 4, 0, 4, 1, 0, 1, 1, 0, 0, 4, 1, 1,
       1, 1, 1, 3, 1, 1, 4, 4, 0, 1, 4, 4, 3, 1, 4, 4, 1, 3, 1, 1, 4, 3,
       4, 1, 4, 4, 0, 0, 4, 0, 1, 4, 4, 1, 4, 4, 4, 1, 1, 4, 1, 3, 3, 0,
       4, 0, 4, 4, 3, 0, 1, 4, 1, 4, 4, 4, 1, 1, 1, 0, 4, 4, 1, 1, 1, 1,
       4, 1, 0, 4, 4, 4, 4, 4, 4, 4, 4, 4, 1, 0, 0, 0, 1, 4, 0, 4, 4,
       4, 4, 4, 4, 4, 4, 4, 4, 4, 0, 0, 4, 4, 1, 4, 4, 4, 0, 4, 4, 4, 4,
       4, 1, 1, 4, 1, 1, 1, 4, 4, 1, 1, 1, 1, 4, 4, 4, 1, 1, 4, 1, 4, 1,
       0, 4, 4, 4, 4, 0, 1, 2, 4, 4, 4, 4, 1, 1, 4, 4, 4, 1, 4, 0, 0, 1,
       4, 4, 1, 1, 0, 4, 4, 1, 4, 1, 4, 1, 4, 3, 4, 4, 1, 1, 1, 4, 1, 4,
       4, 4, 4, 4, 4, 1, 4, 4, 4, 4, 4, 4, 4, 4, 4, 4, 4, 0, 0, 4,
       4, 4, 4, 1, 4, 4, 4, 4, 4, 3, 4, 0, 4, 0, 4, 4, 0, 0, 4, 4, 4, 4,
       1, 1, 1, 4, 1, 4, 4, 4, 4, 0, 4, 4, 0, 4, 4, 1, 4, 1, 0, 0, 0, 0,
       4, 4, 4, 0, 4, 4, 4, 1, 4, 4, 4, 1, 1, 4, 1, 1, 1, 1, 1, 1, 1, 4,
       4, 1, 4, 0, 1, 4, 4, 4, 1, 4, 4, 4, 1, 4, 4, 4, 4, 0, 4, 4, 4, 4,
       4, 1, 4, 3, 0, 4, 4, 4, 4, 1, 1, 4, 1, 4, 4, 1, 1, 4, 1, 4, 1, 1,
       4, 1, 4, 4, 4, 1, 4, 4, 4, 4, 4, 4, 1, 4, 4, 4, 4, 0, 0, 4, 1,
       4, 4, 1, 0, 4, 1, 0, 0, 0, 4, 1, 4, 4, 4, 4, 4, 4, 4, 4, 4, 0, 4,
       1, 4, 4, 4, 4, 0, 4, 4, 4, 4, 0, 1, 1, 4, 4, 4, 4, 0, 4, 1, 1, 4,
       1, 4, 1, 1, 4, 4, 1, 0, 1, 0, 4, 4, 4, 0, 4, 4, 4, 0, 0, 1, 4, 4],
      dtype=int32)
```

Figure 4.24: *Code snippet to get cluster indices of the dataset*

XMeans is a typical parametric model of clustering. It goes with the hard-statistical assumption that data of individual clusters are normally distributed. It may give inaccurate results if, in reality, this assumption does not hold good.

Density-based clustering

The density-based approach tries to find clusters with the concept of reachability. Unlike center-based algorithms, it does not have any mean based centroid computation, which is highly dependent on values rather than actual reachability. We will discuss one of the density-based clustering approaches next.

DBSCAN clustering

DBSCAN creates clusters around a point by finding a number of close points within certain reachability. Density here is defined by how many data points are there in a point's neighborhood. There are a few specific types of points in DBSCAN's nomenclature:

- **Core points:** These points are the backbone of the entire cluster setup. Around these points, the clusters will be defined. It is analogous to the centroids of KMeans clustering, but mathematically these are not mean value of other data points. A point is declared a core point if there are a defined number

(`MinPts`) of points within a defined radius (`Eps`) around it. So, instead of being a mean value, rather, it relies on reachability. `MinPtsandEps` are externally seeded parameters of DBSCAN. Eps is a distance metric, and most commonly, Euclidean Distance is computed here. Pictorially, a core point can be shown as below:

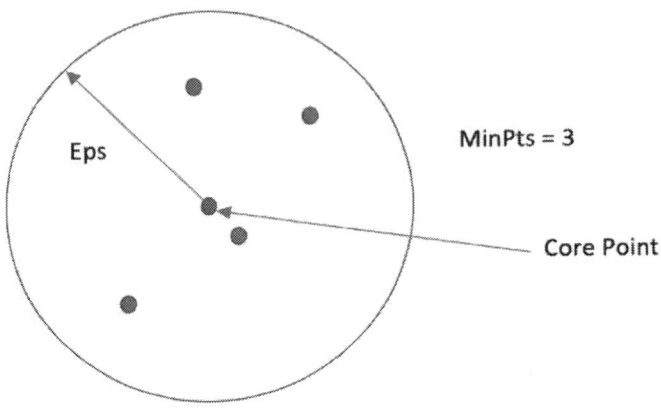

Figure 4.25: Core point and Eps of DBSCAN

- **Border points:** Data points that are within the distance `Eps` around a core point are declared as border points. A border point cannot be a core point. Below diagram shows it:

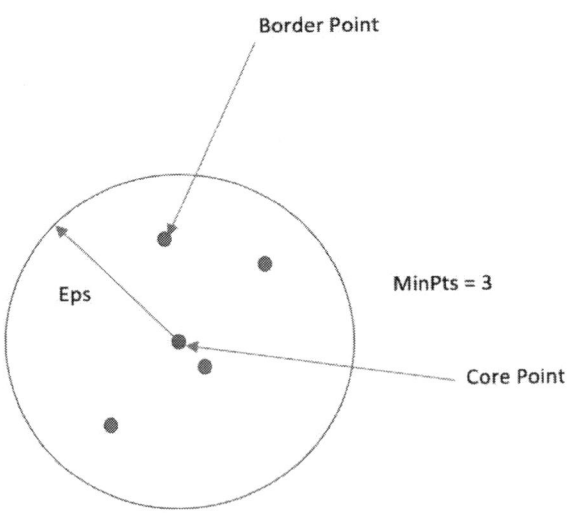

Figure 4.26: Core point, Border Point, and Eps of DBSCAN

- **Noise points:** Data points that are neither core nor border points are declared as noise points. These are outliers or anomalies (refer to *Chapter 7: Miscellaneous Unsupervised Learning*).

DBSCAN algorithm starts its execution by labeling all points as the core, border, or noise points. Then it picks up each point and computes distances with all other, and if it finds there are minimum `MinPts` number of data points are there within a distance `Eps`, then that point is declared as a core point. Within the boundary of `Eps`, all other points become border points. This process goes on until all points are covered. Unlike KMeans, DBSCAN does not expect the number of clusters as a parameter. It determines clusters dynamically. The number of clusters at the end equals to the number of core points.

Python implementation of DBSCAN clustering

The `scikit-learn` has a library for DBSCAN. We will use the same Wholesale Customer's dataset as our source data and the same preprocessing.

```
from sklearn.pipeline import Pipeline
from sklearn.cluster import DBSCAN

dba = DBSCAN(eps=0.65, min_samples=10)
dbscan_pl = Pipeline(steps = [
                        ('col_preprocessor', preprocessor),
                        ('dbscan', dbs)
                        ]
            )
dbscan_pl.fit(df)

Pipeline(memory=None,
        steps=[('col_preprocessor',
                ColumnTransformer(n_jobs=None, remainder='drop',
                        sparse_threshold=0.3,
                        transformer_weights=None,
                        transformers=[('numerical',
                                        StandardScaler(copy=True,
                                                with_mean=True,
                                                with_std=True),
                                        ['Fresh', 'Milk', 'Grocery',
                                         'Frozen', 'Detergents_Paper',
                                         'Delicassen']),
                                        ('categorical',
                                        OneHotEncoder(categorical_features=None,
                                                categories=None,
                                                drop=None,
                                                dtype=<class 'numpy.float64'>,
                                                handle_unknown='ignore',
                                                n_values=None,
                                                sparse=True),
                                        ['Channel', 'Region']]],
                        verbose=False)),
                ('dbscan',
                DBSCAN(algorithm='auto', eps=0.65, leaf_size=30,
                        metric='euclidean', metric_params=None, min_samples=10,
                        n_jobs=None, p=None))],
        verbose=False)
```

Figure 4.27: Code snippet of the pipeline for DBSCAN

We have used 0.65 and 10 as values for `Epsandmin_samples` (`MinPts`) parameters, respectively. DBSCAN class does not define a predict method like KMeans. Instead, it has one attribute `labels_` of type array which holds predicted cluster labels of all data points:

```
dbs.labels_

array([ 1,  1, -1,  0, -1,  1, -1,  1,  0, -1, -1, -1, -1, -1, -1,  0,  1,
       -1, -1,  0,  1,  0, -1, -1, -1, -1,  0,  0, -1, -1, -1,  0,  0, -1,
        0,  1, -1, -1, -1, -1, -1, -1, -1, -1, -1, -1, -1,  1, -1,  0,
        0, -1, -1,  0,  0, -1, -1,  0,  0, -1, -1,  1, -1,  0, -1,  0, -1,
       -1,  0,  0, -1, -1, -1,  1,  0, -1, -1,  0,  0, -1,  1,  0, -1,
       -1, -1, -1, -1, -1,  0,  0, -1, -1, -1,  0, -1,  0,  0,  0, -1, -1,
        1, -1,  0,  0,  1, -1,  1, -1,  0, -1, -1,  0,  0,  0,  0,  0,  0,
        0,  0,  0,  0, -1, -1, -1,  0, -1,  0, -1,  0,  0,  0,  0,  0,  0,
       -1,  0,  0,  0, -1, -1, -1,  0,  0, -1,  0,  0,  0, -1,  0,  0,  0,
        0,  0, -1,  1,  0,  1, -1,  1,  0,  0, -1, -1, -1,  1,  0,  0,  0,
       -1, -1,  0, -1,  0,  1, -1, -1,  0,  0, -1, -1, -1, -1,  0,  0,  0,
       -1, -1, -1, -1,  0, -1,  0,  0, -1, -1,  2,  2, -1, -1, -1,  2,
        2, -1,  2, -1, -1, -1,  2, -1,  2, -1, -1, -1, -1,  2, -1,  2,  2,
       -1, -1, -1,  2,  2, -1,  2, -1, -1, -1, -1, -1,  2, -1, -1,  2, -1,
        2, -1, -1, -1, -1,  2,  2, -1, -1,  2,  2,  2, -1,  2, -1, -1, -1, -1,
       -1,  2, -1, -1, -1,  2, -1, -1, -1, -1, -1, -1, -1,  2, -1,  2,
       -1, -1,  0,  0, -1, -1,  0,  1,  0,  1, -1, -1, -1, -1,  0,  0,  0,
       -1,  0,  0,  0, -1, -1, -1, -1, -1, -1, -1, -1, -1, -1, -1, -1, -1,
       -1,  3,  3, -1, -1, -1, -1,  3,  3, -1,  3, -1, -1,  3, -1, -1,  3,  3,
       -1, -1, -1, -1, -1, -1, -1,  3, -1, -1, -1, -1, -1,  3, -1, -1, -1,
        1,  1,  0, -1,  0,  0, -1, -1,  0, -1,  0, -1,  0, -1, -1,  0,  0,
       -1, -1,  0,  0,  0,  0,  0,  0,  1,  0,  0,  0,  0, -1,  0, -1,  1,
        0,  0, -1, -1,  0, -1,  0,  0, -1,  0, -1,  0,  0,  0,  0,  0,  0,
        0,  0, -1,  0,  0, -1,  0,  0,  0, -1, -1, -1, -1,  0,  0, -1, -1,
       -1, -1,  0, -1, -1, -1,  0,  1, -1,  0, -1,  0, -1,  1,  0, -1, -1,
       -1, -1, -1,  0,  0, -1, -1,  0,  0,  0, -1, -1, -1,  0,  0])
```

Figure 4.28: Code snippet to get cluster indices of DBSCAN

Cluster label -1 indicates that it is a noise point. We can get the number of generated clusters from the length of `lables_` array:

```
len(set(dbs.labels_)) - (1 if -1 in dbs.labels_ else 0)

4
```

Figure 4.29: Code snippet to get the number of clusters of DBSCAN

So, the optimal number of clusters is 4 in this case.

Visualization of clusters

Like KMeans, we will do a cluster plot with original variables as well as the first two PCs.

- **Using any two variables and cluster indices**

    We will plot computed cluster indices with respect to `Milk` and `Grocery`:

```
import matplotlib.pyplot as plt

plt.figure(figsize=(25,15))

plt.scatter(x=df.iloc[dbs.labels_==-1, [3]].values, y=df.iloc[dbs.labels_==-1, [4]].values, s=100, color='red')
plt.scatter(x=df.iloc[dbs.labels_== 0, [3]].values, y=df.iloc[dbs.labels_== 0, [4]].values, s=100, color='green')
plt.scatter(x=df.iloc[dbs.labels_== 1, [3]].values, y=df.iloc[dbs.labels_== 1, [4]].values, s=100, color='blue')
plt.scatter(x=df.iloc[dbs.labels_== 2, [3]].values, y=df.iloc[dbs.labels_== 2, [4]].values, s=100, color='magenta')
plt.scatter(x=df.iloc[dbs.labels_== 3, [3]].values, y=df.iloc[dbs.labels_== 3, [4]].values, s=100, color='orange')

plt.title('DBSCAN Cluster with Milk & Grocery', fontsize=16)
plt.ylabel('Grocery', fontsize=16)
plt.xlabel('Milk', fontsize=16)
plt.xticks(rotation='vertical');
```

Figure 4.30: Code snippet to plot the DBSCAN cluster using two main features

This time we have used normal `pyplot` library's `scatter` function instead of `seaborn` library's `scatterplot` function. The `scatter` function is invoked multiple times separately for each plotting cluster and that too with different color codes. Data points with cluster indices -1 is plotted with red. These are noise points, as discussed earlier. The entire plot looks like below:

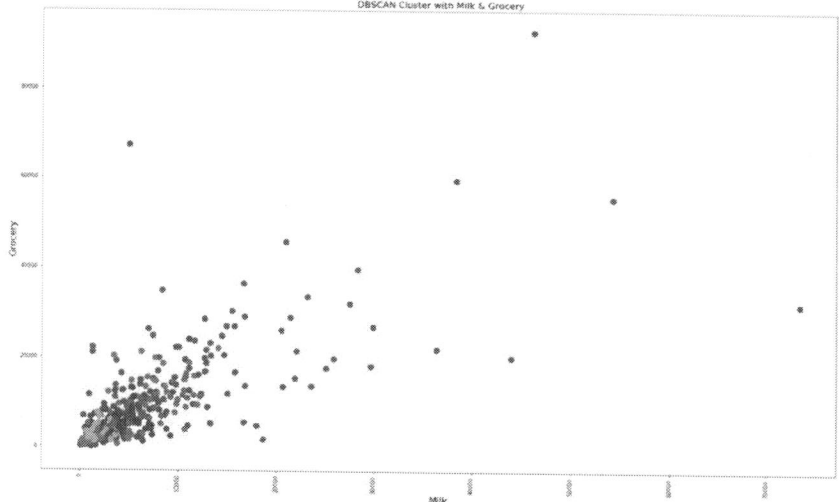

Figure 4.31: *DBSCAN cluster plot with noise points*

We can see that DBSCAN generated clusters are far more irregular shaped than KMeans. Noise points are separated, and these are quite far away from other data points.

- **Using the first two principal components and cluster indices**

  The pipeline for these principal generating components can be defined in the same manner as earlier.

```
from sklearn.decomposition import PCA

pca_pl = Pipeline(steps = [     ('col_preprocessor', preprocessor),
                                ('pca', PCA(n_components=2))
                        ]
                )
pca_vectors = pca_pl.fit_transform(df)
pca_vectors
array([[ 4.56510987e-01, -4.15233235e-01],
       [ 6.90371107e-01, -4.13859584e-01],
       [ 9.86235647e-01,  7.46248727e-01],
       [-9.07106282e-01,  6.34782984e-01],
       [ 3.35755338e-01,  1.13006219e+00],
       [ 1.19396372e-01, -4.41716878e-01],
       [-3.80732985e-02, -6.87171852e-01],
       [ 4.02827403e-01, -3.49837686e-01],
       [-5.74674443e-01, -6.28149912e-01],
       [ 1.83178373e+00, -7.01265659e-01],
       [ 8.92241713e-01, -4.66822617e-01],
       [-6.27745123e-01, -4.47404670e-01],
       [ 1.16474959e+00,  6.41779558e-01],
       [ 1.07665725e+00, -1.32861412e-01],
       [ 1.05696458e+00,  1.03528532e-01],
       [-1.00284796e+00, -5.12217369e-01],
       [ 8.52259604e-01, -1.08773107e+00],
       [-4.68200766e-01,  2.39988299e-01],
       [ 5.30761279e-01,  3.30717861e-01],
```

Figure 4.32: *Code snippet for the pipeline of DBSCAN using first two PCs*

Now, DBSCAN can be applied on top this `pca_vectors` to know the cluster labels:

```
cluster_labels = DBSCAN(eps=0.2, min_samples=5).fit(pca_vectors).labels_
cluster_labels

array([ 0,  0, -1,  0, -1,  0,  0,  0,  0,  3,  0,  0, -1,  0, -1,  0,  1,
        0, -1,  0, -1,  0, -1, -1, -1,  0,  0,  0, -1,  0, -1,  0,  0,  2,
        0,  1,  2, -1, -1, -1, -1,  0,  1, -1,  1, -1,  4, -1,  0, -1,  0,
        0, -1,  1,  0,  0, -1,  1,  0,  0,  0, -1,  0,  3,  0, -1, -1,  0,
        0,  0,  0, -1,  0, -1,  0,  0,  0, -1,  0,  0,  0, -1,  0,  0,  0,
       -1, -1, -1,  0,  2,  0,  0, -1, -1,  1,  0, -1,  0,  0,  0,  0,  3,
        1, -1,  0,  0,  1,  3,  0,  4,  0,  3,  0,  0,  0,  0,  0,  0,  0,
        0,  0,  0,  0,  0,  0, -1,  0, -1,  0,  0,  0,  0,  0,  0,  0,  0,
       -1,  0,  0,  0,  0, -1,  2,  0,  0, -1,  0,  0,  0,  0,  0,  0,  0,
        0,  0, -1,  1,  0,  1, -1,  1,  0,  0, -1,  1, -1,  0,  0,  0,  0,
        1, -1,  0, -1,  0,  1, -1,  0,  0, -1, -1,  1, -1,  0,  0,  0,  0,
        0,  1,  1,  0,  0,  0,  1,  0,  2, -1,  1,  0,  0, -1, -1, -1,  0,
        0, -1,  0,  0,  0, -1,  0, -1,  0,  1,  0, -1,  0, -1,  0,  0,  0,
        0,  0,  0,  0,  0, -1,  0,  0,  0, -1,  0,  0,  0,  0,  0,  0,  0,
        0, -1, -1,  0,  0,  0,  0,  1,  0,  0,  0,  0,  0,  0, -1,  0, -1, -1,
        0,  0,  0, -1, -1,  0,  0,  0,  0, -1, -1,  3,  0, -1,  0,  0,  0,
        0,  0,  0,  0,  2, -1,  0,  0,  0,  0, -1,  0, -1,  0,  0,  0,  0,
        0,  0,  0,  0,  1,  0,  0,  0,  0,  1,  0,  0,  4,  1, -1, -1,  1,
        4,  0,  0,  0,  4,  0,  0, -1,  0,  0,  0,  0, -1,  0,  0,  0,  0,
        0,  0, -1,  0,  0,  0,  0, -1,  0, -1, -1, -1,  0,  0,  0,  0,
        1,  1,  0, -1,  0,  0,  1, -1,  0, -1,  0, -1,  0, -1,  2,  0,  0,
       -1, -1,  0,  0,  0,  0,  0,  0,  0,  0,  0,  0,  2,  0,  0, -1,
        0,  0,  0,  0,  0, -1,  0,  0, -1,  0, -1,  0,  0,  0,  0,  2, -1,
        0,  0,  2,  0,  0,  0,  0,  0,  0,  0, -1,  0,  0,  0,  0,  2, -1,
        0,  0,  0,  0, -1, -1,  0,  0,  1,  0, -1,  0,  1,  0,  0,  0,  0,
       -1, -1, -1,  0,  0,  0,  2,  0,  0,  0, -1,  0, -1,  0,  0])
```

Figure 4.33: Code snippet to run DBSCAN on PC vectors and get cluster indices

We have used `Eps` as 0.2 and `min_samples` (MinPts) as 5. Now, we these `cluster_labels` can be the plot in the same manner:

```
import matplotlib.pyplot as plt

plt.figure(figsize=(25,15))

plt.scatter(x=pca_vectors[cluster_labels==-1, 0], y=pca_vectors[cluster_labels==-1, 1], s=100, color='red')
plt.scatter(x=pca_vectors[cluster_labels==0, 0], y=pca_vectors[cluster_labels==0, 1], s=100, color='green')
plt.scatter(x=pca_vectors[cluster_labels==1, 0], y=pca_vectors[cluster_labels==1, 1], s=100, color='blue')
plt.scatter(x=pca_vectors[cluster_labels==2, 0], y=pca_vectors[cluster_labels==2, 1], s=100,
            color='magenta')
plt.scatter(x=pca_vectors[cluster_labels==3, 0], y=pca_vectors[cluster_labels==3, 1], s=100, color='orange')
plt.scatter(x=pca_vectors[cluster_labels==4, 0], y=pca_vectors[cluster_labels==4, 1], s=100, color='black')

plt.title('DBSCAN Cluster setup with first 2 PC', fontsize=16)
plt.ylabel('Principal Component 2', fontsize=16)
plt.xlabel('Principal Component 1', fontsize=16)
plt.xticks(rotation='vertical');
```

Figure 4.34: DBSCAN Cluster plot with respect to the first two PCS

The code snippet of *Figure 4.35* produces the following plot.

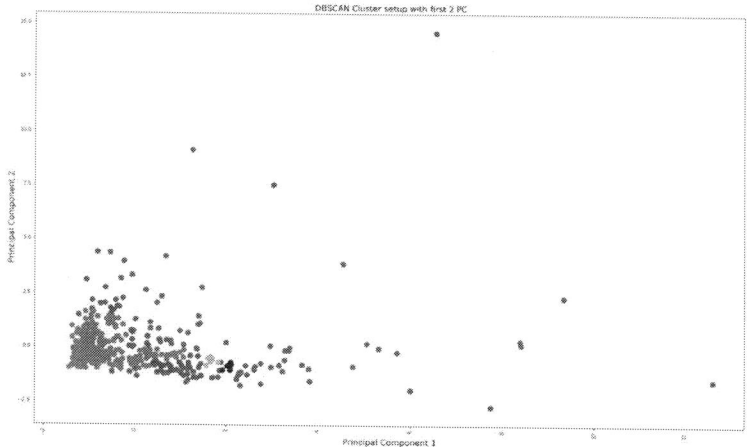

Figure 4.35: Code snippet to plot the DBSCAN cluster using the first two PCs

We can visually confirm that with principal components, clusters look quite well-formed rather than that with the original variable. It is also proof that DBSCAN works better when the number of dimensions is less.

Advantages of DBSCAN

- DBSCAN can find clusters of varying shapes and sizes. Unlike KMeans, it does not try to form globular clusters always. Datasets that tend to form arbitrary shaped clusters are a good fit for DBSCAN. For example, finding patterns in geolocation data could be a good use case for DBSCAN.

- DBSCAN works well where sufficient domain knowledge is there, which may help in determining Eps and MinPts.

Disadvantages of DBSCAN

- It suffers from high run-time complexity. Its worst-case complexity is O(n2), where n is the number of data points.

- It performs poorly for the very high-dimensional dataset. We already visualized this phenomenon.

DBSCAN can automatically find out outliers from a dataset as a result. So, this algorithm can also be used for anomaly/outlier detection. We will see it in detail in *Chapter 6: Miscellaneous Unsupervised Learning*.

Determining optimal parameters of DBSCAN

There is no hard and fast rule for determining optimal `Eps` and `MinPts` for DBSCAN. Most of the cases, domain knowledge, helps to find proper values of those. But with some heuristic approach and visual interpretation, an estimated optimal value can be determined.

`MinPts` value typically comes from domain knowledge only. One heuristic estimate is to use log N as `MinPts` value where N is the total number of data points.

K-distance plot for determining Eps

K-distance plot shows the behavior of the distance from a data point to its kth nearest neighbor. Distances of all points for a specific *K* are computed first, and then these values are sorted in increasing order and plotted as a curve. The curve looks like an inverted *L*. We can set *k* as log *N* as discussed previously and analyze the k-distance plot. Optimal `Eps` value will be distance value found at the elbow-shaped corner of the graph.

We can write a Python function to plot *K*-distance using the same dataset discussed earlier:

```python
from sklearn.neighbors import NearestNeighbors
from math import log
import numpy as np

def plot_k_distance():
    t_df = preprocessor.fit_transform(df)
    K = round(log(len(t_df)))
    nn = NearestNeighbors(n_neighbors=K)
    nn.fit(t_df)
    distances, indices = nn.kneighbors(t_df)

    distances = np.sort(distances, axis=0)
    distances = distances[:,1]
    plt.plot(distances)
```

Figure 4.36: Code snippet of plot_k_distance function

We should transform all the variables and then use it in finding nearest neighbors. `scikit-learn` provides a class `NearestNeighbors` to do that. It takes K as a parameter. Its `neighbors` function returns distances and the corresponding data point indices.

Finally, the `plot_k_distance` function can be called to get the graph:

```
plot_k_distance()
```

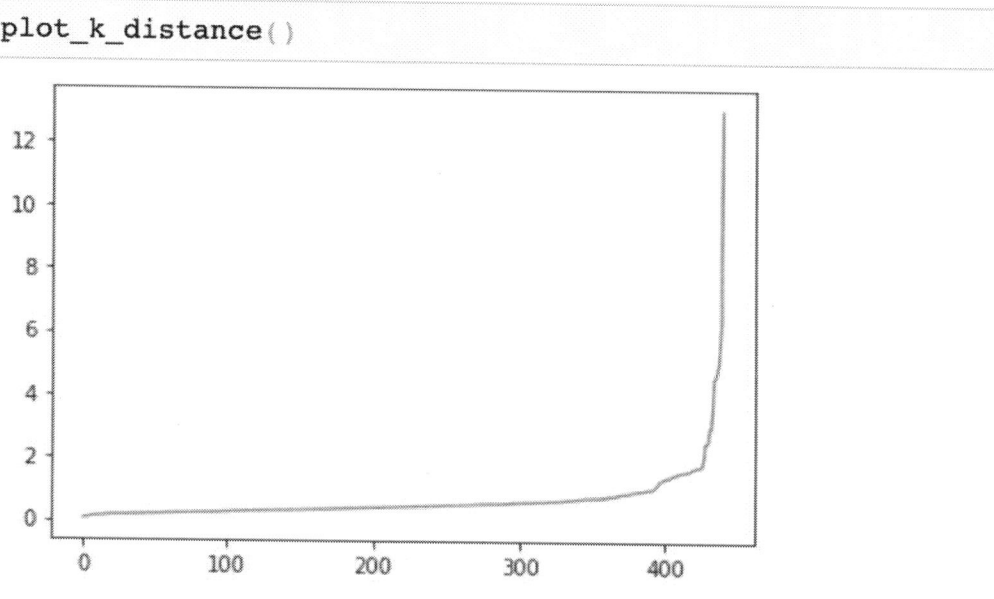

Figure 4.37: *k distance plot of the dataset*

We can visually confirm that the sharp elbow corner is observed at a distance of around **1.5**, and hence optimal `Eps` is **1.5**. This value is on the same scale as all transformed variables.

Hierarchical clustering

Clustering models discussed so far can only assign one single cluster for a data point. One cluster is nothing but a group. What if there are sub-groups, sub-sub-groups, and so on, that is, the existence of parent-child relationships in clusters? There are techniques to generate these types of cluster hierarchies from a dataset. We will discuss one of the generic approach called **Agglomerative clusteringnext**.

Agglomerative clustering starts with individual pairs of points and merges them one by one. This merging decision is taken by the proximity of points of two different clusters. One-by-one cluster gets merged and form parent clusters. One sample hierarchical cluster is shown below:

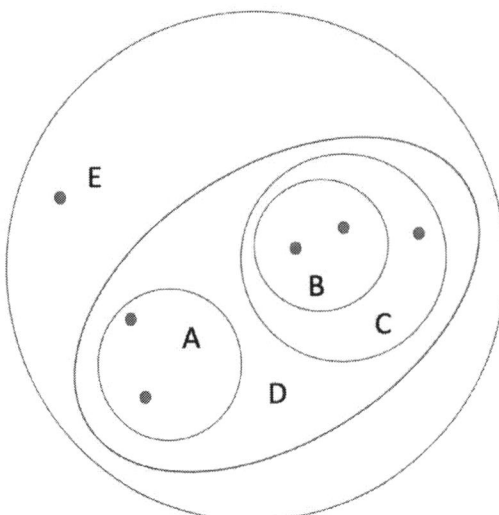

Figure 4.38: Sample Hierarchical Cluster

E is the top-most cluster in the hierarchy. A, B, C, and D are other sub-clusters. There are few strategies to determine the link between different sub-clusters or create a sub-cluster, as discussed next.

- **Min (or Single):** Min strategy defines the distance between two clusters as the minimum distance between any two points of the two clusters. It starts with an M × M matrix of points where M is the total number of points in the dataset. Each cell in the matrix contains distances between any two points. The algorithm picks up the minimum distance from M × M and joins the corresponding two points as a single cluster. In the next step, it computes the distance between other points and that single cluster and makes another cluster on top of it based on minimum distance. It continues the same process until no points are left.

Now, let us see the minimum distance computing mechanism between two clusters in a 2D feature space. Suppose, there are two clusters C1 and C2.

Data points under C1 and C2 are given below:

C_1 = {(3,5), (2,8), (6,1)}

C_2 = {(8,5), (9,2)}

Min-Distance (C_1, C_2) = min {distance {(3, 5), (8, 5)}, distance {(3, 5), (9, 2)},
distance {(2,8), (8,5)}, distance {(2,8), (9,2)},
distance {(6,1), (8,5)}, distance {(6,1), (9,2)}}

= min {5, 6.7, 6.7, 10, 4.47, 3.16}

= 3.16

- **Max (or Complete):** Mechanism of max is exactly same as min with the only difference that it computes distance as maximum between any two points instead of minimum.

Ward: Ward method defines the distance between two clusters as the increase in SSE when two are merged. It chooses to merge those two clusters where the possible increase in SSE is minimum, among others. For SSE computation, it follows the same principle as KMeans, as explained in earlier sections.

Python implementation of Agglomerative clustering

The scikit-learn's class `AgglomerativeClustering` does the hierarchical clustering with different link strategies discussed earlier. We will use the same dataset and `ColumnTransformer` here also to design the pipeline:

```
from sklearn.cluster import AgglomerativeClustering
from sklearn.pipeline import Pipeline

agc = AgglomerativeClustering(n_clusters = 5)

agc_pl = Pipeline(steps = [
                         ('col_preprocessor', preprocessor),
                         ('agc', agc)
                         ]
            )
agc_pl.fit(df)
```

```
Pipeline(memory=None,
        steps=[('col_preprocessor',
               ColumnTransformer(n_jobs=None, remainder='drop',
                                sparse_threshold=0.3,
                                transformer_weights=None,
                                transformers=[('numerical',
                                              StandardScaler(copy=True,
                                                            with_mean=True,
                                                            with_std=True),
                                            ['Fresh', 'Milk', 'Grocery',
                                             'Frozen', 'Detergents_Paper',
                                             'Delicassen']),
                                            ('categorical',
                                              OneHotEncoder(categorical_features=None,
                                                            categories=None,
                                                            drop=None,
                                                            dtype=<class 'numpy.float64'>,
                                                            handle_unknown='ignore',
                                                            n_values=None,
                                                            sparse=True),
                                            ['Channel', 'Region'])],
                                verbose=False)),
               ('agc',
               AgglomerativeClustering(affinity='euclidean',
                                      compute_full_tree='auto',
                                      connectivity=None,
                                      distance_threshold=None,
                                      linkage='ward', memory=None,
                                      n_clusters=5,
                                      pooling_func='deprecated'))],
        verbose=False)
```

Figure 4.39: Code snippet of the pipeline for Hierarchical cluster

We have used the award method for linking. Link strategy is mentioned in the linkage parameter, and by default, `AgglomerativeClustering` is instantiated with the ward. Other possible parameter values are complete, average, and single. We have mentioned n_clusters as five which denotes the total number of clusters wanted.

Now, we can get cluster indices for all data points using `labels_` attribute:

```
agc.labels_

array([2, 2, 2, 0, 2, 2, 2, 2, 1, 2, 2, 2, 2, 2, 2, 1, 2, 1, 2, 1, 2, 1,
       0, 0, 2, 2, 1, 1, 2, 0, 1, 1, 0, 0, 1, 2, 0, 2, 2, 2, 0, 0, 1, 2, 2,
       2, 2, 2, 4, 2, 2, 1, 1, 0, 2, 0, 1, 4, 2, 1, 1, 2, 4, 2, 2, 1, 4,
       1, 2, 1, 1, 0, 0, 0, 2, 0, 0, 2, 1, 1, 1, 2, 2, 0, 2, 4, 4, 0,
       0, 0, 1, 0, 4, 0, 2, 1, 2, 1, 1, 0, 2, 2, 2, 0, 1, 1, 2, 2, 2, 2,
       1, 2, 0, 1, 0, 1, 1, 1, 1, 0, 1, 0, 1, 1, 2, 0, 0, 0, 2, 1, 0, 0, 1,
       1, 1, 1, 1, 1, 1, 1, 1, 1, 0, 0, 0, 0, 2, 1, 1, 1, 0, 1, 1, 0, 1,
       1, 2, 2, 0, 2, 2, 2, 1, 0, 2, 2, 2, 2, 1, 1, 1, 2, 2, 1, 2, 1, 2,
       0, 1, 1, 1, 1, 0, 1, 3, 1, 1, 1, 1, 2, 2, 0, 1, 1, 2, 1, 1, 0, 0, 2,
       1, 1, 2, 2, 0, 1, 1, 2, 1, 2, 1, 2, 1, 4, 1, 1, 2, 1, 2, 1, 2, 1,
       1, 1, 1, 0, 1, 1, 2, 1, 1, 1, 0, 1, 1, 1, 1, 1, 1, 1, 0, 0, 1,
       1, 1, 1, 2, 1, 1, 1, 1, 1, 4, 1, 0, 0, 1, 1, 1, 0, 0, 1, 1, 1, 1,
       2, 0, 2, 1, 2, 1, 1, 1, 1, 0, 1, 1, 0, 0, 0, 2, 1, 2, 0, 0, 0, 0,·
       1, 0, 1, 0, 1, 1, 1, 2, 1, 2, 1, 2, 2, 1, 2, 2, 2, 2, 2, 2, 2, 1,
       1, 2, 0, 1, 2, 1, 1, 2, 1, 1, 1, 2, 1, 1, 1, 1, 0, 1, 1, 0, 1,
       1, 2, 1, 4, 0, 2, 1, 0, 0, 0, 2, 2, 1, 2, 1, 1, 2, 2, 1, 2, 1, 2,
       1, 2, 0, 1, 0, 2, 0, 1, 0, 1, 1, 1, 1, 2, 1, 1, 0, 1, 0, 0, 1, 2,
       1, 1, 2, 0, 1, 2, 0, 0, 0, 1, 0, 1, 1, 0, 1, 1, 0, 1, 1, 0, 1, 1,
       2, 0, 0, 1, 1, 0, 0, 0, 0, 1, 0, 2, 2, 1, 1, 1, 1, 0, 0, 2, 2, 1,
       2, 1, 1, 2, 0, 2, 2, 0, 1, 0, 1, 1, 1, 0, 0, 1, 1, 0, 0, 2, 1, 1])
```

Figure 4.40: Code snippet to get cluster indices of Hierarchical Cluster

Now, the question may arise what is the role of `n_clusters` over here? `AgglomerativeClustering` anyway builds a hierarchy. It will keep on merging clusters one by one until there are only `n_clusters` remaining. Then`_clusters` and `distance_threshold` parameters are mutually exclusive. If `n_clusters` is not mentioned, then the algorithm keeps on doing merging operation if the distance between any two clusters is less than `distance_threshold`.

Visualization of clusters

We will similarly use the first two PCs like earlier models for visualization:

```
from sklearn.decomposition import PCA

pca_pl = Pipeline(steps = [  ('col_preprocessor', preprocessor),
                             ('pca', PCA(n_components=2))
                          ]
                 )
pca_vectors = pca_pl.fit_transform(df)
pca_vectors

array([[ 4.56510987e-01, -4.15233235e-01],
       [ 6.90371107e-01, -4.13859584e-01],
       [ 9.86235647e-01,  7.46248727e-01],
       [-9.07106282e-01,  6.34782984e-01],
       [ 3.35755338e-01,  1.13006219e+00],
       [ 1.19396372e-01, -4.41716878e-01],
       [-3.80732985e-02, -6.87171852e-01],
       [ 4.02827403e-01, -3.49837686e-01],
       [-5.74674443e-01, -6.28149912e-01],
       [ 1.83178373e+00, -7.01265659e-01],
       [ 8.92241713e-01, -4.66822617e-01],
       [-6.27745123e-01, -4.47404670e-01],
       [ 1.16474959e+00,  6.41779558e-01],
       [ 1.07665725e+00, -1.32861412e-01],
       [ 1.05696458e+00,  1.03528532e-01],
       [-1.00284796e+00, -5.12217369e-01],
       [ 8.52259604e-01, -1.08773107e+00],
       [-4.68200766e-01,  2.39988299e-01],
       [ 5.30761279e-01,  3.30717861e-01],
```

Figure 4.41: Code snippet of the pipeline to computing first two PCs of the dataset

And after that, applying `AgglomerativeClustering` on the PCs:

```
cluster_labels = AgglomerativeClustering(n_clusters = 5).fit_predict(pca_vectors)
cluster_labels
array([0, 0, 2, 2, 2, 0, 0, 0, 4, 0, 0, 4, 2, 0, 0, 4, 0, 2, 0, 0, 0, 4,
       2, 2, 2, 0, 4, 4, 0, 2, 2, 4, 4, 2, 4, 0, 2, 0, 0, 2, 2, 2, 0, 0,
       0, 0, 0, 3, 0, 0, 4, 0, 2, 0, 2, 4, 0, 0, 4, 0, 0, 3, 0, 0, 4, 3,
       0, 0, 2, 4, 2, 2, 2, 2, 0, 2, 2, 0, 4, 4, 4, 0, 0, 4, 0, 3, 3, 2,
       2, 2, 4, 2, 3, 2, 0, 4, 0, 4, 4, 4, 0, 0, 2, 4, 4, 0, 0, 0, 0,
       4, 0, 2, 4, 4, 4, 4, 2, 4, 4, 4, 0, 2, 2, 2, 0, 2, 4, 4,
       4, 4, 4, 4, 0, 0, 2, 4, 2, 2, 2, 2, 4, 0, 4, 4, 4, 2, 4, 4, 4, 4,
       4, 0, 0, 4, 0, 0, 0, 4, 4, 0, 0, 0, 0, 4, 4, 4, 0, 0, 4, 4, 0,
       2, 2, 4, 2, 0, 1, 0, 1, 4, 4, 4, 0, 0, 0, 2, 4, 4, 0, 4, 2, 2, 0,
       4, 4, 0, 0, 2, 4, 0, 4, 0, 0, 0, 4, 3, 4, 0, 0, 0, 0, 4, 0, 4,
       4, 0, 4, 4, 4, 4, 0, 4, 0, 0, 0, 4, 4, 2, 4, 4, 4, 2, 4, 2, 2, 2,
       4, 4, 0, 0, 4, 4, 4, 4, 4, 3, 2, 0, 2, 2, 4, 4, 2, 2, 4, 4, 4, 4,
       0, 2, 0, 2, 0, 4, 4, 4, 0, 2, 4, 4, 2, 2, 2, 0, 4, 0, 2, 2, 2, 2,
       4, 2, 4, 2, 4, 4, 4, 0, 2, 0, 4, 0, 0, 4, 0, 0, 0, 0, 0, 0, 4,
       4, 0, 2, 2, 0, 4, 0, 4, 4, 4, 0, 4, 4, 4, 4, 2, 1, 4, 4, 2, 4,
       4, 0, 2, 3, 2, 0, 4, 2, 2, 2, 0, 0, 0, 4, 0, 0, 0, 4, 0, 4, 0,
       4, 0, 2, 4, 2, 0, 2, 4, 4, 4, 4, 4, 0, 4, 4, 4, 4, 2, 2, 2, 0,
       4, 4, 0, 2, 4, 0, 2, 2, 2, 4, 2, 4, 4, 4, 4, 4, 4, 4, 2, 4, 4,
       0, 2, 4, 4, 4, 2, 2, 2, 2, 4, 2, 0, 0, 2, 4, 2, 0, 2, 4, 0, 0, 0,
       0, 4, 0, 0, 4, 4, 0, 2, 0, 2, 4, 4, 0, 2, 4, 4, 4, 2, 2, 0, 4, 4])
```

Figure 4.42: *Code snippet to get cluster indices of Hierarchical clusters on PC features*

The fit_predict function builds the clustering model and returns cluster indices for all data points altogether.

Finally, plotting data points and cluster indices using different color labels:

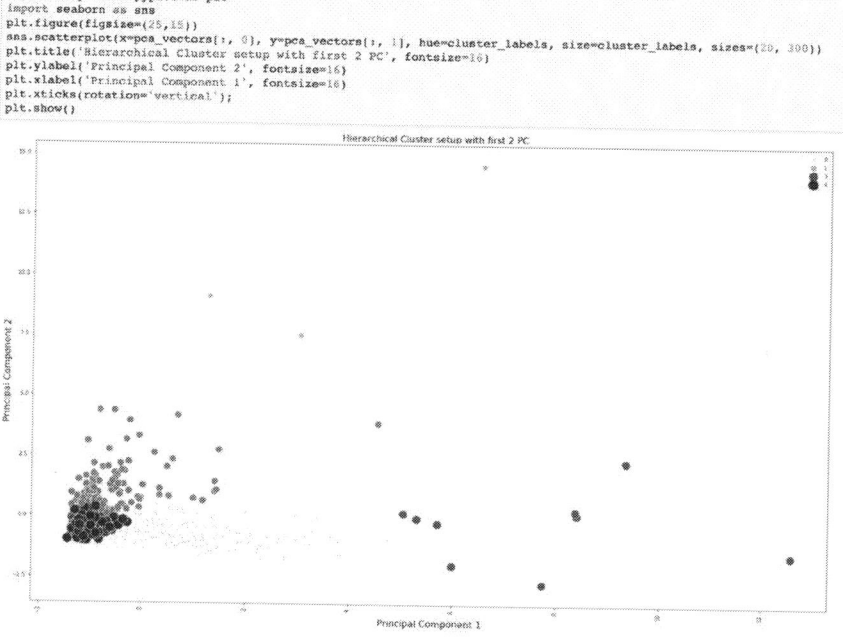

Figure 4.43: *Code snippet to plot Hierarchical clusters on PC features*

The above cluster plot does not show the hierarchy. It shows the last remaining and assigned n_clusters to each data point.

Visualization of hierarchical clusters with a dendrogram

A dendrogram is an alternative pictorial representation for hierarchical clusters. It has complete or partial rectangular boxes joined one after another in a tree-like hierarchical fashion. Each box connects two points or clusters.

We will use Python library scipy's linkage function to generate hierarchical clusters from the same dataset and plot the dendrogram. Generally, the dendrogram has too many miniature clusters at the bottom. To avoid that and for our convenience, we will show only the last 20 merged clusters:

```python
from scipy.cluster.hierarchy import dendrogram, linkage

z = linkage(preprocessor.fit(df).transform(df), 'ward')
plt.figure(figsize=(25, 10))
plt.title('Hierarchical Clustering Dendrogram')
plt.xlabel('index')
plt.ylabel('distance')
dendrogram(
    z,
    leaf_rotation=90.,
    leaf_font_size=8.,
    p=20,
    truncate_mode='lastp',
)
plt.show()
```

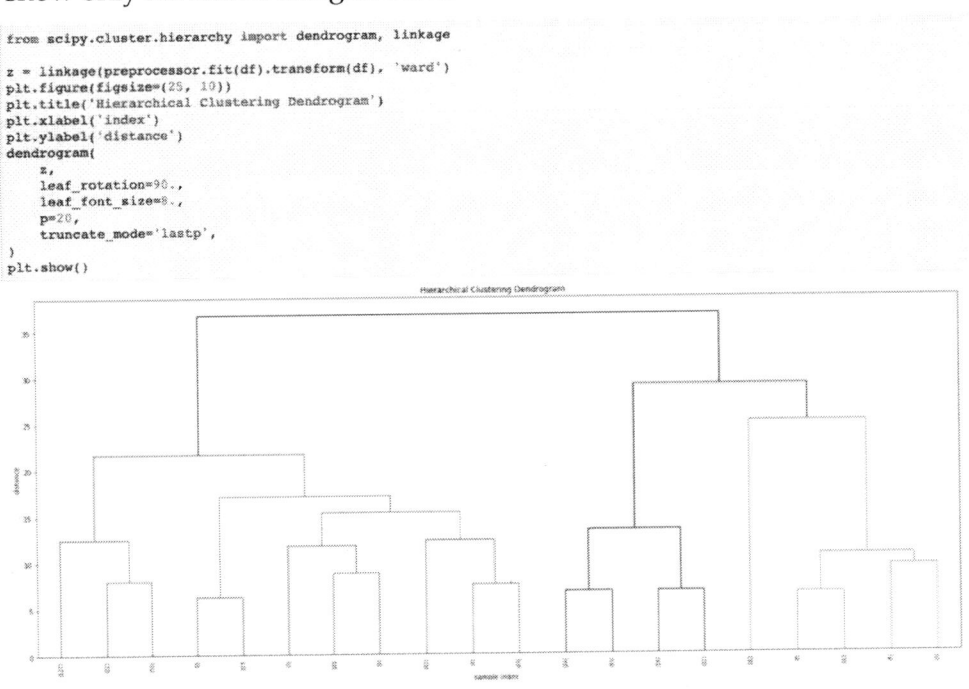

Figure 4.44: Code snippet to generate visualize dendrogram generated from clusters

Parameters p and truncate_mode are set values 20 and lastp, respectively. The truncate_mode function ensures that the hierarchy tree is cut down to some extent for convenience. We have used ward method for generating clusters here.

Clustering to solve a classification problem

Clustering can be used as an alternative technique to solve any classification problem. It may not be a primary model, but definitely can be added as an option in a set of ensembles.

Computation of class probabilities

As clustering is an unsupervised learning technique, we will not include class labels of a dataset in computation while building the clusters. Apart from the class label feature, all other features will be considered in the distance computation of clustering. Once the clusters are formed, the probabilities of each class would be computed per cluster. The class that has maximum probability would be the representative class of a cluster.

Mathematically, if M_j is number of records that belong to cluster j and m_{cj} is the number of records having class label c under cluster j, then

$$P_{cj} = \frac{m_{cj}}{M_j}, c \in \{C\}, j < K$$

Where K is the total number of possible clusters in the entire setup, and C is the set of all possible class labels in the dataset.

Now, the probability of the representative class label $\hat{C}$ of the cluster, j is given by:

$$P_j(Y = \hat{C}) = \max \{P_{cj}\}, \quad c \in \{C\}, j < K$$

It means the class which has the maximum probability becomes the representative class of a cluster j.

The entire training process involves cluster formation and computation of class probabilities like above. At the end of it, each cluster will be mapped with a representative class label. This *cluster-class* mapping, along with the original cluster setup, should be used as a complete model.

Classification process

We have the cluster setup and the mapped class label per cluster as a model. Classification from here is a two-step process. Firstly, for an unknown data instance, the corresponding cluster index can be found from the cluster setup. Secondly, the representative class for that can be found from the cluster-class mapping, which takes cluster index as input. And this one becomes the predicted class label. We can also use the maximum class probability as the match score of the classification.

Python implementation of the model

We can use either of KMeans or DBSCAN as our clustering algorithm. For our convenience, we will use previously discussed XMeans as it automatically computes the number of possible clusters. We will use the EEG Brainwave dataset from Kaggle (https://www.kaggle.com/birdy654/eeg-brainwave-dataset-feeling-emotions) for this.

This dataset contains brain wave signals values (probably Fourier transformed values) and three class labels – *positive, negative,* andneutral tagged with each record. It represents the mental state corresponding to the brainwave signals. Our objective is to build a model that can predict mental state from the signal values. A sample from the dataset is shown below:

```
import pandas as pd

df = pd.read_csv('../data/emotions.csv')
df.head()
```

mean_d_1_a	mean_d_2_a	mean_d_3_a	mean_d_4_a	...	fft_741_b	fft_742_b	fft_743_b	fft_744_b	fft_745_b	fft_746_b	fft_747_b	fft_748_b	fft_749_b	label
0.411	-15.70	2.06	3.15	...	23.5	20.3	20.3	23.5	-215.0	280.00	-162.00	-162.00	280.00	NEGATIVE
1.680	2.88	3.83	-4.82	...	-23.3	-21.8	-21.8	-23.3	182.0	2.57	-31.60	-31.60	2.57	NEUTRAL
3.360	90.20	89.90	2.03	...	462.0	-233.0	-233.0	462.0	-267.0	281.00	-148.00	-148.00	281.00	POSITIVE
-0.284	8.82	2.30	-1.97	...	299.0	-243.0	-243.0	299.0	132.0	-12.40	9.53	9.53	-12.40	POSITIVE
-5.790	3.06	41.40	5.52	...	12.0	38.1	38.1	12.0	119.0	-17.60	23.90	23.90	-17.60	NEUTRAL

Figure 4.45: Code snippet read & display EEG Brainwave dataset

The target variable is the label, and other attributes are brainwave signal values. All these are continuous except for the target variable.

As a first step, we will split the dataset in X and Y variables where X would be featured and Y would be the target and then split it into training and testing sections:

```
from sklearn.model_selection import train_test_split

Y = df['label']
X = df.drop('label', axis = 1, inplace=False)

train_x, test_x, train_y, test_y = train_test_split(X, Y, test_size=0.2)
```

Figure 4.46: Code snippet to split train and test dataset

We will use the same XMeans class for clustering and can write a custom Estimator which builds the cluster first (all variables are scaled first using a StandardScaler), computes class probabilities and creates cluster-class mapping:

```
from sklearn.preprocessing import StandardScaler

class Clustering_Classifier(BaseEstimator):

    def __init__(self, max_k):
        self.clusterer_ = XMeans(max_k)
        self.cluster_class_labels_ = {}
        self.scaler_ = StandardScaler()

    def _determine_cluster_class_(self, y, cluster_labels, cluster_index, unique_labels):
        current_cluster_y = y[cluster_labels == cluster_index]
        current_cluster_records_count = len(current_cluster_y)

        max_probability = -1.0
        cluster_class_label = None
        for label in unique_labels:
            current_class_proba = current_cluster_y[current_cluster_y == label].count()/current_cluster_records_count
            if current_class_proba > max_probability:
                max_probability = current_class_proba
                cluster_class_label = label

        return cluster_class_label

    def fit(self, X, y=None):
        self.scaler_.fit(X)
        X = self.scaler_.transform(X)
        self.clusterer_.fit(X)
        cluster_labels = self.clusterer_.predict(X)
        unique_labels = y.unique()
        for cluster_index in range(self.clusterer_.optimal_k):
            current_cluster_class = self._determine_cluster_class_(y, cluster_labels, cluster_index, unique_labels)
            self.cluster_class_labels_[cluster_index] = current_cluster_class

        return self

    def predict(self, X):
        predicted_cluster_labels = self.clusterer_.predict(self.scaler_.transform(X))
        predicted_class_labels = []
        for predicted_cluster_label in predicted_cluster_labels:
            predicted_class_labels.append(self.cluster_class_labels_[predicted_cluster_label])
        return predicted_class_labels
```

Figure 4.47: Code snippet of Clustering_Classifier as Estimator

The _determine_cluster_class_ is a private function that iterates through all the class labels and computes class counts per cluster and corresponding probabilities. But it only returns the class label, which has maximum probability (as per the theory discussed earlier). It could also have returned maximum class probability (max_probablity) along with class labels, which may be used as a probability match score of the prediction. Inside fit function _determine_cluster_class_ is called iteratively for each cluster to get the representative class, and one global mapping (cluster_class_label) is created for all. The predict function just utilizes the cluster setup and the created cluster_class_label mapping to get the clustered index and corresponding predicted class labels.

We can use this class to train and build the model:

```
cc = Clustering_Classifier(max_k=20)
cc.fit(train_x, train_y)
```

```
Clustering_Classifier(max_k=None)
```

Figure 4.48: Code snippet train Clustering_Classifier

Internally, we are using the XMeans algorithm, so the number of clusters was generated automatically. We can get the number optimal number of K from the API itself:

```
cc.clusterer_.optimal_k
```

```
12
```

Figure 4.49: Code snippet to get optimal K from the internal cluster

So, there isa total of 12 clusters, and each one has one representative class.

Visualization of clusters and classification accuracy

It is a very high-dimensional dataset, so we will have to use the top two PCs to visualize it in 2-D. First, we will the class distribution plot using the training data:

```
%matplotlib inline

from sklearn.decomposition import PCA
from sklearn.preprocessing import StandardScaler

import seaborn as sns
import matplotlib.pyplot as plt

pca = PCA(n_components=2)
pca_x = pca.fit_transform(cc.scaler_.transform(train_x))
sns.set(font_scale=2)
plt.figure(figsize=(15,10))
sns.scatterplot(x=pca_x[:, 0], y=pca_x[:, 1], hue=train_y)
plt.title('Class Distribution plot with first 2 PC', fontsize=16)
plt.ylabel('Principal Component 2')
plt.xlabel('Principal Component 1')
plt.xticks(rotation='vertical');
plt.show()
```

Figure 4.50: Code snippet to plot the Class distribution of EEG Brainwave dataset using the first 2 PCs

Code snippet of *Figure 4.50* generates the following plot:

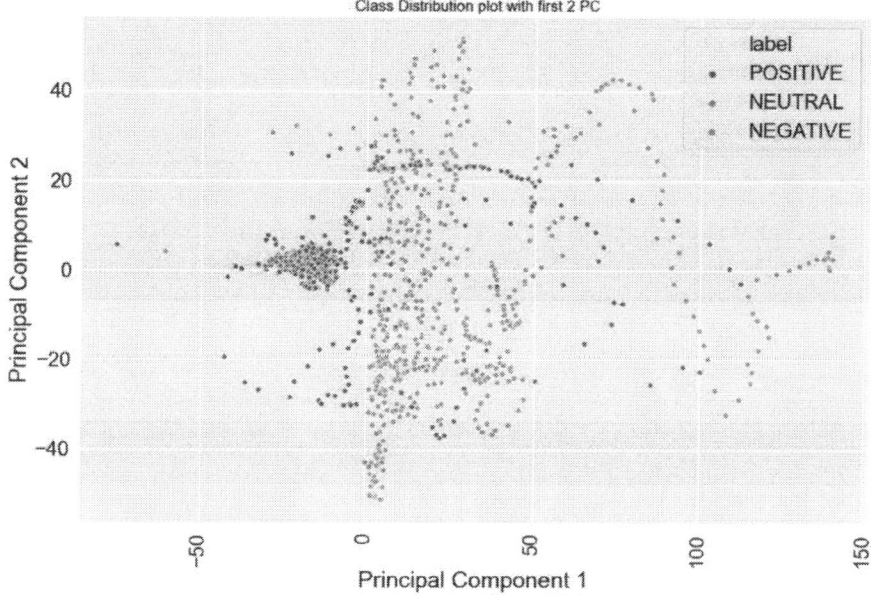

Figure 4.51: Class distribution plot of EEG Brainwave dataset

It is a typical scatter diagram plot for a multi-class classification problem. We used the scatterplot function of the seaborn library. Parameter hue carries the class label information as an array. NEGATIVE is a little dominant class in the distribution. Now, let's see how to do a cluster plot with a representative class for each.

We will define one function which can format the typical numeric cluster labels with added representative class label information:

```
def format_cluster_labels(cluster_class_labels, cluster_labels):
    formatted_cluster_labels = []
    for c_l in cluster_labels:
        class_name = cluster_class_labels[c_l]
        formatted_cluster_labels.append(str(c_l) + '-' + class_name)
    return formatted_cluster_labels
```

Figure 4.52: Code snippet of format_cluster_labels function

We will use this `format_cluster_labels` function to do a cluster plot:

```
formatted_cluster_labels = format_cluster_labels(cc.cluster_class_labels_,
                                                 cc.clusterer_.optimal_clusterer.labels_)
plt.figure(figsize=(15,10))
sns.scatterplot(x=pca_x[:, 0], y=pca_x[:, 1], hue=formatted_cluster_labels,
                palette=sns.color_palette(n_colors=cc.clusterer_.optimal_k))
plt.title('Cluster setup plot with first 2 PC', fontsize=16)
plt.ylabel('Principal Component 2')
plt.xlabel('Principal Component 1')
plt.xticks(rotation='vertical');
plt.show()
```

Figure 4.53: Code snippet to plot clusters of EEG Brainwave features

And it will produce cluster plot like below:

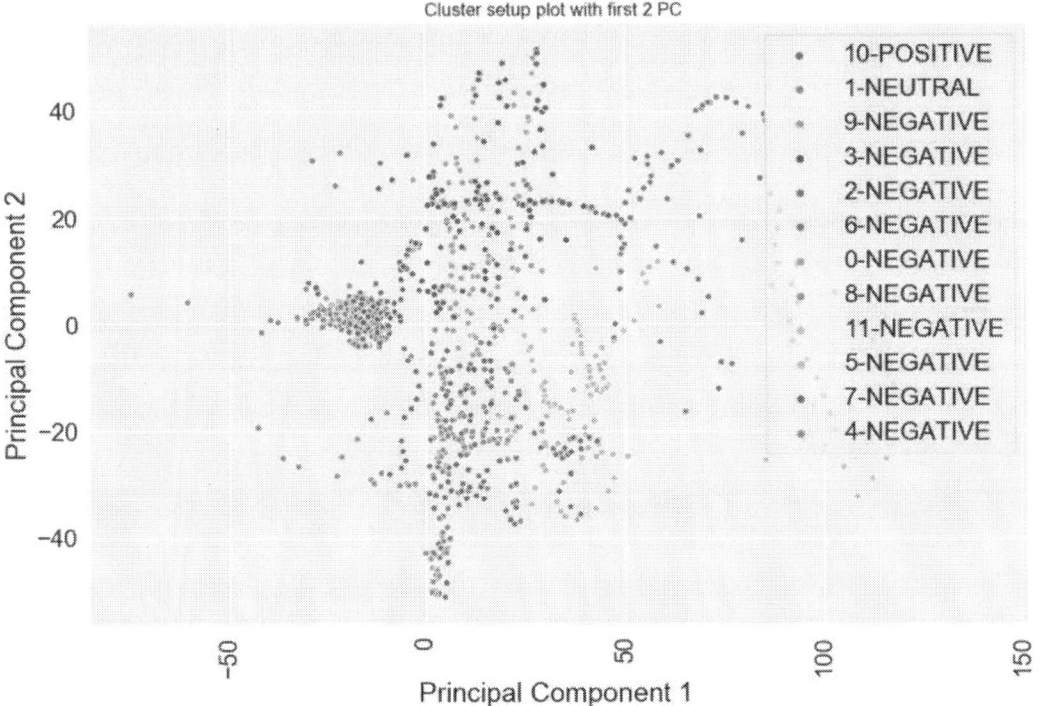

Figure 4.54: Cluster plot of EEG Brainwave dataset with class labels

Cluster labels are attached to class labels. For example, 10-POSITIVE says that the 10th cluster has POSITIVE as a representative class. So, any data point that belongs to the 10th cluster should be labeled as POSITIVE. If we compare *Figure 4.51* and *Figure 4.53*, we will able to see the similarities between a class distribution and orientation of representative classes of each cluster.

Now, let's see the classification accuracy on the test dataset.

```
from sklearn.metrics import accuracy_score

predicted_y = cc.predict(test_x)
accuracy_score(test_y, predicted_y)
```

0.9133489461358314

Figure 4.55: Code snippet to compute classification accuracy

We got almost 91% accuracy.

Key points to remember about clustering-based classification

- There can be multiple clusters representing a single class label. It completely depends on relationships between the features and the class distribution.

- It may give biased results if the class imbalance is there in the dataset. There is no direct technique to handle class imbalance here. But to mitigate the problem, we should always keep the number of clusters (K) greater than the number of unique class labels in the dataset. As a result, there will be higher chances that at least one cluster would have the least dominant class as a representative class. Not only for class imbalance problems, it also helps in normal scenarios to have at least one cluster for each class.

- It is better not to use this as a single and main model. Preferably it should be added in a set of ensembles where we need to get alternative ways to predict class labels.

- It can be used in scenarios where traditional models are failing to understand hidden data patterns which are inferring class labels.

- A proper clustering algorithm should be chosen to get a better result.

Though the choice of clustering algorithm depends on the dataset, the still center-based approach theoretically is well-suited here as there is always a concept of representative or center-class of the model.

Conclusion

In this chapter, we discussed clustering as one of the unsupervised learning and how it can form groups from a dataset without the knowledge of any target variable. We saw different clustering strategies like centroid based, density-based, hierarchical, and corresponding algorithms like KMeans, DBSCAN, and more. Different ways of determining cluster parameters were also discussed. In the end, we discussed how classification could be done with the help of the clustering algorithm.

We learned about each clustering algorithms pros and cons and the situations where these will be applicable on a case to case basis. Visualization plays an important role in clustering. We learned how to do that using `seaborn` and other libraries. Just doing a 2-D plot using principal components of a very high-dimensional dataset can show cluster formation from a high level.

In the next chapter, we will discuss a completely different way of doing predictive ML modeling using deep learning and neural networks. Deep learning-based techniques can solve traditional classification and regression related problems differently and generically. We will discuss the details of these and different types of neural networks.

CHAPTER 5
Deep Learning

So far, we have seen several supervised and unsupervised learning techniques; and different algorithms. Under supervised learning, we have seen how to do classification and regression analysis on the dataset. In this chapter, we will discuss another entirely different and generic supervised approach to solving these types of problems. It is known as **deep learning**. It is a process of learning with successive layers of increasingly meaningful representation. Basically, in short, a layered and supervised learning approach. We will see in detail what are the building blocks and functions of these layers through our discussion.

Structure

In this chapter, we will discuss:

- Definition of deep learning
- What arethe neural network and its anatomy
- Different activation functions and their mathematical form
- Training process of neural network
- How to use a neural network for classification and regression problem
- Details of convolution neural network (CNN)

Objective

After finishing this chapter, we will be able to

- Build a neural network model to solve classification and regression problem
- Use the neural network for image analysis and classification

What is deep learning?

We will start with a very general question: *How do we differentiate a car's picture from a dog's picture?* This may sound silly, but there isa lot of complicated processing happens inside the human brain to perform this task. First, we check the structure of two objects: car and dog. One is a vehicle, and another one is an animal. So obviously, there will be differences, and then the question of color comes into our mind. A car can have any color, but a dog has a limited set of body colors. And there are a lot of other details. Our minds can process all of this information and can make a decision. The human brain consists of *neurons*, and these are capable of taking this type of granular level decisions. And these neurons are structured in a layered fashion so that the information flows through them from one layer to another. This layered structure can be very deep. It is very deep for all of us. It is up to the person that how much of these layered neurons can be used, and this usage determines the intelligence level of that person. Now, the branch of machine learning, which can simulate this type of learning process, is known as **deep learning**. Here *deep* does not infer a very deeper understanding of the subject; rather, it tells how deep the layered architecture is.

Why is deep learning required?

Many problems cannot be solved by traditional machine learning techniques discussed in previous chapters. Even the problem is solved; it may suffer from poor accuracy. Especially if we are dealing with a *perception driven* learning approach, then traditional techniques may not work well. By perception driven learning, we mean, looking at the data, if we can think about its inner meaning or try to make a perception about it. It happens especially with images, video, and audiodata. We need a learning process which can map human thinking into a mathematical or computer science-driven model. We can say deep learning technique is a mapped version of the human brain's working process.

Moreover, it is a generic way of solving problems. Whatever classification or regression techniques we have seen so far, all can be solved by deep learning models. It is far more complicated (we will discuss in detail) than traditional models, and sometimes also it overcomplicates the problem-solving procedure. So, a detailed analysis and understanding of the data are required before taking a call on whether it is to be solved by deep learning or traditional methods.

Neural network

Deep learning models are implemented using a neural network. It consists of *neurons*, actually of type *perceptron*, which is a special type of neuron. A neuron is analogous to the **Neuron of Human Brain**. It stores some information, and several neurons are interconnected with each other, thus build a network. As this network is artificially generated, unlike the human brain network, it is also called an **Artificial Neural Network (ANN)**. A typical diagram of an ANN is shown below:

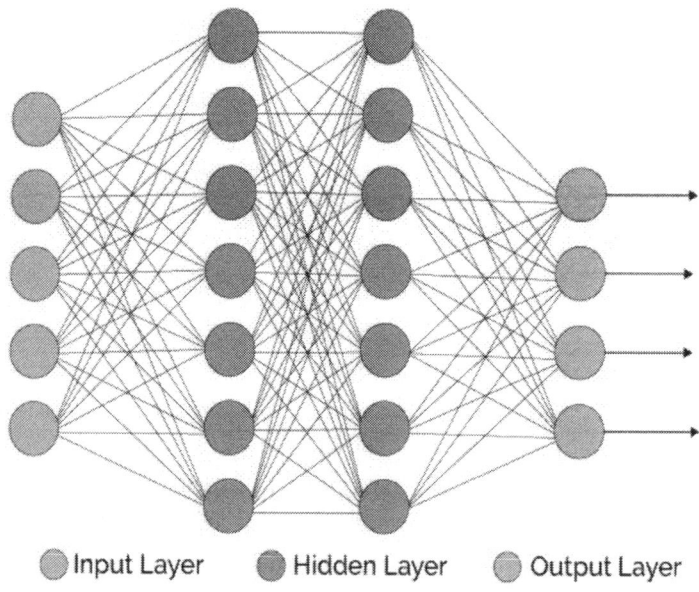

Figure 5.1: *General Network Architecture of an ANN*

Each of these green, saffron, and blue nodes is perceptions. And as discussed earlier, it is visible that this ANN is built of several layers. We will discuss the significance of these later. All perceptions are connected via edges. We can say that ANN is a connected graph.

Anatomy of a neural network

A neural network consists of several components: *perceptions' layers, loss function,* and *optimizers*. We have already seen how layers are organized in the above diagram. We will discuss in detail all components one-by-one.

Perceptron

Perceptron is a composite computing unit containing a weighted sum of feature variables and one activation function unit. A weighted sum is passed to the activation function unit, and one single value is returned from there. In short, it captures signals from the features and forwards the signal to the next available perceptions for further processing. Below diagram shows the internal structure of a perceptron:

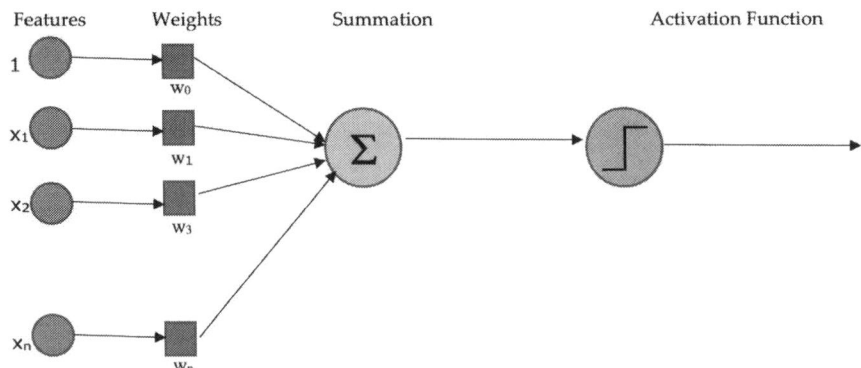

Figure 5.2: *General architecture of a perceptron*

Mathematically, summation node's operation can be written as below:

$$y = w_0 + \sum_{i=1}^{n} w_i x_i$$

It is completely analogous to the linear regression expression, as explained in *Chapter 2: Classification*. A single perceptron mimics the multivariate linear regression operation. Here weights are associated with edges connecting two perceptrons, and w_0 is the bias of the perceptron. After computation, the value of y is passed to the activation function node.

Activation function

Neural networks are non-linear models by nature. And the activation function is the component responsible for giving non-linear flavor to this model. There are various types of activation functions, as described below.

Sigmoid or logistic

It squashes the output between 0 and 1. The mathematical expression is given by:

$$sigmoid(x) = \frac{1}{1 + e^{-x}}$$

If this function is plotted, then it looks like an S-shaped curve like below:

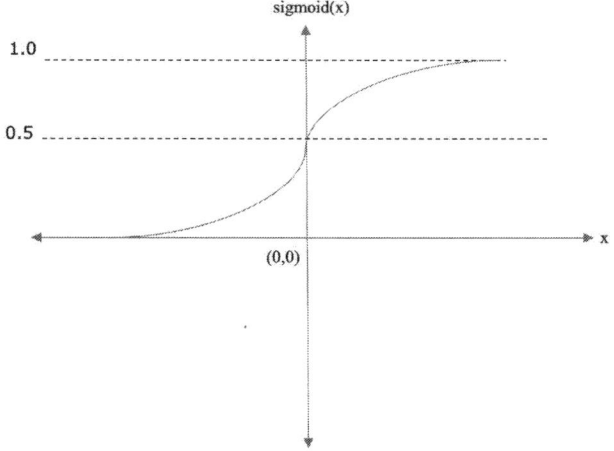

Figure 5.3: Ideal sigmoid function

Sigmoid is useful in those cases, where we have to predict the probability of a data instance belonging to a class (like in logistic regression)

Tanh

It squashes the output between –1 and 1. The mathematical expression of tanh is:

$$\tanh(x) = \frac{e^x - e^{-x}}{e^x + e^{-x}}$$

Basically it is shifted *sigmoid* function and it also looks like an *S* shaped curve:

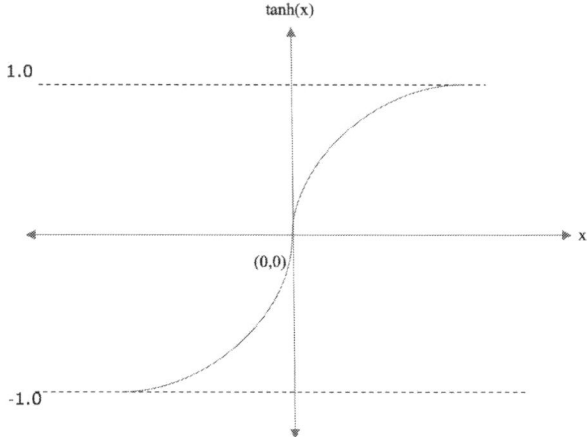

Figure 5.4: Ideal tanh function

This function maps negative inputs to strongly negative values and zero inputs of near-zero value. This is useful in binary classification problems.

ReLU (Rectified Linear Unit)

It just passes a strong positive value out of everything. The mathematical expression is:

$$relu(x) = \begin{cases} 0 \; if \; x < 0 \\ x \; otherwise \end{cases}$$

It looks like a straight line originating from *(0, 0)*:

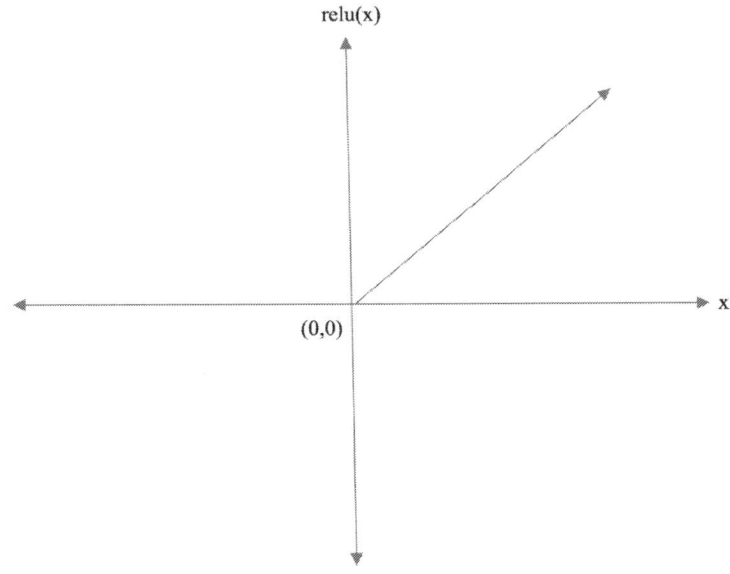

Figure 5.5: Ideal ReLU function

It ranges from 0 to infinity. **ReLU** is a strongly positive function and ideal for regression problems with positive values. It is also very useful in hidden layers of a feed-forward neural network. We will see it later.

Linear

It is a simple pass-through function. The mathematical expression is:

$$linear(x) = x$$

It looks like a straight line passing through (0, 0):

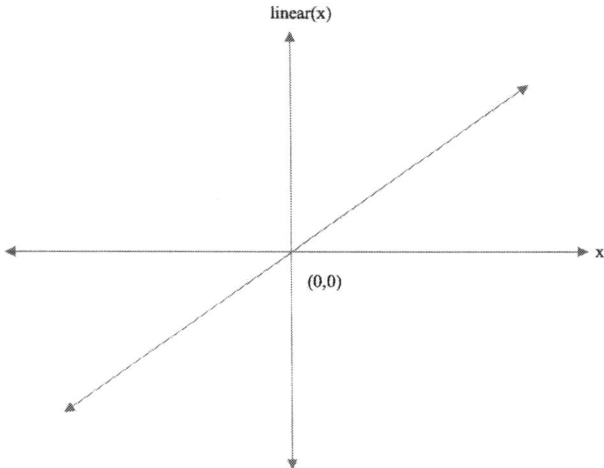

Figure 5.6: *Ideal linear function*

It ranges from -infinity to +infinity. This is used for normal regression problems where output can have any values.

Layers

One layer consists of an array of the perceptron. Within one layer, perceptrons are not interconnected, but across the layer, these are. It is shown in *Figure 5.1*. Outputs from perceptrons of one layer enter as inputs to the perceptrons of the next layer. At high-level, there can be three types of layers, as explained below:

- **Input layer:** This is the first layer of any neural network, as shown in the above diagram. Features of any dataset are directly seeded into this layer. There can be only one input layer in any neural network.

- **Hidden layer:** This is a purely computing layer. There can be many hidden layers connected. The job of this layer is to do feature engineering, and it generates intermediate features that are seeded to the next hidden layer or the output layer.

- **Output layer:** It generates the required output for the problem. The output may vary depending on the problem type. If it is classification, then the output layer may generate a probability for the classes, or if it is regression, then the value for the target variable.

Each time an input data enters from the input layer goes through several hidden layers for actual computation and goes out from the output layer as signals.

Loss function

It measures the inconsistency between the predicted value ($\hat{y}$ and it comes from the output layer of the neural network) and the actual label (y). The output of the loss function is a non-negative value, which helps to tune the model and making it perfect during the learning phase. Loss functions should always be differentiable so that loss can be optimized to build a perfect model. There are various types of loss functions. Two of those are discussed below.

Mean Squared Error (MSE)

It is the average square of the absolute difference between the predicted and actual value. The mathematical expression is given below:

$$L = \frac{1}{n}\sum \left(y_i - \widehat{y_i}\right)^2$$

The target of MSE is to minimize the error or residual sum of squares. This loss function is used mainly for regression problems.

Cross-Entropy Loss

When the output layer gives the probability of each class for a classification problem, the loss function is used. It gives the average entropy, that is, average negative log-probability measure. The mathematical expression is given by:

$$L = -\frac{1}{n}\sum \sum_{K=1}^{C} p_k \log\left(p_k\right)$$

Where p_k = probability of each class k and C = total no of classes.

Optimizer

The objective of the *optimizer* is to find out the optimal values of the weights(w) of the hidden layer, as shown in the above equation. It does so by minimizing the output from loss function. Weight values (w) change in a continuous and iterative learning process. We already discussed the learning process of linear regression in *Chapter 2: Classification*. If we consider a single layer and single perceptron neural network, its learning process becomes quite similar to the linear regression one. There are various types of optimizers. Two of these are discussed below.

Stochastic Gradient Descent (SGD)

Generally, neural network-based models are trained with a large set of data. SGD, as explained in *Chapter 2: Classification*, is not suitable for this as it would take a very long time and resource to converge. SGD updates each weight by following mathematical expression:

$$w_{i+1} = w_i + \alpha \frac{\partial L}{\partial w}$$

Where, L = Loss function, w = weight, and i = iteration number.

One big disadvantage here that this update happens very slowly, and there are high chances of reaching local minimum value, which yields an overfitted model at the end.

Mini-batch Gradient Descent

To overcome the problem of overfitting, instead of updating weights in each iteration, small batches of the test dataset is used at a time. So, the update happens only after iterating through each batch. It is a tradeoff between the traditional Gradient Descent and Stochastic Gradient Descent technique.

There are other advanced optimizers like Adam, AdaGrad, and more. These are out of the scope of this discussion.

Building a neural network model

As mentioned earlier, deep learning andneural networks-based approach are ideal for perception driven learning (visual perception, auditory perception, and more.) where human brain activities play an important role. Though it can be applied for normal problems of very much non-linear response patterns where classical machine learning algorithms fail.

Training process of neural network

Training of the neural network starts with seeded features into the first input layer. All weights of hidden layers are randomly initialized. The entire process can be divided into two stages: forward and backward propagation. We will consider a small neural network of 2 hidden layersandthree input features to discuss these. We will consider only partial connections within the network for our convenience.

Forward propagation

Below diagram shows the forward propagation mechanism:

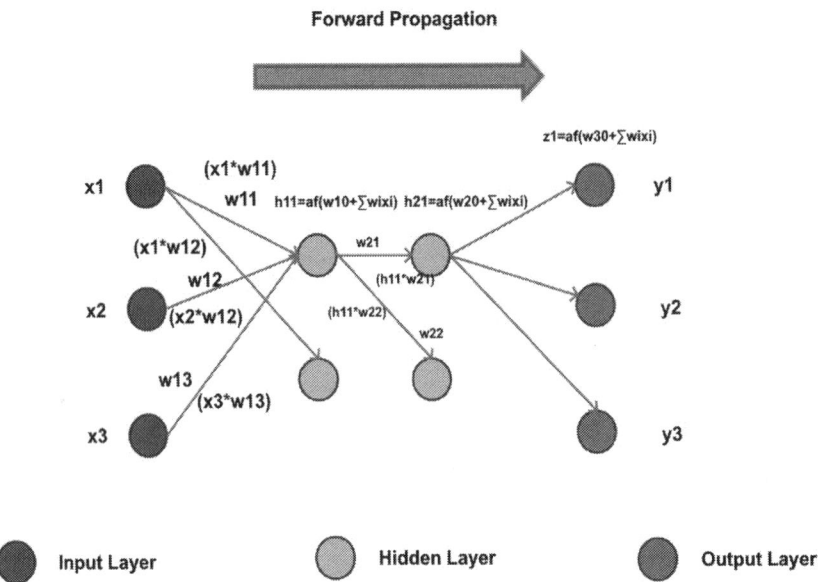

Figure 5.7: Forward Propagation Architecture

Each connecting edge contains the weights associated with it. For example, *w11* denotes the weight of 1st hidden layer associated with *x1* and similarly for *w12*. The bias of nodes is denoted by *w10, w20,* and more. Data flow happens from left to right direction for **forwarding propagation**. Features *x1, x2,* and more are seeded into the first layer, and these get multiplied by corresponding weight for each edge while traversing into the next layer. As the next layer is hidden, all of these multiplied weight-feature combinations and bias get added, and an activation function is applied on top of it. As shown, *h11* computed as $af(w_{10} + \sum w_i\, x_i)$. Here af is the activation function. This *h11* becomes the input for the next hidden layer and is similarly multiplied by a weight *w21*. The same holds while computing *h21*. Ultimately, the value coming out from output layer becomes $z_1 = af(w_{30} + \sum w_i\, x_i)$. If they're more than two hidden layers, value propagation happens similarly from layer to layer.

Backward propagation

This stage computes total error occurred at the output layer and propagates it back to the previous layers using a proper combination of *loss function and optimizer*. While propagating back, weight at each edge is updated with gradient calculated at that point to mitigate the effect of the error. Below diagram shows the data flow from right to left:

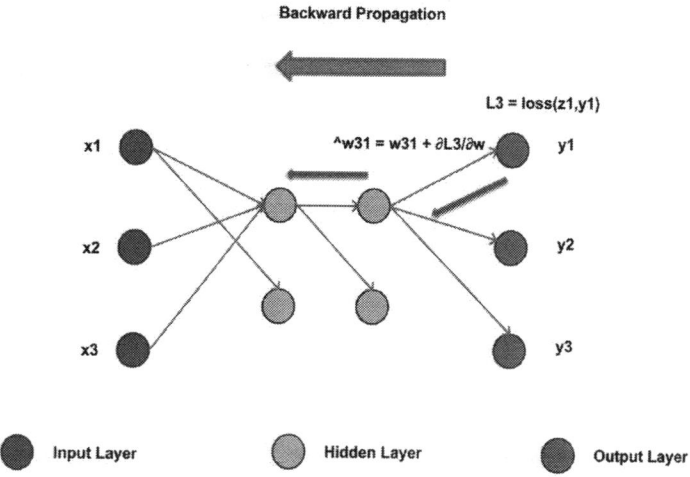

Figure 5.8: *Backward propagation architecture*

Loss is first computed at the last layer using the proper loss function, and then the weight is updated with the gradient $\left(\dfrac{\partial L_3}{\partial w}\right)$ like:

$$\widehat{w_{31}} = w_{31} + \alpha\frac{\partial L_3}{\partial w}$$

(Here α is the learning rate. We can tune α to control the training process. An optimal value of α can be found by proper hyperparameter tuning.)

This flow propagates in the same way to the first layer until all weights are updated.

Stopping criteria

This forward and backward propagation continues cyclically until & unless either a pre-decided threshold accuracy is reached or a certain no of pre-decided iterations are complete. We already know from our knowledge that *accuracy* is problem-specific, and its definition varies. At the end of the process, we will be having all our hidden layer weights with properly adjusted values. Then this network model can be used for prediction or any other purpose.

Applying neural network for classification and regression problem

As discussed above, we can use a neural network for building classifiers and regressors. This is appropriate if the class boundary or the regression problem is non-linear and if it is of a perception driven learning.

Deciding the number of hidden layers and perceptrons

We can set the number of hidden layersand perceptron as hyperparameters and test with various combinations. There is no hard and fast rule of deciding these. Generally, for a specific type of problem area, this decision can be taken after having the experience of building several models.

Classification problem

We will be using the Adult dataset (https://archive.ics.uci.edu/ml/datasets/adult) of UCI repository for building a classifier using a neural network. We will be using `pandas` and `scikit-learn` library of Python to exploring data and model building.

Dataset is already divided into train and test. First, let's explore the training dataset and identify our target variables and feature variables:

```
import pandas as pd

adult_train = pd.read_csv("../data/adult.data", header=None)
adult_train
```

	0	1	2	3	4	5	6	7	8	9	10	11	12	13	14
0	39	State-gov	77516	Bachelors	13	Never-married	Adm-clerical	Not-in-family	White	Male	2174	0	40	United-States	<=50K
1	50	Self-emp-not-inc	83311	Bachelors	13	Married-civ-spouse	Exec-managerial	Husband	White	Male	0	0	13	United-States	<=50K
2	38	Private	215646	HS-grad	9	Divorced	Handlers-cleaners	Not-in-family	White	Male	0	0	40	United-States	<=50K
3	53	Private	234721	11th	7	Married-civ-spouse	Handlers-cleaners	Husband	Black	Male	0	0	40	United-States	<=50K
4	28	Private	338409	Bachelors	13	Married-civ-spouse	Prof-specialty	Wife	Black	Female	0	0	40	Cuba	<=50K
5	37	Private	284582	Masters	14	Married-civ-spouse	Exec-managerial	Wife	White	Female	0	0	40	United-States	<=50K
6	49	Private	160187	9th	5	Married-spouse-absent	Other-service	Not-in-family	Black	Female	0	0	16	Jamaica	<=50K
7	52	Self-emp-not-inc	209642	HS-grad	9	Married-civ-spouse	Exec-managerial	Husband	White	Male	0	0	45	United-States	>50K

Figure 5.9: Code snippet to read the Adult dataset and the result

In the actual dataset, columns are not named properly. But in the problem description section of the UCI portal, these are mentioned as `age`, `workclass`, `fnlwgt`, `education`, and more. And our target variable is column no 14, that is, whether a person makes $50K a year or not. It has two value `<=50K` and `>50K`. Feature variables are from column 0 to 13. We can separate these variables for training purpose:

```
adult_train_x = adult_train[adult_train.columns[0:14]]
adult_train_y = adult_train[adult_train.columns[14:15]]
```

Figure 5.10: Code snippet to split the dataset into train and test

There are some categorical variables in features like 1, 3, 5, 6, and more are of a categorical type. And as it is a classification problem, the target variable 14 itself is categorical. So, all these have to be converted to numerical because the neural network only understands the numerical variable. We will do one-hot-encoding using the `get_dummies` function of `pandas`. We need to pass there a list of categorical column names or indices for which this conversion is necessary:

```
adult_train_x_encoded = pd.get_dummies(adult_train_x,columns=[1,3,5,6,7,8,9,13])
adult_train_y_encoded = pd.get_dummies(adult_train_y, columns=[14])
```

Figure 5.11: Code snippet to apply one-hot-encoder

Now, the features look like below:

```
adult_train_x_encoded.head()
```

	0	2	4	10	11	12	1_?	1_Federal-gov	1_Local-gov	1_Never-worked	...	13_Portugal	13_Puerto-Rico	13_Scotland	13_South	13_Taiwan	13_Thailand	13_Trinadad&Tobago	13_United-States	13_Vietnam
0	39	77516	13	2174	0	40	0	0	0	0	...	0	0	0	0	0	0	0	1	0
1	50	83311	13	0	0	13	0	0	0	0	...	0	0	0	0	0	0	0	1	0
2	38	215646	9	0	0	40	0	0	0	0	...	0	0	0	0	0	0	0	1	0
3	53	234721	7	0	0	40	0	0	0	0	...	0	0	0	0	0	0	0	1	0
4	28	338409	13	0	0	40	0	0	0	0	...	0	0	0	0	0	0	0	0	0

5 rows × 108 columns

Figure 5.12: One-hot-encoded features

And the target variable looks like:

```
adult_train_y_encoded.head()
```

	14_<=50K	14_>50K
0	1	0
1	1	0
2	1	0
3	1	0
4	1	0

Figure 5.13: One-hot-encoded target variable

We can see that the original variables have been decomposed into separate variables.

We can easily understand, feature variables are at a different scale, especially after one-hot-encoding and neural network optimization gets heavily affected by this. So, we have to use a `StandardScaler` to bring those down on the same scale:

```
from sklearn.preprocessing import StandardScaler

adult_train_x_arr = StandardScaler().fit_transform(adult_train_x_encoded)
adult_train_x_arr
```

```
array([[ 0.03067056, -1.06361075,  1.13473876, ...,  0.34095391,
        -0.04540836, -0.02217266],
       [ 0.83710898, -1.008707  ,  1.13473876, ...,  0.34095391,
        -0.04540836, -0.02217266],
       [-0.04264203,  0.2450785 , -0.42005962, ...,  0.34095391,
        -0.04540836, -0.02217266],
       ...,
       [ 1.42360965, -0.35877741, -0.42005962, ...,  0.34095391,
        -0.04540836, -0.02217266],
       [-1.21564337,  0.11095988, -0.42005962, ...,  0.34095391,
        -0.04540836, -0.02217266],
       [ 0.98373415,  0.92989258, -0.42005962, ...,  0.34095391,
        -0.04540836, -0.02217266]]])
```

Figure 5.14: Code snippet to apply StandardScaler on features and the result

Output becomes a numpy array instead of a data frame.

Now, we can use this to build a neural network. We will use a 2-layer simple one. The scikit-learn library has a class named MLPClassifier for this. We can sequentially mention over there all layer details and the number of nodes under it.

The heuristic approach of deciding the number of nodes in hidden layers

Generally, we can keep the number of nodes in the hidden layer as (number_of_input_features/2).

Here, the total number of features after one-hot-encoding:

```
adult_train_x_arr.shape[1]
```

```
108
```

Figure 5.15: Shape of the transformed features

So, we can use two 54 (108/2) node hidden layers for our classifier and train it:

```
from sklearn.neural_network import MLPClassifier

mlp_classifier = MLPClassifier(hidden_layer_sizes=(54, 54))
mlp_classifier.fit(adult_train_x_arr,adult_train_y_encoded)
```

```
/Users/avnag/Library/Python/3.6/lib/python/site-packages/sklearn/neural_network/multilayer_perceptron.py:566: Converg
enceWarning: Stochastic Optimizer: Maximum iterations (200) reached and the optimization hasn't converged yet.
  % self.max_iter, ConvergenceWarning)
```

```
MLPClassifier(activation='relu', alpha=0.0001, batch_size='auto', beta_1=0.9,
              beta_2=0.999, early_stopping=False, epsilon=1e-08,
              hidden_layer_sizes=(54, 54), learning_rate='constant',
              learning_rate_init=0.001, max_iter=200, momentum=0.9,
              n_iter_no_change=10, nesterovs_momentum=True, power_t=0.5,
              random_state=None, shuffle=True, solver='adam', tol=0.0001,
              validation_fraction=0.1, verbose=False, warm_start=False)
```

Figure 5.16: Code snippet to train the neural network model

The fit function trains the model. To avoid the warning, we can set other hyperparameters. From the parameter details, we can see that by default, for hidden layers, ReLU is used as activation function and Adam as the optimizer. `MLPClassifier` also gives options to change these parameters according to our needs.

We will see the training accuracy now:

```
mlp_classifier.score(adult_train_x_arr, adult_train_y_encoded)
```

```
0.9219004330333835
```

Figure 5.17: Code snippet to get the accuracy of the Neural Network model

It is almost 0.92 or 92%.

Now, we can read the test data and do some kind of pre-processing like one-hot-ending and scaling to make it ready for use:

```
adult_test = pd.read_csv("../data/adult.test", header=None)
adult_test_x = adult_test[adult_test.columns[0:14]]
adult_test_y = adult_test[adult_test.columns[14:15]]
adult_test_x_encoded = pd.get_dummies(adult_test_x,columns=[1,3,5,6,7,8,9,13])
adult_test_y_encoded = pd.get_dummies(adult_test_y, columns=[14])
```

Figure 5.18: Code snippet to transform test data with one-hot-encoder

There is a challenge in one-hot-ended results in test data. There can be discrepancies between one-hot-encoded training and testing dataset. It was also explained in *Chapter 2: Classification*. Some data instances of a particular category under a categorical variable may be present in the test dataset, which is absent in training. For this, one-hot-encoded transformed dimensions will be different for both, and any classifier will fail. We can remove this difference by filling it with zero:

```
adult_test_x_encoded = adult_test_x_encoded.reindex(columns = adult_train_x_encoded.columns, fill_value=0)
```

Figure 5.19: Code snippet to re-index test data

Now, we can do the same *StandardScaler* transformation and use the model for testing accuracy

```
adult_test_x_arr = StandardScaler().fit_transform(adult_test_x_encoded)
mlp_classifier.score(adult_test_x_arr, adult_test_y_encoded)
```

```
0.8268533873840673
```

Figure 5.20: *Code snippet to apply StandardScaler on test data*

Testing accuracy is almost 0.8268 or 82.68%. We can see the loss curve of the model:

```
%matplotlib inline
pd.DataFrame(mlp_classifier.loss_curve_).plot()
```

```
<matplotlib.axes._subplots.AxesSubplot at 0x12ac2fa90>
```

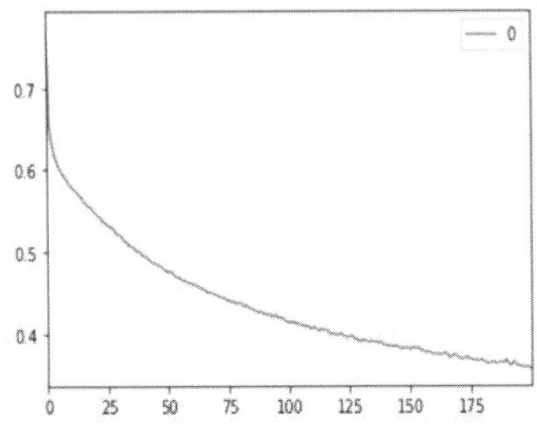

Figure 5.21: *Code snippet to plot loss curve of the Neural Network model*

As it is a classification problem, this plot is for log-loss function. The x-axis contains the iteration number, and *Y*-axis contains loss function value. We can observe that loss is decreasing as the number of iterations is increasing, and the model is converging to a stable state. It is the expected behavior of any neural network-based model.

Now, we can use this model to predict an incoming data instance. We will do with a randomly selected test data instance:

```
adult_test_x_encoded[6:7]
```

	0	2	4	10	11	12	1_?	1_Federal-gov	1_Local-gov	1_Never-worked	...	13_Portugal	13_Puerto-Rico	13_Scotland	13_South	13_Taiwan	13_Thailand	13_Trinadad&Tobago	13_United-States	13_Vietnam	Yu
6	29	227026	9	0	0	40	1	0	0	0	...	0	0	0	0	0	0	0	1	0	

1 rows × 108 columns

```
adult_test_y_encoded[6:7]
```

	14_<=50K.	14_>50K.
6	1	0

```
mlp_classifier.predict(adult_test_x_arr[6:7])
```
```
array([[1, 0]])
```

Figure 5.22: Code snippet to test the classifier with an unknown data

So, the predicted income category is <=50K, which is the same as the original.

Regression problem

We will use US Census Demographic data from Kaggle (https://www.kaggle.com/muonneutrino/us-census-demographic-data) for our regression problem. We will explore the dataset first to see what's there:

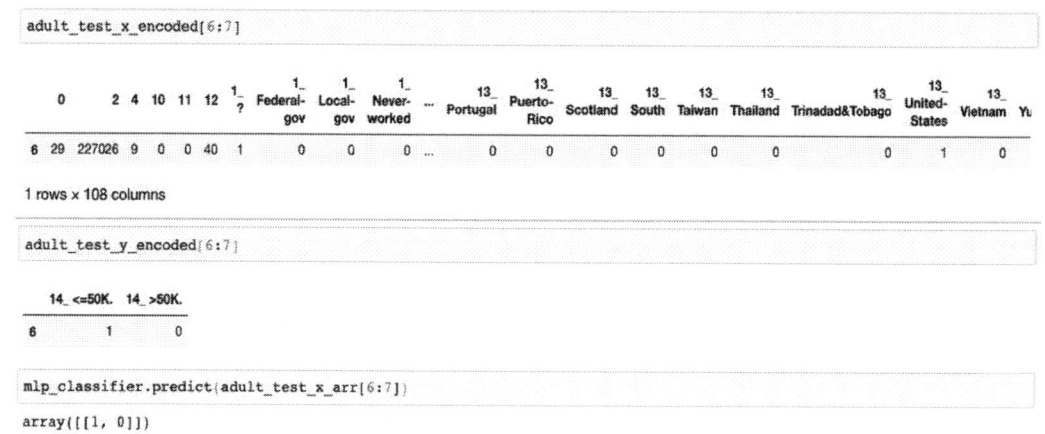

```
import pandas as pd

census_df = pd.read_csv("../data/acs2017_census_tract_data.csv")
census_df
```

	TractId	State	County	TotalPop	Men	Women	Hispanic	White	Black	Native	...	Walk	OtherTransp	WorkAtHome	MeanCommute	Employ
0	1001020100	Alabama	Autauga County	1845	899	946	2.4	86.3	5.2	0.0	...	0.5	0.0	2.1	24.5	8
1	1001020200	Alabama	Autauga County	2172	1167	1005	1.1	41.6	54.5	0.0	...	0.0	0.5	0.0	22.2	8
2	1001020300	Alabama	Autauga County	3385	1533	1852	8.0	61.4	26.5	0.6	...	1.0	0.8	1.5	23.1	14
3	1001020400	Alabama	Autauga County	4267	2001	2266	9.6	80.3	7.1	0.5	...	1.5	2.9	2.1	25.9	18
4	1001020500	Alabama	Autauga County	9965	5054	4911	0.9	77.5	16.4	0.0	...	0.8	0.3	0.7	21.0	47
5	1001020600	Alabama	Autauga County	3620	1765	1855	3.0	70.7	25.1	0.0	...	0.7	3.5	8.0	21.1	13
6	1001020700	Alabama	Autauga County	3420	1459	1961	4.0	78.0	13.7	0.6	...	0.0	0.0	0.0	16.4	14

Figure 5.23: Code snippet to read census dataset and the result

Our target variable is Income, that is, mean household income of the County. We have to predict it from the other feature variables. It is a continuous variable, and hence it is a regression problem.

First, we need to separate feature and target variables and truncate TractId as it is unnecessary:

```
census_x = census_df[[x for x in census_df.columns if x not in('Income','TractId')]]
census_y = census_df[['Income']]
```

Figure 5.24: Code snippet to split feature and target variable

Next, we have to apply one-hot-encoding to categorical variables and then StandardScaler to all variables:

```
from sklearn.preprocessing import StandardScaler

census_x_encoded = pd.get_dummies(census_x,columns=['State','County'])
census_x_arr = StandardScaler().fit_transform(census_x_encoded)
census_x_arr

array([[-1.13943709, -1.12329429, -1.11757897, ..., -0.00636723,
        -0.0073523 , -0.00367607],
       [-0.99272938, -0.88412665, -1.06610599, ..., -0.00636723,
        -0.0073523 , -0.00367607],
       [-0.44852003, -0.55750218, -0.3271634 , ..., -0.00636723,
        -0.0073523 , -0.00367607],
       ...,
       [-0.97209159, -1.0322678 , -0.88115224, ..., -0.00636723,
        -0.0073523 , -0.00367607],
       [-0.00211583, -0.17287064,  0.16488338, ..., -0.00636723,
        -0.0073523 , -0.00367607],
       [-0.62080065, -0.72706133, -0.49641353, ..., -0.00636723,
        -0.0073523 , -0.00367607]]])
```

Figure 5.25: Code snippet to apply StandardScaler on features

As we don't have separate test dataset, so will divide the existing dataset into training and testing part:

```
from sklearn.model_selection import train_test_split

census_train_x, census_test_x, census_train_y, census_test_y = train_test_split(census_x_arr, census_y)
```

Figure 5.26: Code snippet to split the dataset into train and test

In the entire dataset, there is a lot of entries with missing values. These will create problems while computation, so we need to replace those with some computed values. We have to do data imputation here and will apply the mean imputation strategy:

```
from sklearn.impute import SimpleImputer
import numpy as np

census_train_x = SimpleImputer(missing_values=np.nan, strategy='mean').fit_transform(census_train_x)
census_train_y = SimpleImputer(missing_values=np.nan, strategy='mean').fit_transform(census_train_y)
```

Figure 5.27: Code snippet to do mean based data imputation

Now, the total number of features becomes 2024:

```
census_train_x.shape[1]
```

2040

Figure 5.28: Shape of features

So, as per heuristics, we will keep two hidden layers of size 1020 (2024/2) and create our neural network. The scikit-learn library has one class named MLPRegressor which can solve the regression problem using multilayer perceptron:

```
from sklearn.neural_network import MLPRegressor

mlp_regressor = MLPRegressor(hidden_layer_sizes=(1020, 1020))
mlp_regressor.fit(census_train_x,census_train_y.ravel())
```

```
/Users/avnag/Library/Python/3.6/lib/python/site-packages/sklearn/neural_network/multilayer_perceptron.py:566: Converg
enceWarning: Stochastic Optimizer: Maximum iterations (200) reached and the optimization hasn't converged yet.
  % self.max_iter, ConvergenceWarning)
```

```
MLPRegressor(activation='relu', alpha=0.0001, batch_size='auto', beta_1=0.9,
             beta_2=0.999, early_stopping=False, epsilon=1e-08,
             hidden_layer_sizes=(1020, 1020), learning_rate='constant',
             learning_rate_init=0.001, max_iter=200, momentum=0.9,
             n_iter_no_change=10, nesterovs_momentum=True, power_t=0.5,
             random_state=None, shuffle=True, solver='adam', tol=0.0001,
             validation_fraction=0.1, verbose=False, warm_start=False)
```

Figure 5.29: Code snippet to train a neural network regression model

We can measure training accuracy:

```
mlp_regressor.score(census_train_x,census_train_y)
```

0.9585943417491387

Figure 5.30: Code snippet to compute model accuracy

Accuracy is 0.95. It is the $R2$ score for the regression problem. We can say 95% of the variance in the training data is explained by the model.

We can see the loss function plot:

```
%matplotlib inline

pd.DataFrame(mlp_regressor.loss_curve_).plot()

<matplotlib.axes._subplots.AxesSubplot at 0x13071c080>
```

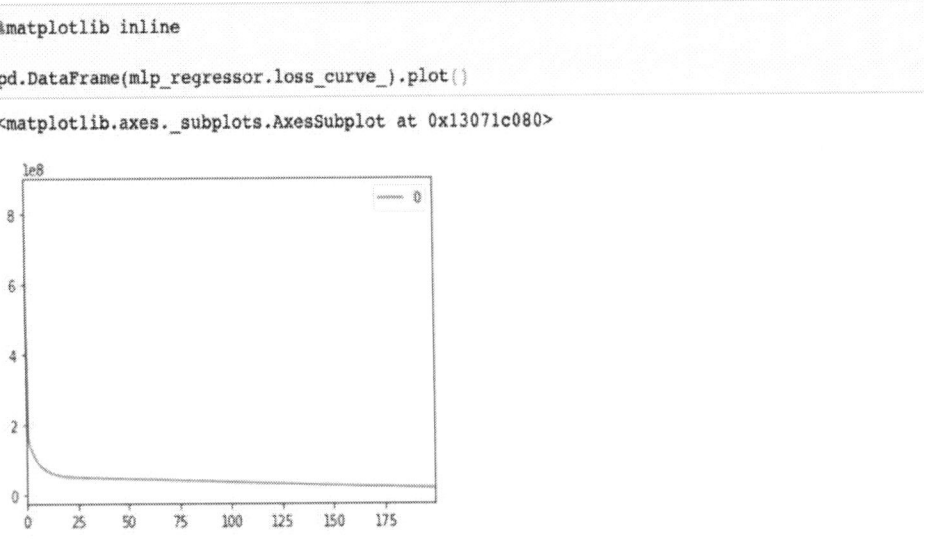

Figure 5.31: Code snippet to plot loss curve of the model

It is a squared-loss plot as the problem is for regression. The *x*-axis contains the iteration number, and *Y*-axis contains the loss function value.

To get the testing accuracy, we can do the same imputation for the testing dataset and measure the score:

```
census_test_x = SimpleImputer(missing_values=np.nan, strategy='mean').fit_transform(census_test_x)
census_test_y = SimpleImputer(missing_values=np.nan, strategy='mean').fit_transform(census_test_y)
mlp_regressor.score(census_test_x,census_test_y.ravel())
```

```
0.7304808094741213
```

Figure 5.32: Code snippet to do mean based data imputation on test data

We can use the model to predict average household income for a data instance taken from testing data:

```
census_test_x[7:8]

array([[-0.27130429, -0.38437337, -0.1518063 , ..., -0.00636723,
        -0.0073523 , -0.00367607]])
```

```
census_test_y[7:8]

array([[41875.]])
```

```
mlp_regressor.predict(census_test_x[7:8])

array([42623.26320453])
```

Figure 5.33: Code snippet to test then model on one sample test data

We can see that the predicted value is quite close to the actual value.

For both classification and regression problems, further tuning is always possible with the right set of hyperparameters. Readers can try it on their own.

Conventions of building MLP (Multilayer Perceptron) model

The above two discussed models are the **Multilayer Perceptron (MLP)** model. It is a special type of ANN. There are some guidelines to build this as discussed below:

1. MLP models are generally built for classification, regression, or outlier detection problems. Choosing the right activation function is very important for a specific type of problem. Activation functions may not be the same across the layers.

   For a binary classification problem, the output layer should have *sigmoid* or *tanh* as activation function as these always squash the output value in the range 0 to 1 or -1 to 1. For classification problems, it helps in identifying appropriate andconcrete class labels. For multi-class problems, we can have the linear function as activation.

   For regression problems, the output layer should have ReLU as activation function as regression can have any real number as output.

2. It is always preferable to keep *ReLU* as the activation function for hidden layers. It helps the network to converge accurately.

   Vanishing Gradient Problem

   If the derivative of the *loss* $\left(\dfrac{\partial L}{\partial w}\right)$ of a perceptron is very small, and it contributes very little while updating weights. Even tuning learning rate parameter α does not do much help. If the large change in the input of activation causes a very small change in the output of it, then this problem occurs. The gradients decrease exponentially as the backpropagation proceeds down the layers. When the backpropagation process reachesthe initial layer, there will be a very small amount of change in the weights. So, the layers won't be able to capture the complex relationships between the features and output variables, and it will cause poor accuracy and early convergence of the model. In short, *gradients will keep on getting vanished down the layer*. This phenomenon is known as **Vanishing Gradient Problem**.

   Activation functions like tanh and sigmoid will cause this problem if these are used repeatedly in hidden layers. This function squashes the output always in between -1 to +1 range. This is a very small range, and a large change in input feature (for example, 20000) may cause a very small amount change (maybe in decimals) for these function outputs. Hidden layers are the heart of the neural network, and if these are not able to capture changes properly, the entire network is bound to fail.

So, as a solution to this problem, ReLU is always preferred activation function for all hidden layers. It has a large range as proportional to the input, and it captures changes perfectly.

3. It is always preferable to transform all input features to the same scale and convert all categorical variables to numerical before putting these into training.

We will discuss different types of neural networks in the next section.

Different types of neural network

So far, whatever we have discussed are all of the type *feed-forward neural network* and works on principles of perceptron and forward-backward propagation. These are also known as MLP. There are other types of networks, like CNN, Auto-Encoder, RNN, GAN, and more. Each one has its purpose. We will only discuss CNN and Auto-Encoder here.

Convolutional Neural Network (CNN)

CNN is based on mathematical convolution operation, as explained below.

Convolution operation

If f is a function and g is filter function, then mathematically, a convolution operation is defined by:

$$f * g = \sum f(a) \cdot g(b) \text{ where } a + b = c$$

If we substitute $b = c - a$ then:

$$f * g = \sum f(a) \cdot g(c - a)$$

Generally, we say convolution is evaluated at point c for a and b. We can say that it is the projection of f by g at given point c.

In practice, if we consider f and g both as tensor or 2D array, then this convolution operation becomes the summation of pairwise multiplication of two array elements. The filter g moves around f with a pre-decided shift or stride parameter, and the elements of two arrays keep getting multiplied and added. The *stride* decides how many steps will be skipped by filter g for the next projection. As a result, we get one output array. Its dimensions would be less than that of f. There is also a concept of **padding**. If, at any point, the convolution filter tries to go out of the input tensor/

matrix while shifting (rather, better to say *striding*), then *padding* operation ensures there are enough cells for computation by adding extra. Like stride, the degree of padding should also be mentioned before applying the filter.

Let us consider *f* like below tensor:

f

1	1	1	0	0
0	1	1	1	0
0	0	1	1	1
0	0	1	1	0
0	1	1	0	0

Figure 5.34: Sample tensor of convolution operation

Then *g* like below:

g

1	0	1
0	1	0
1	0	1

Figure 5.35: Sample tensor of convolution operation

The *g* will start movement from top left corner of *f* and computing and putting convoluted result in the output array. This operation has been shown below:

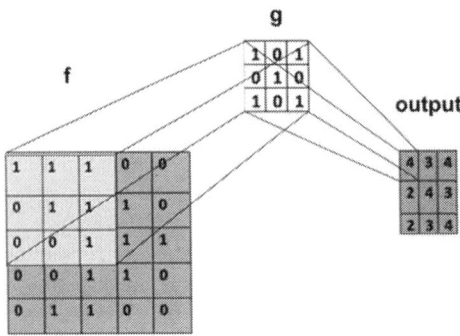

Figure 5.36: Stepwise Convolution operation on f & g

First convoluted output element at *(0, 0)* is computed as per below logic:

$$output\ (0,0) = f(0, 0)\ x\ g(0, 0) + f(0, 1)\ x\ g(0, 1) + f(0, 2)\ x\ g(0, 2) + f(1, 0)\ x\ g(1, 0)$$
$$+ f(1, 1)\ x\ g(1, 1) + f(1, 2)\ x\ g(1, 2) + f(2, 0)\ x\ g(2, 0) + f(2, 1)\ x\ g(2, 1)$$
$$+ f(2, 2)\ x\ g(2, 2)$$
$$= (1\ x\ 1) + (0\ x\ 1) + (1\ x\ 1) + (0\ x\ 0) + (1\ x\ 1) + (1\ x\ 0) + (1\ x\ 0)$$
$$+ (0\ x\ 0) + (1\ x\ 1) = 4$$

With a similar fashion, if the filter g takes stride as 1 then next output at (0,1) will be generated like below:

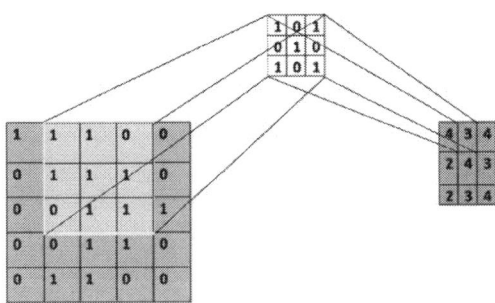

Figure 5.37: Stepwise Convolution operation on f and g

Ans like this way the operation will continue and generate the complete output tensor as shown above.

The practical significance of convolution operation is that it can extract important information from a tensor and project it in a lower dimension.

Significance of convolution in the neural network model

Most of the neural network models deal with sparse and high dimensional data, and the data goes through numerous amounts of computation through different layers. As a result, we often lose out some important features, and it is also very difficult to understand which feature is important and which are not. Due to the complexity of the neural network, it is very important to apply some techniques that can automatically extract out a filtered and important flavor of the data, which contributes significantly to identifying it. We can explain this through the example of image recognition. If we are given a set of animal images and told to build a model which can classify the images, then what would be our first stage? We will start by analyzing the unique and distinguishable features of each animal. Visually, we can do it easily, but how can we make a machine learning model for understanding those features? Like a horse has long tails, but it does not have a trunk like an elephant. So, the horse can be distinguished from the elephant by this feature. Also, the color of the animal matter here a lot. Like this, there can be a lot of small and tiny features that can play an important role. CNN is the solution over here. It can understand image regions, image color schemes, object structure, and more. Not only image recognition, but CNN can also solve audio and video recognition problems easily in this manner. It also works well in understanding text data.

Anatomy of a CNN

Like a normal neural network, CNN also consists of several layers. Apart from normal layers, it will have some special layers, as discussed below.

Convolution layer

Convolution layer will consist of a convolution filter. It can extract out important features from the original feature tensor. Convolution filters are generally square-shaped. There can be multiple convolution filters in a CNN.

Max/average-pool layer

It is a 2D window filter that traverses through convoluted output tensor and picks up the maximum or average value within that window. It works as a dimensionality reduction technique. As we already discussed, for image/audio/video data, choosing high impacting features is very important. Max/average-pool layers just strengthen this process by selecting high impacting signal generating elements from a convoluted tensor. Max-pool layer is explained by the below diagram:

Figure 5.38: Sample Max-Pool operation

A max-pool window of size 2x2 is applied to the above tensor, and it produces just seven as output, which is maximum among the four elements. So, the dimension is reduced from 2x2 to 1x1.

A typical CNN looks like below diagram:

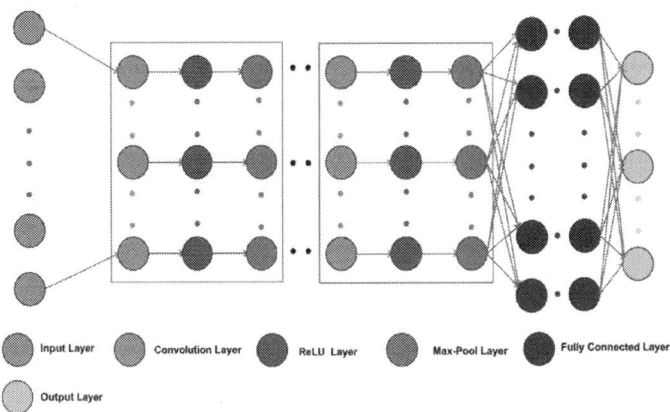

Figure 5.39: Architecture of a CNN

There can be a repeated sequence of Convolution, ReLU, and max-pool layer, as shown above. One fully connected layer maybe there before the final output layer. This layer is optional. Sometimes, a simple linear function layer also works well. The above one is a very generic and open architecture of CNN.

In many cases, it can be far simpler. For example, the max-pool layer may be optional for some cases where we don't want dimensionality reduction. Each convolution layer is responsible for finding out one distinguished and unique feature from the dataset. No of extracted features would be equal to the number of convolution layers used over there. Fully connected layers are responsible for using these convoluted features to do the actual task like classification, regression, and more.

Feature engineering of images using CNN

In any Image recognition problem, the biggest challenge is extracting the right features. Image data are not like normal dataset, whatever we discussed so far. Features are not well defined there. An image consists of $M \times N$ pixels where M is the number of rows (height), and N is the number of columns (width). An image dataset contains a set of images.

Moreover, an image can have different color-coding scheme: RGB (Red, Green, Blue), HSI (Hue, Saturation, Index), LAB (Luminance, a^*, b^*), and more. We will discuss our example with respect to RGB only. RGB is an additive color model. Red, green, and blue are core three base colors in this model. All other colors are generated by mixing different magnitude levels of these three. It is one of the most widely used models in normal image processing. Other models have their special purpose usage on case to case basis. Conversion from one color model to others is also possible using proper mathematical computation.

A brief introduction to PyTorch for designing a neural network

PyTorch is a python based library for developing deep learning solutions. It provides ready-made APIs for designing neural networks shortly and effectively. It has support for most of the activation functions, optimizers required for a neural network. The basic building block and primary data structure of PyTorch are Tensor. A Tensor is a Python **numpy** array with GPU support. We can create a 2D tensor with all zero elements like below:

```
import torch as torch

t2d = torch.zeros(3,4)
t2d

tensor([[0., 0., 0., 0.],
        [0., 0., 0., 0.],
        [0., 0., 0., 0.]])
```

Figure 5.40: Code snippet for sample tensor creation using PyTorch

We can create two random tensors and add them together:

```
x = torch.rand(5,7)
y = torch.rand(5,7)
z = x + y
z
```

```
tensor([[0.9878, 1.7096, 0.3282, 0.9775, 0.6114, 0.1655, 1.0679],
        [0.8106, 0.4962, 1.2823, 1.3246, 0.4356, 0.7809, 0.9264],
        [0.6357, 0.6246, 1.7548, 1.4301, 0.6811, 1.2153, 0.2562],
        [1.0525, 1.0453, 0.1584, 1.8502, 1.3645, 0.9473, 0.8402],
        [0.3934, 0.8277, 1.4104, 1.1622, 1.1136, 1.0378, 0.7441]]])
```

Figure 5.41: Code snippet for the addition of two tensors using PyTorch

Similarly, we can create *n*-D tensors with these APIs.

To design a neural network, a predefined base class `Module` (under PyTorch's nn module) should be extended. We should override two functions there: __init__ and forward. The function __init__ should consist of all layer definitions, their parameters, and hyperparameters. As per Python semantics, __init__ is nothing but the default constructor function. The function forward should declare the flow of the network, that is, how does the output of one layer go as input to another layer. There are many ready-made layer classes in PyTorch. Those can be stacked one after another to develop a complete neural network. For example, `Conv2d, Maxpool2d,` `ReLU`, and more are various layers (as discussed earlier). The `linear` layer is used as the final output layer to get activations. For classification problems, the number of nodes in output (for the linear layer) should be the same as the number of classes in the dataset. The linear layer can be used here. Choosing different layers is completely dependent on the nature and complexity of the problem.

An example of designing a neural network module with PyTorch is given below:

```python
import torch.nn as nn

class NaturalImageClassifierCNNModel(nn.Module):

    def __init__(self, num_classes=8):
        super(NaturalImageClassifierCNNModel,self).__init__()

        self.conv1 = nn.Conv2d(in_channels=3, out_channels=12, kernel_size=3,stride=1, padding=1)
        self.relu1 = nn.ReLU()

        self.maxpool1 = nn.MaxPool2d(kernel_size=2)

        self.conv2 = nn.Conv2d(in_channels=12, out_channels=24, kernel_size=3, stride=1, padding=1)
        self.relu2 = nn.ReLU()

        self.lf = nn.Linear(in_features=32 * 32 * 24, out_features=num_classes)

    def forward(self, input):
        output = self.conv1(input)
        output = self.relu1(output)

        output = self.maxpool1(output)

        output = self.conv2(output)
        output = self.relu2(output)

        output = output.view(-1, 32 * 32 * 24)

        output = self.lf(output)

        return output
```

Figure 5.42: Code snippet for sample image classifier CNN class

We also have to define how this network will be trained and what kind of optimizers and loss functions will be used:

```python
from torch.optim import Adam

cnn_model = NaturalImageClassifierCNNModel()
optimizer = Adam(cnn_model.parameters())
loss_fn = nn.CrossEntropyLoss()
```

Figure 5.43: Code snippet for optimizer and loss function creation

So, we are using **Adam** as optimizer and **CrossEntropyLoss** as the loss function.

We will see a full case study of image classification using PyTorch in *Chapter 9: Case Studies and Storytelling*.

CNN using PyTorch

PyTorch also provides good support for computer vision and audio processing. It treats each data (be it image, audio) as a tensor, as discussed above. RGB color-coded images are decomposed into three channels (red, green, and blue channel respectively) to compute convoluted tensor of that. The convolution operation is applied to each of these channels separately, and then all outputs are summed up to produce a single tensor:

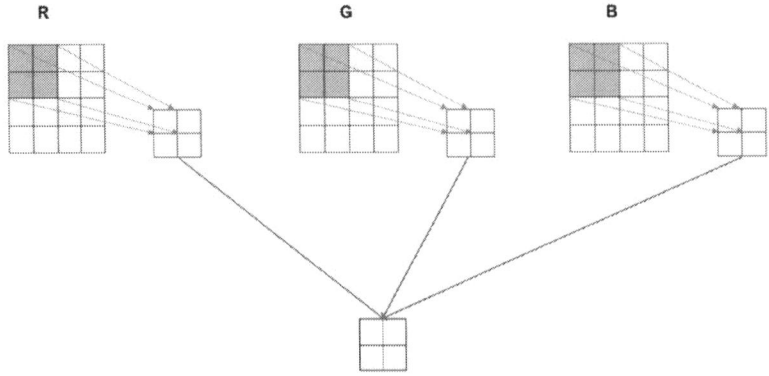

Figure 5.44: Flow of convolution operation in a 3-color channel image

This single tensor is used then in all kinds of computation in successive layers.

Input andoutput channel

Input channels are as usual as three-color codes (red, green, and blue). One convolution filter takes input image tensor as three channeled data and produces an output tensor, as shown in the above diagram. Output channels denote how many these type filters will be applied to the input image tensor.

If we fix input channels as three and output channels as k (k is a number) and feed one image to a convolution layer will produce k number of intermediate images. Each of these images will represent one unique feature of the original image. We will see this through an example.

At first, we will use Python's `PIL` library to read a sample read, apply the appropriate transformation, and display the image:

```
%matplotlib inline

from PIL import Image
import matplotlib.pyplot as plt
import numpy as np
from torchvision.transforms import transforms

transformations = transforms.Compose([
    transforms.ToTensor()
])

sample_image = Image.open("../data/monarch.png")
plt.figure(figsize=(5,5))
sample_image_tensor = transformations(sample_image).float()
sample_image_tensor_tr = np.transpose(sample_image_tensor, (1, 2, 0))
plt.imshow(sample_image_tensor_tr)
```

```
<matplotlib.image.AxesImage at 0x1260d4eb8>
```

Figure 5.45: Code snippet to read and display image from the dataset

It is an image of a `monarch`. Now, we will use `Conv2d` class `PyTorch` to design a convolution filter. We will set `input_channels` as `three` and `output_channels` as 6:

```
import torch.nn as nn
import torch as torch

no_of_images = 6
sample_image_tensor.unsqueeze_(0)
conv = nn.Conv2d(in_channels=3, out_channels=no_of_images, kernel_size=3,stride=1, padding=1)
conv_output = conv(sample_image_tensor)
conv_output.shape
```

```
torch.Size([1, 6, 512, 768])
```

Figure 5.46: Code snippet to design a sample convolution filter

`Conv2d` API expects image data in batches and as a 4D tensor. For that, we have added an extra dimension to our single image to simulate a single batch with a single record. It is done by `sample_image_tensor.unsqueeze_(0)`. It adds the dimension in the first place. Image tensor `sample_image_tensor` is passed in a convolution filter and produced the output tensor. Internally it calls `__call__`function as defined in

`Conv2d` class. This filter produced six intermediate image tensors. We can see that the channel dimension changed from 3 to 6.

Now, we will see the intermediate images produced by the operation:

```
def show_transformed_image(image):
    np_image = image.detach().numpy()
    plt.figure(figsize=(20,20))
    plt.imshow(np.transpose(np_image, (1, 2, 0)))
```

```
from torchvision.utils import make_grid

def display_conv_image(conv_image):
    batch,channel,width,height = conv_image.shape
    conv_image = conv_image.view(batch*channel, -1, width, height)
    show_transformed_image(make_grid(conv_image))
```

```
display_conv_image(conv_output)
```

```
Clipping input data to the valid range for imshow with RGB data ([0..1] for floats or [0..255] for integers).
```

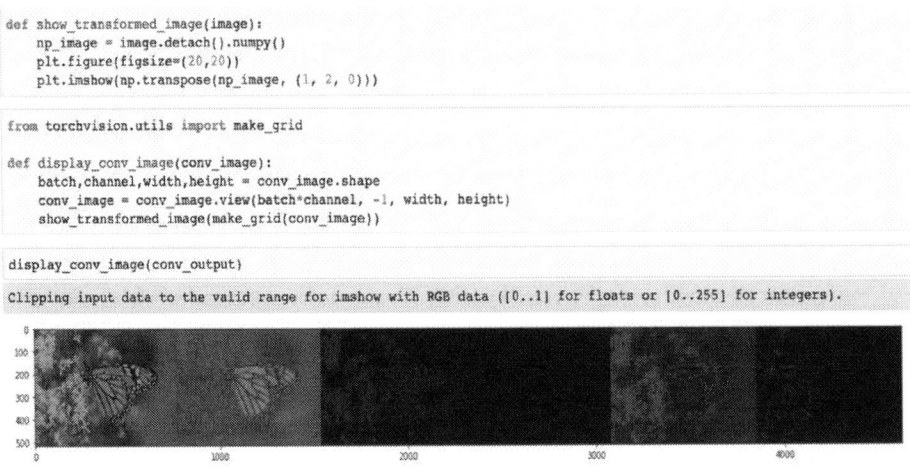

Figure 5.47: Code snippet of show_transformed_image and display_conv_image function

All intermediate images are dark shade grey-level images. This phenomenon can be explained by the mechanism of the convolution network.

As discussed earlier, three input channels are summed up together, and then convolution filters are applied one after another. RGB color model-based pixel consists of three values: red, green, and blue. If we take the average of these three values and assign it to each of red, green, and blue, then it becomes a grey-level pixel, and the entire image turns into a grey-level image (For a grey-level image red, green, and blue pixel color values are same). For example, let's assume the value of a pixel for RGB based image is (100, 201, 230). Now if it is converted into a grey-level image then pixel value becomes (177, 177, 177) because (100+201+230)/3 = 177. Now, for a normalized image, if the sum is taken instead of average, still it becomes a grey-level image. The same thing is happening while applying a convolution filter on input channels. Summing up operation is converting the image into a grey-level one, and as usual, different convolution kernels are producing different grey-level sub-images from the original one.

Each of the convoluted images is depicting some unique features of the original image. Some of these are highlighting designs in the wings of the monarch, and some are highlighting the boundary lines. These can play a major role in classifying any image. These intermediate images can be used as features and feed into a classifier or any other neural network.

We will see how to design a full CNN and use it for image classification with `PyTorch` library in case studies of *Chapter 9: Case Studies and Storytelling*.

Auto-Encoder

Auto-Encoder is a special type of neural network which comes under *unsupervised learning*. It can reproduce the same features of a dataset in the output layer. We use auto-encoder where we don't know the output/target variable and try to understand the data. A typical auto-encoder consists of an encoding layer, hidden compressing/coding layer, and decoding layer, as shown in the below diagram:

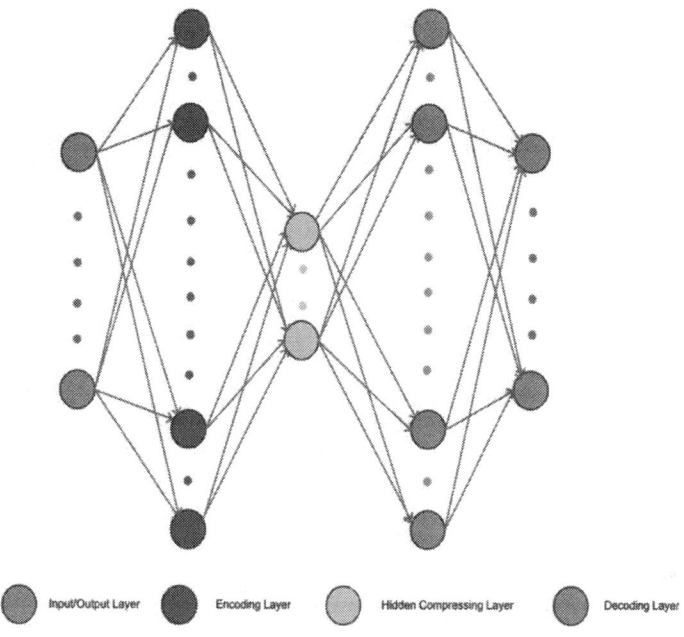

Figure 5.48: Architecture of an Auto-Encoder

Auto-encoders are trained with the same feature variables as input and output. For example, if X $(x_1, x_2, x_3, ... x_n)$ is the set of features in a dataset, then for an auto-encoder, X will be seeded in the input layer as well as in output layer. As said above, the purpose of the network is to re-generate the same input through encoding and decoding. The network is trained until and unless a fixed number of iterations are not done, or certain magnitude similarities are not found between input and output. We will see the practical use of Auto-Encoder in *Chapter 6: Miscelleneous Unsupervised Learning*.

Disadvantages of deep learning and neural network

So far, we discussed many practical usages of neural networks and deep learning. But, along with these, there isa risk/disadvantage associated with this:

- Neural networks are highly complex and difficult to tune. There are no hard and fast rules to decide parameters/hyperparameters of neural networks. Data scientists mostly rely on a heuristic approach for this.

- Any deep learning-based technique needs a large amount of data. If there are shortages of collected data, then it is always better to go for traditional techniques rather than deep learning.

- As the hidden layers and weights represent the virtual feature set of the data, neural networks are difficult to be used in **descriptive ML** practice. It cannot explain a certain behavior by a model. We should rely on traditional techniques for this. And it is also difficult to relate deep learning with the business context of the data. Deep learning models are always difficult to be explained to Business Analysts or target stakeholders who are not from a data science background. These are only ideal for the use case where we need perfect predictions.

- Deep learning techniques always need high-end hardware/infrastructure support. It may not always be possible to start developing/deploying deep learning models without a larger enterprise-level plan.

It is always preferable to think and analyze datasets, and requirements thoroughly decide applying deep learning models. It is better to explore other simpler models even though as long as the accuracy we are getting from those has a negligible difference.

Conclusion

In this chapter, we covered the architecture and mathematical details of neural networks, the concept of deep learning thoroughly. We learned about different components of a neural network and its anatomy. We have also learned how to develop a neural network using Python libraries and apply it to solving classical machine learning problems of classification and regression.

We have also learned how many different types of neural networks can be there. Among those, we studied **Convolution Neural Network (CNN)** in-depth and saw how to use it for analyzing images.

In the next chapter, we will learn a few unsupervised techniques, the definition of an outlier, and techniques to find them.

CHAPTER 6
Miscellaneous Unsupervised Learning

We know that unsupervised learning works with unlabeled data and without any knowledge of the target variable. We saw in *Chapter 4: Clustering* that how does it, group, objects without any predefined tags, which is an example of unsupervised learning. But clustering is not the only unsupervised technique. There are many more. Each one has different objectives. In this chapter, we will discuss more of this technique to solve another two primary problems in Machine Learning: *Dimensionality reduction and outlier detection.*

Structure

In this chapter, we will discuss:

- What we mean by dimensionality reduction and its importance
- **Principal Components Analysis (PCA)** as a primary dimensionality reduction technique and its application in classification and regression
- What do we mean by outlier detection and its importance
- Different unsupervised outlier detection techniques using Auto-Encoder, DBSCAN clustering, and Isolation tree.

Objective

After finishing this chapter, we will be able to

- Apply dimensionality reduction techniques like PCA in traditional classification and regression technique
- Apply specific outlier detection technique depending on the use case

Dimensionality reduction

In previous chapters, we studied various techniques of classification, regression, deep learning, clustering, and more. All of those dealing with a certain amount of data with various dimensions. Sometimes, dimension size is so huge that it creates a lot of problems in terms of optimization and performance of the ML model. As we know, dimensions are nothing but features of the model. But, do we need all the features to build a model? We will try to find the answer to this question from an example. Let us try to understand a picture of a landscape. We can easily identify rivers, trees, hills from it. When we see it from close, the identification process is easier. But, when we see it from a considerable distance, we can still do it. So, looking at it from far does not stop us from recognizing individual natural objects. We may not need very minute details of a river, hill, or tree to identify it. Just an overall idea of the shape and color is sufficient for it. This is dimensionality reduction. We already saw a small technical example of it in *Chapter 3: Regression* chapter. There we implemented the Forward Selection algorithm to choose the right set of features for linear regression modeling. It reduces the number of features. Dimensionality reduction helps us to understand the dataset more easily, reduce noise, reduce computationally, and operational cost of the algorithm without or with a very negligible compromise in the accuracy.

There are many dimensionality reduction techniques available. But here, we will discuss only **Principal Component Analysis (PCA)** in the next section.

Principal Component Analysis (PCA)

It says about transforming the coordinate system of the feature set into a new one in an unsupervised manner. The transformed features will be chosen by the dataset itself without any prior knowledge. New features will contain the most variant part of the dataset so that maximum information can be carried forward. These transformed features are known as **Principal Components (PC)** of the original features. There can be multiple PCs, and each one is directionally orthogonal or perpendicular to another one if projected in a vector space. Forward Selection of Linear Regression approach selects a small set of original and physical features among all others. For example, if the original feature consists of 10 features, say $f_1, f_2,.., f_{10}$, then maybe by *forwarding Selection*, four of them are selected, say f_3, f_6, f_9 & f_{10}. So, these are the original features only. But, in the case of PCA, features get transformed. We cannot say whether PC 1 is f_1 or f_2 or not. These are transformed, and virtual representation of original features and do not exist physically in the dataset.

Let us consider a sample 2D plot of the two-dimensional dataset:

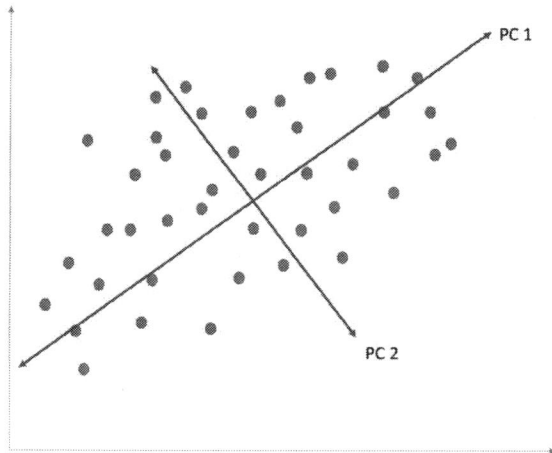

Figure 6.1: *Principal Components Co-ordinate Systems*

PCsproduce new co-ordinate axes. In the above scatter plot, maximum variability in the data is captured by **PC 1** and **PC 2** axes. Just having the axes does not produce principal component values directly. These axes are just like normal X and Y axes in a different dimension to hold the data point values. We have to do the actual transformation of values to map those in these new dimensions. Projections of data points (as shown in below plot) on PC axes are the transformed PC values.

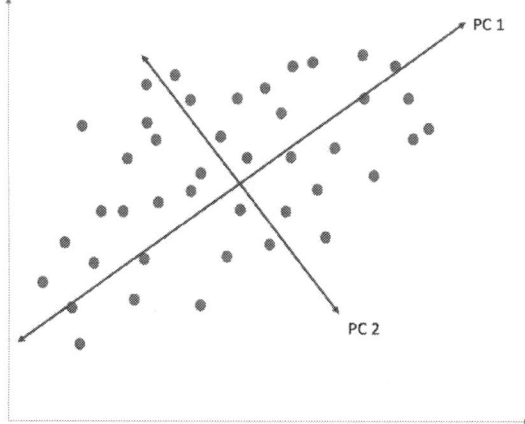

Figure 6.2: *Projection of a data point on PC co-ordinate system*

To explain things better, let us consider a pair of linear relations

$$y_1 = b_1 + w_1 x_1 + w_2 x_2$$

$$y_2 = b_2 + w_3 x_3 + w_4 x_4 + w_5 x_5$$

y_1 is a transformed variable from x_1 and x_2, whereas y_2 is from x_3, x_4, and x_5. So, to summarize, we can say that by the pair of linear transformations, a set of 5 variables: x_1, x_2, x_3, x_4, and x_5 are transformed into a pair of variables y_1 and y_2. If any two data points p_1 and p_2 have certain variability in the original five variables co-ordinate space, then a certain percentage of it can also be maintained in the new y_1 and y_2 based co-ordinate space. In simpler and high-level terms, if p_1 and p_2 can be separated by a distance d, then in new co-ordinate space, they can be separated by a certain percentage of d.

Principal components are orthogonal to each other. If there are n number of PCs, then these are all perpendicular (orthogonal) to each other in N-dimensional coordinate space. We can extract our maximum n number of PCs from N-dimensional original features. But, in practice, we would want to generate the number of dimensions quite less than n. There are multiple ways to compute principal components. We will discuss one of them in the next section.

Computation of PC from Covariance and Eigenvectors

We already discussed Eigenvectors and Eigenvalues in *Chapter 1: Introduction to Machine Learning*. We will use these to compute PCs. We know that the purpose of principal components is to capture most variability in the data. It also means that it should preserve the variance and reduce the dimensions. The variance of the multi-dimensional dataset can be obtained from the covariance matrix. It is a N x N matrix where $(i, j)^{th}$ element is the covariance between the ith and j^{th} feature. Below are the steps of computing PCs from a dataset:

1. Standardize all variables by zero mean and unit variance.
2. Compute the covariance matrix between all possible variable combinations.
3. Compute Eigenvectors and Eigenvalues of the covariance matrix.
4. Project principal component values by multiplying all original variables with Eigenvectors.

Eigenvalues obtained from the computation shows how much variance is explained by each of the principal components.

We will now create a set of dummy features and compute the principal components using Python library **numpy**. First, we will create a 1000 sample data records of

5-dimension and later will use PCA to reduce it to 2-dimension:

```
from numpy.random import randint

dataset = randint(low=10, high=650, size=(1000, 5))
dataset
```

```
array([[582, 409, 248, 113, 207],
       [390, 591, 193, 646, 163],
       [311, 558, 547,  80, 164],
       ...,
       [352, 520, 423, 579, 210],
       [ 42, 619, 181, 275, 141],
       [ 73, 454, 529, 326, 446]])
```

Figure 6.3: Code snippet to create a random dataset

Next, intervariable covariance will be computed after transforming using a StandardScaler (For making the distribution to have zero mean and unit variance):

```
from numpy import cov
from sklearn.preprocessing import StandardScaler

scaled_dataset = StandardScaler().fit_transform(dataset)
A = cov(scaled_dataset)
A
```

```
array([[ 1.03085333,  0.06713458,  0.52376508, ..., -0.10941273,
        -0.05925923, -0.58544404],
       [ 0.06713458,  1.34964611, -0.15831764, ...,  0.72295648,
         0.82031135, -0.34674728],
       [ 0.52376508, -0.15831764,  1.36692089, ...,  0.15670598,
         0.59875293,  0.41382997],
       ...,
       [-0.10941273,  0.72295648,  0.15670598, ...,  0.55932057,
         0.53025287,  0.01455662],
       [-0.05925923,  0.82031135,  0.59875293, ...,  0.53025287,
         1.3837021 ,  0.49935759],
       [-0.58544404, -0.34674728,  0.41382997, ...,  0.01455662,
         0.49935759,  0.92007999]])
```

Figure 6.4: Code snippet to compute the covariance matrix from the dataset

Eigenvalues and Eigenvectors can be computed by `eig` function which takes covariance matrix as input and returns a tuple:

```
from numpy.linalg import eig

eig_vals, eig_vectors = eig(A)
```

Figure 6.5: Code snippet to compute Eigenvalues & Eigenvectors

In the next step, a dot product of scaled features and Eigenvectors will produce all possible principal components. We will only take the top 2 of those:

```
import numpy as np

np.dot(eig_vectors.T, scaled_dataset)[:,[0,1]]
array([[-21.51829045+0.j       ,   4.34499193+0.j        ],
       [ 15.92213644+0.j       , -18.12735671+0.j        ],
       [  6.42322197+0.j       ,   2.10609466+0.j        ],
       ...,
       [  0.14388496+0.j       ,   0.14388496+0.j        ],
       [  0.43805401+0.12720919j,   0.43805401+0.12720919j],
       [  0.43805401-0.12720919j,   0.43805401-0.12720919j]])
```

Figure 6.6: Code snippet to get principal components

We had to transpose the Eigenvector matrix to match the dimensions required for dot product. As a final result of all steps described above, a five-dimensional dataset got converted to a two dimensional one.

We will now discuss PCA with a real dataset. The `scikit-learn` already has a class named PCA for this, which can be added in a pipeline along with other preprocessing transformers. We have to do standard scaling like the previous example before doing PCA.

We will use Wholesale Customer's dataset from the UCI Machine Learning Repository (https://archive.ics.uci.edu/ml/datasets/Wholesale+customers) for understanding PCA. Let's explore the dataset first:

```
encoded_df = pd.get_dummies(df, columns=['Channel','Region'])
encoded_df.head()
```

	Fresh	Milk	Grocery	Frozen	Detergents_Paper	Delicassen	Channel_1	Chanı
0	12669	9656	7561	214	2674	1338	0	
1	7057	9810	9568	1762	3293	1776	0	
2	6353	8808	7684	2405	3516	7844	0	
3	13265	1196	4221	6404	507	1788	1	

Figure 6.7: Code snippet to read Wholesale Customer's dataset and result

This dataset holds information about product wise sales across different channels and regions. From the description available in the UCI portal, we can observe that channel and region are categorical variables, and the rest is all continuous. Though channel and region contain integer values, these are repetitive, so as per theory, we can consider these as categorical. Our objective is to study variable relationships and apply PCA to reduce dimensions.

We can convert the categorical variables (`Channel` and `Region`) using `get_dummies` function of `pandas` and get the encoded dataframe:

```
encoded_df = pd.get_dummies(df, columns=['Channel','Region'])
encoded_df.head()
```

	Fresh	Milk	Grocery	Frozen	Detergents_Paper	Delicassen	Channel_1	Channel_2	Region_1	Region_2	Region_3
0	12669	9656	7561	214	2674	1338	0	1	0	0	1
1	7057	9810	9568	1762	3293	1776	0	1	0	0	1
2	6353	8808	7684	2405	3516	7844	0	1	0	0	1
3	13265	1196	4221	6404	507	1788	1	0	0	0	1
4	22615	5410	7198	3915	1777	5185	0	1	0	0	1

Figure 6.8: Code snippet to apply One-Hot-Encoder transformation

We can now study the relationship between `Detergents_Paper` and `Milk` using scatter plot:

```
%matplotlib inline

import matplotlib.pyplot as plt

plt.scatter(encoded_df['Detergents_Paper'], encoded_df['Milk'])
plt.xlabel('Detergents_Paper')
plt.ylabel('Milk')
plt.show()
```

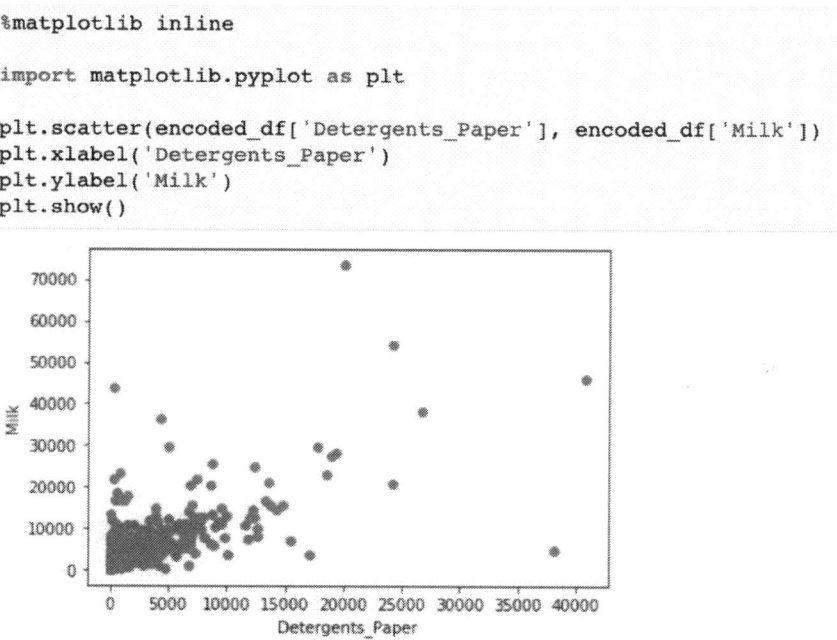

Figure 6.9: Code snippet to plot Detergent Paper vs. Milk from the dataset

Some high concentration is there between 0-5000 units of `Detergents_Paper` and 0-10000 units of `Milk`. Now let us take the first two principal components of just these two variables using a pipeline. The `scikit-kit` provides a class named PCA to do that:

```
from sklearn.decomposition import PCA
from sklearn.preprocessing import StandardScaler
from sklearn.pipeline import Pipeline

pca_1 = PCA(n_components = 2)
pca_pl_1 = Pipeline(steps = [('scaler', StandardScaler()),
                            ('pca', pca_1)])
pca_pl_1.fit(encoded_df[['Detergents_Paper','Milk']])
pca_transformed_1 = pca_pl_1.transform(encoded_df[['Detergents_Paper','Milk']])
pd.DataFrame(pca_transformed_1).head()
```

	0	1
0	0.339411	-0.401026
1	0.446089	-0.323891
2	0.383089	-0.194671
3	-0.793804	0.088694
4	-0.201041	-0.126941

Figure 6.10: Code snippet to design a pipeline for PCA

PCA class takes one parameter n_components, which specifies how many principal components we want to generate from the data. It can take the number of original features likethe maximum value. As PCA is unsupervised, no target variable was mentioned, and it generates components by understanding the existing dataset (as per theory explained earlier).

PCsare transformed values in a different coordinate space, so ranges will be completely different. Just by looking at it, we will not understand the significance.

Let us plot the PCs and see the pattern:

```
plt.scatter(pca_transformed_1[:,0], pca_transformed_1[:,1])
plt.xlabel('PC 1')
plt.ylabel('PC 2')
plt.show()
```

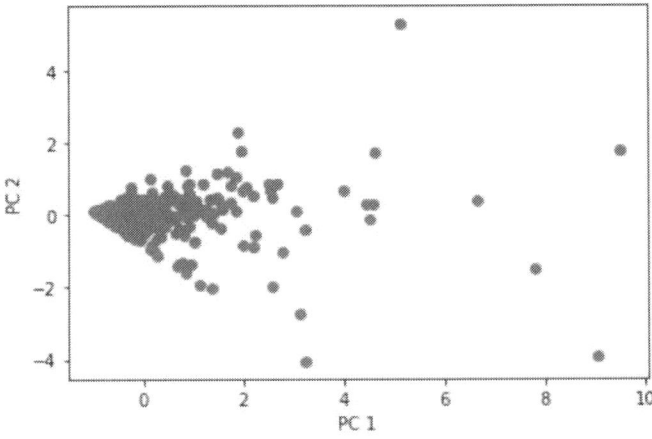

Figure 6.11: Code snippet to plot two primary PCs from the dataset

We can observe that it is explaining the same pattern of the original variables. As it is a two-variable case, it may be easy to understand from the plot, but for a multi-variable case, we have to analyze the correlation between them.

We can see the explained variance by each of the PCs as an array (size of the array equals the number of PCs):

```
pca_1.explained_variance_ratio_
```

```
array([0.83090784, 0.16909216])
```

Figure 6.12: Code snippet to get explained variance ratio of the PCs

It is quite obvious that the first PC is the most important one and explaining maximum variance in the data (83%).

Now, we can write another pipeline by taking all the features and computing PCA from there:

```
%matplotlib inline

from sklearn.decomposition import PCA
from sklearn.preprocessing import StandardScaler
from sklearn.pipeline import Pipeline

pca_95 = PCA(0.95)
pca_pl_95 = Pipeline(steps = [('scaler', StandardScaler()),
                              ('pca', pca_95)])
pca_pl_95.fit(encoded_df)
pd.DataFrame(pca_95.explained_variance_ratio_).plot()
plt.show()
```

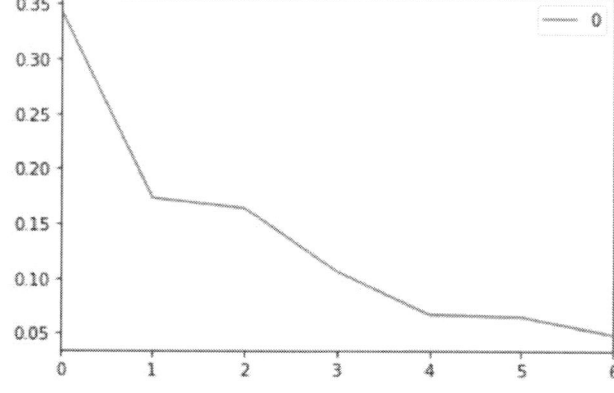

Figure 6.13: Code snippet to plot explained variance ratios of all PCs from the dataset

One important thing to be noticed here. We used PCA(0.95) constructor instead of the PCA(n_components) in the above example. Both two have different meanings. PCA(0.95) says that a set of PCs is needed that will explain a total sum of 95% variance of the data. How many PCs needed is never mentioned there, unlike PCA(n_components). It will dynamically decide the number of components. We plotted the PC number vs. Percentage Variance Explained. So, a total 95% variance is explained by 7 PCs. And Percentage Variance Explained is decreasing with an increasing PC number. From the plot, we can observe that around 34% variance is explained by PC 0, around 17.5% by PC 1, and so on.

We can also see the cumulative plot of variance explained:

```
import numpy as np

pd.DataFrame(np.cumsum(pca_95.explained_variance_ratio_)).plot()
plt.show()
```

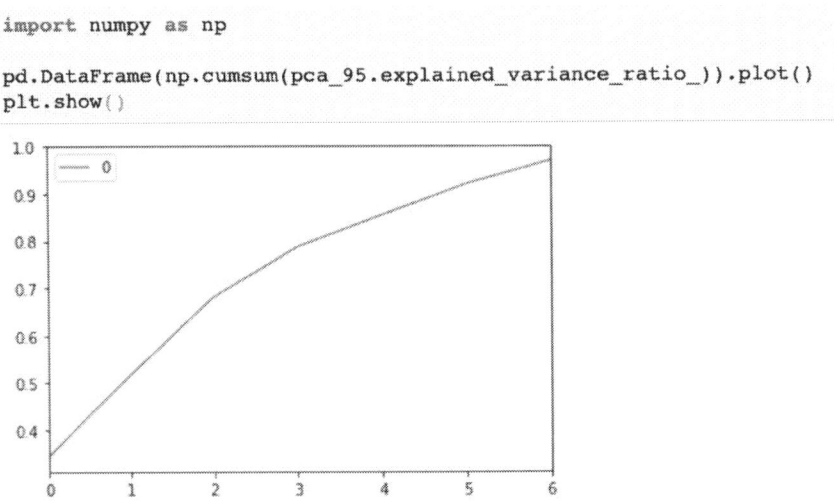

Figure 6.14: Code snippet to plot cumulative explained variance ratios of all PCs from the dataset

The cumulative plot shows how the explained variance increases when the number of principal components increases. There is a junction point where an increasing principal component does not do a significant increase in variance explained part. We can get the optimal number of PCs from there. In the above plot, there is a junction point at PC 3, which almost explains around 79% (probable) of the variance. So, three here is the optimal number of PCs.

PCA and Co-relation coefficient

PCs can reduce the correlation between the transformed variables. It helps in optimizing many models. We can first observe the co-relation coefficients between all pairs of original variables:

```
encoded_df.corr().style.background_gradient(cmap='coolwarm').set_precision(2)
```

	Fresh	Milk	Grocery	Frozen	Detergents_Paper	Delicassen	Channel_1	Channel_2	Region_1	Region_2	Region_3
Fresh	1	0.1	-0.012	0.35	-0.1	0.24	0.17	-0.17	-0.033	-0.058	0.067
Milk	0.1	1	0.73	0.12	0.66	0.41	-0.46	0.46	-0.019	-0.033	0.039
Grocery	-0.012	0.73	1	-0.04	0.92	0.21	-0.61	0.61	-0.027	0.046	-0.0092
Frozen	0.35	0.12	-0.04	1	-0.13	0.39	0.2	-0.2	-0.0068	0.069	-0.042
Detergents_Paper	-0.1	0.66	0.92	-0.13	1	0.069	-0.64	0.64	-0.022	0.069	-0.021
Delicassen	0.24	0.41	0.21	0.39	0.069	1	-0.056	0.056	-0.026	-0.045	0.054
Channel_1	0.17	-0.46	-0.61	0.2	-0.64	-0.056	1	-1	0.088	-0.06	-0.033
Channel_2	-0.17	0.46	0.61	-0.2	0.64	0.056	-1	1	-0.088	0.06	0.033
Region_1	-0.033	-0.019	-0.027	-0.0068	-0.022	-0.026	0.088	-0.088	1	-0.16	-0.74
Region_2	-0.058	-0.033	0.046	0.069	0.059	-0.045	-0.06	0.06	-0.16	1	-0.55
Region_3	0.067	0.039	-0.0092	-0.042	-0.021	0.054	-0.033	0.033	-0.74	-0.55	1

Figure 6.15: Code snippet to plot the correlation matrix of original variables

The `corr` function in `pandas` dataframe computes correlation coefficients for all pairs of variable combinations under the calling dataframe. The `cmap` style coolwarm specifies that cells with more reddish and bluish shade have a correlation coefficient close to +1 and -1, respectively.

We will now apply PCA transformation on all of the variables and take the first three principal components:

```
from sklearn.decomposition import PCA
from sklearn.preprocessing import StandardScaler
from sklearn.pipeline import Pipeline

pca = PCA(n_components = 3)
pca_pl = Pipeline(steps = [('scaler', StandardScaler()),
                           ('pca', pca)])
pca_pl.fit(encoded_df)
pca_transformed = pca_pl.transform(encoded_df)
pca_transformed_df = pd.DataFrame({'PC 1': pca_transformed[:, 0],
                                   'PC 2': pca_transformed[:, 1],
                                   'PC 3': pca_transformed[:, 2]})

pca_transformed_df.head()
```

	PC 1	PC 2	PC 3
0	1.511220	0.228095	-1.127748
1	1.697774	0.237829	-1.032925
2	1.798824	1.057406	-0.223328
3	-1.290635	0.953700	-0.200953
4	1.230277	1.199619	-0.153445

Figure 6.16: Code snippet to compute top 3 PCs from the dataset

Now, we can see the co-relation coefficients among those:

```
pca_transformed_df.corr().style.background_gradient(cmap='coolwarm')
                    .set_precision(2)
```

	PC 1	PC 2	PC 3
PC 1	1	-3.1e-16	-3e-16
PC 2	-3.1e-16	1	-4.3e-16
PC 3	-3e-16	-4.3e-16	1

Figure 6.17: Code snippet to plot the correlation matrix of PCs

We can observe that inter PC co-relations are almost close to zero. It is proof of the statement we made earlier that PCsare independent of each other.

We can also compute the cosine similarities between the PCs:

```
from sklearn.metrics.pairwise import cosine_similarity

cosine_sim = cosine_similarity(pca_transformed_df.transpose())
cosine_sim_df = pd.DataFrame(data={'PC 1': cosine_sim[:, 0],
                                   'PC 2': cosine_sim[:, 1],
                                   'PC 3': cosine_sim[:, 2]}, index=['PC 1', 'PC 2', 'PC 3'])

cosine_sim_df.style.background_gradient(cmap='coolwarm').set_precision(2)
```

	PC 1	PC 2	PC 3
PC 1	1	-3.5e-16	-3.3e-16
PC 2	-3.5e-16	1	-4.2e-16
PC 3	-3.3e-16	-4.2e-16	1

Figure 6.18: Code snippet to plot cosine similarity matrix of PCs

So, inter-PC cosine similarities are showing close to zero; that is, these are orthogonal or perpendicular (900 angles as `cos (900) = 0`) to each other.

Classification using principal components

As discussed earlier, PCsare actually alternative features which can be used in any model. We saw how to use Naïve Bayes Classifier in *Chapter 1: Classification*. We used the **Online Shoppers Intentions** dataset there. This time also will use the same for PCA based approach and build the model. We have to do featuresand target variable separation, train, and test data splitting in the same manner. We will skip discussing those and jump into the direct pipeline building for the model. Here, one extra step will be the PCA after `StandardScaler`.

```
from sklearn.decomposition import PCA
from sklearn.pipeline import Pipeline
from sklearn.preprocessing import StandardScaler
from sklearn.naive_bayes import GaussianNB

gnb_pca = PCA(0.98)
gnb_pipeline = Pipeline(steps = [
                        ('cat_var_encoder',
                         CategoricalVariableEncoder(categorical_features=['Month','VisitorType','Weekend'])),
                        ('scaler', StandardScaler()),
                        ('pca', gnb_pca),
                        ('nb_clf', GaussianNB())
                        ]
                 )
gnb_pipeline.fit(train_x, train_y)
```

Figure 6.19: Code snippet to design pipeline for building a classifier with PCA

We have used the same `CategoricalVariableEncoder` estimator, as done in *Chapter 1: Classification*. We have to `GaussianNB` as PCA produces all continuous features.

We can test the model accuracy:

```
gnb_pipeline.score(test_x, test_y)
```

```
0.8049472830494728
```

Figure 6.20: Code snippet to compute the accuracy of the PCA based classifier

It is giving better accuracy than Naïve Bayes without PCA.

Naïve Bayes Classifier relies on the conditional independence of the features. Most of the time, original features are not at all conditionally independent of each other. Finding out pairs of such features is a long and computationally heavy process. PCA sometimes helps here by finding out un-correlated features and which have the potential to be used as conditionally independent. Though, statistically, there is no assurance that un-correlated features will always be conditionally independent. Co-relation coefficient just says how the change in one feature affects the other feature, whereas conditional independence deals with the influence of the occurrence of events on each other.

We had a total 29 features as below:

```
len(pd.get_dummies(page_visits_x, columns=['Month','VisitorType','Weekend']).iloc[0,:])
29
```

Figure 6.21: Code snippet to get the total number of features

Now, PCA reduced it to 11 features:

```
len(gnb_pca.explained_variance_ratio_)
```

```
11
```

Figure 6.22: Code snippet to get the total number of PCs

So, there is a significant drop in the number of features. It will have a major impact on the performance of the classifier.

Regression using principal components

We can use PCA for regression exactly in a similar fashion like Classification and build the pipeline. PCA reduces the multi-collinearity (refer *Chapter 3: Regression*) problem and produces a set of features having co-linearity almost zero. These features can be used in building the pipeline for Linear Regression, Lasso, or Ridge Regression.

Key points to remember about PCA

- PCA helps to reduce the complexity and training time of the model a lot. Principal components can be used as alternative features in place of the original features in any model. These are especially useful in situations where having an independent feature set is a prior requirement.

- PCA can never tell the underlying physical feature combination. By graphical plot, we can intuitively assume some of its structure, but that is also not fool-proof. In that sense, it is a black box.

- PCA sometimes lose out important characteristics of the data. For that, it is always preferable to use PCA very carefully. As it is a linear projection of the data, using PCA on the dataset having a very complex non-linear feature combination can cause a lot of information loss.

PCs are linear projections of original variables. It is always preferable to use it in building linear models rather than non-linear. The moment we use PCs, it vanishes off the non-linear flavors of the data and only captures the linear part. It is always better to do a proper experiment with the data before making any final decision.

Unsupervised outlier detection

Outlier a.k.a. Anomaly is the data object which is different from most of the other objects. In general, any domain of datasets contains objects sharing some common characteristics. We discussed earlier that the primary objective of Machine Learning is to find that common pattern of the characteristics. But many times, there are also objects which don't follow these patterns. These objects can be there in any dataset. Most of the time, we build models by including them, and it affects accuracy. Many systems and business applications need outliers to be detected at the earliest to avoid loss or major failure. For example, in credit card transactions, identifications of a fraudulent one are very important. It saves the customer from losing a lot of money. A fraudulent transaction is an outlier over here, which is different from other normal transactions.

Another example could be network intrusion detection. These intrusions are nothing but attacks on computer networks or systems. These attacks result in huge security threats or system failure causing **DoS (Denial of Service)**. If we study network logs, then we can see that these attacks have some abnormal network statistics different from normal ones and indicate of being an outlier.

Most of the use cases we discussed earlier don't come with a tagged outlier flag. We may not have the knowledge base of the proper definition of an outlier so that a model can be trained on it. So, the problem becomes unsupervised as per ML theory like Clustering. Like clustering, outliers can be spotted from a scatter diagram. We can see a sample 2-D plot and outliers below:

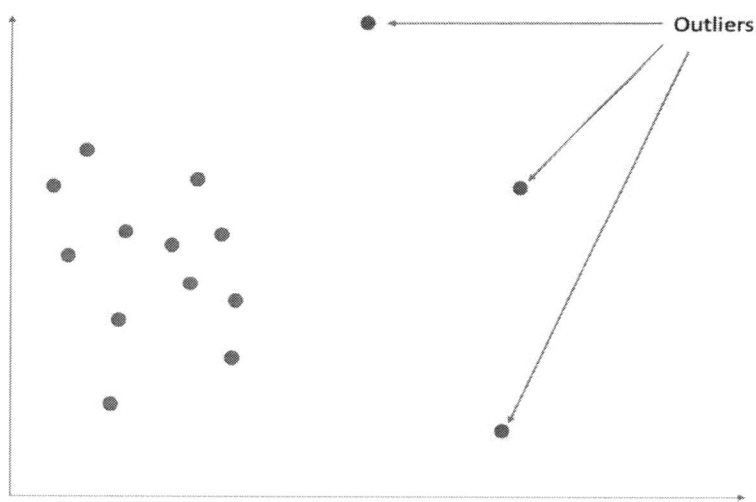

Figure 6.23: Sample outliers for a 2-D dataset

We can see that outliers (data points in red) lie far away from other data points. There are significant distances present within the outliers also.

Generally, the number of outliers is very few as compared to normal data points. If we take the ratio number of outliers/number of total data points, then it will come close to zero in most of the cases. Statistically, it can be said that outliers are rare events, and the probability of rare events is close to zero or less than some predefined threshold. This threshold is domain-specific and should be supplied externally.

In the next section, we will discuss some of the unsupervised techniques to determine potential outliers from a dataset.

Outlier detection using Auto-Encoder

We have already seen a basic architecture of Auto-Encoder in the Deep Learning chapter. It is a special type of feed-forward Neural Network where input and output layer features are the same. Before that, we will discuss the problem statement and the dataset.

For this, we will use Credit Card Fraud Detection dataset from Kaggle (https://www.kaggle.com/mlg-ulb/creditcardfraud). We will explore the data first:

```
import pandas as pd

df = pd.read_csv('../data/creditcard.csv')
df.head()
```

V5	V6	V7	V8	V9	...	V21	V22	V23	V24	V25	V26	V27	V28	Amount	Class
-0.338321	0.462388	0.239599	0.098698	0.363787	...	-0.018307	0.277838	-0.110474	0.066928	0.128539	-0.189115	0.133558	-0.021053	149.62	0
0.060018	-0.082361	-0.078803	0.085102	-0.255425	...	-0.225775	-0.638672	0.101288	-0.339846	0.167170	0.125895	-0.008983	0.014724	2.69	0
-0.503198	1.800499	0.791461	0.247676	-1.514654	...	0.247998	0.771679	0.909412	-0.689281	-0.327642	-0.139097	-0.055353	-0.059752	378.66	0
-0.010309	1.247203	0.237609	0.377436	-1.387024	...	-0.108300	0.005274	-0.190321	-1.175575	0.647376	-0.221929	0.062723	0.061458	123.50	0
-0.407193	0.095921	0.592941	-0.270533	0.817739	...	-0.009431	0.798278	-0.137458	0.141267	-0.206010	0.502292	0.219422	0.215153	69.99	0

Figure 6.24: Code snippet to read & display Credit Card Fraud dataset

The dataset contains transaction details done through credit cards. Column **Amount** is the spent money through the card, and **Class** denotes whether the transaction is fraudulent or not. Value 1 for **Class** says it is fraudulent, and 0 says it is not. Features **V1** to **V28** is the virtual features. These are the first 28 PCs taken from the original physical features of transactions. As per Kaggle, original features were not given for security reasons.

Now, this question may arise that as we already have records tagged with 0 or 1, which denotes fraudulent or non-fraudulent, then why are we talking about unsupervised techniques? There is a reason. While building the model, we will never consider a `Class` variable in computation and will do it in a completely unsupervised manner. Later, to match the accuracy of our solution, we will use this `Class`.

Let us now understand the concept of an outlier from the dataset. At first, we will separate the `target` variable `Class` from the rest of the features. For our convenience, we will also not consider variable `Time` present in the dataset:

```
Y = df['Class']
X = df.drop(['Time','Class'], axis = 1, inplace=False)
```

Figure 6.25: Code snippet to divide the dataset into feature & target

Now, we will compute the class probabilities from the entire dataset:

```
prob_1 = Y[Y==1].count()/len(Y)
prob_0 = Y[Y==0].count()/len(Y)
prob_1,prob_0
```
```
(0.001727485630620034, 0.9982725143693799)
```

Figure 6.26: Code snippet to compute class probabilities from the entire dataset

The probability of class 1 is close to zero, thus making it a very rare event. By definition, records with class 1 are an outlier. We need to find records with class 1 in an unsupervised manner without involving the `Class` variable in the model.

Architecture of the Auto-Encoder for outlier detection

Including *Amount*, there isa total of 29 features in the dataset. As the *neural network* can be used for both supervised and unsupervised learning, we will use an *Auto-Encoder*, which takes 29 input features and produces the same 29 features as output. The architecture is shown below:

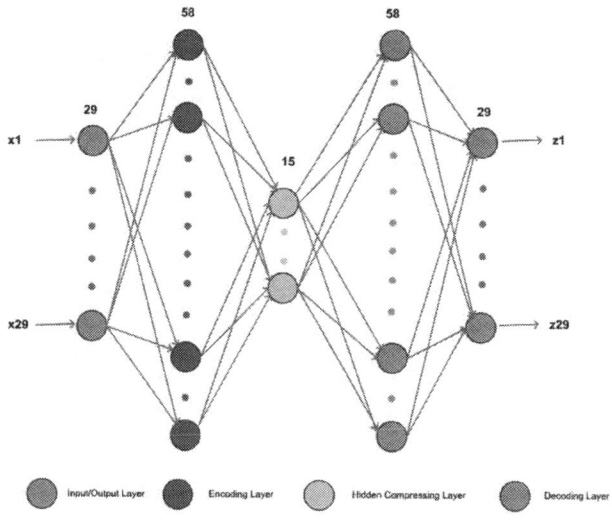

Figure 6.27: Architecture of the Auto-Encoder for Credit Card Fraud dataset

The *auto-encoder* consists of 5 layers, including three hidden layers. Layer structure looks like *29->58->15->58->29*. A multiply divide by powers of 2 rule is applied for deciding the number of nodes in each layer ($58 = 29 * 2$, $15 = 58 / 2^2$). It is quite a common convention in typical autoencoder architecture. Layer 1, Layer 2, and Layer 3 are responsible for encoding, compression, and decoding. The final output will come out from Layer 5. Outputs are the reconstructed version of the input. The entire network will try to find out common hidden patterns and apply the reverse procedure to reconstruct it at the end. It is analogous to the multivariable regression network. Any predictive ML model produces a certain amount of errors in the process, and so does the *auto-encoder*. As outliers present in the data don't follow the common hidden pattern of the majority, those tend to produce more errors at the end. The process of outlier detection is to capture these errors. Data instance, which causes more error production, tends to be a potential outlier.

Metric to measure outlier factor

We need a metric to capture reconstruction error at the end. We will use this as *Outlier Factor* to decide which are more potential outliers in a dataset.

If X_i is a data instance having d number of features and $X = (x_1, x_2, ..., x_d)$ and Z_i is the reconstructed version of X_i from the output layer, then *outlier factor* for the data instance X_i is OF_i and is given by the expression:

$$OF_i = \frac{1}{d} \sum_{j=1}^{d} \left| z_{ij} - x_{ij} \right|$$

It is the average absolute error generated across the features for a data instance. We can also take the square of the error instead of modulus. This factor also has to be scaled properly so that we can have a domain and feature independent metrics to compare data points.

Training of Auto-Encoder

As discussed earlier, an auto-encoder should be trained with the same set of features as both input and output. First, we will split the dataset into training and testing set:

```python
from sklearn.model_selection import train_test_split

train_x, test_x, train_y, test_y = train_test_split(X, Y, test_size=0.2)
```

Figure 6.28: Code snippet to split the dataset into train & test

Next, we will write a customer `Estimator` which will work as Auto-Encoder:

```python
from sklearn.base import BaseEstimator
from sklearn.neural_network import MLPRegressor
from sklearn.metrics import r2_score
from sklearn.preprocessing import MinMaxScaler
from statistics import mean
import numpy as np

class AutoEncoder(BaseEstimator):

    def __init__(self, layers):
        self.mlp_reg = MLPRegressor(hidden_layer_sizes=layers)
        self.min_max_scaler = MinMaxScaler(feature_range=(0, 10))
        self.loss_ = None
        self.model_r2_ = None
        self.outlier_factors_ = None

    def _compute_outliers_factors_(self, X_Input, X_Output):
        dimension = len(X_Input[0])
        n = len(X_Input)
        outlier_factors = []
        for index in range(n):
            value_differences = []
            for dim_index in range(dimension):
                value_differences.append(abs(X_Input[index, dim_index] - X_Output[index, dim_index]))

            outlier_factors.append(mean(value_differences))

        return np.asarray(outlier_factors).reshape(-1, 1)

    def fit(self, X, y=None):
        self.mlp_reg.fit(X, X)
        self.loss_ = self.mlp_reg.loss_curve_
        X_Output = self.mlp_reg.predict(X)
        self.model_r2_ = r2_score(X, X_Output)
        outlier_factors = self._compute_outliers_factors_(X, X_Output)
        self.min_max_scaler.fit(outlier_factors)
        self.outlier_factors_ = self.min_max_scaler.transform(outlier_factors)
        return self

    def decision_function(self, X):
        X_Output = self.mlp_reg.predict(X)
        outlier_factors = self._compute_outliers_factors_(X, X_Output)
        return self.min_max_scaler.transform(outlier_factors)
```

Figure 6.29: Code snippet of AutoEncoder class as custom Estimator

As discussed earlier, auto-encoder is a multivariable regressor network; we have used `MLPRegressor` as the neural network class (refer *Chapter 5: Deep Learning for more details*). Inside the fit function, we have trained the `MLPRegressor` with the same feature array X as input and output. The `_compute_outlier_factors_` calculates outlier factors for the dataset and returns those as an array. We have used the mean of the absolute differences of features as outlier factor. Later these factors are scaled by a `MinMaxScaler` to give it a value range between 0 and 10 for convenience.

Before actual training, features have to be scaled using `StandardScaler` to reduce cross-feature variance as we are using a regressor over here. However, `StandardScaler` cannot reduce the effect of outliers in the dataset. Everything can be added in a pipeline and trained on the training dataset.

```python
from sklearn.neural_network import MLPRegressor
from sklearn.preprocessing import StandardScaler
from sklearn.pipeline import Pipeline

auto_encoder = AutoEncoder(layers=(53,15, 53,))
auto_encoder_pl = Pipeline(steps=[('scaler',StandardScaler()),
                                  ('auto_encoder', auto_encoder)])
auto_encoder_pl.fit(train_x)

Pipeline(memory=None,
         steps=[('scaler',
                 StandardScaler(copy=True, with_mean=True, with_std=True)),
                ('auto_encoder', AutoEncoder(layers=None))],
         verbose=False)
```

Figure 6.30: Code snippet to design the pipeline of the AutoEncoder

We can see the previously discussed layer structure (58, 15, 58) is passed in the constructor of `AutoEncoder` class.

We can now get the R2 measure of the internal regression process:

```
auto_encoder.model_r2_

0.9784853319522269
```

Figure 6.31: Code snippet to get R2 of the regressor

Almost 97% variance is explained by the network, which is quite scored!! But, it also depends on how many outliers are present in the dataset.

We can plot the loss generated in the entire iterative process:

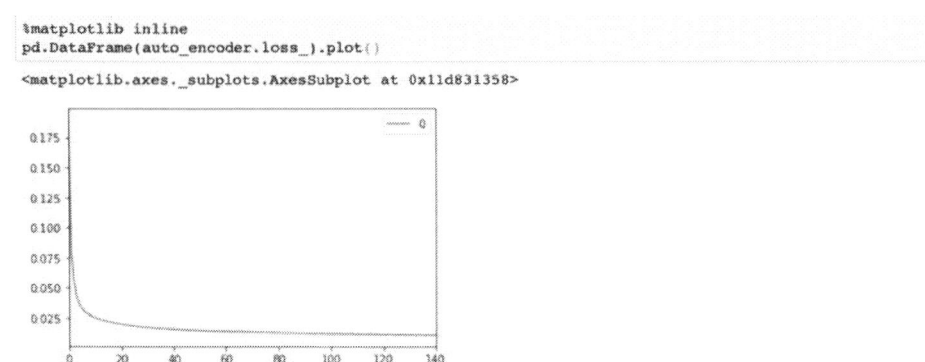

Figure 6.32: Code snippet to plot the loss curve of AutoEncoder regressor

Loss is showing a negative exponential pattern, which is a good sign. Now, we will see a histogram plot of the outlier factors:

```
import matplotlib.pyplot as plt

plt.figure(figsize=(25,15))
plt.hist(auto_encoder.outlier_factors_, bins='auto')
plt.title("Histogram for Outlier factors")
plt.show()
```

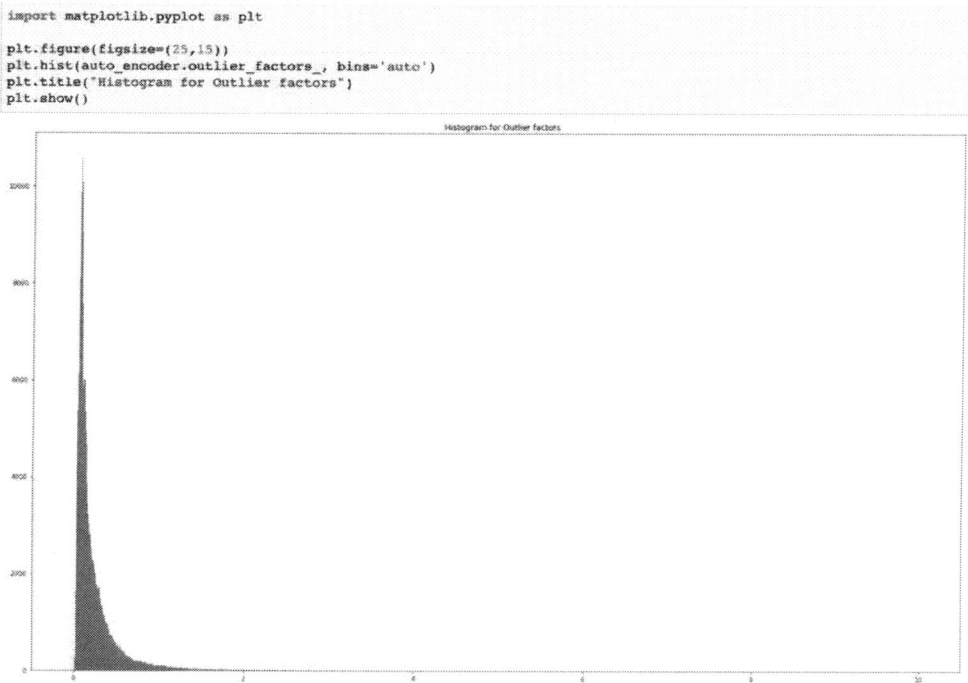

Figure 6.33: Code snippet to plot the histogram of outlier factors

It automatically bins the outlier factor values and counts how many data instances fall under that (Y-axis is the count of data instances, and the X-axis is the outlier factor values). We can see a clear pattern that lower outlier factor values have higher counts, which is quite normal. It means that a larger number of data instances produce less reconstruction error.

We visually confirm a threshold outlier factor around 2.0 (could also be around 2.3) from the plot. There are quite a smaller number of data points having an outlier factor above 2.0. So, the derived conclusion is that data points having outlier factor higher than 2.0 are potential outliers. We can save this information as a trained model along with trained `MLPRegressor` and `MinMaxScaler`.

Visual confirmation of threshold may not always be possible and not recommended, especially models trained on production systems. We may have to check the underlying statistical distribution, and if it follows Gaussian, then $\mu \pm n\sigma$ rule can be applied to get proper threshold value in a non-manual and automated way.

We can get the statistical properties of the outlier factors by converting it into a `pandas` dataframe and calling `describe` function:

```
pd.DataFrame({'OF': auto_encoder.outlier_factors_[:,0]}).describe()
```

	OF
count	227845.000000
mean	0.078820
std	0.106502
min	0.000000
25%	0.028436
50%	0.049265
75%	0.096321
max	10.000000

Figure 6.34: Code snippet to get statistical properties of outlier factors

But, we have to remember that if the distribution of outlier factors is not Gaussian, then $\mu \pm n\sigma$ may give the wrong result. So, some statistical tests can be done to be sure about the distribution.

Testing the result

We can compute outlier factors for test data and apply the threshold 2.0 on it to get the list of potential outliers. We will use the trained model for this.

```
outlier_factors_test = auto_encoder_pl.decision_function(test_x)
predicted_y = np.where(outlier_factors_test < 2.0, 0, 1)
```

Figure 6.35: Code snippet to apply decision function on test data

As the process is unsupervised, there are no produced `target` variable values to get and compare. But, from the outlier factor values, we can create one and compare it with the original test data.

Data instance having factor value greater than 2.0 is tagged with 1 (potential outlier) otherwise 0. Thus, we can get an array (named as `predicted_y`) of 0 and 1, which is similar in structure to test data array `test_y` for target variable `Class`.

The `decision_function` defined in the `AutoEncoder` class predicts the reconstructed value first and then applies the outlier factor computation technique to get the scaled factor value. It uses the same trained `MLPRegressor` and `MinMaxScaler`.

We will now see how the outliers are placed in a series of 2-D plots. Each plot will be for a pair of principal components as given in the feature set. We can write a generic function for this:

```
import matplotlib.pyplot as plt

def plot_outliers(X, Y, var_index_1, var_index_2):
    plt.scatter(x=X.iloc[Y == 1, [var_index_1]].values,
                y=X.iloc[Y == 1, [var_index_2]].values,
                s=20, color='red', marker='>')
    plt.scatter(x=X.iloc[Y == 0, [var_index_1]].values,
                y=X.iloc[Y == 0, [var_index_2]].values,
                s=20, color='green', marker='+')
    plt.xlabel('V' + str(var_index_1 + 1))
    plt.ylabel('V' + str(var_index_2 + 1))
```

Figure 6.36: Code snippet of plot_outliers function

Now, this function is called with different variable indices:

```
predicted_y_shaped = predicted_y.reshape(1,-1)[0]
plt.figure(figsize=(10,10))
plt.subplot(321)
plot_outliers(test_x, predicted_y_shaped, 0, 1)
plt.subplot(322)
plot_outliers(test_x, predicted_y_shaped, 2, 3)
plt.subplot(323)
plot_outliers(test_x, predicted_y_shaped, 4, 5)
plt.subplot(324)
plot_outliers(test_x, predicted_y_shaped, 6, 7)
plt.subplot(325)
plot_outliers(test_x, predicted_y_shaped, 8, 9)
plt.subplot(326)
plot_outliers(test_x, predicted_y_shaped, 10, 11)
```

Figure 6.37: Code snippet to plot outliers for w.r.t each pair of PCs

And it produces the following plot:

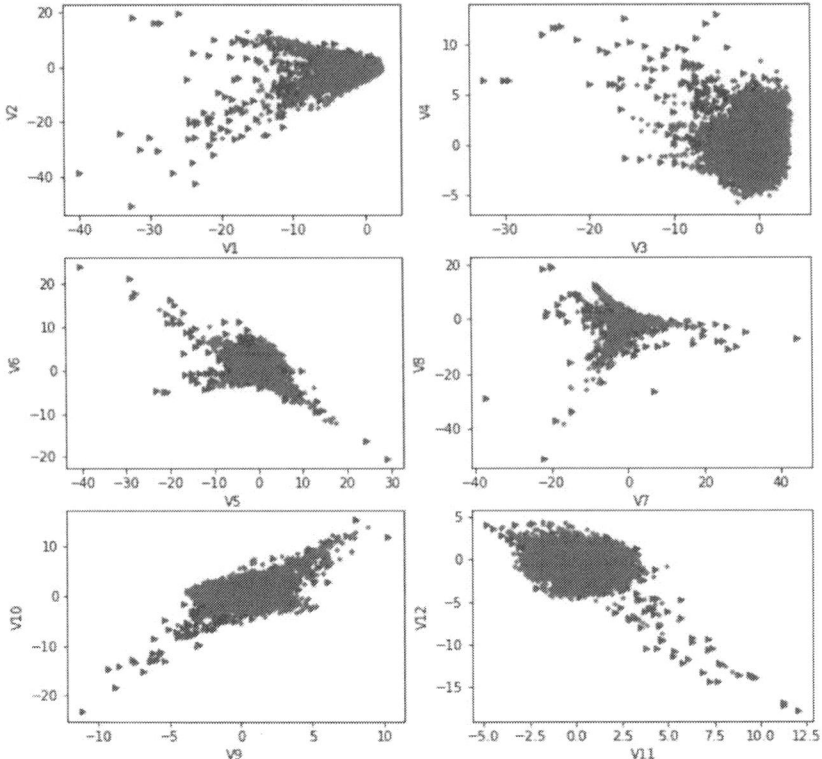

Figure 6.38: *Plot of outliers (in red points) w.r.t each pair of PCs*

Red points denote outliers. We can observe that those are mostly well separated. As we are visualizing with respect to only two variables, a little bit of overlapping would be there. Including a greater number of variables will give a better separated picture.

We can apply the normal classification accuracy metric to compare `predicted_y` and `test_y`:

```
from sklearn.metrics import accuracy_score
accuracy_score(test_y, predicted_y)
0.9960675538078017
```

Figure 6.39: *Code snippet to compute the accuracy of outlier detection*

Almost 99% of accuracy is achieved.

Key points to remember about Auto Encoder based outlier detection

1. By virtue of the deep learning, auto-encoders are excellent in finding out complex hidden patterns present in very large dimensional datasets. It captures non-linearity present in the data well.

2. By default, `MLPRegressor` uses Adam optimizer, but we can try with other optimizers to experiment on case to case basis.

3. Auto-Encoders should not be used if sufficient training data is not available.

4. Similar to other deep learning models, it needs sufficient memory and other hardware support for quick and successful execution.

In general, `AutoEncoder` based approach works well in outlier detection in Computer Vision or Digital Signal data (like voice or video) based problem.

Outlier detection using clustering

We already know that the clustering algorithm can group unlabeled data points and identify patterns. It is an unsupervised technique and can be used to find potential outliers from the dataset. We will discuss several clustering approaches and their ability for outlier detection.

Center-based clustering algorithm for outlier detection

The silhouette coefficient metric of the center-based clustering algorithm can give some idea of a potential outlier. A Silhouette coefficient value close to zero for a data point indicates that it should not belong to any cluster properly. Though the process, it gets an assigned cluster; ideally, it should have been left alone. Absolute values of Silhouette coefficients for all data points can be sorted in increasing order to get top *n* outliers.

Though the approach stated above is partially correct, but the problem lies in the basic formation of some center-based approach like KMeans. The silhouette coefficient-based approach would only work in situations where cluster formation is perfect. It assumes that the centroid location is perfectly balanced. But, as the statistical measure mean itself is very sensitive to outliers, so computing means (for KMeans) from a dataset having a lot of extreme values as outliers would produce a very skewed value. It will heavily affect the cluster formation, and the centroids will not showcase the proper information center. So, outlier detection using the Silhouette coefficient will also be affected, and practically it will leave out actual outliers. Instead of KMeans, we could use KMedoids, which considers the statistical median as a cluster center instead of the mean. But it is not also completely foolproof.

Keeping all limitations in mind, it is preferable not to use center-based clustering algorithms for outlier detection.

Density-based clustering algorithm for outlier detection

We have already discussed DBSCAN in *Chapter 4: Clustering*. It is based on density or reachability and does not use any central tendency metric for cluster center computation. It rejects out noise data points at the end, which are not possible to be put into any cluster. We can say that these noise points are outliers.

For this one also, we will use the same Credit card Fraud Detection dataset. But, as DBSCAN is a very computationally expensive algorithm, it may take a lot of resources and time to finish the task. That's why for our convenience, we will shrink the data size a bit by repetitive splitting and use the final split as train and test dataset:

```
from sklearn.model_selection import train_test_split

train_x_1, _, train_y_1, _ = train_test_split(X, Y, test_size=0.25)
train_x_2, _, train_y_2, _ = train_test_split(train_x_1, train_y_1, test_size=0.25)
train_x_3, _, train_y_3, _ = train_test_split(train_x_2, train_y_2, test_size=0.25)
train_x, test_x, train_y, test_y = train_test_split(train_x_3, train_y_3, test_size=0.25)
```

Figure 6.40: Code snippet to shrink the dataset for convenience

Like the Auto-Encoder approach, we will not use the tagged target variable `train_y` anywhere in the model building. We will validate the result with the `test_y` exactly in the same fashion as done earlier.

We will use the same heuristics and visual confirmation approach for determining DBSCAN parameters `EpsandMinPts`, as discussed in the *Chapter 4: Clustering*. For that, we need to do a K-distance plot of data points under `train_x` with heuristically determined *K* as a log of the record size. Before that, we need to use `StandardScaler` to normalize `train_x`:

```
from sklearn.preprocessing import StandardScaler

standard_scaler = StandardScaler()
standard_scaler.fit(train_x)
scaled_train_x = standard_scaler.transform(train_x)
```

Figure 6.41: Code snippet to apply standard scaler on the variables

We will use the same `plot_k_distance` function as defined in *Chapter 4: Clustering*:

```
from sklearn.neighbors import NearestNeighbors
from math import log
import numpy as np
import matplotlib.pyplot as plt

def plot_k_distance(X):
    K = round(log(len(X)))
    nn = NearestNeighbors(n_neighbors=K)
    nn.fit(X)
    distances, indices = nn.kneighbors(X)

    distances = np.sort(distances, axis=0)
    distances = distances[:,1]
    plt.plot(distances)
```

Figure 6.42: Code snippet of plot_k_distance function

The function should be called with `scaled_train_x`:

```
plot_k_distance(scaled_train_x)
```

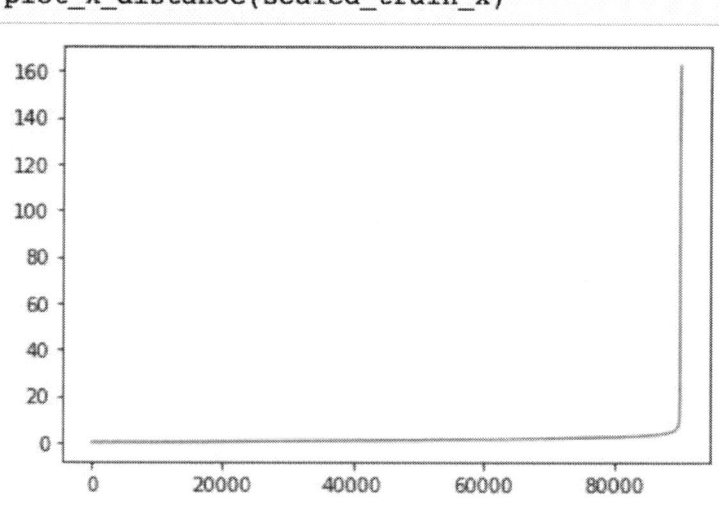

Figure 6.43: K distance plot of the dataset

We can observe an elbow point at around the Y-axis value 5.0, and it can be used as `Eps`. It is a rough estimation based on the visual confirmation only. The actual value may differ a bit.

Now, clustering should be done on the data points under `scaled_train_x`. We will get a list of noise points as outliers from the training data. Our end goal is to use this as a model so that we can predict outliers from the testing dataset. But DBSCAN does not give any direct technique to do that. We can design an algorithm like below:

1. Get the list of core points from the model.
2. For a test data point, compute its distances from all core points.
3. Find the minimum of the computed distances of Step 2.
4. Declare the test data point as an outlier if the minimum distance is greater than `Eps`; otherwise, declare it as non-outlier.
5. Go to Step 2 for the next test data point.

So, the concept is pretty simple. A test data point is an outlier if its minimum distance from any of the core points is greater than `Eps`. We can design a custom `Estimator` like we have done so far for other models.

```python
from sklearn.base import BaseEstimator
import multiprocessing
from sklearn.metrics.pairwise import euclidean_distances
from sklearn.cluster import DBSCAN

class DBSCANOutlierDetector(BaseEstimator):

    def __init__(self, eps, min_pts):
        self.dbs_clusterer = DBSCAN(eps=eps, min_samples=min_pts, n_jobs=(multiprocessing.cpu_count() - 1))
        self.core_pts = None

    def fit(self, X, y=None):
        self.dbs_clusterer.fit(X)
        self.core_pts = X[self.dbs_clusterer.core_sample_indices_]
        return self

    def predict(self, X):
        core_pts_distance = euclidean_distances(X, self.core_pts, squared=False)
        x_n = len(X)
        outlier_ind = []
        for index in range(x_n):
            distance_core_pt = min(core_pts_distance[index,:])
            if (distance_core_pt <= eps):
                outlier_ind.append(0)
            else:
                outlier_ind.append(1)

        return np.asarray(outlier_ind)
```

Figure 6.44: Code snippet of DBSCANOutlierDetector as Estimator

`DBSCANOutlierDetector` defines an overridden fit function that runs a DBSCAN cluster creation process with the given `Eps` and `MinPts`. The`core_pts` array stores all of the core point indices of the training data. We have implemented the previously discussed algorithm for the prediction of test data inside `predict` function. The function returns a 1-D array of 0 or 1, where 1 indicates an outlier.

We should add `DBSCANOutlierDetector` in a pipeline. We could have used `scaled_train_x` directly, but to make the pipeline reusable for test data, we will use `train_x` and add a `StandardScaler` stage separately:

```python
from sklearn.pipeline import Pipeline

eps = 5.0
min_pts = round(log(len(train_x)))
dbscan_outlier_pl = Pipeline(steps = [
                            ('scaler', StandardScaler()),
                            ('dbscan', DBSCANOutlierDetector(eps=eps, min_pts=min_pts))
                            ]
                        )
dbscan_outlier_pl.fit(train_x)

Pipeline(memory=None,
        steps=[('scaler',
                StandardScaler(copy=True, with_mean=True, with_std=True)),
               ('dbscan', DBSCANOutlierDetector(eps=None, min_pts=None))],
        verbose=False)
```

Figure 6.45: Code snippet to design pipeline with DBSCANOutlierDetector

We have used the estimated value 5.0 from the elbow plot for `Eps` and a heuristic estimate of the log of the total number of training records for `MinPts`.

We can now use this pipeline's `predict` function to get the array of outlier indicators for test data:

```
outlier_ind = dbscan_outlier_pl.predict(test_x)
```

Figure 6.46: *Code snippet to apply trained pipeline on test data*

We will use the same function defined in Auto-Encoder section for visualization of outliers:

```
plt.figure(figsize=(10,10))
plt.subplot(321)
plot_outliers(test_x, outlier_ind, 0, 1)
plt.subplot(322)
plot_outliers(test_x, outlier_ind, 2, 3)
plt.subplot(323)
plot_outliers(test_x, outlier_ind, 4, 5)
plt.subplot(324)
plot_outliers(test_x, outlier_ind, 6, 7)
plt.subplot(325)
plot_outliers(test_x, outlier_ind, 8, 9)
plt.subplot(326)
plot_outliers(test_x, outlier_ind, 10, 11)
```

Figure 6.47: *Code snippet to plot outliers for w.r.t each pair of PCs*

And it produces the following plot:

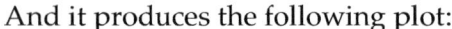

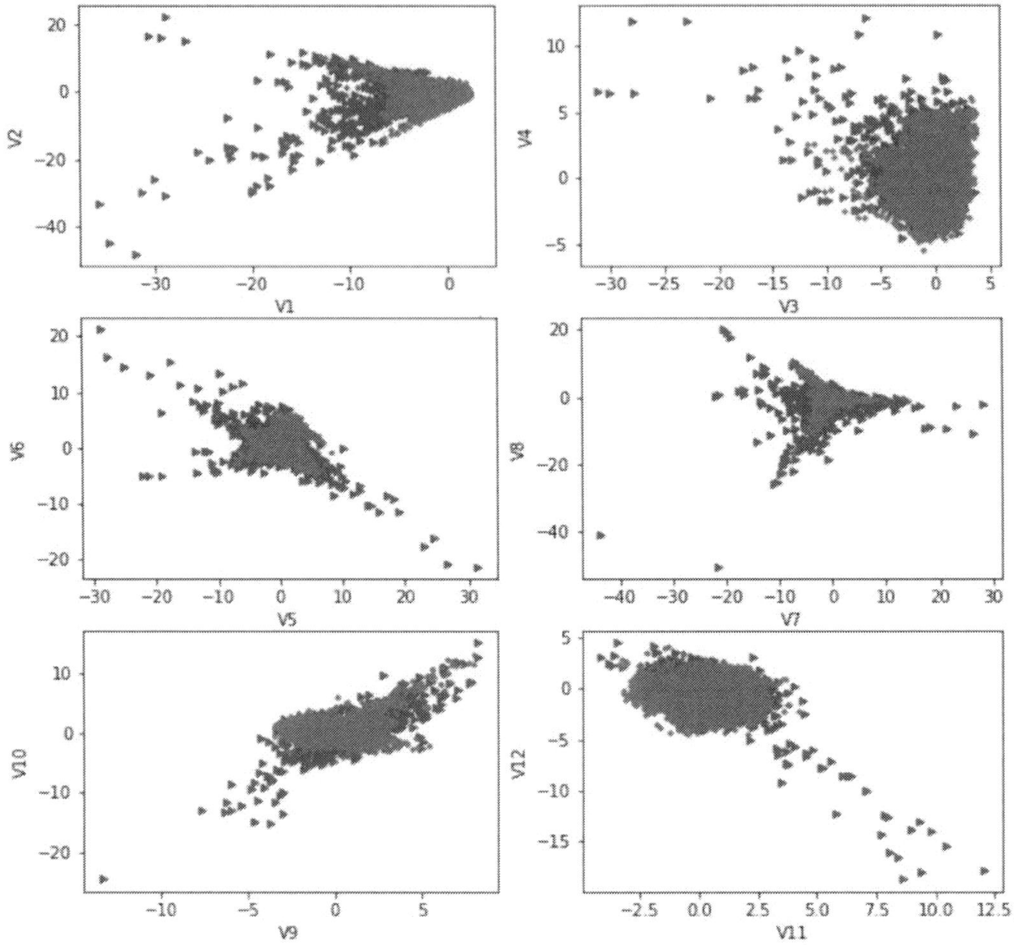

Figure 6.48: Plot of outliers (in red points) w.r.t each pair of PCs

We can see a similar kind of plots. But it seems like separation of outliers is better than Auto-Encoder results.

Testing the accuracy

We can test accuracy with the `test_y` dataset by conventional classification accuracy metric:

```
from sklearn.metrics import accuracy_score

accuracy_score(test_y, outlier_ind)
```

0.9812570743724616

Figure 6.49: *Code snippet to test the accuracy*

Almost 98% of accuracy is achieved.

Key points to remember about DBSCAN based outlier detection

1. DBSCAN can identify arbitrary shapes in the data. It helps in determining outliers where decision boundaries are very complex.

2. DBSCAN can work well even if there are fewer data.

3. The main challenge with DBSCAN approach is the performance and resource consumption. It is a greedy approach, and run-time complexity is very high (refer to *Chapter 4: Clustering*). Also, it does not give a good result with very high dimensional data.

DBSCAN based outlier detection technique can be a very good fit for finding abnormalities in geolocation data. Having some random patterns is very commonly observed there which DBSCAN can identify and throw out noises from there well.

Outlier detection using Isolation Forest

Isolation Tree is a special kind of binary decision tree that tries to search a data point at each level, depending on feature values. The name Isolation indicates that the search procedure is a step by step narrowing down or separation process. It works on the similar principals of a typical **Binary Search Tree** (BST). Let us first create a BST from a random array [56, -27, 19, 30, 2104, 34, 35, 47, 40]. The process of creating BST is just to keep on inserting elements one by one and maintain the node property. Created BST will look like below:

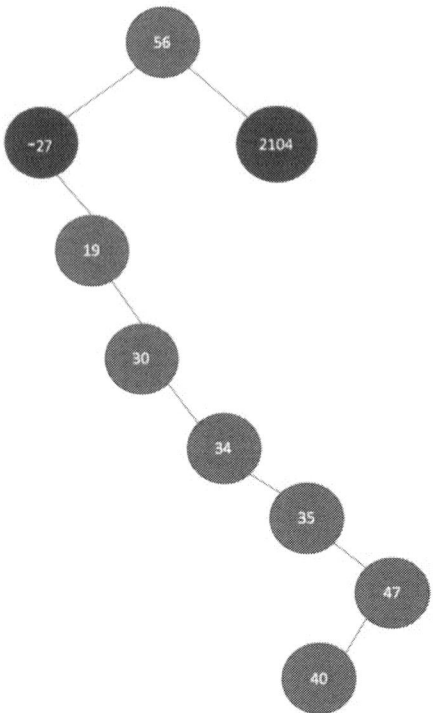

Figure 6.50: A typical BST with outliers/noisy data

Now, if we have to search for 34 in this BST, we need to travel down fourlevels to reach there. But, in the case of -21 or 2104, just 1 level travel is sufficient for finding them out. Just by looking at the array, we can figure out manually that -21 and 2104 are outliers. So, in BST, outliers are highly probable to stay at the higher level of the tree and can be found out earlier than those others. The length of the path needed to be traveled maybe a score to determine how potentially strong these outliers are. A lower value of the path length indicates a strong outlier that can be separated earlier than others. But one condition is applied over here. The array elements should be completely randomly generated. If the array is sorted or if the BST is made height-balanced after each time an element is inserted, then the property of potential outlier discussed earlier may be lost.

Isolation Tree

An Isolation Tree should have a similar property as potential outliers have in BST. But the formation of the tree from a dataset is done a bit differently than BST. The algorithm is given below:

If A is a set of attributes where $A = \{A_1, A_2,..., A_d\}$ and X is a data point where $X = \{x_1, x_2, ..., x_d\}$ then

1. Create a current node, and a randomly selected attribute A_p is chosen from the set$A$ and a random split value q is chosen from A_p values.

2. Two branch nodes T_l & T_r are created such that T_l having values $A_p < q$ and T_r having valued $A_p > q$

3. Choose T_l & T_r as current nodes and repeat from Step 1 if either one of the condition met:

    a. If at any node $|A| = 1$, that is, no more attributes are pending to be chosen.

    b. If the node contains data points having the same values.

    c. If the certain predefined height of the tree is reached.

Unlike traditional BST, split value is not the middlemost value of the sorted array or the current element in that array (In normal case, BST is constructed by setting the first element of the array as the root node. In the previous example, 56 was the root element). It is done to have a random nature in the tree to boost the outlier identification process. A more balanced tree lessens the outlier finding chances. An external node of the Isolation Tree is the node where the tree-building process ends. It is analogous to the leaf node of BST. Reaching to an external node while searching an item indicates an unsuccessful search; otherwise, it is considered successful. The entire approach is unsupervised as the target label was never considered or not even known to us.

Isolation Forest

Isolation Forest is an ensemble of Isolation Trees like Random Forest. Dataset is divided into several sub-samples, and a collection of Isolation Tree is built from each of these sub-samples.

We need to have an outlier score for a data point search. One rough estimation could be the direct path length from root to the corresponding node where the search ends. But this metric could grow proportionately with n (total records) and is not stable. For an alternative metric, we need several other metrics to be defined as follows:

* $h(x)$: Path length of a search for data point x in an Isolation Tree.

* $c(n)$: Average path length of unsuccessful search for data point x given n. It can be formularized from the theory of BST like below:

$$c(n) = 2H(n-1) - \frac{2(n-1)}{n}$$

where,

$$H(n-1) = \log(n-1) + 0.577$$

- $E[h(x)]$: Average path length of the search for a data point in the ensemble (collection of Isolation Trees, a.k.a Forest). From all of the above metrics, the final outlier score is formulated as:

$$s(x, n) = 2^{-\frac{E[h(x)]}{c(n)}}$$

$s(x, n)$ is bounded between 0 and 1. A higher value close to 1 indicates a strong outlier. The score can be further normalized to have positive and negative values for better understanding.

We will use the same **Credit Card Fraud** detection dataset here also to build and test this model. We will follow the same approach of not considering the target variable `Class` to make it unsupervised.

We will do similar training and testing data splitting:

```
from sklearn.model_selection import train_test_split

train_x, test_x, train_y, test_y = train_test_split(X, Y, test_size=0.25)
```

Figure 6.51: Code snippet to split the dataset into train & test

The training dataset has to be scaled properly using `StandardScaler` to get a better result. We will use scikit-learn's `IsolationForest` class to do the actual task. Both of these two can be added in a pipeline and trained using the fit function:

```
from sklearn.pipeline import Pipeline
from sklearn.ensemble import IsolationForest
from sklearn.preprocessing import StandardScaler
import multiprocessing

isf_pl = Pipeline(steps=[('scaler',StandardScaler()),
                  ('isolation_forest', IsolationForest(n_jobs = (multiprocessing.cpu_count() - 1)))])
isf_pl.fit(train_x)
```

Figure 6.52: Code snippet to design the pipeline with IsolationForest

The `decision_function` can compute the outlier scores, normalize it using an offset, and return the scores for all data points as an array.

We will get scores for all data points of the test dataset using the trained model above:

```
outlier_scores = isf_pl.decision_function(test_x)
```

Figure 6.53: Code snippet to apply the trained pipeline on test data

We can plot the `outlier_scores` using histogram:

```
%matplotlib inline
import matplotlib.pyplot as plt

plt.hist(outlier_scores, bins='auto')
plt.title("Histogram for Outlier Scores from Isolation Forest")
plt.show()
```

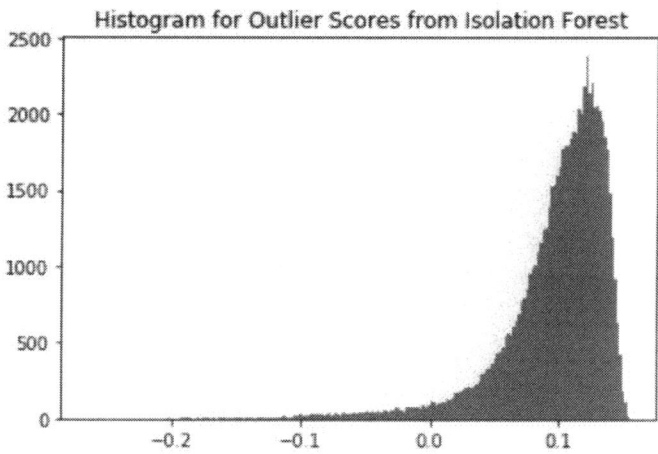

Figure 6.54: Code snippet to plot the histogram of outlier scores

It shows record counts of scores stored in auto-generated bins. From there, we can observe, a low score has a lower record count. It means data points having low scores are rare in the dataset and are potential outliers. As per sciki-learn's documentation, scores are adjusted by an offset, and anything less than zero can be tagged as the outlier.

We can now generate class labels from the scores. Any data point having scored less than zero will be tagged as 1 (outlier) otherwise 0 (normal):

```
import numpy as np
predicted_y = np.where(outlier_scores < 0, 1, 0)
```

Figure 6.55: Code snippet to tag (0 or 1) outliers based on scores

Now, we will use the same `plot_ouliers` function defined in previous models for plotting the data points:

```
plt.figure(figsize=(10,10))
plt.subplot(321)
plot_outliers(test_x, predicted_y, 0, 1)
plt.subplot(322)
plot_outliers(test_x, predicted_y, 2, 3)
plt.subplot(323)
plot_outliers(test_x, predicted_y, 4, 5)
plt.subplot(324)
plot_outliers(test_x, predicted_y, 6, 7)
plt.subplot(325)
plot_outliers(test_x, predicted_y, 8, 9)
plt.subplot(326)
plot_outliers(test_x, predicted_y, 10, 11)
```

Figure 6.56: *Code snippet to plot outliers for w.r.t each pair of PCs*

It will produce scatter plots with outliers in red:

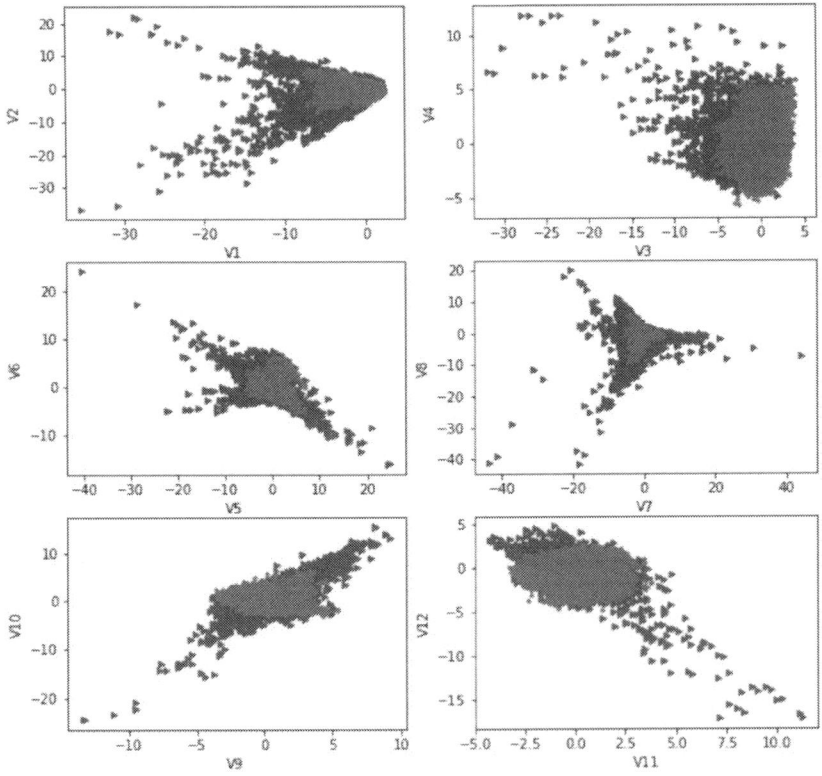

Figure 6.57: *Plot of outliers (in red points) w.r.t each pair of PCs*

This model is detecting more data points as outliers than DBSCAN or Auto-Encoder.

Accuracy

Accuracy can be computed similarly like other models:

```
from sklearn.metrics import accuracy_score

accuracy_score(test_y, predicted_y)
```
0.9631471026094772

Figure 6.58: Code snippet to test the accuracy

Almost 96% is achieved.

Key points to remember about Isolation Forest-based outlier detection

1. Isolation Forest works very well even for small datasets, unlike Auto-Encoder.

2. Both training time and prediction processes are very fast as compared to DBSCAN or Auto-Encoder. It is more suitable to integrate with very real-time systems wherefast response time is expected.

Isolation Forest is well suited for the use cases having a lot of irrelevant attributes and a lack of domain knowledge about the data.

Conclusion

This chapter gave a detailed analysis of unsupervised techniques for outlier detection and dimensionality reduction using principal components. It has explained what dimensionality reduction is, how does it help to boost performance, how does PCs reduce dimensions, and more. The definition of outliers has been explained. Three major unsupervised techniques of outlier detection have been given explained.

We got an idea about how to use principal components in any classical ML problems like *classification* or *regression* to reduce complexity. We discussed three different techniques of outlier detection and the corresponding model description. We also learned about the advantages/disadvantages of each technique and the typical use case where these are well suited.

In the next chapter, we will discuss how to process textual data, making it ready to use for any ML model (different vector space model to represent text actually) and solve typical problems of text classification and clustering.

CHAPTER 7
Text Mining

So far, we have discussed about problems that contains categorical and numerical data types. In the real world, the text is another widespread form of data type. Some of the very common text data we see in day to day life are emails, resumes, reviews of any restaurant or movies, any form of technical tutorials, and many others. Standard **machine learning (ML)** techniques like classification and clustering are very relevant in text data. For example, by reading a movie plot, we can say whether it is good or bad, or we can group similar movies by reading the plot. Text mining is the process of solving these types of problems by analyzing text, extract meaningful information from it. In this chapter, we will discuss various techniques for text representation and ML models for solving standard problems.

Structure

In this chapter, we will discuss:

- Techniques of text analysis and preprocessing
- Different vector space models: TF-IDF, Word2Vec, and Doc2Vec
- Comparison of different vector space models and typical scenarios for best use
- Standard text classification and clustering techniques
- Text visualization using bar chart and word cloud

Objective

After finishing this chapter, we will be able to

- Apply standard text preprocessing techniques and appropriate vector space models for text classification or clustering.
- Use different text visualization techniques for better representation.

Analyzing text

Categorical variables can be most similar to text data. But we consider categories as a whole and don't bother about its grammatical meaning. In almost all ML models, every feature has to be converted into some sort of numbers. Categorical data also get converted into numbers by transformations like One-Hot-Encoding. This is one of the characteristics of ML models that only understand numbers. So, to be on the same line, for building models using text, it has to be converted into numbers. But the question is, how? We will discuss some standard models for converting text into numbers. These are called **vector space models** (For more details about *vector space*, please refer to *Chapter 1: Classification*). Before applying these models, several pre-processing of text is needed. We will discuss those steps one-by-one.

What are a corpus and document?

A corpus is a collection or dataset of texts for a particular domain or multiple domains. In simple terms, we can say: the in-memory version of a corpus is an array of texts. We will be using this term many times in our discussion.

A text is also sometimes referred to as a document. We will be using this interchangeably with *text*.

Pre-processing of text

We all know that a text can contain verbs, adjectives, nouns, pronouns, conjunctions, and interjections. These are *parts of speech*. Apart from these, a text also contains punctuations and other symbols. If we see thoroughly, most of the meaningful information is contained by verbs and nouns. In a word, verbs and nouns primarily set the context of the text. So, before putting a text into a vector space model, a series of pre-processing steps are required. We can also call this as *cleaning*. By cleaning, we mean the removal of unwanted parts (which may not be that much relevant to ML algorithm) from text to make it more meaningful and context-aware.

If we don't do the *cleaning* then it does not mean that vector space model conversion is not possible, or any machine learning algorithm will not work. Those will work, but the accuracy and relevancy will be very low.

Steps of cleaning text

It is a typical unwanted parts removal process. It may contain a series of standards steps as given below:

1. Conversion to lower case.
2. Removal of extra spaces.
3. Removal of punctuations.
4. Removal of integers and numbers.
5. Removal of any unwanted tags like `<html>`, `<p>`, `<b>` (specially which are all for indentation or formatting purpose).
6. Removal of stop words like the, and, too, and more.
7. Stemming (conversion to the root form).

All other steps are self-explanatory except stemming. This is a technique that converts all verbs to its root or basic form from any kind of tense. Let's say if a text contains three words like 'play, "playing," played,' then we will convert all three into root-form play. It may happen that root form is not present in the text, but for our convenience, we will consider the root form only. In the above example, had there been only two words: 'played' and 'playing,' we would consider only 'play,' which is the root form.

We will see a practical example of the cleaning process by Python code. We will use Python library `gensim` for all these operations:

```python
import gensim.parsing.preprocessing as gsp

from gensim import utils as gs_utils

filters = [
            gsp.strip_tags,
            gsp.strip_punctuation,
            gsp.strip_multiple_whitespaces,
            gsp.strip_numeric,
            gsp.remove_stopwords,
            gsp.strip_short,
            gsp.stem_text
          ]

def clean_text(s):
    s = s.lower()
    s = gs_utils.to_unicode(s)
    for f in filters:
        s = f(s)
    return s
```

Figure 7.1: The cleaning process

Now, we will see the effect of applying `clean_text` on an example text:

```
str_1 = "<i>Hello</i> <b>World</b>! Th3    weather is really good today, isn't it?"
clean_text(str_1)
```

```
'hello world weather good todai isn'
```

Figure 7.2: Example of cleaning

All unwanted characters, spaces, and punctuations are removed. Though the cleaned text looks a little odd, it is essential for the execution of the model. We will see another example:

```
str_2 = "John loves playing football. He plays it regularly"
clean_text(str_2)
```

```
'john love plai footbal plai regularli'
```

Figure 7.3: Example of cleaning

We can see how stemming is working above. Sometimes correct spelling of the stemmed words gets changed. It depends on the type of stemmer being used. But it does not matter as long as it is holding the context of the text.

Vector space models of text

Vectors are n-dimensional data type of numbers. A vector space model converts a text into numbers, which are nothing but vectors. By this, texts get converted into real features. These features are then used in any machine learning algorithms instead of the original text. All vector space-related operations are appliedtothe text once it gets converted into a vector. We can measure similarity (refer to *Chapter 1: Classification*), take a norm, do summation, and more. Each of these pulls out meaningful information from the text. There are different types of vector space models available for text. We will discuss these in the next section.

Most of the vector space model needs tokenization of text before proceeding. Tokenization means splitting text by spaces. We will see an example:

```
clean_text(str_1).split()
```

```
['hello', 'world', 'weather', 'good', 'todai', 'isn']
```

Figure 7.4: Tokenization of text

So, text got split into an array of tokens, a.k.a. terms. This array is seeded into the vector space models.

TF-IDF model

TF-IDF model stands for **Term Frequency-Inverse Document Frequency**. It is so far the simplest vector space model. There are two concepts as described below:

*   **Term-Frequency (TF):** No of times a term/token appears in a text document of a corpus.
*   **Inverse Document Frequency (IDF):** No text documents in a corpus containing a particularterm/token.

Mathematically, IDF is expressed as an inverse function of the no of documents a term appears. TF-IDF is calculated for each term/token of a text document.

The mathematical expression of TF-IDF for a term is given by:

$$\left(TF\_IDF\right)_{i,j} = TF_{i,j} \times \log\left(\frac{N}{IDF_j}\right)$$

where $TF_{(i,j)}$ = number of occurrences of term j in document i.

N = total number of documents in a corpus.

IDF_j = number of documents containing term j.

$(TF\_IDF)_{(i,j)}$ = *tf-idf* measure of term j in document i.

So, for a document, *TF-IDF* becomes an array of numbers, that is, a vector. It represents the relative position/importance of that document in the entire corpus.

There are other different strategies to compute TF and IDF with different formulae (for example, log-normalization of *TF*).

Here, we will see the computation of *TF-IDF* with the formulae mentioned above through an example.

Let's take a sample corpus of three text documents like below:

*   Weather is really good today, isn't it?
*   Yesterday's weather was really bad!!

After cleaning texts, entire *TF-IDF* distribution per document looks like the below matrix:

Terms Documents	Weather	good	today	isn't	yesterday'	bad
Document 1	1 × log(2/2) = 0	1 × log(2/1) = 0.3	1 × log(2/1) = 0.3	1 × log(2/1) = 0.3	0 × log(2/1) = 0	0 × log(2/1) = 0

Document	1 × log(2/2)	0 × log(2/1)	0 × log(2/1)	0 × log(2/1)	1 × log(2/1) =	1 × log(2/1)
2	= 0	= 0	= 0	= 0	0.3	= 0.3

Table 7.1: Sample TF-IDF distribution

After cleaning, some of the tokens are removed. So, TF-IDF representation of documents can be written as vectors like below:

- *Weather is really good today, isn't it? = (0, 0.3, 0.3, 0.3, 0, 0)*

- *Yesterday's weather was really bad!! = (0, 0, 0, 0, 0.3, 0.3)*

Now, these vectors can be used in any ML algorithm instead of the original texts. We can use Python `scikit-learn` library for computing TF-IDF of a corpus. Below code can do that:

```
from sklearn.feature_extraction.text import TfidfVectorizer
corpus = [
    clean_text('Weather is really good today, isn't it?'),
    clean_text('Yesterday's weather was really bad !!')
]
vectorizer = TfidfVectorizer()
X = vectorizer.fit_transform(corpus)
print('TF-IDF matrix shape ' ,  X.shape)
print(X)
```

```
TF-IDF matrix shape   (2, 6)
  (0, 2)          0.534046329052269
  (0, 3)          0.534046329052269
  (0, 1)          0.534046329052269
  (0, 4)          0.37997836159100784
  (1, 0)          0.6316672017376245
  (1, 5)          0.6316672017376245
  (1, 4)          0.4494364165239821
```

Figure 7.5: TF-IDF computation

The differences in values are coming due to different strategies/formulas for calculating TF and IDF separately. This TF-IDF vector can also be used to find out the similarity of the texts. We will see it later.

Word2Vec model

This model works with words rather than complete texts. It is a vectored representation of words present in the corpus. But it helps in vector generation of complete texts. Unlike TF-IDF, Word2Vec tries to find out the contextual meaning of any particular word rather than just telling the raw frequencies. It is a much more complex model than TF-IDF.

There are two variants of this model: Skip-Gram and **CBOW (Continuous Bag of Words)**. Both techniques are dependent on the same common concept of analyzing neighborhood words of a particular word. There is a parameter called `window_size`, which has to be mentioned beforehand. `window_size` is the size of the neighborhood of word, that is, how many words are there within the specified window on both sides of a particular word.

Both of above mentioned two models are made of Neural Networks (please refer *Chapter 5: Deep Learning*) and are of a Multi-Layered perceptron in nature.

Skip-Gram Word2Vec model

It is a neural network made with three layers. The input layer is a one-hot-encoded word vector, the hidden layer is pass-through layer without any activation function, and the output layer is made of Softmax Probability function and spits out the probability of occurring each neighborhood word. The target word, that is, for which is we are trying to find out word vectors, is set into the input layer and neighborhood words into the output layer.

This network is trained by keeping the input the same with the target word and varying the output with different neighborhood words in a single batch. Training happens for all words in the corpus. In the end, values of hidden layer coefficients are used as word vector representation for each word. Input and output layers are just for the training purpose. Unlike normal neural network, our objective is not to get the values from the output layer, but from the hidden layers which capture the context the word intelligently.

We will see this for the sample text. *The quick brown fox jumped over the lazy dog.*

If we clean this text, then the content becomes a `quick brown fox jump lazi dog`. Now for a `window_size` of two, input and output training data become like following:

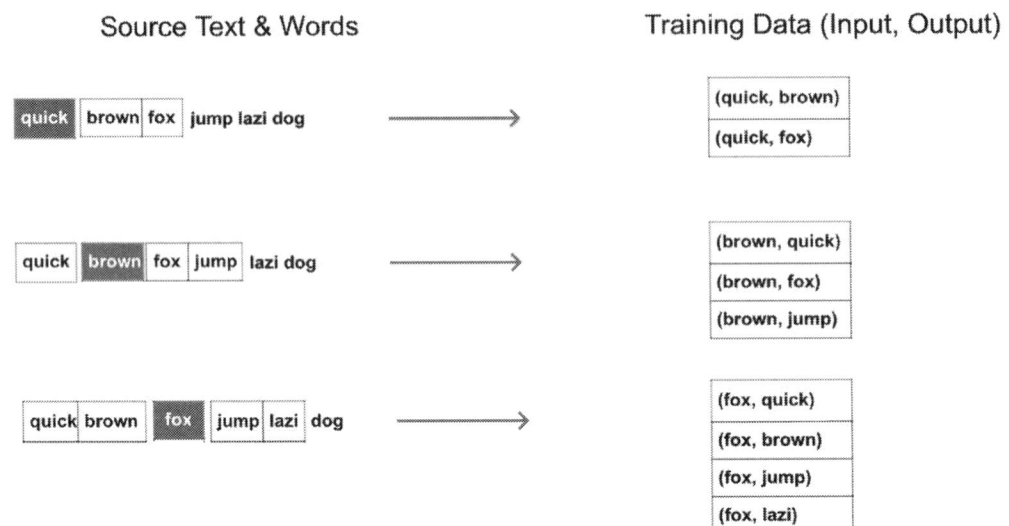

Figure 7.6: Word2Vec window analysis

The input word is the target word for which we are trying to get the word vectors, and output words are context words. From the training data combination, we can see that the input word is kept fixed, and output context words are kept varying.

This input, output combination is seeded in a neural network, as shown below:

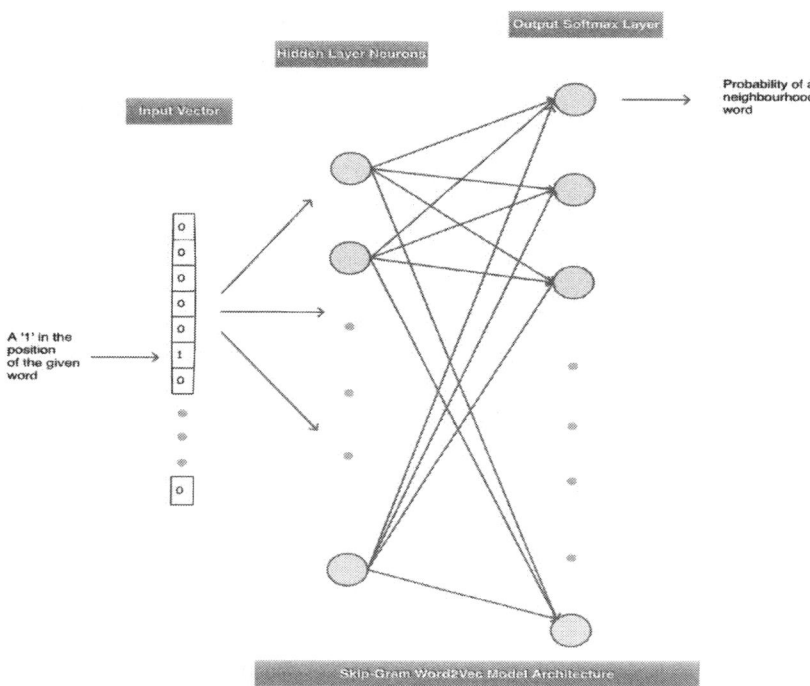

Figure 7.7: Word2Vec – Skip Gram Model

Each word of the corpus is trained separately with this neural network. At the end of the process, for each word, a vector representation is obtained from the hidden layer. That's our objective, and we can use that as a feature of the word in any ML algorithm.

CBOW (Continuous Bag of Words) Word2Vec model

A neural network architecture in CBOW is similar to Skip-Gram with one difference. Here target word is kept at the output layer, and context words are kept at the input layer, just an opposite situation of Skip-Gram. We try to predict a target word from its context. So, the input-output combination will be like this: [(brown, quick), (fox, quick)], [(quick, brown), (fox, brown), (jump, brown)],. And more. The output is kept fixed, and input is kept varying.

For both Skip-Gram and CBOW models, maintaining a proper size of the word vector is important. The size of word vectors is nothing but the size of the hidden layer in the Neural Network shown above. Generally, this size is kept at any value between 100 and 300. But, it is also a matter of experiment, and optimal value can be found by proper hyperparameter tuning.

Comparison of Skip-Gram and CBOW

CBOW is faster than Skip-Gram. But, Skip-Gram is always preferred in situations where we have infrequent but very domain-specific important words that carry a lot of context by their single presence.

Example of Word2Vec using python gensim library

Python's `gensim` library provides ready-made Word2Vec API. It uses the CBOW model of word vector generation. We will use a small sample corpus of three sentences and train the model. The default size of the word vector is 100 as per the API. Below code snippet gives an example of using `gensim` for Word2Vec:

```
from gensim.models import Word2Vec

sentences = [
        clean_text('The quick brown fox jumped over the lazy dog.').split(),
        clean_text('lazy dog always eats & sleeps').split(),
        clean_text('fox is a very clever animal').split()
]

w2v_model = Word2Vec(sentences, min_count=1)
w2v_model.train(sentences, total_examples=w2v_model.corpus_count, epochs=w2v_model.epochs, report_delay=1)

(6, 65)
```

Figure 7.7: Code snippet for training Word2Vec

Gensim does not have the `fit, transform,` and `predict` function combinations for any model, unlike `scikit-learn`. The `train` function above builds the model. The `min_count` parameter specifies that words having frequencies lower than this would be ignored. So, for our very small corpus, it is better to set it as 1. We can get the trained vector for any word like below:

```
w2v_model.wv['fox']
array([ 7.1389548e-04, -2.6116157e-03,  2.3899733e-03,  3.8155084e-03,
        3.5063776e-03,  4.0421989e-03, -1.8547628e-03,  3.0672151e-04,
       -1.6146308e-03,  4.1430378e-03, -4.3945787e-03,  1.6343076e-03,
       -1.7896242e-03,  4.3383106e-03, -4.0001902e-03,  4.8638876e-03,
        4.0260958e-03,  3.8172253e-03,  9.0236228e-04,  3.1559062e-03,
       -4.6137515e-03,  1.2563978e-03, -1.5235897e-03, -6.6659697e-05,
        8.0185430e-04,  3.5787257e-03,  3.6964237e-03,  2.5144350e-03,
        2.2449130e-03,  2.7306732e-03, -4.7686119e-03, -4.0213014e-03,
       -1.2074590e-03, -2.3785776e-03,  8.3335489e-04,  2.7944120e-03,
       -2.1570676e-03,  3.0105545e-03, -1.7749957e-03,  2.5714641e-03,
        2.7155136e-03,  3.9767558e-03, -8.3640782e-04,  2.0396828e-03,
        3.6737903e-03,  1.1100413e-03,  4.0761656e-03,  1.1594077e-03,
        1.7091498e-03, -2.1585757e-03, -2.7006508e-03, -2.0589800e-05,
       -4.3599927e-03,  1.8858127e-03,  4.9626082e-03,  3.3768364e-03,
       -4.5533860e-03,  4.7867470e-03,  1.5455976e-03,  1.0103919e-03,
       -4.8780679e-03,  5.1233947e-04, -4.8284880e-03, -2.2195068e-03,
        1.1239417e-04,  2.7535355e-03,  4.1526882e-03, -1.9736991e-04,
       -1.2923805e-04,  1.1842650e-03, -4.5934338e-03,  8.4561115e-04,
        1.6058665e-03,  7.3723041e-04,  2.1343010e-03, -3.5216040e-03,
       -2.4574075e-03,  2.4573163e-03, -4.3262248e-03,  2.0205604e-04,
       -5.0454523e-04,  2.6510938e-03, -1.9989018e-03, -2.1524925e-03,
       -1.7415507e-03, -3.5632055e-03,  4.5476574e-03, -5.5480079e-04,
       -4.8824335e-03,  2.1640682e-03, -4.4516651e-03,  2.2508781e-03,
       -9.7279734e-04, -1.0441840e-03, -7.2264631e-04,  2.7170437e-03,
       -4.2457674e-03, -1.8857830e-03,  1.2540387e-03, -3.5179944e-03],
      dtype=float32)
```

Figure 7.8: Code snippet for getting Word2Vec

So, a simple word fox got decomposed into a 100-length vector.

Doc2Vec model

Doc2Vec can generate vectors for the entire document/text (like TF-IDF) but in a context-sensitive way like Word2Vec. It is based on the concept of paragraph vectors, which are again one-hot-encoded vectors of all texts in the corpus. There are three ways of generating Doc2Vec, as discussed next.

Average of Word2Vec

It is the simplest of the Doc2Vec models available so far. If a document contains k number of words, then this Doc2Vec for model takes the average of k Word2Vec vector values of those words. Vector length becomes the same as Word2Vec.

Distributed Memory Model (PV-DM) of Doc2Vec

In this model, all word vectors and paragraph vectors are concatenated and trained together with the hidden layer of the neural network. It is analogous to the CBOW model of Word2Vec. The output layer is again a vector of randomly sampled words from a sliding window (like Word2Vec model). Word Vectors are shared across different training iterations, but paragraph vectors are not. These keep changing for each text/paragraph. At the end of the training, the tuned paragraph vector becomes a document vector or Doc2Vec for the corresponding text.

Entire network diagram is shown below:

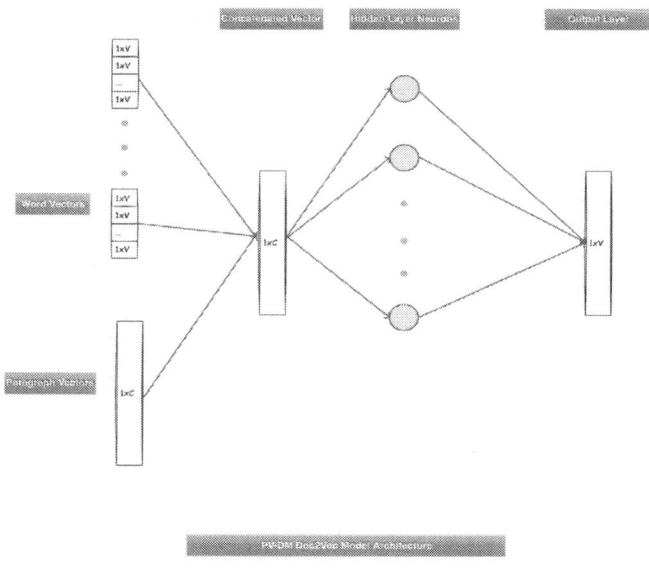

Figure 7.9: Doc2Vec – PV DM Model

Distributed Bag of Words of Paragraph Vectors Model (PV-DBOW) of Doc2Vec

This model is analogous to the Skip-Gram model of Word2Vec. It predicts the probability of all context words randomly sampled from the paragraph to the output. The diagram shows it.

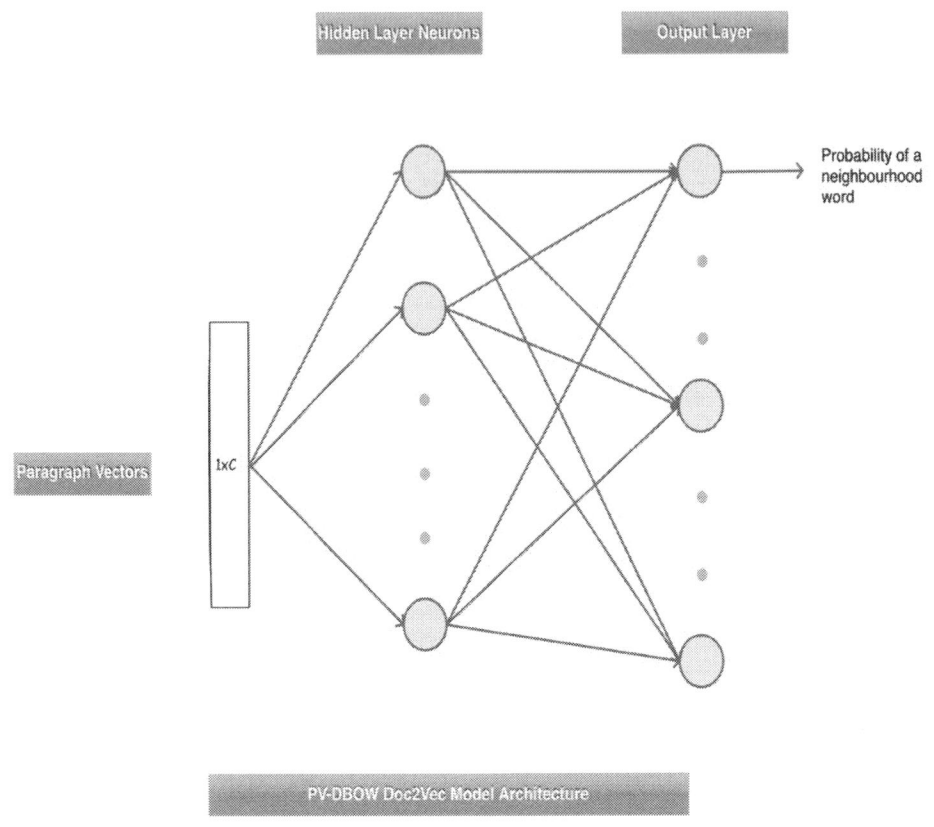

Figure 7.10: *Doc2Vec – PV DBOW Model*

Comparison of different Doc2Vec models

Average schemed Doc2Vec is very simple to implement. Many times, it is used when proper implementation library support is not there for Doc2Vec. But accuracy wise it not so perfect as compared to PV-DM or PV-DBOW. For document vector generation, the PV-DM model is superior, but PV-DBOW consumes less memory. So, it is a good practice to use a proper combination of both these models.

Example of Doc2Vec using python gensim library

Python's `genism` library has a direct API to generate Doc2Vec for a corpus. We will see the generation of it for three documents corpus like the previous example. Here each document will be referred by a string tag token.

```python
from gensim.models.doc2vec import Doc2Vec, TaggedDocument

documents = [TaggedDocument(doc, ['tag_' + str(i)]) for i, doc in enumerate(sentences)]
d2v_model = Doc2Vec(documents, min_count=1)
d2v_model.docvecs['tag_1']
```

```
array([-1.5683484e-03,  1.2750727e-03,  3.1947626e-03,  3.1726300e-03,
        4.0903678e-03, -1.4084670e-03,  1.1938852e-03, -1.7150403e-03,
        1.5353727e-03,  7.8599644e-04, -3.6693888e-03,  1.8381681e-03,
        8.4936392e-04,  2.1692074e-03,  1.8554020e-03,  7.8372651e-04,
        4.8418256e-04, -3.8350152e-04,  2.8157840e-03, -2.2225084e-03,
        7.7009224e-04,  4.1419244e-03,  7.5378991e-04, -3.0480828e-03,
        4.1223401e-03,  3.9683077e-03, -1.1481444e-03, -3.0051267e-03,
       -8.4251381e-04,  6.6914759e-04,  2.0858964e-03,  2.0775434e-03,
       -3.7229082e-03, -3.4163448e-03, -4.7055581e-03,  2.5871894e-03,
        3.7388024e-03, -3.2429013e-03,  3.3142294e-03,  3.4578398e-04,
        2.5457866e-04, -2.7491134e-03, -9.7664182e-05,  3.6116818e-03,
        3.1354101e-03, -1.6634837e-04,  3.4500153e-03,  4.2528557e-03,
        1.6178339e-03, -1.3906679e-03, -7.0449454e-04,  4.8540537e-03,
        3.9452268e-03,  1.4192550e-03,  2.8374153e-03, -2.2079123e-03,
        2.8362628e-03, -2.6379984e-03, -3.4001095e-03, -2.0208249e-03,
        1.4175337e-03, -4.1882959e-04,  4.9212640e-03,  3.1222058e-03,
       -4.1013523e-03,  3.3258942e-03, -3.5097662e-03,  1.2171763e-03,
       -3.8229348e-03,  1.4664852e-03, -1.9219243e-03, -2.2408573e-03,
       -2.4188196e-03,  7.1484456e-04,  1.4745049e-03, -4.2936285e-03,
       -4.4843541e-03, -2.4188382e-03, -1.4762285e-03, -2.4300681e-03,
        3.9725532e-03, -2.0395836e-03,  4.4545977e-04, -3.3707065e-03,
        3.2660514e-03, -2.6336615e-03, -4.3446682e-03, -1.0662524e-03,
        4.8143929e-03, -3.5005754e-03,  1.9762729e-05,  4.6791155e-03,
        3.8871968e-03, -1.4176170e-03,  1.0027719e-03,  3.7726719e-04,
        5.8826094e-04, -4.0514326e-05,  2.7222428e-03,  2.3834268e-03],
      dtype=float32)
```

Figure 7.11: Code snippet for Generation of Doc2Vec

We got the document vectors of the sentence tagged with token `tag_1`.

Comparisons of different vector space models

TF-IDF is a simple model, easy to compute, and is better suited for modeling small-sized text-based corpus. But it is very difficult to scale with a large vocabulary set or very sophisticated text. Because in that case, the number of distinct tokens per document also increases at a larger rate, and it starts consuming a lot of memory. The biggest problem with TF-IDF is that it fails to understand the context of the text;that is, if different texts are written using different words, but the overall meaning is the same, and then TF-IDF fails to capture it. Its raw token frequency-based approach is responsible for that. But, TF-IDF works well in modeling very domain-specific texts where the existence of a word/token infers a lot of meaning. For example, if we have to analyze and classify the error category from the logs of a specific networking device, then just the existence of some particular words may infer the class/category of the logs. TF-IDF will be able to model it well.

Doc2Vec & Word2Vec models are far more complex and able to capture the contextual meaning of the text. Even if different texts are written using different words, but the mood is the same, then these models work better than TF-IDF. Especially for long texts, these models may be preferable, as these will cut down it to fixed-length vectors. In that sense, Doc2Vec or Word2Vec can work as an automatic dimensionality reduction technique for text processing. But, there is one restriction also. Texts have to be grammatically and syntactically perfect for Doc2Vec & Word2Vec to work. If it is not, then these models fail. In the above example of network device logs, texts are rough, and some scenarios are mentioned in short sentences with an emphasis on networking specific keywords. Doc2Vec may not work here perfectly, and an inferior model like TF-IDF may work better there. Modeling *Wikipedia* texts can be an ideal example of Doc2Vec usage.

Text classification techniques

We already saw standard classification models in *Chapter 2: Classification*. All those models are also applicable in text classification. But some models specifically give good results for text classification as compared to other classification cases. Basic pre-processing like text cleaning (as discussed earlier) and standard vector space model conversion are essential here before applying the actual classification model. Once we do vector space model conversion, texts become vectors of numbers. Then these vectors can be used as features.

We will take a sample dataset and see how it works. We will use *BBC Text Articles* dataset from Kaggle (https://www.kaggle.com/yufengdev/bbc-fulltext-and-category). Before going ahead, first, we will just read the first few records of the dataset and see how it looks:

```python
import pandas as pd
pd.set_option('display.max_colwidth', 300)
bbc_text_df = pd.read_csv('../data/bbc-text.csv')
bbc_text_df.head()
```

	category	text
0	tech	tv future in the hands of viewers with home theatre systems plasma high-definition tvs and digital video recorders moving into the living room the way people watch tv will be radically different in five years time. that is according to an expert panel which gathered at the annual consumer e...
1	business	worldcom boss left books alone former worldcom boss bernie ebbers who is accused of overseeing an $11bn (£5.8bn) fraud never made accounting decisions a witness has told jurors. david myers made the comments under questioning by defence lawyers who have been arguing that mr ebbers was not ...
2	sport	tigers wary of farrell gamble leicester say they will not be rushed into making a bid for andy farrell should the great britain rugby league captain decide to switch codes. we and anybody else involved in the process are still some way away from going to the next stage tigers boss john wel...
3	sport	yeading face newcastle in fa cup premiership side newcastle united face a trip to ryman premier league leaders yeading in the fa cup third round. the game - arguably the highlight of the draw - is a potential money-spinner for non-league yeading who beat slough in the second round. conference ...
4	entertainment	ocean s twelve raids box office ocean s twelve the crime caper sequel starring george clooney brad pitt and julia roberts has gone straight to number one in the us box office chart. it took $40.8m (£21m) in weekend ticket sales according to studio estimates. the sequel follows the master cr...

Figure 7.12: Code snippet for BBC Text Articles Understanding

There are five different categories and we need to classify text as one of these categories. It is a typical multi-class classification problem.

Visualization techniques for text

Before doing any sort of model building, we will learn some visualization techniques for text. These will help us understand the text data quickly.

First, we will clean off the entire corpus and concatenate all texts in a single one. We can write a function to do that:

```python
def concatenate_all_texts(text_df):
    clean_texts = text_df['text'].apply(lambda x : clean_text(x))
    single_text = ''
    for text in clean_texts:
        single_text = single_text + ' ' + text

    return single_text
```

Figure 7.13: Code snippet for the function to clean & concatenate entire corpus

Now, we will call this function with the text data frame:

```python
all_texts = concatenate_all_texts(bbc_text_df)
```

Figure 7.14: Code snippet to call concatenate_all_texts function

This `all_texts` variable will help us in doing the visualization. We will discuss the next two visualization approaches.

Histogram

To plot a histogram, we have to generate token frequency distribution from the corpus. We will do it using `Counter` class from the collections library of Python. There are a lot of tokens in the corpus, so they will be interested in getting the first 15 high-frequency tokens. The `most_common` function of `Counter` gives us the topmost high-frequency tokens and their respective frequencies as tuples:

```python
from collections import Counter

c = Counter(all_texts.split())
common_tokens = [word[0] for word in c.most_common(15)]
common_tokens_counts = [word[1] for word in c.most_common(15)]
common_tokens_counts_df = pd.DataFrame({'Tokens': common_tokens, 'Token Count': common_tokens_counts})
```

Figure 7.15: Code snippet to generate a token frequency distribution

We can see from the code snippet (*Figure 7.15*) that tokens and respective frequencies are added into a data frame for better access.

We will use the `seaborn` library for plotting a histogram:

```python
import matplotlib.pyplot as plt
import seaborn as sns

fig = plt.figure(figsize=(30,15))
sns.set(font_scale=3)
bar_plot = sns.barplot(data=common_tokens_counts_df, y='Token Count', x='Tokens')
plt.title('Histogram of Token Distribution')
plt.show()
```

Figure 7.16: Code snippet to plot the histogram

The `barplot` function of `seaborn` takes x and y variable names. These should be the same as data frame key names. The code snippet in *Figure 7.16* produces bar plot like below:

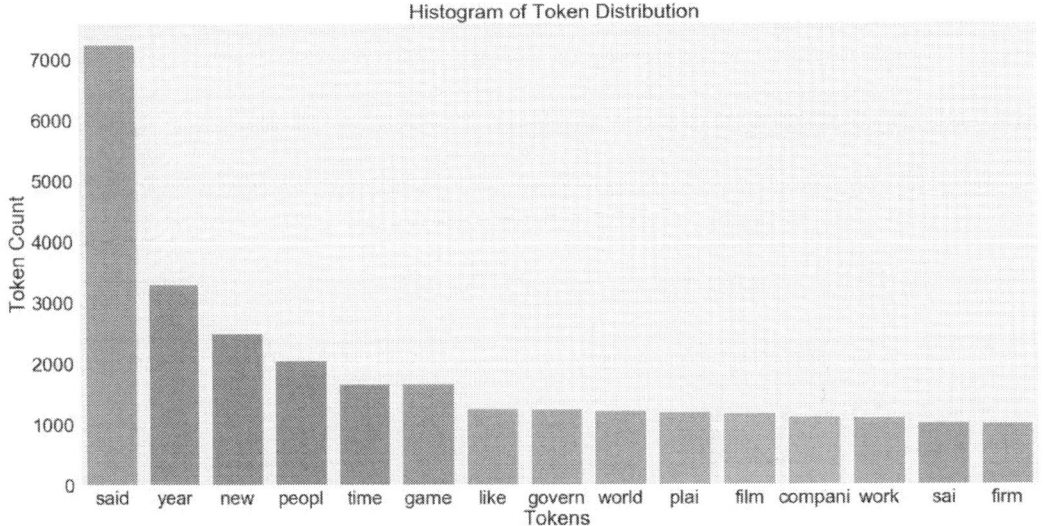

Figure 7.17: Histogram for Token distribution

We can see from *Figure 7.16* that **said, year, new,** and more. Are the most high-frequency tokens in the entire corpus? We can also get the least frequency tokens from the corpus. Readers can try it on their own.

Word Cloud

It is another way of representing token distribution where all tokens form a zig-zag cloud with larger font size for high-frequency ones.

There is a separate library for plotting the word cloud with the same name. We will seed the `all_texts` variable there like below:

```
from wordcloud import WordCloud

wordcloud_instance = WordCloud(width = 800, height = 800,
            background_color ='black',
            stopwords=None,
            min_font_size = 10).generate(all_texts)

plt.figure(figsize = (8, 8), facecolor = None)
plt.imshow(wordcloud_instance)
plt.axis("off")
plt.tight_layout(pad = 0)
plt.show()
```

Figure 7.18: Code snippet to generate Word Cloud

The code snippet in *Figure 7.18* produces word cloud like below:

Figure 7.19: Word Cloud for the entire corpus

We can see from *Figure 7.19* that high-frequency tokens have a bigger font size. Word cloud gives a better visualization to get a quick idea about any corpus. It is a better choice than a histogram where the exact frequency is not needed, but dominant tokens have to be identified and displayed in a user-friendly way.

Naïve Bayes Classifier for text

We will now come back to the actual work of building a classifier for BBC Text Articles.

We need to divide the total dataset into the feature and target variable, split the dataset into train and test:

```
from sklearn.model_selection import train_test_split

df_x = bbc_text_df['text']
df_y = bbc_text_df['category']
train_x, test_x, train_y, test_y = train_test_split(df_x, df_y)
```

Figure 7.20: Code snippet for train-test split

We will use both the TF-IDF & Doc2Vec vector space model with the Naïve Bayes classifier.

TF-IDF with Naïve Bayes classifier

We can write a custom transformer that cleans the text and apply the TF-IDF model on top of it. We will use TfIdfVectorizer class of scikit-learn library inside our transformer class:

```
from sklearn.feature_extraction.text import TfidfVectorizer
from sklearn.base import BaseEstimator

class Text2TfIdfTransformer(BaseEstimator):

    def __init__(self):
        self._model = TfidfVectorizer()

    def fit(self, X, y=None):
        X_arr = X.apply(lambda x : clean_text(x))

        self._model.fit(X_arr)
        return self

    def transform(self, X):
        X_arr = X.apply(lambda x : clean_text(x))
        return self._model.transform(X_arr).todense()
```

Figure 7.21: Code snippet for TfIdf Transformer class

Now, we will build the pipeline with `Text2TfIdfTransformer` and `GaussianNB` as all TF-IDF features are continuous:

```python
from sklearn.pipeline import Pipeline
from sklearn.naive_bayes import GaussianNB

nb_pl = Pipeline(steps = [('tf_idf', Text2TfIdfTransformer()),
                          ('gnb', GaussianNB())])
nb_pl.fit(train_x, train_y)
```

Figure 7.22: Code snippet for Naïve Bayes pipeline with TF-IDF

We can get the accuracy ofthe test data.

```python
nb_pl.score(test_x, test_y)
```

0.8922800718132855

Figure 7.23: Code snippet for accuracy of GaussianNB with TF-IDF

We got almost 89% accuracy!

Doc2Vec with Naïve Bayes classifier

The `scikit-learn` does not provide a Doc2Vec API, so we will use the same one from `gensim` like earlier. But we have to wrap it inside a custom transformer:

```python
from gensim.models.doc2vec import Doc2Vec, TaggedDocument
import numpy as np

class Text2Doc2VecTransformer(BaseEstimator):

    def __init__(self):
        self._model = None

    def fit(self, X, y=None):
        X_arr = X.apply(lambda x : clean_text(x))
        tagged_doc = [TaggedDocument(doc, ['tag' + str(i)]) for i, doc
                      in enumerate(X_arr)]
        self._model = Doc2Vec(tagged_doc, vector_size=300)
        return self

    def transform(self, X):
        X_arr = X.apply(lambda x : clean_text(x))
        return np.asmatrix(np.array([self._model.infer_vector(row.split())
                           for index, row in enumerate(X_arr)]))
```

Figure 7.24: Code snippet for custom Doc2Vec transformer

This time we set the vector size of Doc2Vec as 300 for a better result. We can create a pipeline with the Text2Doc2VecTransformer like below:

```
from sklearn.pipeline import Pipeline
from sklearn.naive_bayes import GaussianNB

nb_doc2vec_pl = Pipeline(steps = [('doc2_vec', Text2Doc2VecTransformer()),
                        ('gnb', GaussianNB())])
nb_doc2vec_pl.fit(train_x, train_y)
```

```
Pipeline(memory=None,
        steps=[('doc2_vec', Text2Doc2VecTransformer()),
               ('gnb', GaussianNB(priors=None, var_smoothing=1e-09))],
        verbose=False)
```

Figure 7.25: Code snippet for Naïve Bayes pipeline with Doc2Vec

We can test the trained pipeline with the test data:

```
nb_doc2vec_pl.score(test_x, test_y)
```

```
0.2513464991023339
```

Figure 7.26: Code snippet for accuracy of GaussianNB with Doc2Vec

Poor accuracy is an indicator that these text documents are not a good fit for a Doc2Vec model. There may be unstructured sentences that could hamper the doc2vec creation.

Measuring text similarity

We can measure how close any two text documents are using vector similarity techniques. Anyway, texts are getting converted to vectors, so standard vector similarity measures like cosine similarity (refer *Chapter 1: Introduction to Machine Learning*) will work over here. We will take two sample texts from our previously discussed corpus and measure their similarity and use cosine_similarity function from metrics.pairwise library of scikit-learn:

One sample text:

```
train_x[1041], train_y[1041]
```

```
('aviator  creator  in oscars snub the man who said he got oscar-nominated movie the aviator off the ground and signe
d up leonardo dicaprio has been shut out of the academy awards race.  charles evans jr battled over his role with the
people who eventually made the film  and won a producer s credit. but he is not on the list of producers who can win
a best film oscar due to a limit on the number of nominees. the oscars organisers have picked two of the aviator s fo
ur producers to be nominated for best film.  up to three producers can be named per film but the studios behind the a
viator and million dollar baby failed to trim their credits - so the academy of motion pictures arts and sciences (am
pas) has done it for them. the aviator s nominated producers are michael mann and graham king - with mr evans and san
dy climan  mr mann s former deputy  left off. mr evans sued mr mann in 2001  claiming he came up with the idea  spent
years developing it and persuaded dicaprio to play hughes - but said he was later excluded from the project. the two
sides settled out of court in a deal that has remained secret apart from the fact mr evans  name has appeared as a pr
oducer when the film s credits roll. at the golden globes  mr evans - who was named among the winners when the film w
on best drama film - evaded a security guard to have his photo taken with dicaprio  director martin scorsese  mr mann
and mr king.  ampas decided to limit the number of producers who could be nominated after shakespeare in love s victo
ry in 1999 saw five producers collect awards. the eligible names for the aviator and million dollar baby were decided
by ampas  producers branch executive committee on wednesday. the decision also saw clint eastwood get his third perso
nal nomination for million dollar baby. he is now named in the best film category as well as being nominated for best
director and best lead actor. the academy awards ceremony will be held in hollywood on 27 february. chinese actress z
iyi zhang  star of crouching tiger  hidden dragon  hero and house of flying daggers  is the latest name to be added t
o the list of presenters on the night.',
 'entertainment')
```

Figure 7.27: One sample text from the corpus

Another sample text:

```
train_x[947], train_y[947]
```

```
('connick jr to lead broadway show singer and actor harry connick jr is to star in a broadway revival of 1950s hit mu
sical the pajama game.  he will play the supervisor of a us pajama factory who has a romance with a union activist du
ring labour unrest. jeffrey richards  the show s co-producer  said connick was  an actor of enormous charisma and ski
ll  a wonderful singer and a bona fide star . he has recently starred in hit us comedy will and grace as the husband
of grace  played by debra messing. the musical will open in november  said mr richards  who added that no other casti
ng had been announced yet.  the original book by george abbott and richard bissell will be revised by playwright pete
r ackerman  who co-wrote the screenplay for the movie ice age. it has a score by richard adler and jerry ross  and ad
ler is writing two new songs for the score  which includes numbers including hey there  small talk and steam heat. co
nnick appeared with his band on broadway in 1990  and he wrote the score for a musical based on emile zola s novel th
erese raquin  called thou shalt not. it had a three-month run on broadway in 2001.',
 'entertainment')
```

Figure 7.28: One sample text from the corpus

We cannot directly measure the similarity between the two. We have to use any of the vector space models to convert these into features. So, we will use the same `Text2TfIdfTransformer` and convert the entire corpus into feature array like below:

```
tfidf_vectors = Text2TfIdfTransformer().fit(train_x).transform(train_x)
```

Figure 7.29: Code snippet to generate TF-IDF vectors for the entire corpus

Now, the cosine similarity:

```
from sklearn.metrics.pairwise import cosine_similarity

cosine_similarity(tfidf_vectors[947],tfidf_vectors[1041])

array([[0.05921244]])
```

Figure 7.30: Code snippet to get Cosine similarity between vectors

Both of the documents belong to the `entertainment` category, and their similarity score is `0.05`. We may also use `Doc2Vec` as our vector space model to calculate similarity.

If we take (`1 - cosine_similarity`) as a metric, it will give a distance/dissimilarity metric. We can use this as a distance metric for text corpus. Traditional Euclidean distance does not work well with text data as it is an absolute measure. It relies on the raw difference in features rather than the orientation/direction of features. It matters a lot in the case of text data. Euclidean distance fails to handle those cases where a small text can be more similar to a large text rather than another similar-sized large text with almost the same token/word distribution.

Text clustering

We have already discussed clustering techniques in *Chapter 4: Clustering*. We can use these to group text documents in an unsupervised manner. Here also conversion to vector space model is a pre-requisite. We will use the previous example of a text corpus as our dataset. To make it unsupervised, we will ignore class labels or `category` fields in the dataset and only focus on the `text` field.

The scikit-learn's KMeans API does not provide cosine similarity as the distance metric, which works well for text corpus. We will use `KMeansClusterer` from `nltk` as an alternative. It comes with cosine similarity as an option. But as it does not follow the pipeline API structure of `scikit-learn`, we have to wrap it inside a custom transformer.

```python
from nltk.cluster import KMeansClusterer, cosine_distance

class TextKMeansClusterer(BaseEstimator):

    def __init__(self, k):
        self._model = KMeansClusterer(num_means=k, distance=cosine_distance, repeats=3)
        self.clusters_labels_ = None
        self.text_vectors_ = None

    def fit(self, X, y=None):
        self.text_vectors_ = X
        self.clusters_labels_ = self._model.cluster(vectors=np.array(X),
                                        assign_clusters=True, trace=False)
        return self

    def transform(self, X):
        _cluster_labels_ = []
        X = np.array(X)
        for x in X:
            _cluster_labels_.append(self._model.classify(x))
        return np.array(_cluster_labels_)
```

Figure 7.31: Code snippet for Custom Transformer for KMeans clustering with text

This transformer is independent of the vector space model. We can pass any kind of text vectors (TF-IDF or Doc2Vec) to it. `KMeansClusterer` API takes a parameter repeats. We have set it as 3. It uses the specified number of randomized attempts to find a set of commonly occurring means to choose as initial centroids for the KMeans algorithm.

We will build a pipeline to do clustering on the text vectors. Pipeline stages would be Text2TfIdfTransformer and TextKMeansClusterer respectively, and it will be trained on train_x:

```python
from sklearn.pipeline import Pipeline
from sklearn.naive_bayes import GaussianNB

txt_clusterer = TextKMeansClusterer(k=5)
clustering_pl = Pipeline(steps = [('tf_idf', Text2TfIdfTransformer()),
                             ('txt_kmeans', txt_clusterer)])
clustering_pl.fit(train_x)
```
```
Pipeline(memory=None,
        steps=[('tf_idf', Text2TfIdfTransformer()),
               ('txt_kmeans', TextKMeansClusterer(k=None))],
        verbose=False)
```

Figure 7.32: Code snippet of Pipeline for text clustering

We have used a 5-cluster setup just to keep it the same with the number of categories or class labels.

We can see the dimensions of the text vectors:

```python
txt_clusterer.text_vectors_.shape
```

```
(1668, 16801)
```

Figure 7.33: Code snippet to get dimensions of text vectors

As it is quite high dimensional, we have to reduce dimensions to visualize cluster setup. We will use the top 2 principal components of text vectors for this purpose and do the plotting:

```python
%matplotlib inline

from sklearn.decomposition import PCA
import seaborn as sns
import matplotlib.pyplot as plt

pca = PCA(n_components=2)
pca_tf_idf_vectors = pca.fit_transform(txt_clusterer.text_vectors_)
sns.set(font_scale=2)
plt.figure(figsize=(15,10))
sns.scatterplot(x=pca_tf_idf_vectors[:, 0], y=pca_tf_idf_vectors[:, 1], hue=txt_clusterer.clusters_labels_)
plt.title('Text Cluster setup with first 2 PC', fontsize=16)
plt.ylabel('Principal Component 2')
plt.xlabel('Principal Component 1')
plt.xticks(rotation='vertical');
```

Figure 7.34: Plotting clusters with twoprincipal components

Above code snippet (*Figure 7.34*) produce the following cluster setup:

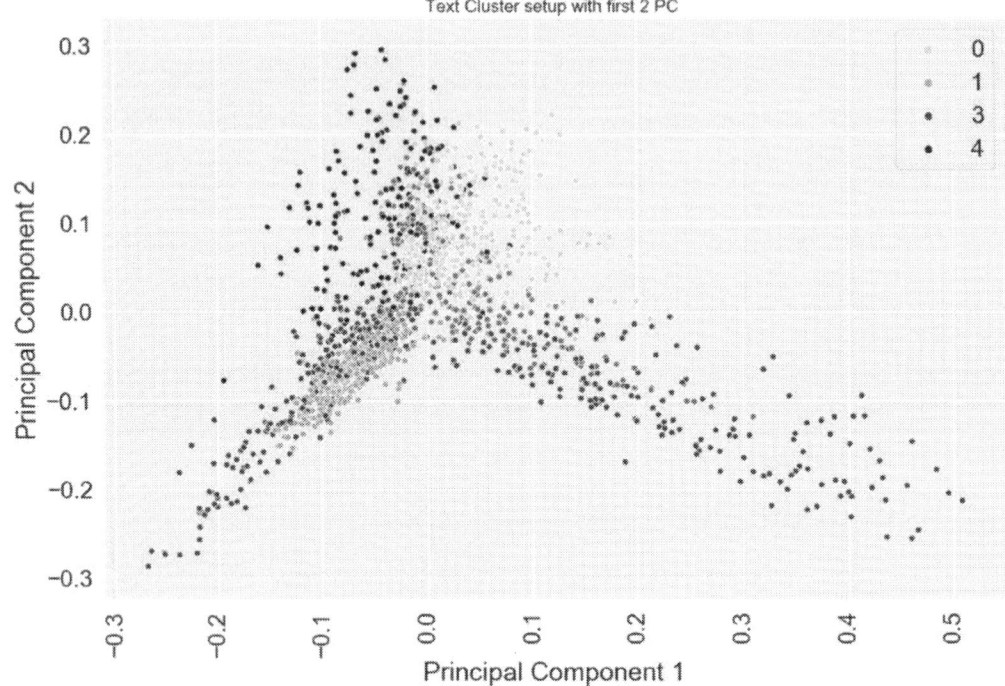

Figure 7.35: Text cluster setup with first 2 PC

We can validate the cluster setup with the actual class distribution plot. Here we have to use class labels (`train_y`) instead of `txt_clusterer.clusters_labels_` variable:

```
plt.figure(figsize=(15,10))
sns.scatterplot(x=pca_tf_idf_vectors[:, 0], y=pca_tf_idf_vectors[:, 1], hue=train_y)
plt.title('Class distribution setup with first 2 PC', fontsize=16)
plt.ylabel('Principal Component 2')
plt.xlabel('Principal Component 1')
plt.xticks(rotation='vertical');
```

Figure 7.36: Code snippet to generate class distribution plot with first 2 PC

And it generates the following plot:

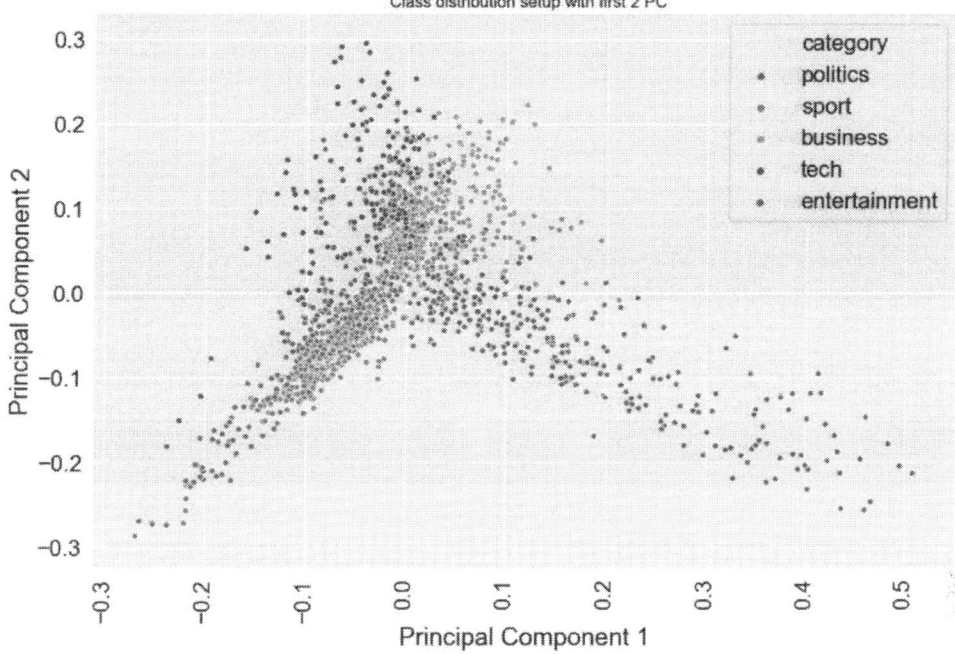

Figure 7.37: Class distribution setup with first 2 PC

If we compare *Figure 7.35* and *Figure 7.37*, then we can see that the distributions of cluster and class labels are almost similar. At a high level, each cluster represents one class label. This validates the accuracy of the cluster setup.

Conclusion

In this chapter, we discussed how to process, and model text data for ML, how to extract meaningful information from unstructured text. We discussed several vector space models and their integration with traditional ML techniques of classification and clustering. We discussed two approaches of text visualization: histogram and word cloud. We will see more examples in the case studies chapter.

We learned how to preprocess text data before building any model. As the choice of the vector space model is very important, we learned about various factors that can influence this choice. We learned about the pros and cons of each model and applied those in traditional text classification and clustering.

From Chapters 1 to 7, we have been discussing building models using mostly small datasets. But scalability becomes a big challenge once the dataset becomes quite large, especially in the production environment. In the next chapter, we will discuss this and will also go through the standards of exporting ML models in a platform-independent form.

CHAPTER 8
Machine Learning Models in Production

So far, what we have discussed is all about designing a **machine learning (ML)** model for research purposes. The objective was to see how the model works with the dataset provided. But, those models were not production-ready. We cannot ship the proof of concept-based models directly into production. Either we need to put architecture around the model or else some kind of *As a Service* layer has to be there before the models. The question of scalability also will come over here. In this chapter, we will discuss what the various options and industry standards available to make a model production ready are.

Structure

In this chapter, we will discuss:

- Challenges of machine learning models in a production environment
- Saving and loading a model with Flask
- Scalable architecture with Big Data and Spark
- Predictive Model Markup Language (PMML)

Objective

After finishing this chapter, we will be able to

- Understand techniques of building a scalable ML model
- Expose the ML model as a service using PMML
- Separate small POC and final production-grade ML model

Challenges of putting a model into production

There are a few common problems that have to be taken care while shipping a model into production systems:

- **Exposing model as a service:** It is very difficult for any specific language-based monolithic model to be integrated into a large production system. That's why the SaaS-based approach works out here well. Models should be exposed as a REST endpoint to the outside systems.

- **Adding scalability support:** Monolithic and language-specific models often fail with a large dataset. Failure may come both at training time as well as testing or actual running time in the production box. So, proper frameworks and technologies should be used to build a model in a scalable way.

- **Building platform-independent model descriptor:** Models can be developed in a language or platform which may be completely different from the consumer/client platform. So, in that case, a platform-independent view/descriptor is required, which can be exchanged in place of the original native model?

- **Building overall architecture:** Probably, this is the biggest challenge in the current industry. The architecture will vary depending on the use case.

We will now discuss solutions for each these challenges in a chronological order

Exposing model as a service

This technique is analogous to the **Machine Learning as a Service(MLaaS)** concept. In a typical **Machine Learning as a Service (MLaaS)** based system, all models are exposed as REST API endpoints. Models should be trained and saved in file format and can be loaded from there later. One advantage of using this technique is consumer/client doesn't have to create monolithic language/library-specific data structures for interacting with the model. The client can rely easily on HTTP based JSON API structures for data exchange.

We will discuss here a technique of exposing the Python `scikit-learn` based model as Python Flask REST API endpoint.

Save and load a model

To make anML model production-ready, we have to save it in filesystems or any database after training, and later we can load it on a need basis. We will build a Ridge regression model using the Concrete Strength Dataset of *Chapter 3: Regression* and save it in `.joblib` format.

```python
import pandas as pd
from sklearn.preprocessing import StandardScaler
from sklearn.pipeline import Pipeline
from sklearn.linear_model import Ridge
from joblib import dump, load

cs_df = pd.read_csv("../data/Concrete_Data_Yeh.csv", header=0)
df_x = cs_df[['cement','slag','water','superplasticizer','coarseaggregate','fineaggregate','age']]
df_y = cs_df[['csMPa']]

model_pl = Pipeline(steps=[('scaling',StandardScaler()),('ridge_lm',Ridge())])
model_pl.fit(df_x, df_y)

dump(model_pl, 'ridge_model.joblib')
saved_model = load('ridge_model.joblib')
saved_model.predict(df_x[3:4])

array([[67.94777033]])
```

Figure 8.1: Code snippet of a sample pipeline and saving it as joblib format

Python's `joblib` library has functions for model persistence. A model can be saved using the **dump** function and can be loaded again using **load** function (as done above). We saved the entire pipeline as our ML model as `.joblib` file format. By this, we can port the model file anywhere and load and use it as per need basis.

So, we can put a REST API endpoint on top of the saved model and can use it to get predictions. We will now see how to develop REST API for it.

A brief introduction to Flask

Flask is a Python-based library for creating UI and backend services. We will use Flask for creating REST APIs on top of ML models. A very simple *hello world* flask API can be developed like below:

```
from flask import Flask
app = Flask(__name__)

@app.route('/hello', methods=['GET'])
def say_hello():
    return 'Hello World !!'

if __name__ == '__main__':
    app.run(debug=False, port=5000)
```

```
* Serving Flask app "__main__" (lazy loading)
* Environment: production
  WARNING: This is a development server. Do not use it in a production deployment.
  Use a production WSGI server instead.
* Debug mode: off
* Running on http://127.0.0.1:5000/ (Press CTRL+C to quit)
127.0.0.1 - - [03/Sep/2019 14:54:48] "GET / HTTP/1.1" 404 -
127.0.0.1 - - [03/Sep/2019 14:54:54] "GET /hello HTTP/1.1" 200 -
```

Figure 8.2: Code snippet of a sample Hello World Flask REST API

The path of the REST API should be mentioned under the @app.route annotation element. There can be multiple functions like say_hello annotated with different paths for handling different HTTP requests. Calling app.run makes the program run continuously and listen to the mentioned port for any incoming request. It starts working like an indigenous server.

We can now hit the API and get the result:

```
curl http://127.0.0.1:5000/hello

Hello World !!
```

Exposing model as Flask REST API

As we can see, the model takes the object of a DataFrame object as input. It is a specific data structure of Python library pandas. But we should never expose this type of language-specific data structure to the consumer. That's why HTTP based REST API plays a significant role over here. We should rely only on XML or JSON based structure for data exchange, which is language and platform-independent data standards. Inside the Flask based REST API, we can convert the incoming XML or JSON to a Python-specific data structure like pandasDataFrame. Generally, for accepting large data frame style input, HTTP POST is always preferred over GET. Now we will develop a Flask API for our model.

```
from flask import Flask, request
from flask.json import jsonify

model_app = Flask(__name__)

ml_model = load('ridge_model.joblib')

@model_app.route('/models/predictions/concrete_strength', methods=['POST'])
def predict_concrete_strength():
    input_features = request.data
    input_df = pd.read_json(input_features)
    result = ml_model.predict(input_df)
    return jsonify(result.tolist())

if __name__ == '__main__':
    model_app.run(debug=False, port=6666)

 * Serving Flask app "__main__" (lazy loading)
 * Environment: production
   WARNING: This is a development server. Do not use it in a production deployment.
   Use a production WSGI server instead.
 * Debug mode: off
 * Running on http://127.0.0.1:6666/ (Press CTRL+C to quit)
```

Figure 8.3: Code snippet of Flask REST API on top of Concrete Strength Regression model

We can test this with a sample JSON as payload containing all feature values. We should save this content in a file `sample_test_json_features.json` and send it as POST payload.

```
'[{"cement":332.5,"slag":142.5,"water":228.0,"superplasticizer":0.0,"coarseaggregate":932.0,"fineaggregate":594.0,"age":365}]'
```

Figure 8.4: Sample JSON structure of features for Concrete Strength Regression model

We can invoke the REST API with `curl` to get the response:

```
curl http://127.0.0.1:6666/models/predictions/concrete_strength -d @sample_test_json_features.json --header "Content-Type: application/json"
```

Figure 8.5: Curl command to invoke model REST api

And we get the following output:

```
[[102.98036301698977]]
```

Figure 8.6: Output from the curl command in Figure 8.5

In the REST API, we can see that conversion from JSON data to a `pandas` data frame (using `read_json` function) and from `numpy` array to JSON (using `jsonify` function) This which are essential for exposing any model as a REST service.

Adding scalability support

Most of the time, ML models developed for research purposes or for doing **proof of concept (POC)** are not scalable. *Scalability* is a software quality attribute of systemsthat ensure the handling of large volumes of data. As in our discussion so far, all of the models have been developed using Python, and it is not considered a scalable language/platform for developing models that will be put in the production environment. We can still use Python libraries in production if our data volume is not that large. Then what is the solution? We discussed the *data engineering* activity of an ML project in *Chapter 1: Introduction to Machine Learning*. Data Engineering is the key to achieve scalability. Big Data platforms play a big role here. There are various data computing platforms/frameworks which are quite commonly used in the industry. Apache Spark, Apache Hadoop, Apache Fink, and more, are some of the examples of these types of frameworks.

Scalability for storage

Large scale systems inthe production environment need sufficient & highly available data storage mechanisms. For ML-based systems, most of the data remain in much-unstructured format (for example, text, or image) and have high volume. For our problems so far, we have used CSV or flat files as a data source. But in practical scenarios inthe production environment, these options won't work. Data storage mechanisms for ML-based systems should provide high throughput for reading, high availability, and large-scale data handling support. Most of the ML systems perform frequent read operations rather than write and don't need transaction support that much. So, data storage or databases which are efficient at reading and in-memory caching of data will be ideal. Traditional RDMS like Oracle, MySQL, and PostgreSQL do exactly the opposite. These software support heavy transactions, data consistency, which ultimately ends up in the slow reading and lack of enough caching support. So, these RDMS are not at all suitable for developing ML systems. NoSQL databases like MongoDB, Casandra, Riak, and more, are famous for fast reads, caching support, storing unstructured data, and many more, and these become default choice.

Scalability for computing

Distributed computing platforms are ideal for large scale data handling. The same can also be appliedto ML systems. The training process of any model needs high computational speed and memory support. Apart from adding required hardware, proper platforms are required which can leverage this. For that distributed computing frameworks like Hadoop, Spark, or Flink can be a very good choice for large scale model development. These frameworks can utilize several machines' memory and processor through a single and simplified programming interface.

Apache Spark-MLlib and pipeline

Apache Spark is a distributed computed framework that is well suited for data processing at a very large volume. It is based on Hadoop architecture and can leverage several physical machines' memory and processor at a time with a single programming interface. We can add/remove several machines for its job execution as per need without making any changes in code/architecture. `MLlib` is a library provided by Spark for machine learning-based job execution. It has implementations of more or less major machine learning algorithms with a common interface. Though Spark internals has been developed in *Scala*, Spark supports cross-language interfaces. As of now, it exposes the same API interface in flavors of four different programming languages: Java, Scala, Python, R. Pythonand R API flavors are especially known as **PySpark** and **SparkR** respectively.

Spark typically has master-slave architecture and is configured at the production environment as clusters. Master node itself does not execute anything and just works as a controller. It takes job request details from client program and forwards to slave nodes for actual execution. Actual job execution happens at the slave node and masterworks as the controller. High configuration machines are generally kept as slave nodes. The client program is completely unaware of the slaves, and it can only see the master. It connects to the master node through APIs of different language-based flavors, as shown in the below diagram:

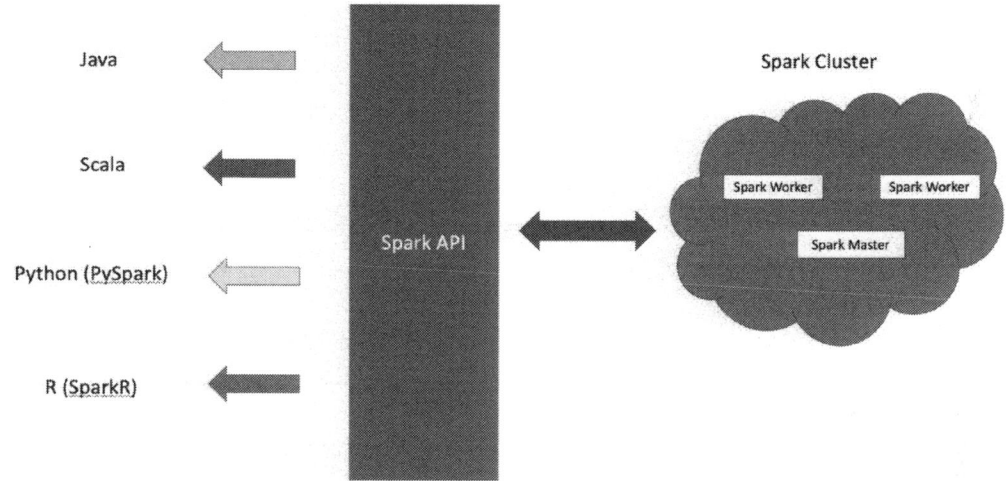

Figure 8.7: Multi-language architecture of Spark

As we are using Python for all our models, so **PySpark** becomes our obvious choice for Spark-ML implementation. This implementation is a typical data engineering activity, as discussed in *Chapter 1: Introduction to Machine Learning*. Usage of PySpark has some major advantages over other language flavors. We can easily leverage some of the rich utility modules of Python while doing this. For example, for any NLP or Text Mining related model development, we can use Python's `Genism` library for cleaning the text and then submit the Spark-ML compliant job to a Spark cluster.

Creating pipelines is a very important design approach for any ML system. We already saw how to create pipelines in *Chapter 2: Classification*. Without using pipelines also, we can develop our models, but reusability and maintainability will be affected a lot. And we all know that these two are the primary software quality attribute of any system, be it ML-based or not. Spark-MLlib has very good support for creating pipeline stages and reuses those stages in multiple places. Stages can be used across different pipelines. A single Spark-MLlib pipeline works as a single composite unit, and it is quite analogous to the scikit-learn pipelines, as discussed in *Chapter 2: Classification*. Pipelines are very useful for doing pre-processing work required for any machine learning algorithm like data cleaning, variable transformation, scaling, and more. A typical pipeline workflow pattern is shown below:

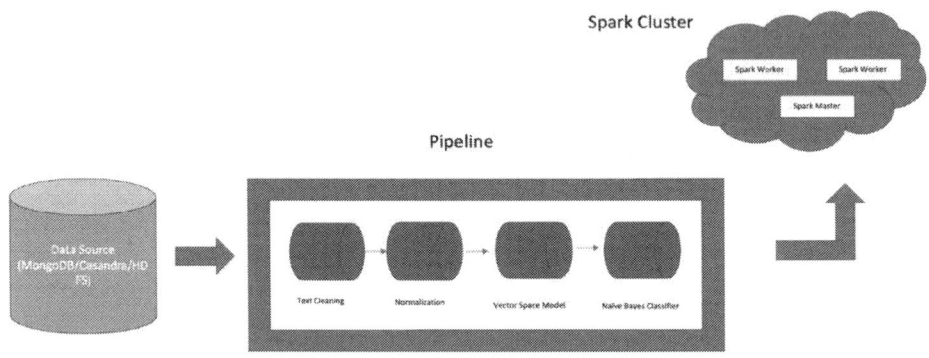

Figure 8.8: Workflow of a typical Spark-ML pipeline

We develop the pipeline workflow in a client system, then Spark master is connected, and the job is submitted to the cluster. Behind the scene, the entire workflow gets executed at slave nodes, and the result is returned to the master. There are some workflow design frameworks like **Oozie**, which will allow developers to create one using XML instead of writing lots of code. These Oozie based workflows can be submitted as Spark jobs. In some very special cases, a customized workflow language can be created to support very domain-specific needs for executing Spark-MLlib based jobs.

So, in summary, to scale up ML systems, a set of typical life cycle stages would be:

1. Design the model using a smaller set of data using Python libraries like scikit-learn, PyTorch, and more.

2. Migrate the model in Big data framework like Spark-MLlib and implement the same algorithm whatever decided in the design phase.

3. Export the model in some form (will be discussed later).

4. Expose it as a service.

Now, the question may come, *Why stage 1 is needed, and why can't we directly start from stage 2?* Reasons are described below:

- For any ML project, a significant amount of research activities is required, which involves quick development and testing of small models using ready-made libraries. It also involves continuous switching between models for A/B testing. Richness and variety of Python libraries are of great help here, and it saves a lot of time and effort.

- Spark-MLlib still has a long way to go in terms of providing support for various advanced ML algorithms. Though it has a good set of ones, still a lot of work is pending. So, random A/B testing with a lack of library support may be difficult.

- It needs a good amount of understanding of Big Data concepts, infrastructure, and distributed computing concepts to start something with Spark or Spark-MLlib. It may work as a bottleneck for some data scientists, especially if they come from Mathematical core background. Also, the concept of distributing computing itself is very complex, and so as Spark APIs and programming style is not straight forward, unlike monolithic Python libraries. So, it will also kill a lot of time at the initial stage.

So, it is always preferable to design the model first using ready-made libraries and then start implementing in Spark-MLlib with a proper timeframe and guideline. It may also happen that once the project team gains sufficient knowledge about the data, the business problem, and kind of models suitable for that, then any fresh design can also start from stage 2 instead of stage 1, that is, directly with Spark-MLlib.

Building platform-independent model descriptor

We saw how to save a model using the `joblib` library. But this technique is Python-specific, and the model cannot be used from another platform or language. Also, the model file format is not at all readable or verbose. We need a redundant and platform-independent standard for the smooth development and deployment of models. This will solve our Model export problem, that is, stage 3, as discussed above.

Predictive Model Markup Language (PMML)

PMML is an XML-based language for describing an ML model. It is an international standard and developed by *The Data Mining Group* (dmg.org), which is an independent consortium managed by the *Center for Computational Science Research, Inc., Illinois* (a non-for Profit Corporation). Since it is XML-based, PMML specification comes as XML-schema. It has predefined tags, each of which carries different aspects of an ML model. For example, coefficients of feature variables, variable transformation and scaling rules, actual algorithm type, and more are some of the contents of a PMML document.

Elements/tags of a PMML document

These are some of the tags of a PMML document:

- **Header:** Contains generic information such as name, description, the purpose of the model, and more.

- **Data dictionary:** Contains details of all features andthe target variable. Details include data type, name, and variable type.

- **Data transformations:** Contains transformation rules, any derived field information (for example, in case of vector space models for text, each derived field will contain the token name and its numeric value).

- **Model:** Contains actual ML model relation information to be used. Details include model name, type, algorithm name, another individual model-specific information (for regression, list of coefficients, for neural networks, number of layers, and more.)

- **Output:** Contains the value of the output variable of the model. It may be the estimated value for a regression model, probability of a class for a classification model, cluster affinity for clustering model, and more.

Generation of PMML document from a model

Instead of going through a sample PMML file, we will generate one from a model developed earlier in our discussion and try to understand its structure.

Installation of required libraries

Standard open source libraries for generating PMML are not very easily available as of now. We have to rely on custom one, and if we can develop something on our own, that is always best. But for our discussion, we will use one very good open-source developed by *Villu Ruusmann* of `opensource.io` (GitHub: `https://github.com/vruusmann`, LinkedIn `https://www.linkedin.com/in/villuruusmann/`). Installation can be done by the following:

```
pip3 install --user --upgrade git+https://github.com/jpmml/sklearn2pmml.git
```

Figure 89: pip3 command to install PMML library

This library does the conversion of `scikit-learn` based Python models to PMML documents.

We also need another library from the same open-source for consumption for PMML document from a client system perspective:

pip3 install jpmml_evaluator

Figure 8.10: pip3 command to install JPMML library

scikit-learn pipeline to PMML conversion

We will take the same example of **Concreate Strength Dataset** and build a Ridge regression model first. But to do that, we have to use `PMMLPipeline` class of `sklearn2pmml` instead of `Pipeline` class of `sciki-learn`:

```
import pandas as pd
from sklearn.preprocessing import StandardScaler
from sklearn.pipeline import Pipeline
from sklearn.linear_model import Ridge
from joblib import dump, load
from sklearn2pmml.pipeline import PMMLPipeline

cs_df = pd.read_csv("../data/Concrete_Data_Yeh.csv", header=0)
df_x = cs_df[cs_df.columns.difference(['csMPa'])]
df_y = cs_df['csMPa']

model_pl = PMMLPipeline([('scaling',StandardScaler()),('ridge_lm',Ridge())])
model_pl.fit(df_x, df_y)

PMMLPipeline(steps=[('scaling', StandardScaler(copy=True, with_mean=True, with_std=True)),
        ('ridge_lm', Ridge(alpha=1.0, copy_X=True, fit_intercept=True, max_iter=None,
        normalize=False, random_state=None, solver='auto', tol=0.001))])
```

Figure 8.11: Code snippet of a model wrapped in PMML pipeline

Now, we can convert the pipeline to a PMML document named `concrete_strength_model.pmml` using `sklearn2pmml` function. It takes the pipeline object and the file name as inputs:

```
from sklearn2pmml import sklearn2pmml
pmml_file = 'concrete_strength_model.pmml'
sklearn2pmml(model_pl, pmml_file, with_repr = True)
```

Figure 8.12: Code snippet to export the model into a PMML file

We can see the partial content of the PMML file generated from code snippet of *Figure 8.12* as given below:

Figure 8.13: Generated PMML file – Part 1

Generated PMML file above contains standard deviation and mean of each field for the Standard Scaler function (under `DerivedField` tag). Now we can see the rest of the content as given below:

```
<Apply function="-">
    <FieldRef field="fineaggregate"/>
    <Constant dataType="double">773.5804854368932</Constant>
</Apply>
<Constant dataType="double">80.13705031241204</Constant>
</Apply>
</DerivedField>
<DerivedField name="standard_scaler(flyash)" optype="continuous" dataType="double">
    <Apply function="/">
        <Apply function="-">
            <FieldRef field="flyash"/>
            <Constant dataType="double">54.18834951456311</Constant>
        </Apply>
        <Constant dataType="double">63.96593010174051</Constant>
    </Apply>
</DerivedField>
<DerivedField name="standard_scaler(slag)" optype="continuous" dataType="double">
    <Apply function="/">
        <Apply function="-">
            <FieldRef field="slag"/>
            <Constant dataType="double">73.89582524271846</Constant>
        </Apply>
        <Constant dataType="double">86.23744840174277</Constant>
    </Apply>
</DerivedField>
<DerivedField name="standard_scaler(superplasticizer)" optype="continuous" dataType="double">
    <Apply function="/">
        <Apply function="-">
            <FieldRef field="superplasticizer"/>
            <Constant dataType="double">6.204660194174758</Constant>
        </Apply>
        <Constant dataType="double">5.970940765272762</Constant>
    </Apply>
</DerivedField>
<DerivedField name="standard_scaler(water)" optype="continuous" dataType="double">
    <Apply function="/">
        <Apply function="-">
            <FieldRef field="water"/>
            <Constant dataType="double">181.56728155339806</Constant>
        </Apply>
        <Constant dataType="double">21.343849922243454</Constant>
    </Apply>
</DerivedField>
</LocalTransformations>
<RegressionTable intercept="35.81796116504855">
    <NumericPredictor name="standard_scaler(age)" coefficient="7.19668934745216"/>
    <NumericPredictor name="standard_scaler(cement)" coefficient="12.337079826943869"/>
    <NumericPredictor name="standard_scaler(coarseaggregate)" coefficient="1.2856118449220513"/>
    <NumericPredictor name="standard_scaler(fineaggregate)" coefficient="1.4629812820085817"/>
    <NumericPredictor name="standard_scaler(flyash)" coefficient="5.4705583226047585"/>
    <NumericPredictor name="standard_scaler(slag)" coefficient="8.784125680891083"/>
    <NumericPredictor name="standard_scaler(superplasticizer)" coefficient="1.7470931961666332"/>
    <NumericPredictor name="standard_scaler(water)" coefficient="-3.318189798225114"/>
</RegressionTable>
</RegressionModel>
</PMML>
```

Figure 8.14: Generated PMML file – Part 2

The file content validates the existence of predefined elements, as discussed earlier. RegressionTable element contains all coefficients of predictors or feature variables.

How to use PMML document

A PMML document, like as shown above, definitely contains all relevant information required to consume a model. We can write a utility module to parse it and implement the consumption mechanism for various ML algorithms. Now, the question may arise, why should we again implement an ML algorithm, where we already saw so many libraries?

So far, what we have learned in different chapters, it is clear that there are two parts in a model, training, and using/validating it. The training part itself is very complex and uses different algorithms separately to train a specific model. But, once the training is done, we will have the required model parameters. Then, we can build a simple in-memory version of the model using any programming language and invoke it. For example, let's consider a Linear Regression model. Training using *Gradient Descent* will give us all coefficients and intercept values. Then we can easily write a function that multiplies feature variables with coefficients, adds intercept value, sums up everything, and return us the total. That's it!! It is the estimated target variable value for the given input of features.

Similarly, we can write utility functions for other models like decision tree, neural network, logistic regression, and more. These lightweight in-memory versions of models can be called as **PMML clients**. It is quite analogous to the stub of a SOAP-based web service.

We don't need the same language library and data structure to invoke a model from a PMML document. It is platform-independent. A model developed in one platform (let's say in Python) can be exported to other (let's say in Java) and can be consumed from there.

Python client for PMML model

We already installed the required library for the client, as given in *Figure 8.10*.

This Python library is a wrapper on top of Java. That's why we need a Py4j gateway to perform the model evaluation:

```python
from jpmml_evaluator.py4j import launch_gateway, Py4JBackend
from jpmml_evaluator import make_evaluator

gateway = launch_gateway()
backend = Py4JBackend(gateway)
evaluator = make_evaluator(backend, pmml_file).verify()

arguments = {
        "age" : 34,
        "cement" : 650,
        "coarseaggregate" : 800,
        "fineaggregate" : 745.7,
        "flyash" : 65.58,
        "slag" : 121.4,
        "superplasticizer" : 2.4,
        "water" : 220
        }

results = evaluator.evaluate(arguments)
print(results)
gateway.shutdown()

{'csMPa': 73.4062541056324}
```

Figure 8.15: Code snippet to use JPMML library in Python

We can see that features are passed as a dictionary to the evaluation function. It again returns the target variable value as a dictionary.

Java client for PMML model

Though in our discussion, all implementations of models are being done with Python. But for this case, we will also see an implementation of a Java client as a matter of proof of platform independence of PMML. Like Python, we need to add certain dependency libraries (in Java, those will be JAR files). We will do it in the pom.xml file of a Maven project.

```xml
<dependency>
    <groupId>org.jpmml</groupId>
    <artifactId>pmml-evaluator</artifactId>
    <version>1.4.11</version>
</dependency>
<dependency>
    <groupId>org.jpmml</groupId>
    <artifactId>pmml-evaluator-extension</artifactId>
    <version>1.4.11</version>
</dependency>
```

Figure 8.16: Maven dependency for PMML library

After doing this, we can write a Java client which will parse the PMML file and invoke the evaluation method like the Python one:

```java
package com.pmml.test;

import java.util.LinkedHashMap;
import java.util.List;
import java.util.Map;

import org.dmg.pmml.FieldName;
import org.jpmml.evaluator.Evaluator;
import org.jpmml.evaluator.EvaluatorUtil;
import org.jpmml.evaluator.FieldValue;
import org.jpmml.evaluator.InputField;
import org.jpmml.evaluator.LoadingModelEvaluatorBuilder;
import org.jpmml.evaluator.TargetField;
import org.jpmml.evaluator.visitors.DefaultVisitorBattery;

/**
 *
 * @author aynag
 *
 */
public class CSMpaRegressionModelTest {

    private static void doSamplePrediction() throws Exception {

        Evaluator evaluator = new LoadingModelEvaluatorBuilder().setLocatable(false)
                .setVisitors(new DefaultVisitorBattery())
                .load(CSMpaRegressionModelTest.class.getClassLoader().getResourceAsStream("concrete_strength_model.pmml")).build();

        evaluator.verify();

        List<? extends InputField> inputFields = evaluator.getInputFields();
        System.out.println("Input fields: " + inputFields);

        List<? extends TargetField> targetFields = evaluator.getTargetFields();
        System.out.println("Target field(s): " + targetFields);

        Map<FieldName, FieldValue> arguments = new LinkedHashMap<FieldName, FieldValue>();

        arguments.put(inputFields.get(0).getFieldName(), inputFields.get(0).prepare(34));
        arguments.put(inputFields.get(1).getFieldName(), inputFields.get(1).prepare(650));
        arguments.put(inputFields.get(2).getFieldName(), inputFields.get(2).prepare(800));
        arguments.put(inputFields.get(3).getFieldName(), inputFields.get(3).prepare(745.7));
        arguments.put(inputFields.get(4).getFieldName(), inputFields.get(4).prepare(65.58));
        arguments.put(inputFields.get(5).getFieldName(), inputFields.get(5).prepare(121.4));
        arguments.put(inputFields.get(6).getFieldName(), inputFields.get(6).prepare(2.4));
        arguments.put(inputFields.get(7).getFieldName(), inputFields.get(7).prepare(220));

        Map<FieldName, ?> results = evaluator.evaluate(arguments);
        Map<String, ?> resultRecord = EvaluatorUtil.decodeAll(results);
        System.out.println("Result ------- > " + resultRecord);
    }

    public static void main(String[] args) throws Exception {
        doSamplePrediction();
    }
}
```

Figure 8.17: Code snippet to use JPMML library in Java

We can execute the code snippet of *Figure 8.17* to get the following output:

```
Input fields: [InputField{name=age, fieldName=age, displayName=null, dataType=double, opType=continuous}, InputField{name=cement, fieldName=cement, displayName=null, dataTyp
Target field(s): [TargetField{name=csMPa, fieldName=csMPa, displayName=null, dataType=double, opType=continuous}]
Result ------- > {csMPa=73.4062541056324}
```

Figure 8.18: Output of Java client in Figure 8.17

Here also, features are passed to the `evaluate` method as `java.util.Map`, which is analogous to a Python `Dictionary`. And from the output, we can confirm that PMML models behave in the same way across the platforms.

PMML documents can also be generated from a Spark-MLlib based model. The above open-source has also support for that.

Building overall architecture

We saw how to expose the model as a service, add scalability, export model in a platform-independent way. But, how to put all of these together and build a complete solution? In real-life applications, there can be two primary technical design approaches at a very high level: Model deployed in batch mode andmodel deployed in ad-hoc/real-time mode. We will discuss both of this one-by-one.

Model deployed in batch mode

By technical terms, *batch mode* means working with a lot of data together at one shot or multiple shots. Each batch handles a predefined set of data. Using Big Data technology stack is always preferable for this type of design. Apache Spark/Flink has capabilities of giving results of prediction/recommendation from an ML model in bulk. This is ideal for the use cases where we want the result from a model as the pre-computed manner and want to store it somewhere for future use. A real-life example would be getting the sales estimate for each month of a year or each week of a month. This design generally does not expose a client-facing API, which can be invoked consecutively. Following architecture diagram can explain it in a better way:

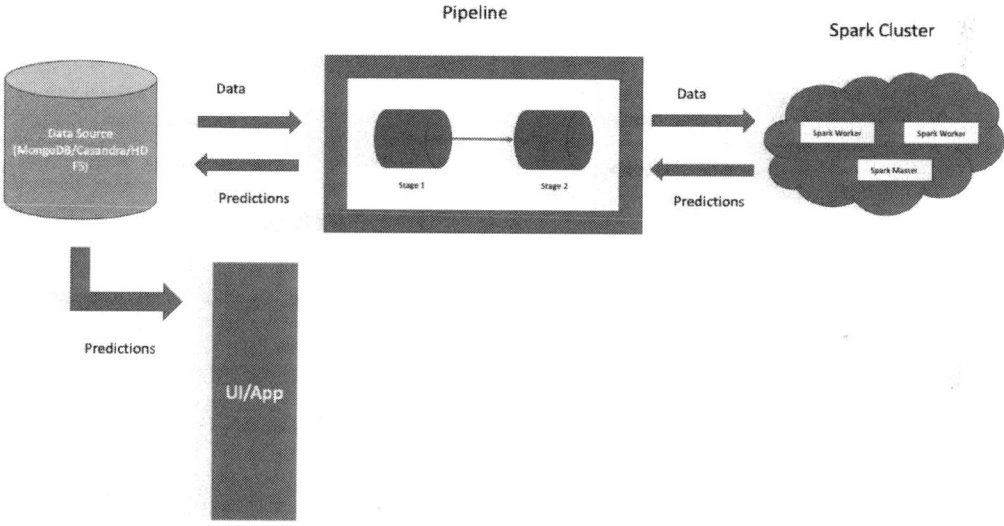

Figure 8.19: Spark Architecture of ML model deployed in batch mode

From the diagram, we can see that the client-facing UI/App neither will have direct access neither to the data processing layer (pipeline or Spark clusters) nor to the underlying model. All model training activities will run separately, and predictions will be stored in the database (NoSQL or HDFS). UI/App will directly get those predictions from the datastore. This is not a suitable real-time use case but will be helpful in a certain case like the *Sales Prediction* example given above.

Model deployed in ad-hoc/real-time mode

By technical terms, *ad-hoc* means something on demand in a stateless mode. Unlike *batch mode*, here, client-facing UI/App will have access to the model. Below diagram explains it well:

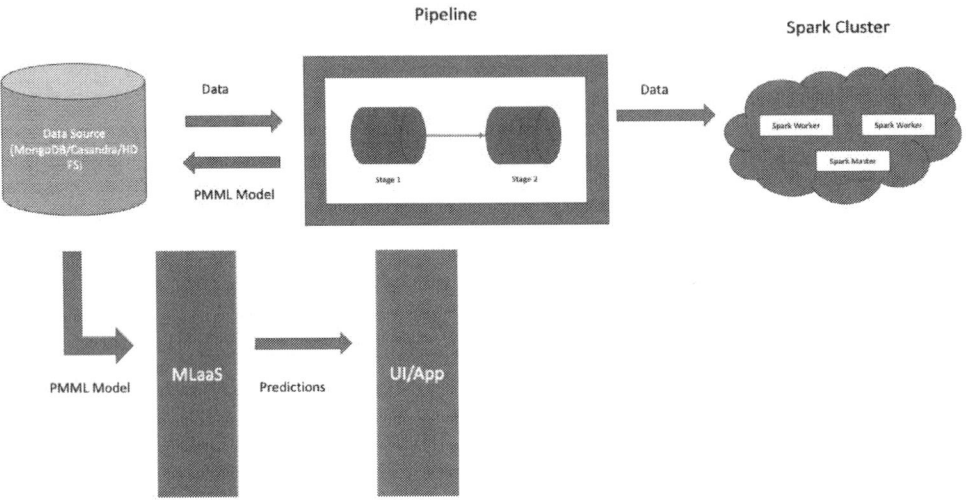

Figure 8.20: Spark Architecture of ML model deployed in ad-hoc mode

Predictions are not made here in a pre-computed manner. It is done on-demand basis. The model can be trained in a Big Data cluster like Spark Cluster, and the generated PMML document is saved back to the datastore. The job of the Spark cluster is just totrain the model and find optimal parameter/hyperparameter is a usual way using the dataset provided. It does not make any kind of predictions, unlike *batch mode* architecture. There is a special **MLaaS (Machine Learning as a Service or better to say as per our use case Prediction as a Service)** layer responsible for exposing APIs which are accessed from client-facing UI/App. This meansthe layer hosts a lightweight in-memory version of the model by parsing the PMML documents (as discussed in the previous section). It can give predictions upon request.

In both of the *batch*and *ad-hoc* mode, the Spark-based Big Data layer is not at all and should never be connected directly to UI/App. Big Data layers like Spark have a very low real-time throughput and should always be avoided from a direct & synchronous call with client-facing systems. In the *batch* mode, we are building a pre-stored prediction/recommendation base which can be referred from UI/App, and in the *ad-hoc* mode, ML models are directly called in a real-time manner via PMML templates.

Conclusion

In this chapter, we discussed all data engineering activities required for putting a machine learning model in production. We discussed scalability techniques, exposing model as service, PMML as a model descriptor, and the architecting ML systems. Our journey of ML started with Mathematical techniques from *Chapter 1: Introduction to Machine Learning* and this chapter gives final shape to it.

We learned about the challenges of putting ML models in the production environment, practical examples of exposing a model as Flask REST API, exporting a model as a PMML document, and how it can be consumed by a Python as well as Java client. In the end, we learned about two different flavors of deploying a model: batch and ad-hoc. We also learned how PMML could be utilized in ad-hoc flavored model deployment.

In the next chapter, we will apply all our knowledge in solving some case studies and will see how to write a proper story in data science.

CHAPTER 9
Case Studies and Storytelling

From the chapter 1 to Chapter 8, our learning path has covered various **machine learning (ML)** techniques, algorithms, practical examples, and of course, the mathematical model behind it. In this chapter, we will discuss how to apply different combinations of those techniques in solving real life. Solutions of those problems have to be shared with the stakeholders who are most of the time may be from the non-ML background. So, it is very important to interpret and represent an ML model in a business context friendly way. A single model can infer a lot of hidden insights from the data. In this chapter, we will discuss techniques of writing a story with a few practical use cases.

Structure

In this chapter, we will discuss:

- Techniques and rules of writing data science stories
- Standard visualization libraries and usage
- Case studies covering regression modeling, multilabel text classification and image classification with CNN

Objective

After finishing this chapter, we will be able to:

- Infer facts from ML models in business terms and user-friendly way
- Learn appropriate visualization for different models and use cases

What is data science storytelling?

Data science is an umbrella over machine learning. ML mainly deals with the mathematical aspect of any problem. The objective of data science practice is to use ML to study data and extract meaningful information related to a business domain. A data science story is a narrative representation of the facts about data with numbers. This story should be written or told in a manner that can reach easily to a larger audience who may or may not have a background in ML or analytics. This practice is known as **data science storytelling**.

A data science story generally consists of the following sections.

Machinelearning model

A Data Science story may have one or more Machine Learning models. This model will be the core of the story. All insights and presentations will be influenced by the models presented there. But, it is also true that a story may not have a model sometimes. In that case, it becomes a narrative of the existing facts.

Visualizations

Proper visualizations are an essential part of a story. Without these, a story becomes very dull and monotonous to the stakeholders. We have to remember the law of Statistics over here: *A picture can tell a thousand words*. Visualization can be of any form: charts, graphs, tabular representation, and more. It depends on the data and the business use case or domain that the story is trying to explain. Usage of different colors also makes a solid impact on the target audience. Below table shows some of the commonly used visualization techniques and the preferred Python libraries for it:

Chart type	Usage	Python library	Function/class
Bar chart	Bar charts or Histograms are ideal for showing group data, counts for categorical data, or any aggregate function applied on clustered data.	seaborn	barplot
Line chart	Line charts are ideal for plotting a function of type y=mx + c. This chart is primarily used for plotting regression lines or relationships between variables.	seaborn	lineplot
	Scatter diagrams are ideal for showing data clusters. The output of a clustering algorithm can be seeded here for display.	seaborn	scatterplot
	Word Cloud is ideal for showing the token distribution of texts. High-frequency tokens are shown in larger fonts and low-frequency ones in smaller fonts. Tokens are randomly aligned with each other in this type of plot and create a meaningful visualization.	wordcloud	WordCloud (instance of WordCloud is passed in imshow function of matplotlib)

Table 9.1 is not at all an exhaustive list of chart/visualization techniques. There are many more. But definitely, these are the most commonly used ones.

Facts

It is the objective of a data science story. Facts are statements with numbers and stakeholders will be most interested in it. So, to give meaning and relevant information, proper domain, and business context should be mixed in facts. A fact should not tell too much low-level technical details, which may be irrelevant to the stakeholders. Rather, it should try to focus on a business context friendly approach of telling the information. Facts can be of two types: *descriptive* and *predictive*. Descriptive facts will tell about the existing information, and predictive will tell about the future. In Predictive fact, outputs of the ML model will matter a lot.

We will now discuss three case studies and try to build data science stories out of those. We will maintain a few conventions here as described below:

- We will discuss the ML model and code, but these should not come in the main story. For our convenience and to make everything clubbed together, we will be doing this.

- The Main Data Science story will be written in italic fonts. The rest of the content will be in normal font. If somebody wants to present the story to the larger audience, he/she should use only those statements which are written in italics.

- We will use Python libraries like `scikit-learn`, `scikit-multilearn`, `PyTorch`, `gensim`, and some libraries from `pypi`.

Case study 1: Analysis of sales-profit for superstore sales data from tableau user group using multivariate regression techniques

Data source and problem definition

We will use **Superstore Sales Data** from **Tableau User Group** (https://community. tableau.com/docs/DOC-1236). Data is available in CSV format.

The objective is to build a model for predicting Profit and study the most important measures and dimensions (apart from customer information) that are affecting Profit and also to what extent.

Data exploration

We will use `pandas` to read the data and display the columns:

```
import pandas as pd

df = pd.read_csv("../data/Sample - Superstore.csv", header=0)
df.head()
```

Customer ID	Customer Name	Segment	Country	City	...	Postal Code	Region	Product ID	Category	Sub-Category	Product Name	Sales	Quantity	Discount	Profit
CG-12520	Claire Gute	Consumer	United States	Henderson	...	42420	South	FUR-BO-10001798	Furniture	Bookcases	Bush Somerset Collection Bookcase	261.9600	2	0.00	41.9136
CG-12520	Claire Gute	Consumer	United States	Henderson	...	42420	South	FUR-CH-10000454	Furniture	Chairs	Hon Deluxe Fabric Upholstered Stacking Chairs,...	731.9400	3	0.00	219.5820
DV-13045	Darrin Van Huff	Corporate	United States	Los Angeles	...	90036	West	OFF-LA-10000240	Office Supplies	Labels	Self-Adhesive Address Labels for Typewriters b...	14.6200	2	0.00	6.8714
SO-20335	Sean O'Donnell	Consumer	United States	Fort Lauderdale	...	33311	South	FUR-TA-10000577	Furniture	Tables	Bretford CR4500 Series Slim Rectangular Table	957.5775	5	0.45	-383.0310
SO-20335	Sean O'Donnell	Consumer	United States	Fort Lauderdale	...	33311	South	OFF-ST-10000760	Office Supplies	Storage	Eldon Fold 'N Roll Cart System	22.3680	2	0.20	2.5164

Figure 9.1: Code snippet for reading Superstore dataset and the result

There isa total of 21 different attributes (dimensions and measures) in the dataset. 'Profit' is the target field, as shown above, which needs to be analyzed with respect to other fields. Few fields are there which can be truncated are: `Customer ID`, `Customer Name`, `ProductID`, `Order ID`) as this analysis will not consider customer information. The objective is to study the data and infer other dimensions and measures which are affecting *Profit*. For `Customer` data analysis, a separate study can be done parallelly.

Data filtering

We can truncate a few columns as described above:

```
df = df.drop(['Row ID','Order ID','Customer ID','Customer Name', 'Product ID'], axis=1)
df.head()
```

	Order Date	Ship Date	Ship Mode	Segment	Country	City	State	Postal Code	Region	Category	Sub-Category	Product Name	Sales	Quantity	Discount	
0	08/11/16	11/11/16	Second Class	Consumer	United States	Henderson	Kentucky	42420	South	Furniture	Bookcases	Bush Somerset Collection Bookcase	261.9600	2	0.00	4
1	08/11/16	11/11/16	Second Class	Consumer	United States	Henderson	Kentucky	42420	South	Furniture	Chairs	Hon Deluxe Fabric Upholstered Stacking Chairs,...	731.9400	3	0.00	21
2	12/06/16	16/06/16	Second Class	Corporate	United States	Los Angeles	California	90036	West	Office Supplies	Labels	Self-Adhesive Address Labels for Typewriters b...	14.6200	2	0.00	
3	11/10/15	18/10/15	Standard Class	Consumer	United States	Fort Lauderdale	Florida	33311	South	Furniture	Tables	Bretford CR4500 Series Slim Rectangular Table	957.5775	5	0.45	-38
4	11/10/15	18/10/15	Standard Class	Consumer	United States	Fort Lauderdale	Florida	33311	South	Office Supplies	Storage	Eldon Fold 'N Roll Cart System	22.3680	2	0.20	

Figure 9.2: Code snippet for truncating few columns of Superstore dataset and the result

Figure 9.2 shows that few columns like various IDs, names are removed as those are not that relevant in ML analysis.

Data pre-processing

Order DateandShip Date are in mm/dd/yy format and have to be decomposed into three fields: data, month, and year for both of these two.

We can write a function to do this like below:

```python
def decompose_date(x):
    parts = x.split('/')
    return parts[0], parts[1], parts[2]
```

Figure 9.3: Code snippet for decompose_date function

We can now use this function to decompose the Order_Date field:

```python
df['Order_Date_Day'], df['Order_Date_Month'],df['Order_Date_Year'] = zip(*df['Order Date'].apply(lambda x :
                                                                         decompose_date(x)))
df = df.drop(['Order Date'], axis = 1)
df.head()
```

City	State	Postal Code	Region	Category	Sub-Category	Product Name	Sales	Quantity	Discount	Profit	Order_Date_Day	Order_Date_Month	Order_Date_Year
son	Kentucky	42420	South	Furniture	Bookcases	Bush Somerset Collection Bookcase	261.9600	2	0.00	41.9136	08	11	16
son	Kentucky	42420	South	Furniture	Chairs	Hon Deluxe Fabric Upholstered Stacking Chairs,...	731.9400	3	0.00	219.5820	08	11	16
Los eles	California	90036	West	Office Supplies	Labels	Self-Adhesive Address Labels for Typewriters b...	14.6200	2	0.00	6.8714	12	06	16
Fort dale	Florida	33311	South	Furniture	Tables	Bretford CR4500 Series Slim Rectangular Table	957.5775	5	0.45	-383.0310	11	10	15
Fort dale	Florida	33311	South	Office Supplies	Storage	Eldon Fold 'N Roll Cart System	22.3680	2	0.20	2.5164	11	10	15

Figure 9.4: Code snippet to decompose 'Order Date' field and the result

In the same way, we can decompose the Ship_Date field:

```
df['Ship_Date_Day'], df['Ship_Date_Month'],df['Ship_Date_Year'] = zip(*df['Ship Date'].apply(lambda x :
                                                                        decompose_date(x)))
df = df.drop(['Ship Date'], axis = 1)
df.head()
```

l-y	Product Name	Sales	Quantity	Discount	Profit	Order_Date_Day	Order_Date_Month	Order_Date_Year	Ship_Date_Day	Ship_Date_Month	Ship_Date_Year
s	Bush Somerset Collection Bookcase	261.9600	2	0.00	41.9136	08	11	16	11	11	16
s	Hon Deluxe Fabric Upholstered Stacking Chairs,...	731.9400	3	0.00	219.5820	08	11	16	11	11	16
ls	Self-Adhesive Address Labels for Typewriters b...	14.6200	2	0.00	6.8714	12	06	16	16	06	16
s	Bretford CR4500 Series Slim Rectangular Table	957.5775	5	0.45	-383.0310	11	10	15	18	10	15
e	Eldon Fold 'N Roll Cart System	22.3680	2	0.20	2.5164	11	10	15	18	10	15

Figure 9.5: Code snippet to decompose 'Ship Date' field and the result

As most of the features are categorical, so these have to be converted to numerical by one-hot-encoding. We will use the default `get_dummies` function of `pandas` to do it. We have to pass the list of feature names eligible for transformation.

```
encoded_df = pd.get_dummies(df,columns=['Ship Mode','Segment','Country','City','State','Postal Code','Region',
                                        'Category','Sub-Category','Product Name','Quantity',
                                        'Order_Date_Day','Order_Date_Month','Order_Date_Year',
                                        'Ship_Date_Day','Ship_Date_Month','Ship_Date_Year'])
encoded_df.head()
```

	Sales	Discount	Profit	Ship Mode_First Class	Ship Mode_Same Day	Ship Mode_Second Class	Ship Mode_Standard Class	Segment_Consumer	Segment_Corporate	Segment_Home Office	...	Ship_
0	261.9600	0.00	41.9136	0	0	1	0	1	0	0	...	
1	731.9400	0.00	219.5820	0	0	1	0	1	0	0	...	
2	14.6200	0.00	6.8714	0	0	1	0	0	1	0	...	
3	957.5775	0.45	-383.0310	0	0	0	1	1	0	0	...	
4	22.3680	0.20	2.5164	0	0	0	1	1	0	0	...	

5 rows × 3205 columns

Figure 9.6: Code snippet to transform using One-Hot-Encoder and the result

Though `Quantity` is a numerical feature, we considered this as categorical because quantity amount varies only from 1 to 14 and that too in whole integer numbers.

Building the model

We will divide the dataset into target and feature variables:

```
df_x = encoded_df[[x for x in encoded_df.columns if x not in('Profit')]]
df_y = encoded_df[['Profit']]
```

Figure 9.7: Code snippet divide the dataset into features and target

We will use a Lasso regression model for our problem. We will achieve two things together over here; first, we will avoid overfitting, and we can automatically get only important feature names as Lasso zero out the coefficients of not so important features. Thus we can get a list of dimensions and measures which are truly affecting Profit.

For fitting the model with Lasso, all features have to scaled by `StandardScaler` first. We will use a `Pipeline` for it:

```
from sklearn.linear_model import Lasso
from sklearn.preprocessing import StandardScaler, MinMaxScaler
from sklearn.pipeline import Pipeline
from sklearn.metrics import r2_score

lasso_model = Lasso()
lasso_pl = Pipeline(steps=[('scaler', StandardScaler()),('lasso', lasso_model)])
lasso_pl.fit(df_x,df_y)
pred_y = lasso_pl.predict(df_x)
lasso_model_r2Val = r2_score(df_y, pred_y)
print('R2 for Lasso Model: ', lasso_model_r2Val)

R2 for Lasso Model:  0.7200601994174354
```

Figure 9.8: Code snippet for Lasso model

Almost 72% of the variance is explained by the model. That is a fair accuracy. However, accuracy can be further improved by the hyper-parameter tuning of Lasso.

We can get the coefficients of all features:

```
coefs = lasso_model.coef_
all_feature_coeffs = []
for index, coef in enumerate(coefs):
    if coef != 0.000:
        feature_coeff = {}
        feature_coeff['Feature Variable'] = df_x.columns[index]
        feature_coeff['Coefficient'] = coef
        all_feature_coeffs.append(feature_coeff)

coeff_df = pd.DataFrame(all_feature_coeffs)
coeff_df_sorted_insc = coeff_df.sort_values('Coefficient')
first_10_coeffs = coeff_df_sorted_insc.head(10)
last_10_coeffs = coeff_df_sorted_insc.tail(10)
```

Figure 9.9: Code snippet to sort all feature coefficients

We sorted the regression coefficients in increasing order. Now we can get the lowest ten and the highest ten coefficients and display:

```
pd.set_option('display.max_colwidth', -1)
last_10_coeffs
```

	Coefficient	Feature Variable
307	5.388959	Product Name_Hewlett-Packard Deskjet 6988DT Refurbished Printer
206	6.495912	Product Name_Canon imageCLASS MF7460 Monochrome Digital Laser Multifunction Copier
505	7.474736	Product Name_Zebra ZM400 Thermal Label Printer
508	8.842331	Quantity_1
162	9.046520	Product Name_Ativa V4110MDD Micro-Cut Shredder
509	9.760329	Quantity_2
91	9.833903	Postal Code_48205
133	15.369593	Sub-Category_Binders
205	23.300587	Product Name_Canon imageCLASS 2200 Advanced Copier
0	197.900762	Sales

```
first_10_coeffs
```

	Coefficient	Feature Variable
221	-87.554917	Product Name_Cisco TelePresence System EX90 Videoconferencing Unit
226	-68.155660	Product Name_Cubify CubeX 3D Printer Double Head Print
227	-60.594993	Product Name_Cubify CubeX 3D Printer Triple Head Print
360	-46.944142	Product Name_Lexmark MX611dhe Monochrome Laser Printer
1	-35.281983	Discount
308	-31.502105	Product Name_High Speed Automatic Electric Letter Opener
264	-28.683737	Product Name_GBC DocuBind P400 Electric Binding System
145	-26.517512	Sub-Category_Tables
372	-25.815289	Product Name_Martin Yale Chadless Opener Electric Letter Opener
213	-21.402621	Product Name_Chromcraft Bull-Nose Wood Oval Conference Tables & Bases

Figure 9.10: *Code snippet to get the highest and lowest ten coefficients and the result*

And the intercept:

```
lasso_model.intercept_

array([28.65689631])
```

Figure 9.11: *Code snippet to get intercept of Lasso Model*

From the coefficients and features names, we can see that decomposed (one-hot-encoded) features have separate coefficients. For example, product Canon ImageCLASS 2200 Advanced Copier and Zebra ZM400 Thermal Label Printer have different coefficients though both of these belong to parent feature Product Name.

Analysis of result and dimension-measure relationships

We have written a utility function for displaying the bar chart:

```
%matplotlib inline

import matplotlib.pyplot as plt
import seaborn as sns

def barplot(X=None, Y=None, df=None, title=None):
    fig = plt.figure(figsize=(18,6))
    bar_plot = sns.barplot(x=X, y=Y, data=df)
    for item in bar_plot.get_xticklabels():
        item.set_rotation(90)
    plt.title(title)
    plt.show()
```

Figure 9.12: Code snippet of barplot function to generate a bar chart

Displaying highest and lowest valued coefficients with this function:

```
sns.set(font_scale=1.3)
barplot(X='Feature Variable',Y='Coefficient', df=pd.concat([first_10_coeffs,last_10_coeffs]))
```

Figure 9.13: Code snippet for calling barplot function to generate a bar chart

And it produces the following chart:

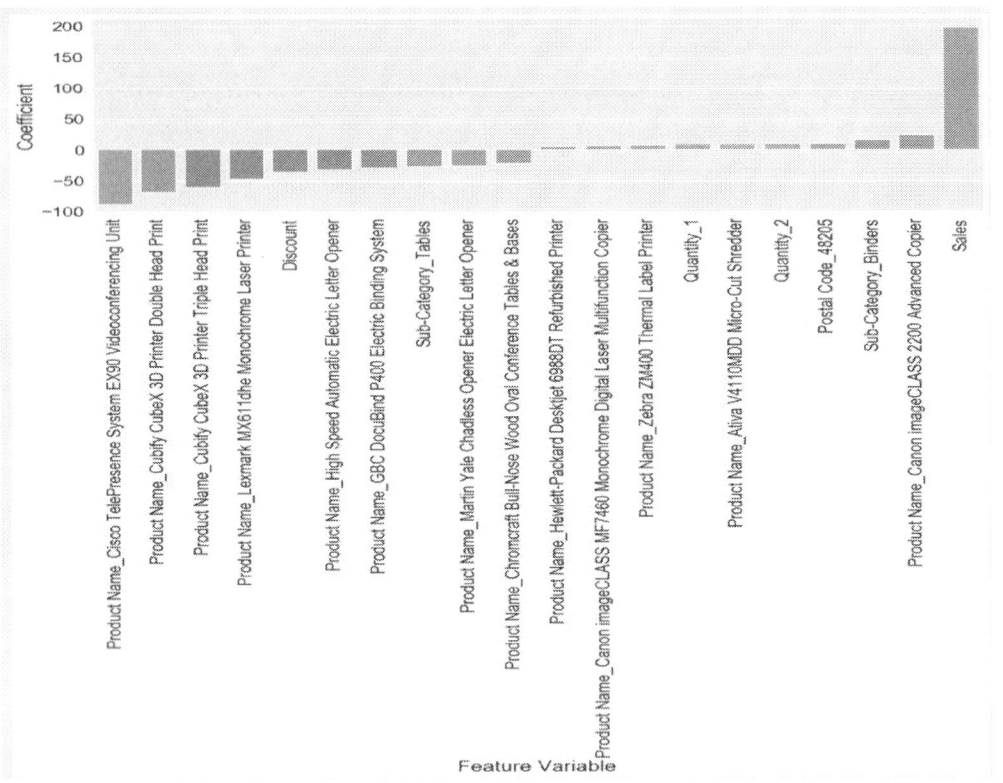

Figure 9.14: Bar Chart for coefficient vs. feature

Twenty of the most important features which are affecting Profit are displayed above. A positive coefficient value indicates that the feature is contributing to increasing the Profit, whereas a negative one is contributing to decreasing it. An unimportant feature will have a coefficient as zero. Some of the important facts that can be inferred from the above analysis are given below:

- A higher `Sales` indicates bigger `Profit`.
- Whenever the product `Cannon ImageCLASS 2200 Advanced Copier` is sold, it has helped to increase the `Profit`.
- `Quantity` amount 1 and 2 both are helping to increase the `Profit`.
- A bigger `Discount` indicates lesser `Profit`.
- Whenever a product named Sub-Category`Tables` has been sold, it has resulted in a decrement in `Profit`.
- Whenever the product `Cubify Cubex 3D Printer Double Head Print` is sold, it has resulted in a decrement in `Profit`.
- `Sales` are the most important factor that is always causing the highest increment in `Profit`, whereas the sale of product `Cisco TelePresence System EX90 Videoconferencing Unit` is always causing the highest decrement in `Profit`.

We can now analyze the dominant features, which are influencing `Profit`.

Subcategory vs.profit analysis

We can compute and display the average profit under each `Sub-Category`:

```
sub_category_avg_series = df.groupby('Sub-Category')['Profit'].mean()
sub_cat_profit_df = pd.DataFrame({'Sub-Category':sub_category_avg_series.index,
                                  'Average Profit':sub_category_avg_series.values})
barplot(X='Sub-Category', Y='Average Profit', df=sub_cat_profit_df, title='Sub-Category vs Average Profit')
```

Figure 9.15: Code snippet to compute and display the average profit per sub-category

And it produces the following bar plot:

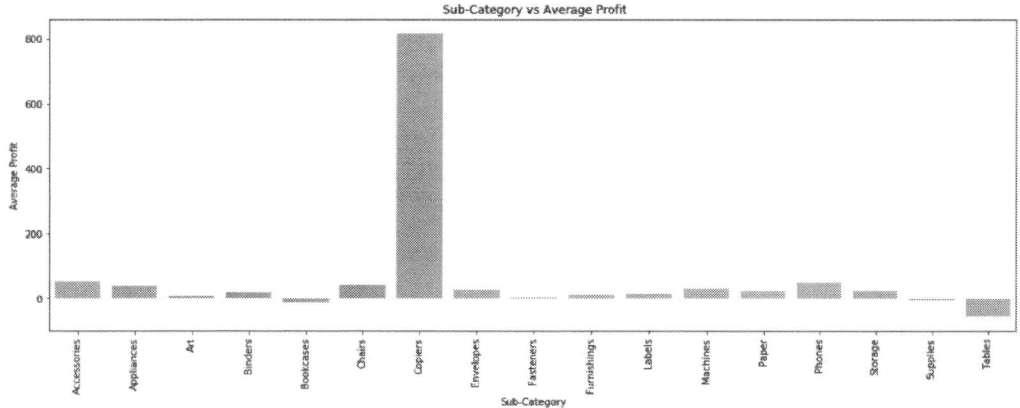

Figure 9.16: Bar chart for Sub-Category vs. Average Profit

Subcategory `Copiers` is giving the highest average `Profit` whereas `Tables` is causing the lowest `Profit` or rather better to say negative profit. From the coefficient analysis, some facts can be inferred as given below:

- Whenever a change happens from subcategory `Binders` to subcategory `Tables`, there is a -9.16 unit change in `Profit`, that is, `Profit` decreases by 9.16 unit. (15.36 – 26.51 = -9.16).

- The opposite change will cause a +9.16 unit change in `Profit`, that is, `Profit` increases by 9.16 units.

The above changes assume that there is no other change in other features are happening; that is, a change in subcategory is assumed, keeping all other features fixed. (Practically, it may not be possible. But still, it gives a useful insight to the analysts).

Quantity vs.profit analysis

We can compute average profit under each quantity (as `Quantity` is also considered as a categorical feature) and display:

```
quantity_avg_series = df.groupby('Quantity')['Profit'].mean()
quantity_profit_df = pd.DataFrame({'Quantity':quantity_avg_series.index, 'Average Profit':quantity_avg_series.values})
barplot(X='Quantity', Y='Average Profit', df=quantity_profit_df, title='Quantity vs Average Profit')
```

Figure 9.17: Code snippet to compute and display the average profit per quantity

And it produces the following plot:

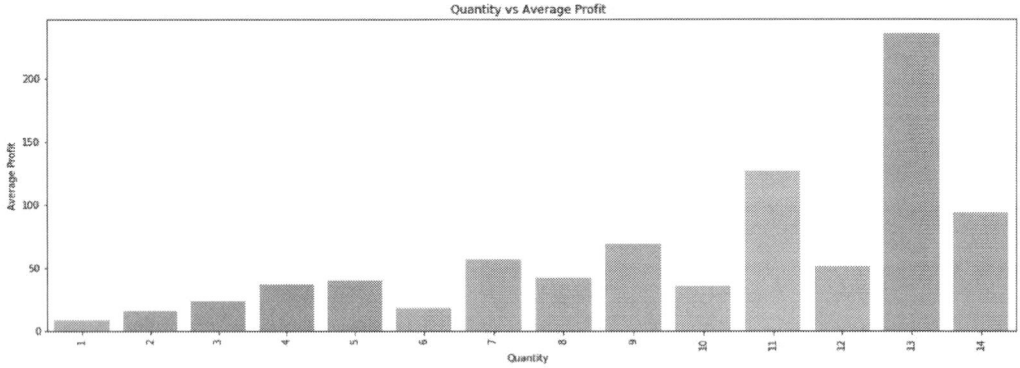

Figure 9.18: Bar chart for quantity vs. average profit

Quantity 13 is giving maximum average profit, and one is giving the minimum. Quantity did not cause any negative profit. From the coefficient analysis, some facts can be inferred as given below:

- Whenever a change happens from `Quantity 1` to `Quantity 2`, there is a corresponding +0.92 (9.76-8.84) unit change in `Profit`.

- Whenever a change happens from `Quantity` 2 to `Quantity` 1, there is a corresponding -0.92 (8.84-9.76) unit change in `Profit`.

Postal code vs.profit analysis

There is lots of `Postal Code` in the dataset. For our convenience, we will compute and display the `Postal Code`, which is giving the highest and lowest profit (first 15 and last 15):

```
postal_code_series = df.groupby('Postal Code')['Profit'].mean()
postal_code_df = pd.DataFrame({'Postal Code':postal_code_series.index, 'Average Profit':postal_code_series.values})
barplot(X='Postal Code', Y='Average Profit', df=postal_code_df.sort_values('Average Profit').tail(15),
        title='Most Profitable Postal Codes vs Averge Profit')
```

Figure 9.19: Code snippet to compute and display average profit per postal code

And it produces the following plot:

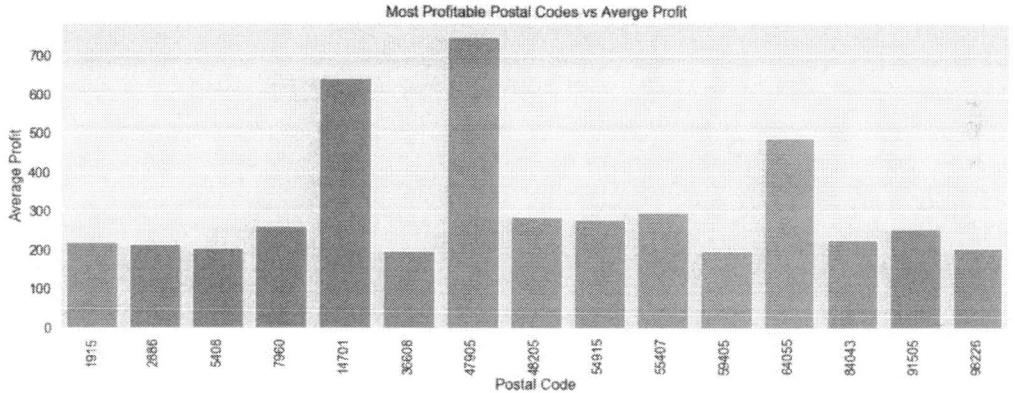

Figure 9.20: Bar plot for most profitable postal codes vs. average profit

Now we can display the least profitable postal codes:

```
barplot(X='Postal Code', Y='Average Profit', df=postal_code_df.sort_values('Average Profit').head(15),
        title='Least Profitable Postal Codes vs Averge Profit')
```

Figure 9.21: Code snippet to compute and display average profit per postal code

And it produces the following plot:

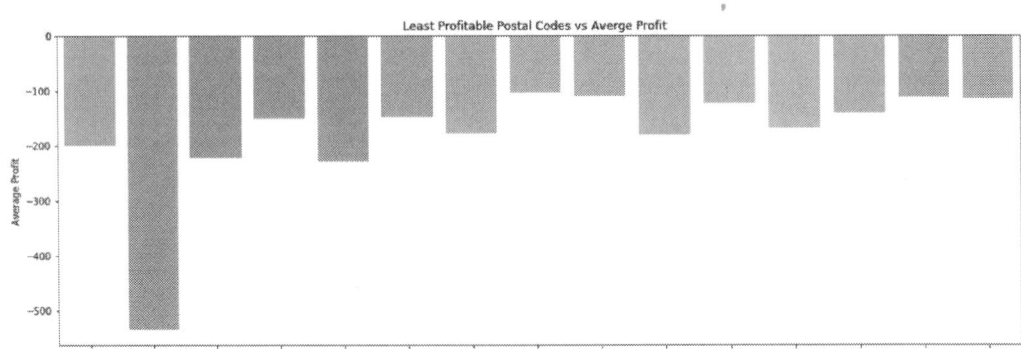

Figure 9.22: Bar chart for the least profitable postal codes vs. average profit

Postal Code 47905 is giving maximum average profit, and 27217 are giving a minimum average profit. Postal Code 48205 is the most dominant feature among other postal codes, as it is coming in the first 20 most important feature lists. And it will give maximum positive change in Profit (+9.83 units) whenever it is chosen in place of other postal codes while selling a product.

Sales vs.profit analysis

As Sales is a continuous feature, we will use the clustering algorithm to group it into different clusters and will compute the average profit under each cluster. We can write a utility function to do clustering and plot. We will use xmeans clustering API from pyclustering library available at pypi repository:

```
from pyclustering.cluster.xmeans import xmeans
from pyclustering.cluster.center_initializer import kmeans_plusplus_initializer
from statistics import mean

def plot_continous_measure_profit(df, measure_name, max_clusters):
    measure_arr = [[float(df.loc[i, measure_name])] for i in range(len(df))]

    initial_centers = kmeans_plusplus_initializer(measure_arr, 2).initialize()
    xm = xmeans(measure_arr, initial_centers, max_clusters)
    xm.process()
    clusters_index = xm.get_clusters()
    centers_centres = xm.get_centers()

    df_enries = []
    for i in range(len(clusters_index)):
        current_clustered_data = []
        profit_data = []
        for j in range(len(clusters_index[i])):
            current_clustered_data.append(measure_arr[clusters_index[i][j]][0])
            profit_data.append(df.loc[clusters_index[i][j], 'Profit'])

        current_cluster_min = min(current_clustered_data)
        current_cluster_max = max(current_clustered_data)

        min_max_key = str(round(current_cluster_min, 2)) + ' ~ ' + str(round(current_cluster_max, 2))
        current_cluster_profit_avg = mean(profit_data)

        df_enries.append({measure_name + ' Group' : min_max_key, 'Average Profit' : current_cluster_profit_avg})

    profit_dist = pd.DataFrame(df_enries)

    barplot(X=measure_name + ' Group', Y='Average Profit', df=profit_dist,
            title=measure_name + ' vs Averge Profit')
```

Figure 9.23: Code snippet for plot_continous_measure_profit function

Above function can generate clusters from any continuous features and plot bar-chart:

```
plot_continous_measure_profit(df, 'Sales', 40)
```

Figure 9.24: Code snippet for plotting bar chart by calling plot_continous_measure_profit

And it generates the following plot:

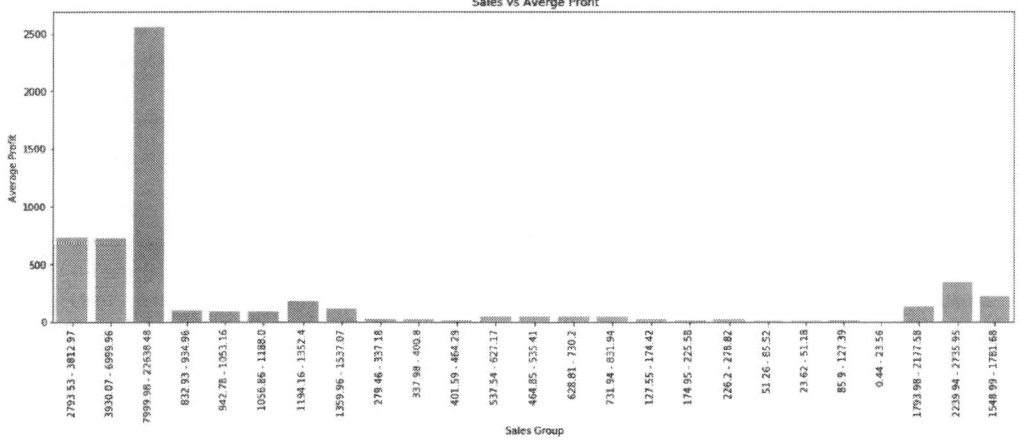

Figure 9.25: Bar chart for sales group cluster vs. average profit

The maximum profit is obtained from the sales range from 7999 to 22638. Sales are always playing a positive factor in increasing Profit, and it is also the most dominant feature. From the coefficient analysis, the following facts can be inferred:

- Increment in Sales results in an increment in Profit and decrement in Sales results decrement in Profit.

- +1 unit change in sales can cause a +197 unit change in Profit, and -1 unit change will cause -197 unit changes in Profit. While changing sales, it is assumed that other feature values are kept fixed.

Discount vs.profit analysis

As Discount is also a continuous feature, we will use the same clustering technique to get average profit per cluster:

```
plot_continous_measure_profit(df, 'Discount', 20)
```

Figure 9.26: Code snippet for plotting bar chart by calling plot_continous_measure_profit

And it produces the following plot:

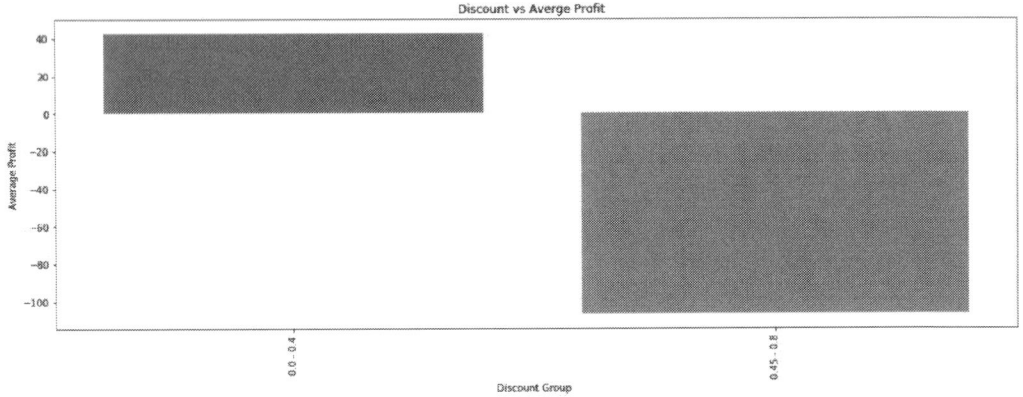

Figure 9.27: Bar chart for discount group cluster vs. average profit

When discount ranges between 0-0.4, it gives a positive Profit, but whenever it goes between 0.45-0.8, Profit becomes negative or at a loss. Discount is one of the dominant factors in determining Profit, and it is associated with a negative coefficient. From there, some facts can be inferred:

- Increment in Discount results in a decrement in Profit and vice versa

- +1 unit change in Discount causes -35 unit change in Profit (that is, a loss) and -1 unit change in Discount causes +35 unit change in Profit. It is assumed that, whenever Discount is changed, other features are kept fixed.

Product name vs.profit analysis

There are lots of `Product Name` in the dataset. For our convenience, we will compute and display the `Product Name`, which is giving the highest and lowest profit (first 15 and last 15):

```
product_name_series = df.groupby('Product Name')['Profit'].mean()
product_name_df = pd.DataFrame({'Product Name':product_name_series.index, 'Average Profit':product_name_series.values})
barplot(X='Product Name', Y='Average Profit', df=product_name_df.sort_values('Average Profit').tail(15),
        title='Most Profitable Product Name vs Averge Profit')
```

Figure 9.28: Code snippet to compute and display the average profit per product name

And it produces the following plot:

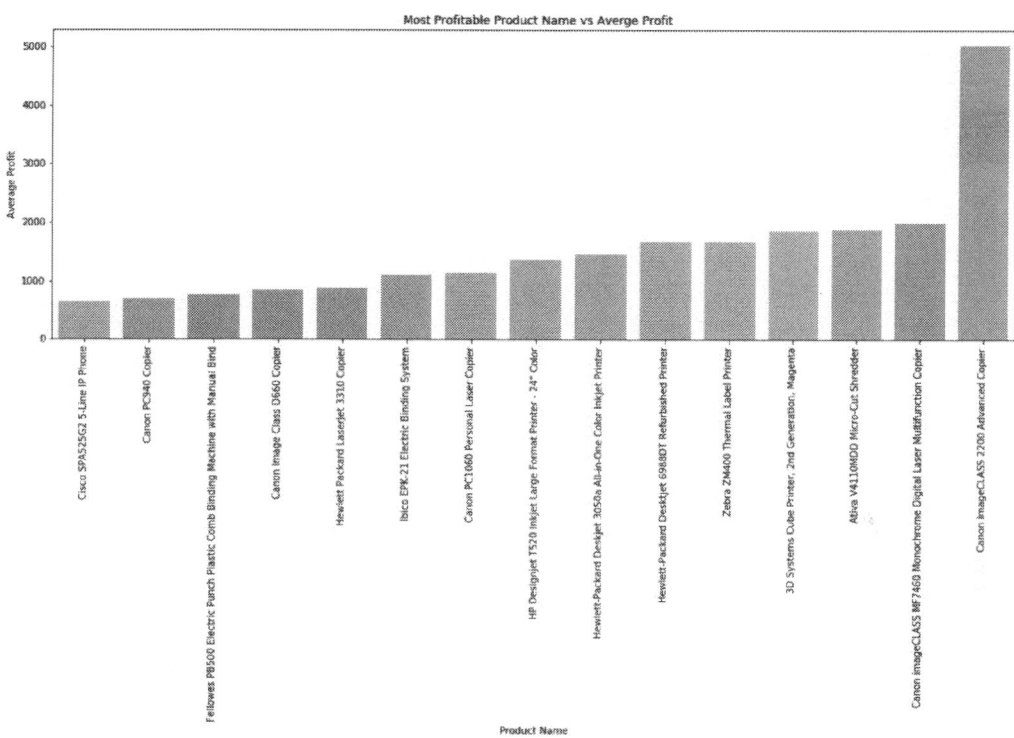

Figure 9.29: Bar chart for most profitable product name vs. average profit

Now we can display the least profitable product names:

```
product_name_series = df.groupby('Product Name')['Profit'].mean()
product_name_df = pd.DataFrame({'Product Name':product_name_series.index, 'Average Profit':product_name_series.values})
barplot(X='Product Name', Y='Average Profit', df=product_name_df.sort_values('Average Profit').head(15),
        title='Least Profitable Product Name vs Averge Profit')
```

Figure 9.30: Code snippet to compute and display the average profit per product name

And it produces the following plot:

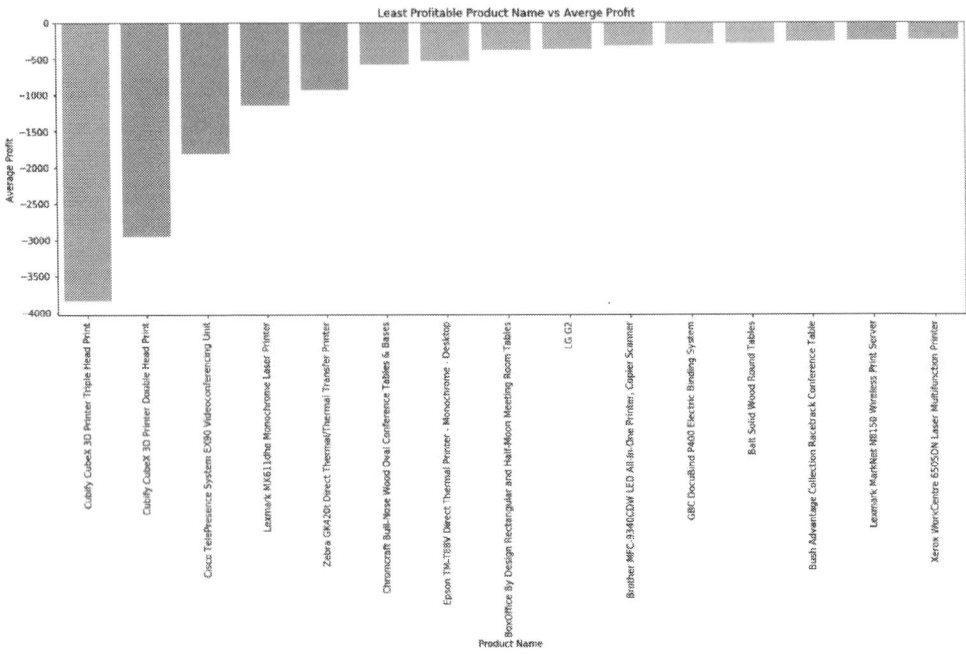

Figure 9.31: Bar chart for the least profitable product name vs. average profit

Product `Cannon ImageCLASS 2200 Advanced Copier` is giving maximum profit whereas `Cubify Cubex 3D Printer Tripple Head Print` is giving minimum profit (basically loss as Profit is negative there). From the coefficient analysis, some facts can be inferred as given below:

- `Cisco TelePresence System EX90 Videoconferencing Unit` is causing maximum negative change (-87 unit) in `Profit` whenever it is sold in place of another product.

- `Cannon ImageCLASS 2200 Advanced Copier` is causing maximum positive change (+23 units) in `Profit` whenever it is sold in place of another product.

Case study 2: Prediction of movie genres with multilabel text classification

Data source and problem definition

We will use CMU Movie Summary Corpus (http://www.cs.cmu.edu/~ark/personas/) as our data source. This dataset contains several CSV files containing movie-metadata, genre, and plot details. One movie plot can have multiple genres attached to it.

The objective is to analyze plot summaries and predict movie genres out of it.

Data exploration

We will use pandas to read the required CSV files, join, and display the required data. Displaying movie metadata:

```python
import pandas as pd

movie_metadata_df = pd.read_csv('../data/MovieSummaries/movie.metadata.tsv', sep = '\t',
                                usecols=[0,8], names=['Wikipedia_movie_ID', 'Genres'])
movie_metadata_df.head()
```

	Wikipedia_movie_ID	Genres
0	975900	{"/m/01jfsb": "Thriller", "/m/06n90": "Science...
1	3196793	{"/m/02n4kr": "Mystery", "/m/03bxz7": "Biograp...
2	28463795	{"/m/0lsxr": "Crime Fiction", "/m/07s9rl0": "D...
3	9363483	{"/m/01jfsb": "Thriller", "/m/0glj9q": "Erotic...
4	261236	{"/m/07s9rl0": "Drama"}

Figure 9.32: Code snippet to display movie metadata and the result

Displaying plot summaries:

```python
movie_plot_summeries = []

file = open('../data/MovieSummaries/plot_summaries.txt', 'r')
lines = file.readlines()
for index, line in enumerate(lines):
    movie_plot = {}
    parts = line.split(sep='\t', maxsplit=2)
    movie_plot['Wikipedia_movie_ID'] = int(parts[0])
    movie_plot['plot'] = parts[1]
    movie_plot_summeries.append(movie_plot)

file.close()
movie_plot_summeries_df = pd.DataFrame(movie_plot_summeries)
movie_plot_summeries_df.head()
```

	Wikipedia_movie_ID	plot
0	23890098	Shlykov, a hard-working taxi driver and Lyosha...
1	31186339	The nation of Panem consists of a wealthy Capi...
2	20663735	Poovalli Induchoodan is sentenced for six yea...
3	2231378	The Lemon Drop Kid , a New York City swindler,...
4	595909	Seventh-day Adventist Church pastor Michael Ch...

Figure 9.33: Code snippet to display plot summaries and the result

Joining these two datasets:

```
movie_id_summary_df = pd.merge(movie_metadata_df, movie_plot_summeries_df, on='Wikipedia_movie_ID', how='inner')
movie_id_summary_df.head()
```

	Wikipedia_movie_ID	Genres	plot
0	975900	{"/m/01jfsb": "Thriller", "/m/06n90": "Science...	Set in the second half of the 22nd century, th...
1	9363483	{"/m/01jfsb": "Thriller", "/m/0glj9q": "Erotic...	A series of murders of rich young women throug...
2	261236	{"/m/07s9rl0": "Drama"}	Eva, an upper class housewife, becomes frustra...
3	18998739	{"/m/0hqxf": "Family Film", "/m/01hmnh": "Fant...	Every hundred years, the evil Morgana returns...
4	6631279	{"/m/06cvj": "Romantic comedy", "/m/0hj3n0w": ...	Adam, a San Francisco-based artist who works a...

Figure 9.34: Code snippet for joining movie metadata and plot summaries and the result

We can see from the above data that multiple genres are tagged with a plot, thus making it a **Multi-Label Text Classification problem**.

Now, we will write a generic `barplot` function to display movie summary and genre data. We will use `seaborn.barplot` for this:

```
import matplotlib.pyplot as plt
import seaborn as sns

def barplot(data, xlabel_txt, ylabel_txt,title):
    fig = plt.figure(figsize=(6,18))
    bar_plot = sns.barplot(data=data, x=xlabel_txt, y=ylabel_txt)
    bar_plot.set(ylabel = ylabel_txt)
    plt.title(title)
    plt.show()
```

Figure 9.35: Code snippet for generic barplot function

We can find out frequency distribution of movie genres using a `Counter`:

```
from collections import Counter

aggregate_counter = Counter()
for row_index,row in movie_id_summary_df.iterrows():
    c = Counter(row['Genres'])
    aggregate_counter += c

common_genres = [word[0] for word in aggregate_counter.most_common(50)]
common_genres_counts = [word[1] for word in aggregate_counter.most_common(50)]
common_genre_count_df = pd.DataFrame({'Genre': common_genres, 'Genre Count': common_genres_counts})
```

Figure 9.36: Code snippet for generating frequency-distribution of most common genres

We can get the total number of unique genres:

```
len(aggregate_counter)
```
```
363
```

Figure 9.37: Code snippet to get a number of unique genres

So, there are 363 different genres. For our case, it would be the total number of unique classes present in the dataset.

There are 363 different genres.

We can now use that custom `barplot` function to view the first 50 most frequency genres in the corpus:

```
barplot(data=common_genre_count_df, xlabel_txt='Genre Count', ylabel_txt='Genre', title='Most Frequent Genres')
```

Figure 9.38: Code snippet to plot the first 50 most frequent genres

The output will be a horizontal `barplot`:

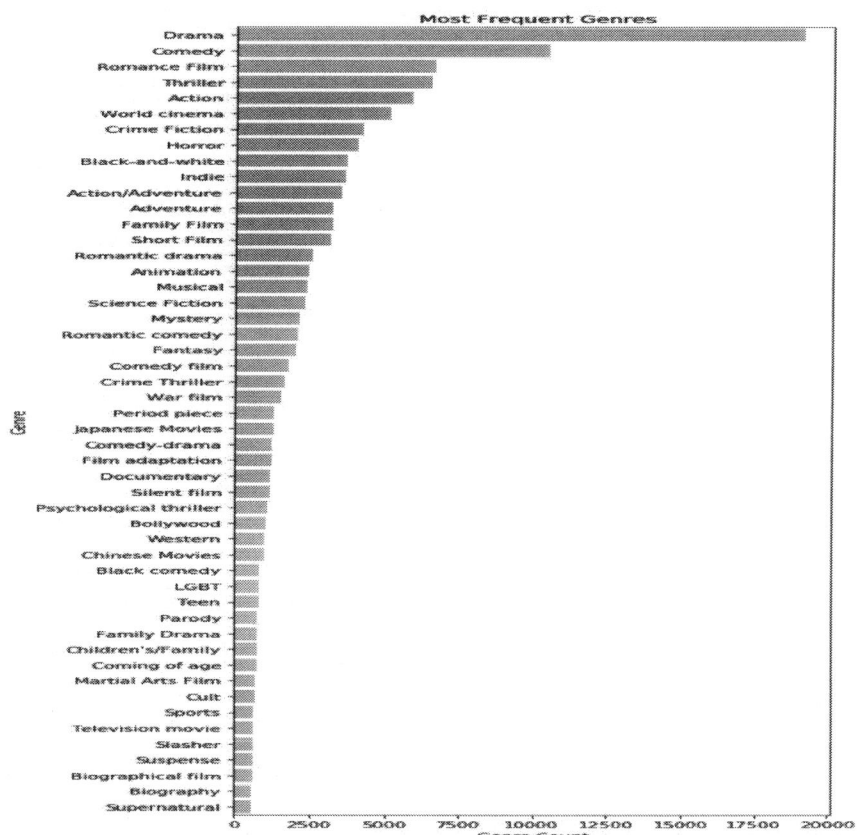

Figure 9.39: Bar chart to show the first 50 unique genres

`Drama,` `Comedy,`and `Romance` films are the first three most frequent genres in the dataset.

We can also find out the least frequent 50 genres and do some kind of barplot:

```
from itertools import islice

def key_token_counter(tupple):
    return tupple[1]

all_genre_counts = sorted(aggregate_counter.items(), key=key_token_counter)
uncommon_genres = [word[0] for word in islice(all_genre_counts, 50)]
uncommon_genres_counts = [word[1] for word in islice(all_genre_counts, 50)]
uncommon_genre_count_df = pd.DataFrame({'Genre': uncommon_genres, 'Genre Count': uncommon_genres_counts})

barplot(data=uncommon_genre_count_df, xlabel_txt='Genre Count', ylabel_txt='Genre', title='Least Frequent Genres')
```

Figure 9.40: Code snippet for generating frequency-distribution of least common genres

And it produces the following plot:

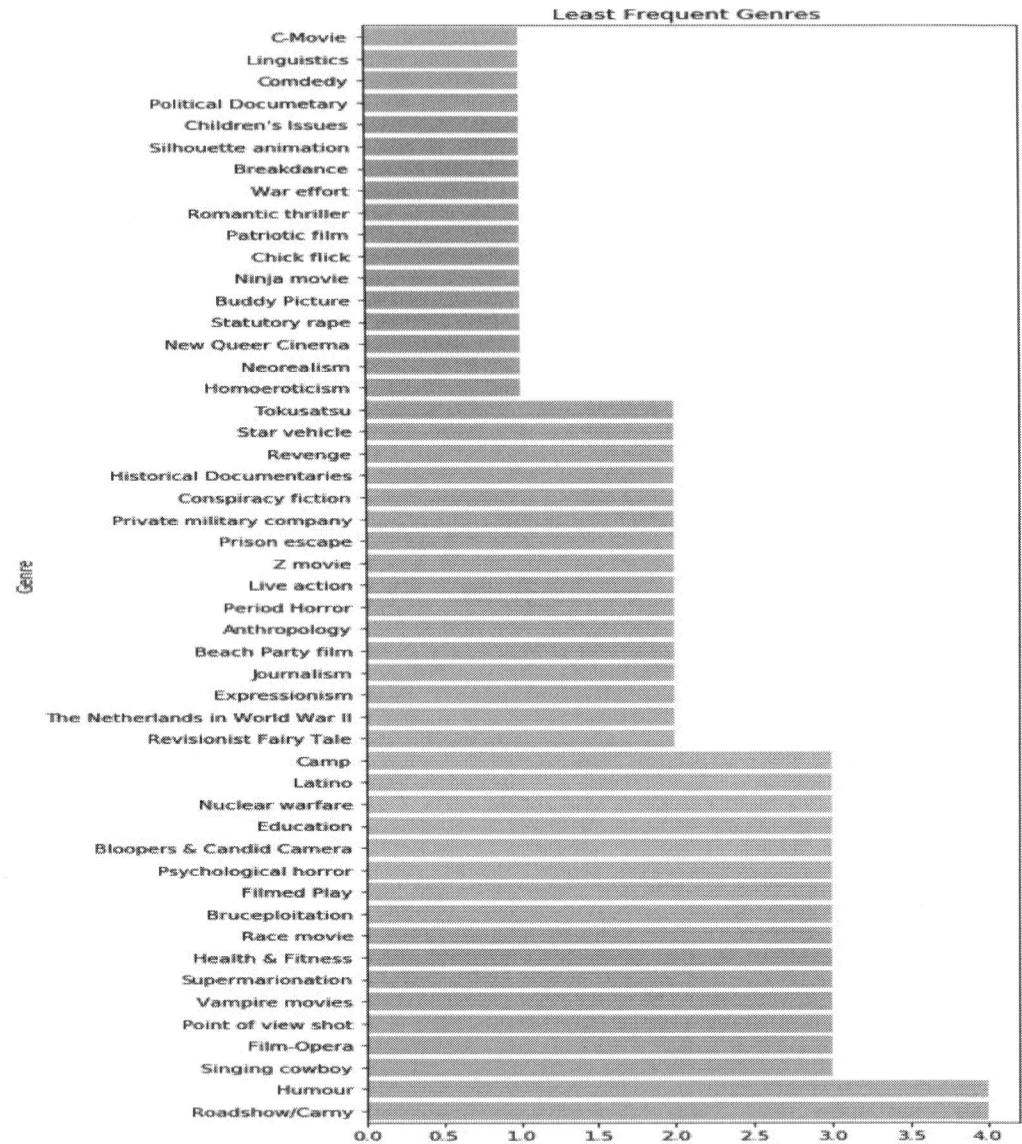

Figure 9.41: Bar chart to show the first 50 unique genres

C-Movie, Linguistics, and Comedy are the first three least frequent movie genres in the dataset.

We should clean the movie plot text before doing any kind of analysis. For cleaning, we can write a function:

```
from gensim import utils
import gensim.parsing.preprocessing as gsp

filters = [
            gsp.strip_tags,
            gsp.strip_punctuation,
            gsp.strip_multiple_whitespaces,
            gsp.strip_numeric,
            gsp.remove_stopwords,
            gsp.strip_short,
            gsp.stem_text
            ]

def clean_text(s):
    s = s.lower()
    s = utils.to_unicode(s)
    for f in filters:
        s = f(s)
    return s
```

Figure 9.42: Code snippet for clean_text function

We can see a sample movie plot first and then apply the above function to clean it:

```
movie_id_summary_df.iloc[3,2]
```

"Every hundred years, the evil Morgana returns to claim Fingall's talisman from the wizard Merlin, with which she in
tends to destroy the world. For the last fourteen hundred years she has failed... now she intends to conquer all. You
ng Ben Clark moves with his parents to a new town, where he befriends his elderly magician neighbor, Milner . Ben ha
s a natural talent for magic and wants to learn all that he can from this old man. Ben carries the same scar as the o
riginal staff-bearer 1,400 years before. Both Morgana and Milner, who is revealed to be Merlin, see this as a sign th
at this time, the battle between good and evil will be stronger and harder than ever. Ben must make his own choice be
tween good and evil as he is drawn into a battle and must draw on his own spirit and magic to decide which path to fo
llow and hence, the fate of the world as we know it.\n"

```
clean_text(movie_id_summary_df.iloc[3,2])
```

'year evil morgana return claim fingal talisman wizard merlin intend destroi world fourteen year fail intend conquer
young ben clark move parent new town befriend elderli magician neighbor milner ben natur talent magic want learn old
man ben carri scar origin staff bearer year morgana milner reveal merlin sign time battl good evil stronger harder be
n choic good evil drawn battl draw spirit magic decid path follow fate world know'

Figure 9.43: Code snippet for cleaning the text by applying clean_text

We will now write a custom **WordCloud** plotting function:

```
from wordcloud import WordCloud
import matplotlib.pyplot as plt

def plot_word_cloud(text):
    wordcloud_instance = WordCloud(width = 800, height = 800,
                background_color ='black',
                stopwords=None,
                min_font_size = 10).generate(text)

    plt.figure(figsize = (8, 8), facecolor = None)
    plt.imshow(wordcloud_instance)
    plt.axis("off")
    plt.tight_layout(pad = 0)
    plt.show()
```

Figure 9.44: Code snippet for plot_word_cloud function

This function shows the frequency of words. We can use this function to do word cloud plotting of all movie plots after cleaning:

```
plots = ''
for index, row in movie_id_summary_df.iterrows():
    plots = plots + ' ' + clean_text(row['plot'])

plot_word_cloud(plots)
```

Figure 9.45: Code snippet for plotting word cloud by applying plot_word_cloud

Figure 9.46: Word Cloud of all genres in corpus

The`tell`, `kill`, `father`, find, and more, are the most frequent tokens in all movie plots across the dataset.

We can write two functions to get a cleaned `plot` for a specific movie genre type and do a word cloud plot:

```
def get_concatened_plots_for_genre(genre):
    genre_specific_plot_str = ''
    genre_specific_plot = movie_id_summary_df[movie_id_summary_df['Genres'].apply(lambda x : genre in list(x))]

    for index, row in genre_specific_plot.iterrows():
        genre_specific_plot_str = genre_specific_plot_str + ' ' + clean_text(row['plot'])

    return genre_specific_plot_str

def word_cloud_of_plot_for_genre(genre):
    genre_specific_plot_str = get_concatened_plots_for_genre(genre)
    plot_word_cloud(genre_specific_plot_str)
```

Figure 9.47: Code snippet for functions to plot the word cloud for a specific genre

We can use the above functions to do word cloud plot for movie genre type `Thriller`.

Thriller is one of the most frequent movie genre types as per the genre type plot shown earlier:

```
word_cloud_of_plot_for_genre('Thriller')
```

Figure 9.48: Code snippet to plot the word cloud for a specific genre

Figure 9.49: Word Cloud for genre'Thriller.'

We can also write a function for the bar plot for genre-specific movie plot tokens:

```
def bar_chart_of_plot_for_genre(genre):
    genre_specific_plot_str = get_concatened_plots_for_genre(genre)
    token_counter = Counter(genre_specific_plot_str.split())
    common_tokens = [word[0] for word in token_counter.most_common(50)]
    common_tokens_counts = [word[1] for word in token_counter.most_common(50)]
    common_tokens_count_df = pd.DataFrame({'Token': common_tokens, 'Token Count': common_tokens_counts})
    barplot(data=common_tokens_count_df,xlabel_txt='Token Count',ylabel_txt='Token', title=str('Most Frequent Tokens i
                                                                                       +' type movie'))

bar_chart_of_plot_for_genre('Thriller')
```

Figure 9.50: Code snippet to generate genre-specific bar chart of movie plot tokens

And it produces the following bar chart for the movie with genre `Thriller`:

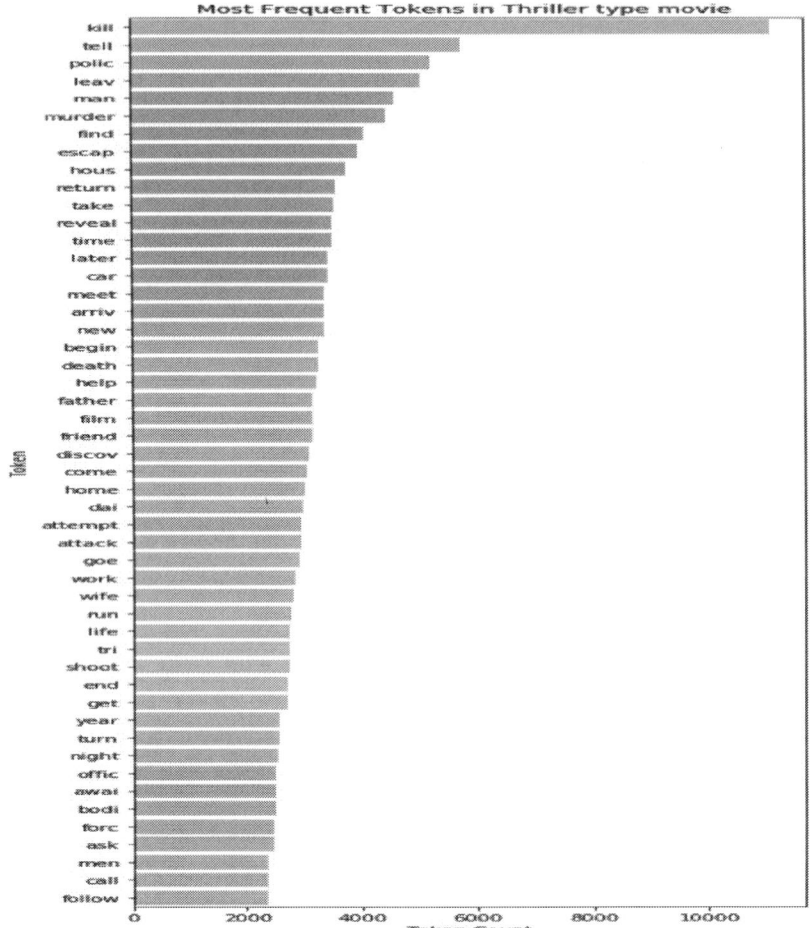

Figure 9.51: Bar chart to show the most frequent tokens in Thriller type movie

The `tell`, `kill`, `leave`, `murder`, `return`, and more, are most frequent tokens in plots of movie genre type `Thriller`. So the existence of these tokens in any given plot infers a high probability that it belongs to genre type `Thriller`.

We can do a similar analysis of one of the least frequent movie genres, `Humour`. First, we will do a word cloud of movie plot tokens. We will use the same `word_cloud_plot_for_genre` function:

```
word_cloud_of_plot_for_genre('Humour')
```

Figure 9.52: Code snippet to plot WordCloud of Humour type movie

And it produces the following plot:

Figure 9.53: Word Cloud of Humour type movie plot tokens

We can also do the bar chart plotting:

```
bar_chart_of_plot_for_genre('Humour')
```

Figure 9.54: Code snippet to generate bar chart of Humour type movie plot tokens

And it produces the following plot:

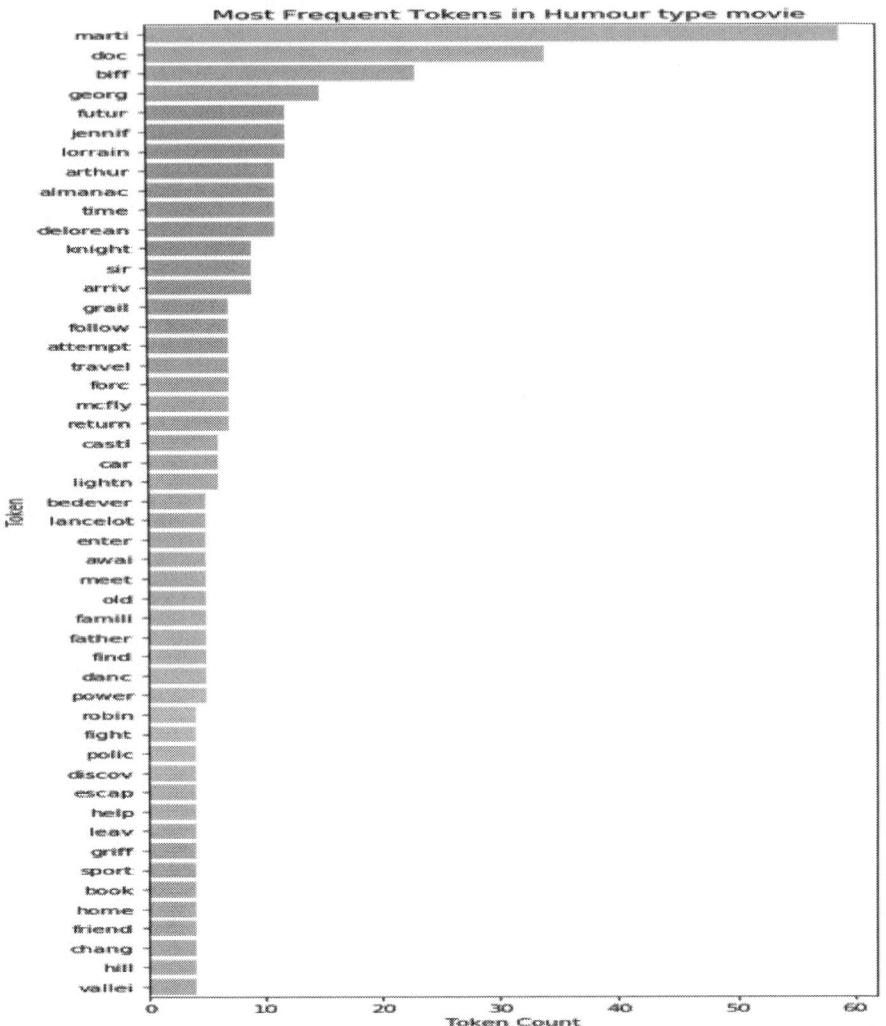

Figure 9.55: Bar chart of Humour type movie plot tokens

The `marti, doc, biff,` and more, are the are most frequent tokens in plots of movie genre type Humour. So the existence of these tokens in any given plot infers a high probability that it belongs to genre type `Humour`.

A similar analysis can be done for other movie genre types, and eventually, it will reveal many of the frequent tokens found in those plots of specific genre types.

Building the model

We need to split the dataset into feature and target variables:

```
df_x = movie_id_summary_df[['plot']]
df_y = movie_id_summary_df[['Genres']]
```

Figure 9.56: Code snippet to divide feature and response variable

As `Genres` is a list of values and it is a multilabel classification problem, conversion to 0 and 1 array is necessary over here. `MultilabelBinarizer of scikit-learn` library can do it:

```
from sklearn.preprocessing import MultiLabelBinarizer

y = []
for index, row in df_y.iterrows():
    y.append(set(row['Genres']))

mlb = MultiLabelBinarizer()
encoded_y = mlb.fit_transform(y)
```

Figure 9.57: Code snippet to apply multilabel binarizer on Genres

Each bit of the array represents one class label (in our case `Genre` type) and a 1 indicates that class is present in the data instance. In our case, there can be multiple 1s in the array due to its multilabel nature.

We need to use a proper vector space model to convert plot text into numerical features. We will try to leverage our understanding from the data exploration and use the TF-IDF model. We can make it dynamic by providing a max number of features and max document frequency ratio as a hyperparameter. As for `TF-IDF`, there is always a tendency of high dimensionality, and in our case, it will be due to a large dataset, this `max_features` will restrict it to concentrate only high-frequency terms.

We can write a generic TF-IDF transformer which can be fit into a pipeline:

```
from sklearn.feature_extraction.text import TfidfVectorizer
from sklearn.base import BaseEstimator

class Text2TfIdfTransformer(BaseEstimator):

    def __init__(self, field, max_features, max_df):
        self._model = TfidfVectorizer(max_features=max_features, max_df=max_df)
        self.field = field

    def fit(self, X, y=None):
        X_arr = X[self.field].apply(lambda x : clean_text(x))

        self._model.fit(X_arr)
        return self

    def transform(self, X):
        X_arr = X[self.field].apply(lambda x : clean_text(x))
        return self._model.transform(X_arr)
```

Figure 9.58: Code snippet of custom text to TF-IDF transformer

The dataset should be divided into training and testing:

```
from sklearn.model_selection import train_test_split

train_x, test_x, train_y, test_y = train_test_split(df_x, encoded_y)
```

Figure 9.59: Code snippet to divide the dataset into train and test

As it is a multilabel classification problem, we will use the `BinaryRelevance` strategy (ref *Chapter 1: Introduction to Machine Learning and Mathematical Preliminaries*) for doing it. We will use the `BinaryRelevance` class from `scikit-multilearn` for it. `BinaryRelevance` will decompose the problem into 363 number of different binary classification problem for each `Genre` type. We will use `RandomForest` as our base binary classifier for each of this problem and build the pipeline with the feature set from TF-IDF transformation:

```
from sklearn.pipeline import Pipeline
from sklearn.ensemble import RandomForestClassifier
from skmultilearn.problem_transform import BinaryRelevance
import multiprocessing

binary_rel_model = BinaryRelevance(RandomForestClassifier(class_weight='balanced',
                                      n_jobs=multiprocessing.cpu_count() - 1))
tf_idf_model = Text2TfIdfTransformer(field='plot', max_features = 10000, max_df=0.8)
multi_label_rf_br_model = Pipeline(steps=[
                            ('tf_idf', tf_idf_model),
                            ('binary_relevance', binary_rel_model)
                          ])
```

Figure 9.60: Code snippet for model pipeline

We have used above 10000 as `max_features` and 0.8 as `max_df` hyper-parameter. As there is a class imbalance, we have used `class_weight` strategy as `balanced`.

We will now train the model:

```
multi_label_rf_br_model.fit(train_x, train_y)
```

```
/Users/avnag/Library/Python/3.6/lib/python/site-packages/sklearn/ensemble/forest.py:245: FutureWarning: The default v
alue of n_estimators will change from 10 in version 0.20 to 100 in 0.22.
  "10 in version 0.20 to 100 in 0.22.", FutureWarning)
/Users/avnag/Library/Python/3.6/lib/python/site-packages/sklearn/ensemble/forest.py:245: FutureWarning: The default v
alue of n_estimators will change from 10 in version 0.20 to 100 in 0.22.
  "10 in version 0.20 to 100 in 0.22.", FutureWarning)
/Users/avnag/Library/Python/3.6/lib/python/site-packages/sklearn/ensemble/forest.py:245: FutureWarning: The default v
alue of n_estimators will change from 10 in version 0.20 to 100 in 0.22.
  "10 in version 0.20 to 100 in 0.22.", FutureWarning)
/Users/avnag/Library/Python/3.6/lib/python/site-packages/sklearn/ensemble/forest.py:245: FutureWarning: The default v
alue of n_estimators will change from 10 in version 0.20 to 100 in 0.22.
  "10 in version 0.20 to 100 in 0.22.", FutureWarning)
/Users/avnag/Library/Python/3.6/lib/python/site-packages/sklearn/ensemble/forest.py:245: FutureWarning: The default v
alue of n_estimators will change from 10 in version 0.20 to 100 in 0.22.
  "10 in version 0.20 to 100 in 0.22.", FutureWarning)
/Users/avnag/Library/Python/3.6/lib/python/site-packages/sklearn/ensemble/forest.py:245: FutureWarning: The default v
alue of n_estimators will change from 10 in version 0.20 to 100 in 0.22.
  "10 in version 0.20 to 100 in 0.22.", FutureWarning)
/Users/avnag/Library/Python/3.6/lib/python/site-packages/sklearn/ensemble/forest.py:245: FutureWarning: The default v
```

Figure 9.61: Code snippet to train the model pipeline

We can ignore the warnings in *Figure 9.57*.

Analysis of result and testing the model

We can measure *hamming loss* and F1 score:

```
from sklearn.metrics import f1_score, hamming_loss

predictions_test_y = multi_label_rf_br_model.predict(test_x)
total_hamming_loss = hamming_loss(y_true=test_y, y_pred=predictions_test_y)
f1_score = f1_score(y_true=test_y, y_pred=predictions_test_y, average='micro')
print('Total Hamming Loss of model :' , total_hamming_loss)
print('F1 score :', f1_score)

Total Hamming Loss of model : 0.009463039659814076
F1 score : 0.19118598683476515
```

Figure 9.62: Code snippet to compute the accuracy of the model

Hamming loss is very good, but the F1 score is showing a little low. F1 score can be improved by setting a threshold probability for each class label.

We will now test the model with a sample data:

```
row_id = 126
movie_id_summary_df['plot'][row_id]
```

'On the planet Krypton, using evidence provided by scientist Jor-El, the Ruling Council sentences three attempted ins urrectionists, General Zod, Ursa and Non, to "eternal living death" in the Phantom Zone. Despite his eminence, Jor-El is unable to convince the Council of his belief that Krypton will soon explode. To save his infant son Kal-El, Jor-El launches a spacecraft containing the child towards Earth, a distant planet with a suitable atmosphere, and where Kal-El\'s dense molecular structure will give him superhuman powers. Shortly after the launch, Krypton is destroyed. Three e years later the ship lands near an American farming town, Smallville, where Kal-El is found by Jonathan and Martha Kent. The Kents take the child back to their farm and raised him as their own son, naming him Clark after Martha\'s m aiden name. At age 18, soon after the death of Jonathan, Clark hears a psychic "call", discovering a glowing green cr ystal in the ship. It compels him to travel to the Arctic, where the crystal builds the Fortress of Solitude, resembl ing the architecture of Krypton. Inside, a vision of Jor-El explains Clark\'s origins, educating him in powers and re sponsibilities. After 12 years, with his powers fully developed, Clark leaves the Fortress with a colorful costume an d becomes a reporter at the Daily Planet in Metropolis. He meets and develops a romantic attraction to coworker Lois Lane, but she sees him as awkward and unsophisticated. Lois becomes involved in a helicopter accident where conventio nal means of rescue are impossible, requiring Clark to use his powers in public for the first time to save her. The r escue of Air Force One and other good deeds make the mysterious "caped wonder" a celebrity. The hero visits Lois at h ome, takes her for a flight over the city, and allows her to interview him for an article in which she names him "Sup erman." Meanwhile, criminal genius Lex Luthor has developed a cunning plan to make a fortune in real estate by buying large amounts of barren desert land and then diverting a nuclear missile test along the San Andreas Fault. The mi ssile will sink California and leave Luthor\'s desert as the new West Coast of the United States, greatly increasing its value. After his incompetent henchman Otis accidentally redirects the first rocket to the wrong place, Luthor\'s girlfriend Eve Teschmacher successfully changes the course of a second missile. Knowing Superman could stop his plan, Luthor lures him to his underground lair and exposes him to Kryptonite. As Superman weakens, Luthor taunts him by rev ealing that the first missile is headed to Hackensack, New Jersey, in the opposite direction, knowing that Superman c annot stop both impacts. Teschmacher is horrified because her mother lives in Hackensack, but Luthor does not care an d leaves Superman to a slow death. Teschmacher rescues Superman on the condition that he will deal with the New Jerse y missile first. He is thus too late to stop the second impact, causing a massive earthquake which he battles to corr ect. While Superman is busy saving others, Lois\'s car falls into the ground due to an aftershock. It quickly fills w ith dirt and debris and she suffocates to death. Distraught at being unable to save Lois, Superman ignores Jor-El\'s warning not to interfere with human history, preferring to remember Jonathan Kent\'s advice that he must be on Earth for "a reason". He travels back in time in order to save Lois, altering history so that her car is never caught in th e aftershock. Superman then delivers Luthor and Otis to prison and flies into the sunrise for further adventures.\n'

```
movie_id_summary_df['Genres'][row_id]
```

dict_values(['Science Fiction', 'Adventure', 'Superhero movie', 'Action/Adventure', 'Family Film', 'Action'])

Figure 9.63: Code snippet to display sample movie plot and genres for testing

The above movie plot has several `Genres` attached to it. We will use our trained model to predict it:

```
test_input_df = pd.DataFrame([{
    'plot' : movie_id_summary_df['plot'][row_id],
}])
predicted_category = multi_label_rf_br_model.predict(test_input_df)
mlb.inverse_transform(predicted_category)

[('Action',
  'Action/Adventure',
  'Adventure',
  'Family Film',
  'Science Fiction',
  'Superhero movie')]
```

Figure 9.64: Code snippet to apply the model on the sample test data instance

So, it is successfully predicting the genres.

We can now write a function to do *ROC curve plotting* for individual binary classifiers:

```
from sklearn.metrics import roc_curve, auc
import numpy as np

def plot_roc_curve(x=None, y=None, classes=[],title=None):

    lw=2
    plt.figure(figsize=(12,6))
    for _class in classes:
        class_index = np.where(mlb.classes_ == _class)[0][0]
        probs = binary_rel_model.classifiers_[class_index].predict_proba(tf_idf_model.transform(x))[:,1]
        model_fpr, model_tpr, _ = roc_curve(y[:,class_index], probs)
        roc_auc = auc(model_fpr, model_tpr)
        plt.plot(model_fpr, model_tpr,
            lw=lw, label='ROC curve -' + _class + '- (area = %0.2f)' % roc_auc)

    plt.plot([0, 1], [0, 1], color='navy', lw=lw, linestyle='--')
    plt.xlim([0.0, 1.0])
    plt.ylim([0.0, 1.05])
    plt.xlabel('False Positive Rate')
    plt.ylabel('True Positive Rate')
    plt.title(title)
    plt.legend(loc="lower right")
    plt.show()
```

Figure 9.65: Code snippet of plot_roc_curve function

We will use this function for plotting ROC curve for classes `Drama, Comedy,` and `Animation` on training and testing data:

```
plot_roc_curve(x=test_x, y=test_y, classes=['Drama','Comedy','Animation'], title='ROC Curve for 3 Genres on test')
```

Figure 9.66: Code snippet for applying plot_roc_curve on the test dataset

And it produces the following plot:

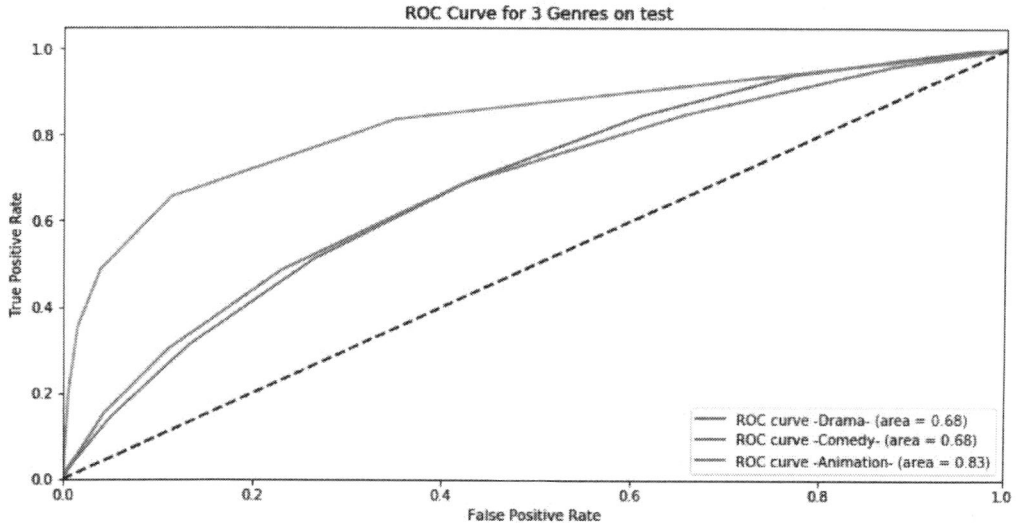

Figure 9.67: ROC of 3 genre classes on test data

We can apply the same on training data:

```
plot_roc_curve(x=train_x, y=train_y, classes=['Drama','Comedy','Animation'], title='ROC Curve for 3 Genres on train')
```

Figure 9.68: Code snippet for applying plot_roc_curve on train dataset

And it produces the following plot:

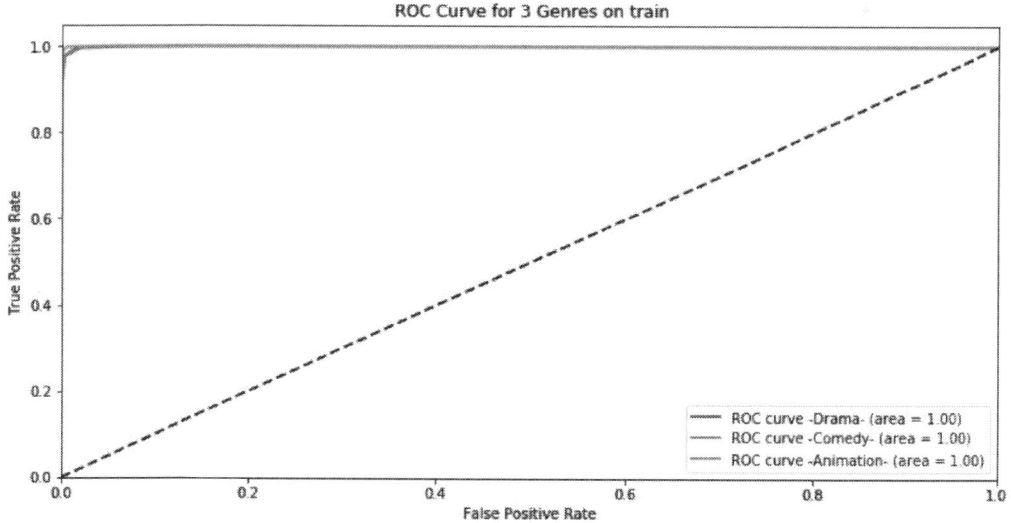

Figure 9.69: ROC of 3 genre classes on train data

ROC curves are showing that coverage area is close to 1, which indicates a good classifier.

Case study 3: Classification of natural images using CNN and PyTorch

Data source and problem definition

We will use the Kaggle dataset of natural images (https://www.kaggle.com/ prasunroy/natural-images). This one contains 6899 images of 8 different categories (classes). These classes are airplane, car, cat, dog, flower, fruit, motorbike, and person.

The objective is to build a classification model to identify images.

Data exploration

The dataset should be explored with visualization (as data here are images of objects) to get a feeling.

We can a function to display images using the PIL library:

```python
from PIL import Image
import numpy as np
import matplotlib.pyplot as plt

def show_image(path):
    img = Image.open(path)
    img_arr = np.array(img)
    plt.figure(figsize=(5,5))
    plt.imshow(np.transpose(img_arr, (0, 1, 2)))
```

Figure 9.70: Code snippet of show_image function

We can use this function to see images present in the dataset:

Figure 9.71: Code snippet for viewing images using show_image

Some transformations are required to be applied to the images to make these ready for processing.

We have to apply normalization and cropping to 64x64 size on these images. We also have to do image and label data separation:

```python
import torchvision.datasets as datasets
from torchvision.transforms import transforms
from torch.utils.data import DataLoader
from torchvision.utils import make_grid

transformations = transforms.Compose([
    transforms.RandomResizedCrop(64),
    transforms.ToTensor(),
    transforms.Normalize((0.5, 0.5, 0.5), (0.5, 0.5, 0.5))
])

total_dataset = datasets.ImageFolder("../data/natural_images", transform = transformations)
dataset_loader = DataLoader(dataset = total_dataset, batch_size = 50)
items = iter(dataset_loader)
image_batch_1, label = items.next()
```

```python
total_dataset.class_to_idx
```

```
{'airplane': 0,
 'car': 1,
 'cat': 2,
 'dog': 3,
 'flower': 4,
 'fruit': 5,
 'motorbike': 6,
 'person': 7}
```

Figure 9.72: Code snippet for pre-processing of images

`DatasetLoader` divides the entire dataset into batches after applying the defined transformations, and class labels are assigned unique indices in this process. We can use these indices as output.

We can write a function to display transformed images:

```
def show_transformed_image(image):
    np_image = image.detach().numpy()
    plt.figure(figsize=(20,20))
    plt.imshow(np.transpose(np_image, (1, 2, 0)))
```

Figure 9.73: Code snippet for show_transformed_image function

This function can be used to show all transformed images for a batch:

```
show_transformed_image(make_grid(image_batch_1))
```

Figure 9.74: Code snippet for applying show_transformed_image function on a batch

The output will look like:

Figure 9.75: Images in a Grid view produced by show_transformed_image

It can be easily observed that the effect of transformations has made images square-shaped (64x64), and color levels changed. Change of color levels is the result of Normalization transformation.

Now, the dimension of the batch tensor can be observed:

```
image_batch_1.shape
torch.Size([50, 3, 64, 64])
```

Figure 9.76: Code snippet to see dimensions of an image batch

We can see one sample transformed image from this batch:

```
plt.figure(figsize=(5,5))
plt.imshow(np.transpose(image_batch_1[11], (1, 2, 0)))
Clipping input data to the valid range for imshow with RGB data ([0..1] for floats or [0..255] for integers).
<matplotlib.image.AxesImage at 0x125ebea90>
```

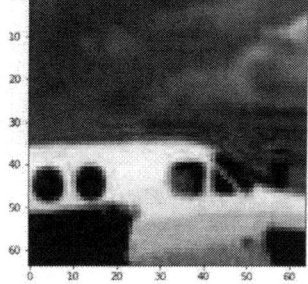

Figure 9.77: Code snippet to view one sample image from the batch and its result

The image looks a little distorted due to the figure size adjustment done with `matplotlib`.

Effect of applying convolution filter

Convolution operation can decompose the image into various sub-images and reveal a lot of important features essential for a Machine Learning algorithm to process.

By default, the `PIL` library will convert the image into a three-channel tensor (as per the RGB color model). PyToch's convolution filter library will n number of kernels of some fixed size, which will produce n number of sub-images as output. As `PyTorch` will sum up three input channels as a single channel for processing and then the convolution will be applied, resultant images will be of grey level type (details have been discussed in *Chapter 6: Miscellaneous Unsupervised Learning*).

We can write a function for convolution and see the effect:

```
import torch.nn as nn
import torch as torch

def generate_conv(image, no_output_layer):
    sample_image_tensor = image
    sample_image_tensor.unsqueeze_(0)
    conv = nn.Conv2d(in_channels=3, out_channels=no_output_layer, kernel_size=3,stride=1, padding=1)
    conv_output = conv(sample_image_tensor)
    return conv_output

conv_output = generate_conv(image=image_batch_1[11], no_output_layer=8)
conv_output.shape

torch.Size([1, 8, 64, 64])
```

Figure 9.78: Code snippet of generate_conv function and result of applying it on an image

We can see that the convolution operation has changed the tensor dimension from 3x64x64 to 8x64x64.

We will see the resultant images produced by convolution:

```
def display_conv_image(conv_image):
    batch,channel,width,height = conv_image.shape
    conv_image = conv_image.view(batch*channel, -1, width, height)
    show_transformed_image(make_grid(conv_image))

display_conv_image(conv_output)
```

Figure 9.79: Code snippet of display_conv_image function

And it will produce the following output:

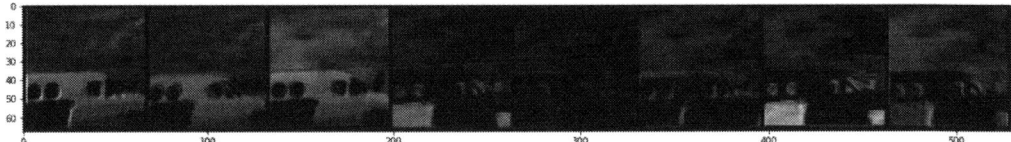

Figure 9.80: Output produced by applying display_conv_image on an image

We can easily observe that the sample image has been converted into eight grey-level images. Each of these images carries very important information that can contribute significantly to ML-based model development. We will apply this convolution while building the actual model.

Building the model

The entire dataset should be divided into training and testing part (80:20 ratio):

```
from torch.utils.data import random_split

train_size = int(0.8 * len(total_dataset))
test_size = len(total_dataset) - train_size
train_dataset, test_dataset = random_split(total_dataset, [train_size, test_size])

train_dataset_loader = DataLoader(dataset = train_dataset, batch_size = 100)
test_dataset_loader = DataLoader(dataset = test_dataset, batch_size = 100)
```

Figure 9.81: Code snippet for splitting the dataset into train and test

Neural network layers should consist of Convolution, **ReLU, Maxpool** in this order. The entire stack should look like below:

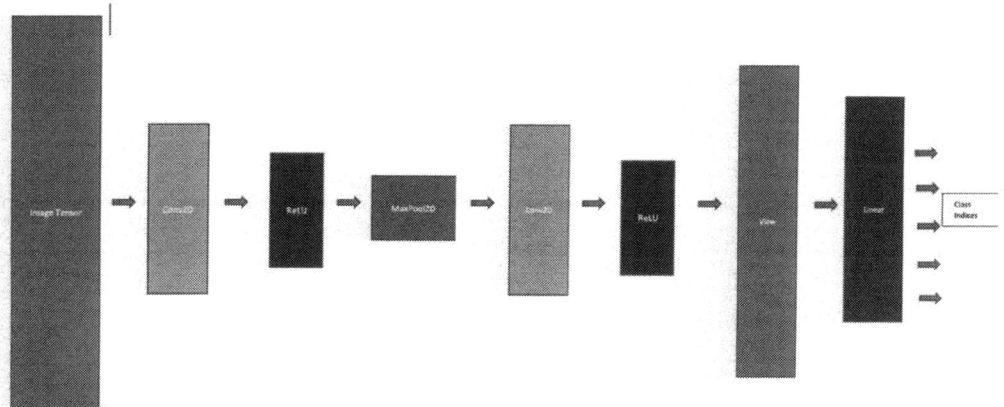

Figure 9.82: Layer Architecture of the CNN

The view layer flattens the **ReLU** output as a one-dimensional tensor, and it is seeded into the **Linear** layer. **The linear** layer is responsible for the mathematical mapping of linear features to output classes. It produces real numbered values for each class, and the highest value at any index in the desired class index (We already saw generated class indices earlier). A number of convolution layers or **ReLU** layers can be chosen depending on the problem complexity. These can be taken hyperparameters, and in that case, the orientation of the above layers will change.

We should extend `torch.nn.Module` and create our custom network class (details discussed in *Chapter 6: Miscellaneous Unsupervised Learning*), which will reflect the layers of architecture displayed above.

```
import torch.nn as nn

class NaturalImageClassifierCNNModel(nn.Module):

    def __init__(self, num_classes=8):
        super(NaturalImageClassifierCNNModel,self).__init__()

        self.conv1 = nn.Conv2d(in_channels=3, out_channels=12, kernel_size=3,stride=1, padding=1)
        self.relu1 = nn.ReLU()

        self.maxpool1 = nn.MaxPool2d(kernel_size=2)

        self.conv2 = nn.Conv2d(in_channels=12, out_channels=24, kernel_size=3, stride=1, padding=1)
        self.relu2 = nn.ReLU()

        self.lf = nn.Linear(in_features=32 * 32 * 24, out_features=num_classes)

    def forward(self, input):
        output = self.conv1(input)
        output = self.relu1(output)

        output = self.maxpool1(output)

        output = self.conv2(output)
        output = self.relu2(output)

        output = output.view(-1, 32 * 32 * 24)

        output = self.lf(output)

        return output
```

Figure 9.83: Code snippet of custom CNN model class

Now, we will have to define optimizer and loss function:

```
from torch.optim import Adam

cnn_model = NaturalImageClassifierCNNModel()
optimizer = Adam(cnn_model.parameters())
loss_fn = nn.CrossEntropyLoss()
```

Figure 9.84: Code snippet for creating instances of CNN, Optimizer, and Loss function

As it is a classification problem, we are using CrossEntropyLoss.

In PyTorch, there is no ready-made training function like scikit-learn. So, we will have to write a function to train the model, calculate loss, and step forward:

```
loss_arr = []
def train_and_build(n_epoches):
    for epoch in range(n_epoches):
        cnn_model.train()
        total_loss = 0
        for i, (images, labels) in enumerate(train_dataset_loader):
            optimizer.zero_grad()
            outputs = cnn_model(images)
            loss = loss_fn(outputs, labels)
            loss.backward()
            optimizer.step()
            total_loss = total_loss + loss
        loss_arr.append(total_loss)
```

Figure 9.85: Code snippet of train_and_build function training CNN model iteratively

The above function takes the number of epochs as an argument. We will call this function with 200 epochs:

```
train_and_build(200)
```

Figure 9.86: Code snippet for calling train_and_build function

Value of the loss function can be plotted:

Figure 9.87: Code snippet for plotting loss curve out of the CNN model

We can observe that loss is decreasing with increasing epochs.

Analysis of result and testing the model

We will now compute the accuracy of the model. Computing accuracy is a little tricky in `PyTorch`. We should be set the model in evaluation mode for so:

```
import torch

cnn_model.eval()
test_acc_count = 0
for k, (test_images, test_labels) in enumerate(test_dataset_loader):
    test_outputs = cnn_model(test_images)
    _, prediction = torch.max(test_outputs.data, 1)
    test_acc_count += torch.sum(prediction == test_labels.data).item()

test_accuracy = test_acc_count / len(test_dataset)
test_accuracy
0.8942028985507247
```

Figure 9.88: Code snippet for computing accuracy of the CNN model

The accuracy of the model is 0.89 or 89%, which is very good!

Calling `cnn_model(test_images)` implicitly calls the `__call__` function of the model. The output of this function is the predicted result from the trained model. Then how many of the predicted results actually match with the original ones need to be checked. Thus we get the accuracy.

Now, we can test the model with two input images from our dataset: one `Motorbike` (class index 6), and one `Fruit` (class index 5):

```
test_image_1_path = '../data/natural_images/motorbike/motorbike_0012.jpg'
show_image(test_image_1_path)
```

```
test_image_1 = Image.open(test_image_1_path)
test_image_tensor_1 = transformations(test_image_1).float()
test_image_tensor_1 = test_image_tensor_1.unsqueeze_(0)
output_1 = cnn_model(test_image_tensor_1)
class_index_1 = output_1.data.numpy().argmax()
class_index_1
```

6

Figure 9.89: Code snippet for testing the CNN model with a sample image

So, the `Motorbike` is correctly predicted. While using the model, we have to set it in `eval` mode, do the necessary transformations the same asthe training process, and then seed the processed image data into the model. As discussed earlier, the tensor index of the maximum value will be the predicted class index.

Similarly, we can use the model for `Fruit`:

```
test_image_3_path = '../data/natural_images/fruit/fruit_0017.jpg'
show_image(test_image_3_path)
```

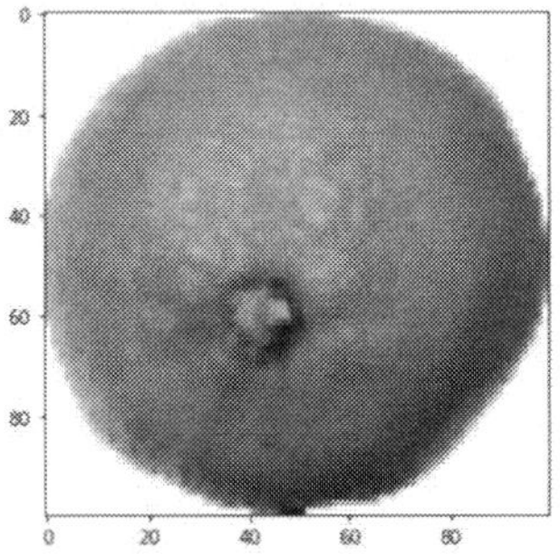

```
test_image_3 = Image.open(test_image_3_path)
test_image_tensor_3 = transformations(test_image_3).float()
test_image_tensor_3 = test_image_tensor_3.unsqueeze_(0)
output_3 = cnn_model(test_image_tensor_3)
class_index_3 = output_3.data.numpy().argmax()
class_index_3
```

5

Figure 9.90: Code snippet for testing the CNN model with a sample image

So, every time it is giving the correct prediction.

Conclusion

In this chapter, we learned what a data science story isand how to write a well-formatted one. We got to know about different visualization techniques and discussed three different use cases of storytelling using practical datasets. This chapter also gave us an idea about how to keep our stories precise so that it can reach a maximum audience of different backgrounds.

Printed in Great Britain
by Amazon